D0590933

FREEDOM
OF THE
PRESS 2007

Freedom of the Press 2007

A Global Survey of Media Independence

Edited by

Karin Deutsch Karlekar

and Eleanor Marchant

Freedom House
New York ▪ Washington, D.C.

Rowman & Littlefield Publishers, Inc.
Lanham ▪ Boulder ▪ New York ▪ Toronto ▪ Plymouth, UK

ROWMAN & LITTLEFIELD PUBLISHERS, INC.

Published in the United States of America
by Rowman & Littlefield Publishers, Inc.
A wholly owned subsidiary of The Rowman & Littlefield Publishing Group, Inc.
4501 Forbes Boulevard, Suite 200, Lanham, Maryland 20706
www.rowmanlittlefield.com

Estover Road, Plymouth PL6 7PY, United Kingdom

ISSN 1551-9163
ISBN-13: 978-0-7425-5581-5 (cloth : alk. paper)
ISBN-10: 0-7425-5581-x (cloth : alk. paper)
ISBN-13: 978-0-7425-5582-2 (pbk. : alk. paper)
ISBN-10: 0-7425-5582-8 (pbk. : alk. paper)

Printed in the United States of America

♾™ The paper used in this publication meets the minimum requirements of
American National Standard for Information Sciences—Permanence of Paper for
Printed Library Materials, ANSI/NISO Z39.48-1992.

Table of Contents

Acknowledgments

Freedom of the Press 2007 could not have been completed without the contributions of numerous Freedom House staff and consultants. The following section, entitled "The Survey Team," contains a detailed list of writers and advisers without whose efforts and input this project would not have been possible.

Karin Deutsch Karlekar, a senior researcher at Freedom House, served as managing editor of this year's survey. Extensive research, editorial, proofreading, and administrative assistance was provided by Eleanor Marchant, assistant editor of *Freedom of the Press*, as well as by Astrid Larson, Thomas Webb, Tyler Roylance, Camille Eiss, Elizabeth Floyd, Jacob Stokes, and Shaina Greiff. Anne Green, of Greenways Graphic Design, and Lori Greenberg Tolchin were responsible for the design and typesetting of the book, while Sona Vogel served as the principal copy editor. Overall guidance for the project was provided by Arch Puddington, director of research, and by Christopher Walker, director of studies. We are grateful for the insights provided by those who served on this year's review team, including Freedom House staff members Arch Puddington, Christopher Walker, Karin Deutsch Karlekar, Eleanor Marchant, Mariam Memarsadeghi, and Celine Senseney, as well as Freedom House visiting fellow Sihem Figuigui and Dan McCarey and Ting Wang of the International Center for Journalists. In addition, the ratings and narratives were reviewed by a number of Freedom House staff based in our overseas offices. This report also reflects the findings of the Freedom House study *Freedom in the World 2007: The Annual Survey of Political*

Rights and Civil Liberties. Statistics on internet usage were taken from www.internetworldstats.com.

We would also like to acknowledge comments and input on various reports from the following members of the International Freedom of Expression Exchange (IFEX) network: Owais Aslam Ali of the Pakistan Press Foundation, Carlos Cortes Castillo of the Fundacion para la Libertad de Prensa (Colombia), Corina Cepoi and Olivia Pirtac of the Independent Journalism Center (Moldova), Gamal Eid of the Arabic Network for Human Rights Information (HRinfo.net), Ronald Koven of the World Press Freedom Committee, H. Naranjargal and Dash Munkhburen of Globe International (Mongolia), Edetaen Ojo of Media Rights Agenda (Nigeria), Julie Payne of Canadian Journalists for Free Expression, Ping Ling of the Hong Kong Journalists Association, and Hans Verploeg of the Netherlands Association of Journalists. Comments were also received from Saad Mohseni, of the Moby Media Group (Afghanistan) and Omar Faruk Osman of the National Union of Somali Journalists.

Freedom House would like to thank the Annenberg Foundation for their generous grant in support of this year's survey. Additional support for our freedom of expression work was provided by the Lynde and Harry Bradley Foundation, the F. M. Kirby Foundation, the Lilly Endowment, the Freedom Forum, and Bette Bao Lord.

The Survey Team

Contributing Authors

Fadeel Al-Ameen is a journalist and author who writes extensively about the status of the contemporary Arab media and has conducted several media-training workshops and seminars for Arab journalists. He worked as editor in chief of *Hi* magazine for three years and is currently a consultant for several media organizations in the D.C. area and the Middle East. He holds an MA in journalism and mass communications from the University of Northern Colorado and completed his graduate degree in international media from Indiana University at Bloomington. He served as a Middle East analyst for *Freedom of the Press*.

Alexis Arieff is a graduate student in international relations at Yale University and a former senior research associate for the Africa program at the Committee to Protect Journalists. She served as an Africa analyst for *Freedom in the World* and *Freedom of the Press*.

Charles Arthur is an analyst and journalist specializing in Caribbean politics and economics. He holds an MA in Latin American government and politics from the University of Essex, United Kingdom. He is a contributing writer for the Economist Intelligence Unit, *Latinamerica Press*, and the IPI *World Press Freedom Review* and is the author of two books about Haiti. He served as the Caribbean analyst for *Freedom of the Press*.

Luis Botello is the director of Latin American programs at the International Center for Journalists. A native Panamanian, he has worked throughout the Americas, conducting training programs and conferences on freedom of expression and the press as well as journalism ethics. He previously served as morning newscast producer, host, and television reporter for Televisora Nacional in Panama, where he covered assignments in Colombia, the United States, and Europe. He holds a BA in journalism and an MA in mass communications from Louisiana State University and has also held several teaching positions. He served as the Central America analyst for *Freedom of the Press.*

Jake Dizard is a research analyst at Freedom House and assistant editor of the annual Freedom House publication *Countries at the Crossroads.* His area of focus is Latin America, with a specific emphasis on the Andean region. He is a 2005 graduate of the Johns Hopkins School of Advanced International Studies. He served as an Americas analyst for *Freedom of the Press.*

Camille Eiss is a research analyst at Freedom House and assistant editor of *Freedom in the World.* Her research focuses on political and human rights developments in Southeast Asia. She previously worked as associate managing editor of the *Washington Quarterly* at the Center for Strategic and International Studies. She holds an MSc in the history of international relations from the London School of Economics, with a focus on political Islam. She served as a Southeast Asia and Middle East analyst for *Freedom of the Press.*

Thomas Gold is a former assistant professor of comparative politics at Sacred Heart University and the author of *The Lega Nord and Contemporary Politics in Italy.* He earned his PhD from the New School for Social Research and received a Fulbright Fellowship to conduct research in Italy. He served as a Western Europe analyst for *Freedom of the Press.*

David Hawk is a human rights advocate specializing in East Asia. He is author of *Hidden Gulag: Exposing North Korea's Prison Camps* and *Thank You Father Kim Il Sung: Violations of Freedom of Thought, Conscience and Religion in North Korea* and, most recently, a Freedom House special report, "Concentrations of Inhumanity: An Analysis of North Korea's Labor Camps." He formerly directed the Cambodia Office of the UN High Commissioner for Human Rights and the U.S. section of Amnesty International. He served as an Asia analyst for *Freedom of the Press.*

Diana Howansky is a staff associate at the Ukrainian Studies Program of Columbia University. She holds an MA in international affairs, with a specialization in Russian-area and Eastern European studies, from the School of Advanced International Studies at Johns Hopkins University, as well as an MS in journalism from Columbia University's Graduate School of Journalism. She has worked in the field of democratic development in various countries in the former Soviet Union. She served as a Former Soviet Union analyst for *Freedom of the Press*.

Sallie Hughes is an assistant professor in the Journalism Program and Spanish-Language Journalism Masters Program at the School of Communication, University of Miami. Her PhD from Tulane University is in Latin American studies, with an emphasis on the media and politics of the region. Her book on the transformation of journalism in Mexico, *Newsrooms in Conflict: Journalism and the Democratization of Mexico*, was published in 2006 by the University of Pittsburgh Press. She served as an Americas analyst for *Freedom of the Press*.

Ana Jelenkovic is an associate at Eurasia Group, focusing on the Caucasus, Southeast Europe, and the broader Black Sea region. She holds an MA in international relations from Columbia University. She has worked on Balkan human rights and media issues at the Committee to Protect Journalists, the Harriman Institute, the Open Society Institute, and Freedom House's New York and Belgrade offices. She served as a Balkans, Eastern Europe, and Caucasus analyst for *Freedom of the Press*.

Karin Deutsch Karlekar is a senior researcher at Freedom House and managing editor of the *Freedom of the Press* survey. She has authored reports and conducted fact-finding missions on press freedom, human rights, and governance issues to a number of countries in Africa and South Asia. She holds a PhD in Indian history from Cambridge University and previously worked as a consultant for Human Rights Watch. She served as a South Asia and Africa analyst for *Freedom of the Press*.

Sanja Kelly is managing editor of the *Countries at the Crossroads* survey at Freedom House. She holds an MA in international relations from Columbia University and previously worked for the U.S. House of Representatives. Her research interests focus on democratic transition and consolidation in the former Yugoslavia and Soviet Union. She served as an Eastern Europe analyst for *Freedom of the Press*.

Daniel Kimmage received his BA from Binghamton University and his MA from Cornell University. He has been the Central Asia analyst at Radio Free Europe/Radio Liberty since December 2003. He served as the Central Asia analyst for *Freedom of the Press*.

John Kubiniec was formerly Freedom House's regional director for Central and Eastern Europe and the Former Soviet Union; he currently serves as a board member of Freedom House Europe. Since 1992, he has lived in several countries in Central and Eastern Europe, where he has worked for human rights and advocacy organizations supporting democratic development and civil society in the Balkans and the former Soviet Union. He studied economics and Slavic languages and literature and speaks Russian and Polish. He served as an Eastern Europe analyst for *Freedom of the Press*.

Astrid Larson is the office manager at Freedom House New York. She holds a BA from Smith College and studied international communication at American University. She served as a Western Europe analyst for *Freedom in the World* as well as the Scandinavia, Africa, and South Pacific analyst for *Freedom of the Press*.

Eleanor Marchant is a research analyst at Freedom House and assistant editor of *Freedom of the Press*. Her research focuses on human rights, particularly press freedom, in West Africa. She holds an MA in international relations from New York University and a BSc in economics and politics from the University of Bristol, United Kingdom. She served as an Africa analyst for *Freedom of the Press*.

Chris W. Ogbondah is a professor of journalism and coordinator of the mass communication program in the Department of Communication Studies at the University of Northern Iowa. He holds a PhD in journalism from Southern Illinois University at Carbondale and is author of *The Press in Nigeria: An Annotated Bibliography; Military Regimes and the Press in Nigeria, 1966 to 1993: Human Rights and National Development;* and *State-Press Relations in Nigeria, 1993–1998: Human Rights and Democratic Development*. He has published articles on press freedom in scholarly journals. He served as a West Africa analyst for *Freedom of the Press*.

Folu Ogundimu is a professor of journalism and former senior research associate for Afrobarometer at Michigan State University. He holds a PhD in mass communication from Indiana University at Bloomington and is coeditor of *Media and Democracy in Africa*. He was founding director of the Ghana Multidisciplinary Studies Program at MSU. He served as a West Africa analyst for *Freedom of the Press*.

Ory Okolloh received her BA in political science from the University of Pittsburgh and her JD from Harvard Law School. She is currently working as legal counsel for Enablis in Johannesburg. She served as an East Africa analyst for *Freedom of the Press*.

Aili Piano is a senior researcher at Freedom House and managing editor of *Freedom in the World*. She was a country report author for several editions of *Nations in Transit*, a Freedom House survey of democratization in East-Central Europe and Eurasia, and for Freedom House's *Countries at the Crossroads 2004* survey of democratic governance. Before joining Freedom House, she worked as a diplomatic attaché at the Estonian Mission to the United Nations. She holds an MA from Columbia University's School of International and Public Affairs. She served as the Baltic States analyst for *Freedom of the Press*.

Mauro P. Porto is assistant professor in the Department of Communications at Tulane University. In 2002, his PhD dissertation in communication from the University of California at San Diego received the Best Doctoral Dissertation Award from the Brazilian Society of Interdisciplinary Communication Studies. His forthcoming book, *Televisao e Politica no Brasil* (*Television and Politics in Brazil*), is based on his dissertation, and he has published on political communication in several academic journals around the world. His teaching interests include media and politics in Brazil and media and democracy in Latin America. He served as a South America analyst for *Freedom of the Press*.

Nanne Priebs von Hahn is a PhD candidate in law at Hamburg University, Germany, and project manager at the Center for Media and Communication Studies at the Central European University in Budapest, Hungary. Her dissertation research focuses on the legal and social implications of the transformation of public service broadcasters in a multichannel media environment. She served as a Western Europe analyst for *Freedom of the Press*.

Arch Puddington is director of research at Freedom House and coeditor of *Freedom in the World*. He has written widely on American foreign policy, race relations, organized labor, and the history of the cold war. He is the author of *Broadcasting Freedom: The Cold War Triumph of Radio Free Europe and Radio Liberty* and *Lane Kirkland: Champion of American Labor*. He served as the United States analyst for *Freedom of the Press*.

David Robie is associate professor of journalism in the School of Communication Studies at New Zealand's Auckland University of Technology and director of the Pacific Media Centre. He holds a PhD in history/politics from the University of the South Pacific, Fiji, where he was former coordinator of the Pacific Region Journalism Program. He is founding editor of *Pacific Journalism Review* and has written several books on Pacific media, including *Mekim Nius: South Pacific Media, Politics, and Education*. He served as an Asia-Pacific analyst for *Freedom of the Press*.

Mark Y. Rosenberg is a doctoral student of political science at the University of California at Berkeley. He is a former researcher and assistant editor of *Freedom in the World* at Freedom House. He is author of the South Africa report for *Countries at the Crossroads 2006* and served as the Southern Africa and Israel/Palestinian territories analyst for *Freedom of the World* and *Freedom of the Press*.

Tyler Roylance is a research and editorial assistant at Freedom House. He holds a BA in classics from Drew University and an MA in history from New York University. He served as a Central and Eastern Europe analyst for *Freedom of the Press*.

Hani Sabra is a human rights professional based in New York. From 2001 to 2005, he was the Middle East and North Africa researcher at the Committee to Protect Journalists. He served as the North Africa analyst for *Freedom in the World* and *Freedom of the Press*.

Janet Steele is an associate professor of journalism in the School of Media and Public Affairs at George Washington University. She received her PhD in history from Johns Hopkins University and has taught courses on the theory and practice of journalism in Southeast and South Asia as a Fulbright senior scholar and lecturer. Her book *Wars Within: The Story of Tempo, an Independent Magazine in Soeharto's Indonesia* focuses on *Tempo* magazine and its relationship to the politics and culture of new-order Indonesia. She served as a Southeast Asia analyst for *Freedom of the Press.*

Leigh Tomppert is a former research and policy associate with the International Gay and Lesbian Human Rights Commission. She holds an MA in the social sciences from the University of Chicago. Previously, she was a researcher at Freedom House and assistant editor of Freedom House's *Women's Rights in the Middle East and North Africa* survey. She served as a Middle East analyst for *Freedom of the Press.*

Thomas Webb is a research assistant at Freedom House and a recent graduate of Vassar College. He served as a Western Europe analyst for *Freedom of the Press.*

Lars Willnat is an associate professor in the School of Media and Public Affairs at George Washington University. Before joining GWU in 1996, he taught at the Chinese University of Hong Kong and was a MacArthur Foundation Fellow at the Indiana Center on Global Change and World Peace. His teaching and research interests include political media effects, theoretical aspects of public opinion formation, and international communication. He received his PhD in mass communication from Indiana University in 1992. He served as an Asia-Pacific analyst for *Freedom of the Press.*

Elijah Zarwan is a Cairo-based researcher for Human Rights Watch. He previously worked as a researcher for the Arabic Network for Human Rights Information, Harvard University, as managing editor of *Cairo* magazine, as an editor at *World Press Review,* and as a freelance journalist in the Middle East. He served as a Middle East analyst for *Freedom of the Press.*

Ratings Review Advisers:

Jon B. Alterman is director of the Middle East Program at the Center for Strategic and International Studies in Washington, D.C. He received his PhD in history from Harvard University, and he has worked on the personal staff of Senator Daniel Patrick Moynihan and on the policy-planning staff at the Department of State. He is the author of *New Media, New Politics?: From Satellite Television to the Internet in the Arab World.* He served as Middle East adviser for *Freedom of the Press.*

Rosental Alves is a professor of journalism at the University of Texas at Austin, where he created the first course in online journalism. For over a decade, he was a foreign correspondent based in Spain, Argentina, Mexico, and the United States, working for *Jornal do Brasil,* one of the most important Brazilian newspapers, in Rio de Janeiro. In 1994, he managed the creation of the *Jornal do Brasil* online edition, making it the first Brazilian newspaper available on the internet. A working journalist since he was 16, he received a BA in journalism from Rio de Janeiro Federal University. He was the first Brazilian awarded a Nieman Fellowship to spend an academic year (1987–1988) at Harvard University. He served as an Americas adviser for *Freedom of the Press.*

Sheila S. Coronel is a professor at the Graduate School of Journalism at Columbia University and head of the Stabile Center for Investigative Journalism at the school. She was a founder and executive director of the Manila–based Philippine Center for Investigative Journalism. She was also a founding director of the Southeast Asian Press Alliance and editor and coauthor of several books, including a study on freedom of information in Southeast Asia. She served as Southeast Asia adviser for *Freedom of the Press.*

Ashley Esarey received his PhD in political science from Columbia University and is currently Luce Fellow of Asian Studies and assistant professor of comparative politics at Middlebury College. His research concerns mass media, the internet, and blogging in Asia and their effect on democratization more generally; he also studies democratic institutions in Japan, Taiwan, South Korea, Hong Kong, and China. He served as East Asia adviser for *Freedom of the Press.*

Festus Eribo is professor of international communication and head of African studies at East Carolina University, Greenville, North Carolina. He received his PhD from the University of Wisconsin at Madison and his MA from St. Petersburg State University and has worked as a journalist in Africa and Russia. He has authored five books, including *Press Freedom and Communication in Africa* and *Window on Africa: Democratization and Media Exposure.* He served as an Africa adviser for *Freedom of the Press.*

Marilyn Greene is an independent media consultant based in Washington, D.C., and recently edited the World Press Freedom Committee's publication *It's a Crime: How Insult Laws Stifle Press Freedom.* She was a 2005 Knight

International Press Fellow in Cameroon, working with Francophone and Anglophone journalists to enhance journalistic professionalism in that country. She served for seven years as executive director of the World Press Freedom Committee and for several years prior as an international affairs reporter for *USA Today,* covering conflicts in Somalia, Kuwait, and Haiti as well as situations throughout Europe, Asia, and the Middle East. She is a graduate of the Medill School of Journalism at Northwestern University and a former fellow in Asian studies at the University of Hawaii and the East-West Center in Honolulu. She served as a global adviser for *Freedom of the Press.*

Tendayi Kumbula is an assistant professor of journalism at Ball State University, Muncie, Indiana. He received his PhD from the University of Southern California and two MA degrees from the University of California at Los Angeles. He has authored or coauthored four books. He has been a reporter and editor in Los Angeles and Indiana and was an editor for four years in Zimbabwe. In 1991 and 2003, he participated in the American Society of Newspaper Editors' Institute of Journalism Excellence, which sends selected journalism educators to spend six summer weeks working in a newsroom. He served as an Africa adviser for *Freedom of the Press.*

Bettina Peters is director of the Global Forum for Media Development, a network of organizations involved in media assistance programs around the world. Until recently, she worked as director of programs at the European Journalism Center, in charge of its international journalism training program. Before joining the EJC, she worked for 10 years at the International Federation of Journalists headquarters in Brussels. She holds degrees in political science and journalism from the University of Hamburg and is author of the chapter entitled "Ethics of Journalists" for the Council of Europe book *Media and Democracy.* She served as Western Europe adviser for *Freedom of the Press.*

Byron T. Scott is professor emeritus and director of the European Union Center at the University of Missouri at Columbia and is a former newspaper and magazine journalist. His special area of interest is the media in transitional nations of the former Soviet bloc. He has worked as a journalist and teacher of journalism throughout the former Soviet bloc, including stints at the American University in Bulgaria, the University of Tirana, and Moscow State University. He served as Eastern Europe/Former Soviet Union adviser for *Freedom of the Press.*

John Virtue is director of the International Media Center of the School of Journalism and Mass Communication at Florida International University. Before joining FIU, he was executive editor of the daily newspaper *El Mundo* in San Juan, Puerto Rico, and for 17 previous years a foreign correspondent and news agency executive in Latin America, based in Sao Paulo, Caracas, and Mexico City. He holds a bachelor of journalism degree from Carleton University, Ottawa, Canada. He served as an Americas adviser for *Freedom of the Press*.

Survey Methodology

The 2007 survey, which provides analytical reports and numerical ratings for 195 countries and territories, expands a process conducted since 1980 by Freedom House. The findings are widely used by governments, international organizations, academics, and the news media in many countries. Countries are given a total score from 0 (best) to 100 (worst) on the basis of a set of 23 methodology questions divided into three subcategories. Assigning numerical points allows for comparative analysis among the countries surveyed and facilitates an examination of trends over time. The degree to which each country permits the free flow of news and information determines the classification of its media as "Free," "Partly Free," or "Not Free." Countries scoring 0 to 30 are regarded as having "Free" media; 31 to 60, "Partly Free" media; and 61 to 100, "Not Free" media. The criteria for such judgments and the arithmetic scheme for displaying the judgments are described in the following section. The ratings and reports included in *Freedom of the Press 2007* cover events that took place between January 1, 2006, and December 31, 2006.

This year, we have added a five-year timeline of ratings under each country report to help readers analyze trends in press freedom over time. More detailed tables with older data are available on our website at www.freedomhouse.org.

Criteria

This study is based on universal criteria. The starting point is the smallest, most universal unit of concern: the individual. We recognize cultural differences, diverse national interests, and varying levels of economic development. Yet Article 19 of the Universal Declaration of Human Rights states:

> Everyone has the right to freedom of opinion and expression; this right includes freedom to hold opinions without interference and to seek, receive, and impart information and ideas through any media regardless of frontiers.

The operative word for this survey is "everyone." All states, from the most democratic to the most authoritarian, are committed to this doctrine through the UN system. To deny that doctrine is to deny the universality of information freedom—a basic human right. We recognize that cultural distinctions or economic underdevelopment may limit the volume of news flows within a country, but these and other arguments are not acceptable explanations for outright centralized control of the content of news and information. Some poor countries allow for the exchange of diverse views, while some economically developed countries restrict content diversity. We seek to recognize press freedom wherever it exists, in poor and rich countries as well as in countries of various ethnic, religious, and cultural backgrounds.

Research and Ratings Review Process

The findings are reached after a multilayered process of analysis and evaluation by a team of regional experts and scholars. Although there is an element of subjectivity inherent in the survey findings, the ratings process emphasizes intellectual rigor and balanced and unbiased judgments.

The research and ratings process involved 33 analysts and 10 senior-level ratings advisers—the largest number to date. The 10 members of the core research team headquartered in New York, along with 23 outside consultant analysts, prepare the draft ratings and country reports. Their conclusions are reached after gathering information from professional contacts in a variety of countries, staff and consultant travel, international visitors, the findings of human rights and press freedom organizations, specialists in geographic and geopolitical areas, the reports of governments and multilateral bodies, and a variety of domestic and international news media. We would particularly like to thank the other members of the International Freedom of Expression Exchange (IFEX) network for providing detailed and timely analyses of press freedom violations in a variety of countries worldwide on which we rely to make our judgments.

The ratings are reviewed individually and on a comparative basis in a series of six regional meetings—Asia-Pacific, Central and Eastern Europe and the Former Soviet Union, Latin America and the Caribbean, Middle East and North Africa, Sub-Saharan Africa, and Western Europe—involving the analysts, ratings advisers with expertise in each region, other invited participants, and Freedom House staff. The ratings are compared with the previous year's findings, and any major proposed numerical shifts or category changes are subjected to more intensive scrutiny. These reviews are followed by cross-regional assessments in which efforts are made to ensure comparability and consistency in the findings. Many of the key country reports are also reviewed by the academic advisers and by other IFEX members.

Methodology

Through the years, we have refined and expanded our methodology. Recent changes are intended to simplify the presentation of information without altering the comparability of data for a given country over the 26-year span or the comparative ratings of all countries over that period.

Our examination of the level of press freedom in each country currently comprises 23 methodology questions divided into three broad categories: the legal environment, the political environment, and the economic environment. For each methodology question, a lower number of points is allotted for a more free situation, while a higher number of points is allotted for a less free environment. Each country is rated in these three categories, with the higher numbers indicating less freedom. A country's final score is based on the total of the three categories: A score of 0 to 30 places the country in the Free press group; 31 to 60 in the Partly Free press group; and 61 to 100 in the Not Free press group.

The diverse nature of the methodology questions seeks to encompass the varied ways in which pressure can be placed upon the flow of information and the ability of print, broadcast, and internet-based media to operate freely and without fear of repercussions: In short, we seek to provide a picture of the entire "enabling environment" in which the media in each country operate. We also seek to assess the degree of news and information diversity available to the public in any given country, from either local or transnational sources.

The **legal environment** category encompasses an examination of both the laws and regulations that could influence media content and the government's inclination to use these laws and legal institutions to restrict the media's ability to operate. We assess the positive impact of legal and constitutional guarantees for freedom of expression; the potentially negative aspects of security legislation, the penal code, and other criminal statutes; penalties for libel and defamation; the existence of and ability to use freedom of information legislation; the independence of the judiciary and of official media regulatory bodies; registration requirements for both media outlets and journalists; and the ability of journalists' groups to operate freely.

Under the **political environment** category, we evaluate the degree of political control over the content of news media. Issues examined include the editorial independence of both state-owned and privately owned media; access to information and sources; official censorship and self-censorship; the vibrancy of the media and the diversity of news available within each country; the ability of both foreign and local reporters to cover the news freely and without harassment; and the intimidation of journalists by the state or other actors, including arbitrary detention and imprisonment, violent assaults, and other threats.

Our third category examines the **economic environment** for the media. This includes the structure of media ownership; transparency and concentration of ownership; the costs of establishing media as well as of production and distribution; the selective withholding of advertising or subsidies by the state or other actors; the impact of corruption and bribery on content; and the extent to which the economic situation in a country impacts the development and sustainability of the media.

Checklist of Methodology Questions for 2007

A. LEGAL ENVIRONMENT (0–30 POINTS)
1. Do the constitution or other basic laws contain provisions designed to protect freedom of the press and of expression, and are they enforced? (0–6 points)
2. Do the penal code, security laws, or any other laws restrict reporting, and are journalists punished under these laws? (0–6 points)
3. Are there penalties for libeling officials or the state, and are they enforced? (0–3 points)
4. Is the judiciary independent, and do courts judge cases concerning the media impartially? (0–3 points)
5. Is freedom of information legislation in place, and are journalists able to make use of it? (0–2 points)
6. Can individuals or business entities legally establish and operate private media outlets without undue interference? (0–4 points)

7. Are media regulatory bodies, such as a broadcasting authority or national press or communications council, able to operate freely and independently? (0–2 points)
8. Is there freedom to become a journalist and to practice journalism? (0–4 points)

B. POLITICAL ENVIRONMENT (0–40 POINTS)

1. To what extent are media outlets' news and information content determined by the government or a particular partisan interest? (0–10 points)
2. Is access to official or unofficial sources generally controlled? (0–2 points)
3. Is there official censorship? (0–4 points)
4. Do journalists practice self-censorship? (0–4 points)
5. Is media coverage robust, and does it reflect a diversity of viewpoints? (0–4 points)
6. Are both local and foreign journalists able to cover the news freely? (0–6 points)
7. Are journalists or media outlets subject to extralegal intimidation or physical violence by state authorities or any other actor? (0–10 points)

C. ECONOMIC ENVIRONMENT (0–30 POINTS)

1. To what extent are media owned or controlled by the government, and does this influence their diversity of views? (0–6 points)
2. Is private media ownership transparent, thus allowing consumers to judge the impartiality of the news? (0–3 points)
3. Is private media ownership highly concentrated, and does it influence diversity of content? (0–3 points)
4. Are there restrictions on the means of journalistic production and distribution? (0–4 points)
5. Does the state place prohibitively high costs on the establishment and operation of media outlets? (0–4 points)
6. Do the state or other actors try to control the media through allocation of advertising or subsidies? (0–3 points)
7. Do journalists receive payment from private or public sources whose design is to influence their journalistic content? (0–3 points)
8. Does the economic situation in a country accentuate media dependency on the state, political parties, big business, or other influential political actors for funding? (0–4 points)

Legend

Country

Status: Free (0–30)
Partly Free (31–60)
Not Free (61–100)

Legal Environment: 0–30 points
Political Environment: 0–40 points
Economic Environment: 0–30 points
Total Score: 0–100 points

Press Freedom in 2006: Growing Threats to Media Independence

Karin Deutsch Karlekar

The state of global press freedom declined in 2006, with particularly worrisome trends evident in Asia, the former Soviet Union, and Latin America. Despite notable improvements in a number of countries, gains were generally overshadowed by a continued, relentless assault on independent news media in a group of geopolitically crucial states, including Russia, Venezuela, Iran, and China, as well as declines in countries with more open press environments, such as Argentina, Brazil, the Philippines, Sri Lanka, and Thailand. Moreover, a growing number of governments moved in 2006 to restrict internet freedom by censoring, harassing, or shutting down sites that provide alternative sources of news and commentary.

These disturbing developments constitute the principal findings of *Freedom of the Press 2007: A Global Survey of Media Independence*, an annual index published by Freedom House since 1980.

The findings reflect a 10-year trend of media freedom stagnation and, in some cases, outright decline in key countries and regions. While press freedom made impressive gains during the 1980s and early 1990s, that progress has stalled in recent years, following a broader pattern of stagnation in political freedom that Freedom House has identified.

Karin Deutsch Karlekar, a senior researcher at Freedom House, served as managing editor of Freedom of the Press 2007. *She holds a Ph.D. from Cambridge University.*

The annual *Freedom of the Press* survey assesses the degree of print, broadcast, and internet freedom in every country in the world, analyzing the events and developments of each calendar year. Ratings are determined through an examination of three broad categories: the legal environment in which media operate; political influences on reporting and access to information; and economic pressures on content and the dissemination of news. Under the legal category, we assess the laws and regulations that could influence media content as well as the government's inclination to use these tools to restrict the media's ability to operate. The political category encompasses a variety of issues, including editorial pressure by the government or other actors; censorship and self-censorship; the ability of reporters to cover the news; and the extralegal intimidation of and violence against journalists. Finally, under the economic category we examine issues such as the structure, transparency, and concentration of media ownership; costs of production and distribution; and the impact of advertising, subsidies, and bribery on content. Ratings reflect not just government actions and policies, but the behavior of the press itself in testing boundaries, even in more restrictive environments. The survey provides a numerical rating from 0 (the most free) to 100 (the least free) for each country and categorizes each country's level of press freedom as "Free," "Partly Free," or "Not Free" based on its numerical rating.

The Global Picture

Out of 195 countries and territories assessed, 74 countries (38 percent) were rated Free, 58 (30 percent) were rated Partly Free, and 63 (32 percent) were rated Not Free. This represented a modest improvement from the 2005 assessment: 73 Free countries, 54 Partly Free countries, and 67 Not Free countries. However, the findings for 2006 represent a negative shift from the survey results of five years ago, which was the last recent high point of press freedom.

In terms of population, the survey found that only 18 percent of the world's inhabitants live in countries that enjoy a Free press, while 39 percent have a Partly Free press and 43 percent have a Not Free press. The relatively negative picture painted by these population figures is due to the impact of two countries—China, with a Not Free rating, and India, with a Partly Free rating—which together account for some two billion of the world's six billion people. The percentage of those enjoying Free media in 2006 improved slightly from 2005, while the percentage of people who live in countries with a Not Free media environment remained steady.

The overall global average score for press freedom worsened slightly in 2006, continuing a five-year downward trend. The global averages for the legal and political categories also worsened, with the legal category showing the largest decline.

Reasons behind the Threats to Media Independence

Driving the decline of global press freedom in recent years is a complex set of factors, some deriving from broad trends in overall freedom and others more specific to the media environment.

1. **Push-Back Against Democracy:** A growing drive to neutralize or eliminate all potential sources of political opposition has emerged in countries as diverse as Russia, Venezuela, and Zimbabwe in recent years. Along with the institutions of civil society, the press has been a principal target of this movement for near absolute political domination and is often one of the first targets of authoritarian regimes. The methods used tend to be legalistic: print or broadcast outlets are taken over by the state or by forces aligned with the political leadership; license renewals are denied; journalists are jailed or hit with heavy fines for libel or defamation. Russia, under President Vladimir Putin, is the template for this phenomenon. During Putin's tenure, the lively and probing press that had emerged during the glasnost and post-Communist periods has been transformed into a toothless sounding board for the opinions of the leadership.

2. **Political Upheaval:** Although not yet a major trend, coups and states of emergency brought on by political unrest or civil war have arisen in a growing number of formerly democratic settings over the past several years, delivering a striking blow to press freedom. This has become an increasingly important factor in Asia, as the media in Bangladesh, Pakistan, Sri Lanka, the Philippines, Thailand, and Fiji have all suffered important setbacks amid political upheaval or mounting polarization.

3. **Violence Targeting Journalists:** The tragic murder of crusading Russian journalist Anna Politkovskaya is but one of the latest examples of what has become a disturbing global trend. The killing and beating of reporters is a particular problem in Latin America, where Mexico has recently replaced Colombia as the most dangerous environment for reporters who investigate controversial subjects. The murder of journalists by both state and nonstate actors has also emerged as an alarming pattern in Russia, Iraq, the Philippines, Pakistan, and Sri Lanka. And in most of these places, a culture of impunity persists, with halfhearted or ineffective efforts being made to punish those responsible.

4. **Legislation Prohibiting Blasphemy, Hate Speech, Insult, and "Endangering National Security":** Governments have increasingly resorted to legal action in their efforts to punish the press for critical reports on the political leadership and for "inciting hatred," commenting on sensitive topics such as religion or ethnicity, or "endangering national security." This has long been a key barrier to media freedom in the Middle East, but it is increasingly occurring in Asia and Africa and in some countries of the former Soviet Union. In Turkey alone, 293 writers and journalists were prosecuted under Article 301 of the revised penal code, which broadly prohibits denigrating "Turkishness."

Regional and Country Declines

Significant numerical declines occurred in Asia, where restrictions on media coverage were imposed following military coups in Fiji and Thailand and states of emergency in the Philippines and Sri Lanka. This led to negative status changes in Fiji, which shifted from Free to Partly Free owing to a crackdown on the media following a coup in December, and Sri Lanka, whose status declined from Partly Free to Not Free as media faced increased restrictions and harassment from both the government and the Tamil Tiger rebels in the context of a general slide back into civil war during the year.

Backsliding in the former Soviet Union continued, with Russia and Kyrgyzstan registering declines. In the Americas, Argentina continued to slide in a negative direction owing to misuse of official advertising, while political turbulence and polarization weakened media freedom in Bolivia and Peru. In several other countries in the region, such as Brazil, Paraguay, and the Dominican Republic, increased violence against journalists covering issues related to drug trafficking or corruption led to declines during the year.

Major declines in a number of countries over the last six years illustrate the broader assault on press freedom. Since 2002, Venezuela has registered a decline of 30 points on a 100-point scale, the greatest decline for a single country. Other major slippages include a 29-point decline for Thailand; a 16-point decline for the Philippines and Ethiopia; a 15-point decline for Eritrea, Russia, and Yemen; and a 12-point decline for Uganda, Argentina, Peru, and Bolivia. The year saw no genuinely positive regional trends; indeed, in practically every region, stagnation or decline was the rule. In the Middle East and North Africa, where progress had occurred over the past several years, governments pushed back against greater openness and livelier coverage of political and social developments, which negatively impacted ratings for a number of countries in the region. Overall trends in the Americas and Asia were also disappointing, as was the case in the former Soviet Union. Sub-Saharan Africa presented a mixed picture.

The year saw setbacks in a number of key countries, many of which had already been on downward trajectories in past years. The most significant numerical declines occurred in Asia, where restrictions on media coverage were imposed following military coups in Fiji and Thailand and states of emergency in the Philippines and Sri Lanka. This led to negative status changes in Fiji, which shifted from Free to Partly Free owing to a crackdown on the media following a coup in December, and Sri Lanka, whose status declined from Partly Free to Not Free as media faced increased restrictions and harassment from both the government and the Tamil Tiger rebels in the context of a general slide back into civil war during the year.

Backsliding in the former Soviet Union continued, with Russia and Kyrgyzstan registering declines. In the Americas, Argentina continued to slide in a negative direction owing to misuse of official advertising, while political turbulence and polarization weakened media freedom in Bolivia and Peru. In several other countries in the region, such as Brazil, Paraguay, and the Dominican Republic, increased violence against journalists covering issues related to drug trafficking or corruption led to declines during the year.

Major declines in a number of countries over the last six years illustrate the broader assault on press freedom. Since 2002, Venezuela has registered a decline of 30 points on a 100-point scale, the greatest decline for a single country. Other major slippages include a 29-point decline for Thailand; a

16-point decline for the Philippines and Ethiopia; a 15-point decline for Eritrea, Russia, and Yemen; and a 12-point decline for Uganda, Argentina, Peru, and Bolivia.

Notable Country Gains

Having been the only European Union member state with a press freedom status lower than Free, Italy stands out among the countries that registered important gains in 2006. The country's ratings had been lowered in 2003 owing to excessive media concentration and political influence over media content during the government of Prime Minister Silvio Berlusconi. His exit from office in 2006 led to Italy's upgrade from the Partly Free to the Free category.

Legal improvements, particularly the decriminalization of libel, led to both Cambodia and the Central African Republic moving from Not Free to Partly Free. General improvements in the political environment, greater respect for media freedom by the government, and the increased ability of journalists to report on important events freely contributed to Cape Verde's upgrade from Partly Free to Free and to positive movement in the Americas as Haiti and Colombia both shifted from Not Free to the Partly Free category.

The final positive category shift to Partly Free, which was accompanied by the largest numerical improvement of the year (19 points), took place in Nepal, where journalists were at the forefront of an effort to end the monarchy's direct rule and restore parliamentary government. Nepal saw dramatic improvements in all aspects of its media environment as harsh laws and decrees were scrapped, censorship was lifted, physical repression and attacks by official forces against journalists eased, and hundreds of private and community radio stations were reopened.

The Internet: Expanding Restrictions on a Key Outlet for Free Expression

The internet has emerged as one of the most potent weapons against censorship and lack of transparency in authoritarian societies. Even in China and Iran, where the authorities have devoted significant resources to the control of internet content, internet-based outlets have remained a vital source of news about social upheaval, labor disputes, official corruption, and acts of state abuse against the citizenry.

Developments in 2006 also reflect the extent to which government authorities are becoming increasingly aware of this phenomenon and acting boldly to curb it. China, Vietnam, and Iran—all restricted media environments in which internet usage has exploded in recent years—continue to convict and imprison large numbers of journalists and "cyberdissidents" who publish political material online, and this trend is spreading to other countries with restrictive media environments where the internet is an important source of unfiltered information. In Russia, legal action was taken against website owners, and the Putin administration has announced plans to regulate internet content. Several African countries with increasingly restrictive press environments, such as Ethiopia and The Gambia, have also moved to impose controls on local and expatriate bloggers and websites, despite the relatively low levels of local internet penetration.

Worst of the Worst

The five worst-rated countries continue to be Burma, Cuba, Libya, North Korea, and Turkmenistan. In these states, which are scattered across the globe, independent media are either nonexistent or barely able to operate, the press acts as a mouthpiece for the ruling regime, and citizens' access to unbiased information is severely limited. The numerical scores for these five countries barely changed from 2005 to 2006, reflecting an extreme level of repression and stagnation for the media. Rounding out the 10 most repressive media environments are two countries in the former Soviet Union—Belarus and Uzbekistan—and three countries in Africa—Equatorial Guinea, Eritrea, and Zimbabwe—where media are heavily restricted.

Regional Trends

Americas: In the Americas, 17 countries (48 percent) were rated Free, 16 (46 percent) were rated Partly Free, and 2 (6 percent) were rated Not Free in 2006. Just under half the countries in the region have media that remain classified as Free, although this includes the Caribbean, whose countries generally have very open media environments, offsetting the less rosy picture in Central and South America.

During the past five years, the percentage of Latin American countries classified as having Free media has slipped from 60 percent to 48 percent. More worrisome, ratings over the past 16 years reflect an overall decline in media freedom in the Americas. The number of Free countries has dropped from 22 in 1990 to 17 in 2006, the most significant decline for any region. The average regional score declined from that of 2005, with drops seen in both the legal and political categories.

Countries of particular concern continue to be Cuba, which has one of the most repressive media environments worldwide, and Venezuela, where the government of President Hugo Chavez has further intensified its efforts to control the press. While **Cuba** has by far the worst score in the hemisphere and ranks in the bottom five worldwide, **Venezuela** has seen one of the most dramatic declines globally over the past six years, with the largest numerical drop (from 44 to 74 points) of any country in the survey. In 2006, Chavez's intention to further squeeze the private media sector was made apparent by the government's December decision not to renew the license of a major television station, RCTV.

The region did have some noteworthy positive developments in 2006, as both Haiti and Colombia registered status changes from the Not Free to the Partly Free category. Colombia's score improved from 61 to 57 owing to the increased willingness of local journalists to report critically on political issues, including the high-level corruption scandals that erupted during the year, as well as a gradually improving security situation. Haiti registered an even more dramatic numerical improvement, from 68 to 59, as the election of a new, more media-tolerant government in April and a reduction in overall political tensions led to openings in the legal and political environment in which journalists operate.

However, these positive developments were overshadowed by negative changes in a number of countries, some of which were continuations of trends noted previously. **Argentina's** score dropped by a further four points, from 45 to 49, to reflect the persistent manipulation of advertising by government officials at both the national and state levels with the intention of influencing media content, either by rewarding supportive outlets or by punishing critical ones. This more subtle form of economic harassment was accompanied by a rise in the number of physical attacks on journalists, often perpetrated by representatives of the state.

Intimidation of and attacks against journalists also appeared to be on the rise in **Peru**, which saw a three-point decline, and in **Bolivia**, primarily in the context of political protests and rallies that took place near the end of the year, resulting in a four-point decline. In several other countries, including **Brazil**, **Paraguay**, and the **Dominican Republic**, rising violence against and harassment of journalists (including murder) was linked to their coverage of sensitive topics like drug trafficking and organized crime.

Continuing the year's negative trend was **Mexico**, where improvements in the legal sphere were outweighed by an appalling level of violence against journalists, who were often the victims of drug lords, and by governmental ineffectiveness in prosecuting those responsible for the murders. Although the **United States** continues to be one of the better performers in the survey, there were continuing problems in the legal sphere, particularly concerning cases in which the authorities tried to compel journalists to reveal confidential sources or provide access to research material in the course of criminal investigations.

Asia-Pacific: The Asia-Pacific region as a whole exhibited a relatively high level of press freedom, with 16 countries (40 percent) rated Free, 10 (25 percent) rated Partly Free, and 14 (35 percent) rated Not Free. Yet the regionwide figures are deceptive, as they disguise considerable subregional diversity. For example, the Pacific islands, Australasia, and parts of East Asia have some of the best-ranked media environments worldwide, while conditions in South Asia, Southeast Asia, and other parts of East Asia are significantly poorer. Among those with poor records of press freedom are large and geopolitically significant countries such as China and Pakistan.

Asia is home to two of the five worst-rated countries in the world, Burma and North Korea, which have extremely repressive media environments, as well as several other poor performers like China, Laos, and Vietnam, all of which use state or party control of the press as the primary tool to restrict media freedom.

The overall level of press freedom in Asia, in terms of the average regional score, declined from the previous year, with drops seen in both the legal and political categories. Two countries received status upgrades and two were downgraded in 2006.

While the majority of the trends noted in 2006 were negative, several bright spots are worth noting. The survey's greatest score jump of the year was in **Nepal**, where wide-ranging political change led to a dramatic opening in the media environment. Following the overthrow of direct rule by the monarchy, the reintroduction of a parliamentary form of government, and the signing of a peace accord with the Maoist rebels, repressive legislation was either scrapped or amended, authorities became more tolerant of media freedom, and hundreds of private and community radio stations were reopened. Nepal's score improved from 77 to 58 and its status shifted to Partly Free as a result of the events of 2006, during which journalists were at the forefront of promoting a more democratic society.

Positive developments in the legal sphere were primarily responsible for **Cambodia**'s upgrade to Partly Free and its score improvement from 61 to 58. Defamation was decriminalized, and there were fewer cases of attacks and harassment as the government adopted a generally more positive attitude toward the media. Defamation was also a key issue in **Indonesia**, whose score improved by four points to 54 in 2006. A Constitutional Court ruling struck down an article of the penal code that criminalized defamation of the president, and several other rulings in high-profile defamation cases were decided in favor of the journalists involved. Meanwhile, media concentration in the small kingdom of **Bhutan** became less pronounced with the opening of the country's first private radio station and the launching of two new private weeklies, leading to a three-point upgrade to 62.

Asia saw many negative developments in 2006, however, continuing the downward regional trajectory noted in the previous year's survey. Coups and military intervention were responsible for the suspension of legal protections for press freedom and new curbs imposed on media coverage in **Fiji**, whose score worsened from 28 to 39 and whose status slipped to Partly Free owing to the government crackdown on the media following a military coup in December. In **Thailand**, the elected government of Prime Minister Thaksin Shinawatra had employed varied forms of harassment of the press, contributing to a slide of 20 points since 2002. In 2006, Thailand's score dropped further, to 59 points, following a bloodless coup in September in which the military deposed Thaksin, introduced a new transitional constitution that does not protect press freedom, and imposed restrictions on media content.

Heightened political and civil conflict during the year in several countries also contributed to declines. **Sri Lanka**'s score declined by five points to 63, and its status was downgraded to Not Free, to reflect new official restrictions on media coverage as well as a rise in attacks against journalists—particularly ethnic Tamils—and media outlets in the north and east, where the government and the Tamil Tiger rebels effectively resumed their civil war. Political violence in April, including debilitating attacks on journalists and media outlets, led to a worsened score for **East Timor** in 2006. An even more significant decline occurred in the **Philippines**, whose score dropped six points to 46, contributing to a dramatic 16-point drop since 2002. The driving forces include the government's clampdown on opposition media during the state of emergency in February, an excessive use of defamation suits to silence criticism of public officials, and the continued threat of attacks on journalists amid a climate of impunity for such crimes.

Heightened restrictions on coverage, as well as harassment of reporters and media outlets that overstep official and unofficial boundaries, contributed to declines in several Asian countries in 2006. In **Malaysia**, official attempts to suppress public discussion of divisive issues such as race and religion led to further restrictions on free reporting, resulting in a three-point decline to 68. The government of **China** also stepped up its restrictions on content, introducing new media regulations, jailing outspoken journalists, and further limiting coverage of breaking news. In **Pakistan**, reporters who attempted to cover sensitive issues such as terrorism, particularly those who were caught between government forces and the Taliban in the tribal areas bordering Afghanistan, faced heightened threats and physical attacks by both sides. Several deaths of journalists and dozens of incidents of intimidation were reported in the country during 2006.

The connected issues of violence and impunity continue to be of serious concern in South and Southeast Asia, particularly in countries such as Bangladesh and the Philippines, where frequent physical threats by both state and nonstate actors, coupled with a deterioration in the rule of law, has had a negative impact on media freedom.

Central and Eastern Europe/Former Soviet Union: For the combined CEE/FSU region, 8 countries (28 percent)—out of a new total of 28 countries, after Montenegro's independence—remain classified as Free, 10 (36 percent) are rated as Partly Free, and 10 (36 percent) are classified as Not Free. These relatively even figures belie the fact that in terms of population, a majority of the people in this region (56 percent) live in Not Free media environments, while only 28 percent have access to Free media.

While the region shares a common history of Communist oppression, the trajectory of those countries in the former Soviet Union has diverged substantially from that of Central and Eastern Europe in terms of respect for fundamental political rights and civil liberties. The press freedom ratings for these subregions reflect a similar divergence.

The repressive media landscape in the former Soviet Union is illuminated by the fact that 10 of the 12 non-Baltic post-Soviet states are ranked as Not Free. The only two that enjoy Partly Free status, Georgia and Ukraine, have recently experienced political upheaval and democratic opening. Of the 10 Not Free countries, none is moving in the direction of more freedom, and most have a decidedly downward trajectory. Of the 195 countries and territories examined in the survey, 3 of the 10 worst press freedom abusers—Belarus, Uzbekistan, and Turkmenistan—are found in the former Soviet Union.

By contrast, all of the countries of Central Europe and the three Baltic states, which themselves needed to overcome a decades-long legacy of Soviet media culture and control, are assessed as Free. Although they contend with the challenges and imperfections that media in democratic systems invariably face, the media from the Czech Republic to Estonia have achieved pluralistic and competitive news environments. In Georgia and Ukraine, which had shown improvement in the wake of democratic transitions in 2003 and 2004, progress has stalled. Indeed in much of the FSU, recent trends have pointed to stagnation or backsliding.

In 2006, the region featured no category shifts and little numerical movement, indicating a general stagnation in the level of press freedom. **Macedonia**'s score improved by four points to 45 as a result of positive developments in the legal environment, including the enactment of a Law on Freedom of Information and the elimination of imprisonment as a penalty for libel.

Most changes in the region were negative, however. **Kyrgyzstan**, whose score had improved in 2005, saw backsliding in 2006 owing to an increase in censorship and attacks against journalists, leading to a three-point decline, for a score of 67. In **Uzbekistan**, where the media environment was already heavily restricted, authorities targeted foreign news outlets and the local stringers they employed in an attempt to close off all remaining avenues of independent information. **Russia**, whose numerical score has deteriorated by 15 points in the last six years to 75 in 2006, saw a worsening of the legal environment and heightened impunity, as demonstrated by the lack of prosecutions of increasingly frequent crimes and attacks against journalists. Russia's attitude toward the media is especially important, as it serves as a model and sponsor for a number of neighboring countries.

Middle East and North Africa: The Middle East and North Africa region continued to show the lowest regionwide ratings, with just 1 country (5 percent) rated Free, 2 (11 percent) rated Partly Free, and 16 (84 percent) rated Not Free in 2006. During the year, the average regionwide score declined, as did the average score in the political subcategory.

Generally, media in the region remain constrained by extremely restrictive legal environments, in which laws concerning libel and defamation, the insult of monarchs and public figures, and emergency legislation continue to hamper the ability of journalists to write freely. Of particular and long-standing concern are **Libya**, **Syria**, **Tunisia**, and the **Israeli-Occupied Territories/Palestinian Authority**, where media freedom remained extremely restricted in 2006. The deteriorating security situation in **Iraq** contributed to a highly dangerous environment for the media, with several dozen journalists and media workers, mostly Iraqis, killed during the year.

During the last several years, we have noted improvements in press freedom in the region as a whole, owing to the continued spread and influence of Pan-Arab satellite television networks and the internet, which serve as alternative sources of news and information. In some countries, print media have also become more critical as journalists have taken the lead in pushing the boundaries of acceptable coverage, even when faced with violence or, more commonly, legal reprisals. However, this trend reversed in 2006, with several countries that had previously shown improvement moving in a negative direction. **Saudi Arabia**'s score declined by three points to 82 to reflect a rise in the number of journalists detained during the year, particularly those who criticized the government and the religious establishment. Conditions in **Iran** deteriorated further as authorities cracked down on independent media outlets and journalists, increasingly targeting internet-based sources of information. In **Egypt**, which had previously seen a considerable improvement, an official push-back against increased press openness halted this positive trend. The legal environment continues to constrain relatively good regional performers such as **Jordan**, **Morocco**, and **Algeria**. In 2006, the use of legal harassment against independent journalists increased in Morocco, with a highly influential editor forced to leave the country because of the threat of crippling fines in a defamation case.

Sub-Saharan Africa: Overall, 8 countries (17 percent) were rated Free, 19 (39 percent) were rated Partly Free, and 21 (44 percent) remained Not Free. Press freedom conditions continue to be dire in **Equatorial Guinea**, **Eritrea**, and **Zimbabwe**, where authoritarian governments use legal pressure, imprisonment, and other forms of harassment to sharply curtail the ability of independent media outlets to report freely. All three countries continue to rank in the bottom 10 performers worldwide.

During the year, the average regionwide level of press freedom declined, as did the average score in the political subcategory. However, the average score in the legal category improved, mostly as a result of reforms detailed below. Trends in individual countries presented a mixed picture, with two positive category changes and a number of positive numerical shifts in some countries balanced by negative movements in others.

In 2006, **Cape Verde**'s score improved from 32 to 29 and its status was upgraded to Free as the continued consolidation of democracy led to a greater opening in the media environment and a decrease in legal harassment and attacks aimed at journalists. In the **Central African Republic**, the government's adherence to the new Press Law and a 2005 constitution that respects freedom of expression and decriminalizes libel were the primary factors behind a status upgrade to Partly Free. Similarly, in **Angola**, the passage of a new Press Law—which, among other things, ended the state monopoly on television broadcasting and allowed truth to be used as a defense for libel—resulted in a three-point upgrade to a score of 62. **Sierra Leone**'s score also improved, to 56, to reflect a decrease in the number of cases brought against journalists under criminal libel legislation. Limited progress in the key Cardoso legal case, coupled with fewer instances of physical harassment of journalists, led to a three-point uptick in the numerical score for **Mozambique**, leaving it with 40 points.

Increased political normalcy also led to improvements for **Togo**, whose score returned to 74 following a period of heightened aggression toward journalists surrounding the 2005 coup and election, and for **Sudan**, where enhanced autonomy in the southern region, coupled with moderately increased freedom for reporters in Khartoum, led to an improvement of four points for a score of 81.

These gains were balanced by declines in a number of countries, several of which were already on a longer-term negative trajectory. **Burundi**'s score worsened by three points to 77 to reflect a targeted official crackdown on critical media outlets, particularly those that questioned the authenticity of an alleged coup attempt that the government used as a justification for its wave of attacks on the opposition. In **Cote d'Ivoire,** blatant attempts by President Laurent Gbagbo and his supporters to control state media content, such as the January takeover of the national radio station by pro-government militias bent on inciting violence, led to a three-point decline, for a score of 68.

Conditions in one of the world's worst performers, **Eritrea**, deteriorated further to a numerical score of 94 as a result of tightened restrictions on foreign reporters traveling inside the country. Over the past six years, Eritrea's score has declined by 15 points. Similarly, in **The Gambia**, whose score has declined by 12 points to 77 over the past six years, independent media activity was further curtailed through the imprisonment, intimidation, and exile of critical journalists. Two countries that registered significant negative movement in 2005 amid long-term negative trends, **Ethiopia** and **Uganda,** showed smaller declines in 2006 as relations between the government and independent media remained rocky.

The internet has not played a major role in most African media environments because of financial and infrastructural constraints. Nevertheless, in a number of countries where the media environment is becoming more restricted and where internet-based news outlets, often run by citizens living abroad, provide a primary source of unfiltered news, authorities made concerted moves to crack down on the promising new medium.

Western Europe: Western Europe continued to boast the highest level of press freedom worldwide; in 2006, 24 countries (96 percent) were rated Free and 1 (4 percent) was rated Partly Free. However, more frequent instances of harassment and threats from far-right and Islamist groups during the year resulted in numerical declines for a number of top-performing countries, particularly those in Scandinavia and northern Europe. A dramatic rise in legal harassment was noted in **Turkey** in 2006 owing to the aggressive use of Article 301 of the revised penal code. Almost 300 journalists and writers were prosecuted for "insulting Turkishness" under the provision, and they were also subject to threats from nationalist groups.

However, in a major positive move, **Italy** was upgraded in 2006 to resume its Free status (with a numerical improvement from 35 to 29), primarily as a result of Prime Minister Silvio Berlusconi's departure from office. While the private broadcast media in Italy are still concentrated in the hands of the Berlusconi-dominated Mediaset, the public broadcaster RAI is no longer under his control. Italy, which had been rated Partly Free since 2003, had stood out as the only European Union member state with a press freedom status other than Free since 1988.

GLOBAL AND REGIONAL TABLES

Rank	Country	Rating	Status
1	Finland	9	F
	Iceland	9	F
3	Belgium	11	F
	Denmark	11	F
	Norway	11	F
	Sweden	11	F
7	Luxembourg	12	F
	Switzerland	12	F
9	Andorra	13	F
	Netherlands	13	F
	New Zealand	13	F
12	Liechtenstein	14	F
	Palau	14	F
	Portugal	14	F
15	Jamaica	15	F
16	Estonia	16	F
	Germany	16	F
	Ireland	16	F
	Monaco	16	F
	Saint Lucia	16	F
	United States	16	F
22	Bahamas	17	F
	Barbados	17	F
	Canada	17	F
	Marshall Islands	17	F
	Malta	17	F
	St Vincent & Grenadines	17	F
	San Marino	17	F
29	Czech Republic	18	F
	Lithuania	18	F
31	Latvia	19	F
	United Kingdom	19	F
33	Costa Rica	20	F
	Dominica	20	F
	Micronesia	20	F
	Saint Kitts & Nevis	20	F
	Slovakia	20	F
	Taiwan	20	F
39	Australia	21	F
	Austria	21	F
	Belize	21	F
	France	21	F
	Hungary	21	F
	Japan	21	F
	Slovenia	21	F
46	Cyprus	22	F
	Poland	22	F
	Spain	22	F
	Suriname	22	F
50	Grenada	23	F
51	Mali	24	F
	Trinidad & Tobago	24	F
	Vanuatu	24	F

Rank	Country	Rating	Status
54	Greece	25	F
55	Ghana	26	F
	Mauritius	26	F
	Kiribati	26	F
	Tuvalu	26	F
59	Nauru	28	F
	South Africa	28	F
61	Cape Verde	29	F
	Guyana	29	F
	Israel	29	F
	Italy	29	F
	Sao Tome & Principe	29	F
66	Benin	30	F
	Chile	30	F
	Hong Kong	30	F
	Namibia	30	F
	Papua New Guinea	30	F
	Samoa	30	F
	Solomon Islands	30	F
	South Korea	30	F
	Uruguay	30	F
75	Tonga	31	PF
76	Bulgaria	34	PF
77	Botswana	35	PF
	India	35	PF
79	Mongolia	36	PF
80	Bolivia	37	PF
	Croatia	37	PF
	Montenegro	37	PF
83	Antigua & Barbuda	38	PF
84	Burkina Faso	39	PF
	Fiji	39	PF
	Serbia	39	PF
87	Dominican Republic	40	PF
	Mozambique	40	PF
89	Ecuador	41	PF
90	Brazil	42	PF
	East Timor	42	PF
	El Salvador	42	PF
	Lesotho	42	PF
	Nicaragua	42	PF
	Peru	42	PF
	Romania	42	PF
97	Panama	43	PF
98	Bosnia	45	PF
	Macedonia	45	PF
100	Philippines	46	PF
	Senegal	46	PF
102	Comoros	48	PF
	Guinea-Bissau	48	PF
	Mexico	48	PF
105	Argentina	49	PF
	Turkey	49	PF

Table of Global Press Freedom Rankings

Rank	Country	Rating	Status	Rank	Country	Rating	Status
107	Albania	50	PF		Maldives	68	NF
	Madagascar	50	PF		United Arab Emirates	68	NF
109	Congo-Brazzaville	51	PF	154	Afghanistan	69	NF
	Honduras	51	PF		Djibouti	69	NF
	Tanzania	51	PF		Gabon	69	NF
112	Malawi	53	PF		Singapore	69	NF
	Ukraine	53	PF	158	Iraq	70	NF
114	Indonesia	54	PF	159	Bahrain	71	NF
	Uganda	54	PF		Oman	71	NF
116	Mauritania	55	PF	161	Chad	74	NF
	Nigeria	55	PF		Togo	74	NF
118	Kuwait	56	PF		Venezuela	74	NF
	Sierra Leone	56	PF	164	Azerbaijan	75	NF
120	Colombia	57	PF		Russia	75	NF
	Georgia	57	PF	166	Brunei	76	NF
122	Cambodia	58	PF		Kazakhstan	76	NF
	Central African Republic	58	PF		Swaziland	76	NF
	Nepal	58	PF		Tajikistan	76	NF
	Niger	58	PF	170	Burundi	77	NF
126	Guatemala	59	PF		Ethiopia	77	NF
	Haiti	59	PF		Gambia	77	NF
	Kenya	59	PF		Vietnam	77	NF
	Lebanon	59	PF	174	Congo-Kinshasa	80	NF
	Thailand	59	PF		Yemen	80	NF
131	Paraguay	60	PF	176	Laos	81	NF
	Seychelles	60	PF		Sudan	81	NF
133	Jordan	61	NF	178	Saudi Arabia	82	NF
134	Algeria	62	NF	179	Syria	83	NF
	Angola	62	NF		Tunisia	83	NF
	Bhutan	62	NF	181	China	84	NF
	Egypt	62	NF		Iran	84	NF
	Morocco	62	NF		IOT/PA*	84	NF
139	Pakistan	63	NF		Rwanda	84	NF
	Qatar	63	NF	185	Somalia	85	NF
	Sri Lanka	63	NF	186	Belarus	89	NF
142	Armenia	64	NF		Equatorial Guinea	89	NF
	Zambia	64	NF		Zimbabwe	89	NF
144	Liberia	65	NF	189	Uzbekistan	91	NF
	Moldova	65	NF	190	Eritrea	94	NF
146	Bangladesh	66	NF	191	Burma	96	NF
147	Cameroon	67	NF		Cuba	96	NF
	Guinea	67	NF		Libya	96	NF
	Kyrgyzstan	67	NF		Turkmenistan	96	NF
150	Cote d'Ivoire	68	NF	195	North Korea	97	NF
	Malaysia	68	NF				

*Israeli-Occupied Territories/Palestinian Authority

Status	Number of Countries	Percent of Total
Free	74	38%
Partly Free	58	30%
Not Free	63	32%
TOTAL	195	100%

19

Sub-Saharan Africa

Rank	Country	Rating	Status	Rank	Country	Rating	Status
1	Mali	24	F		Niger	58	PF
2	Ghana	26	F	26	Kenya	59	PF
	Mauritius	26	F	27	Seychelles	60	PF
4	South Africa	28	F	28	Angola	62	NF
5	Cape Verde	29	F	29	Zambia	64	NF
	Sao Tome & Principe	29	F	30	Liberia	65	NF
7	Benin	30	F	31	Cameroon	67	NF
	Namibia	30	F		Guinea	67	NF
9	Botswana	35	PF	33	Cote d'Ivoire	68	NF
10	Burkina Faso	39	PF	34	Djibouti	69	NF
11	Mozambique	40	PF		Gabon	69	NF
12	Lesotho	42	PF	36	Chad	74	NF
13	Senegal	46	PF		Togo	74	NF
14	Comoros	48	PF	38	Swaziland	76	NF
	Guinea-Bissau	48	PF	39	Burundi	77	NF
16	Madagascar	50	PF		Ethiopia	77	NF
17	Congo-Brazzaville	51	PF		Gambia	77	NF
	Tanzania	51	PF	42	Congo-Kinshasa	80	NF
19	Malawi	53	PF	43	Sudan	81	NF
20	Uganda	54	PF	44	Rwanda	84	NF
21	Mauritania	55	PF	45	Somalia	85	NF
	Nigeria	55	PF	46	Equatorial Guinea	89	NF
23	Sierra Leone	56	PF		Zimbabwe	89	NF
24	Central African Republic	58	PF	48	Eritrea	94	NF

Status	Number of Countries	Percent of Total
Free	8	17%
Partly Free	19	39%
Not Free	21	44%
TOTAL	48	100%

The Americas

Rank	Country	Rating	Status	Rank	Country	Rating	Status
1	Jamaica	15	F	19	Antigua & Barbuda	38	PF
2	Saint Lucia	16	F	20	Dominican Republic	40	PF
	United States	16	F	21	Ecuador	41	PF
4	Bahamas	17	F	22	Brazil	42	PF
	Barbados	17	F		El Salvador	42	PF
	Canada	17	F		Nicaragua	42	PF
	Saint Vincent & Grenadines	17	F		Peru	42	PF
8	Costa Rica	20	F	26	Panama	43	PF
	Dominica	20	F	27	Mexico	48	PF
	Saint Kitts & Nevis	20	F	28	Argentina	49	PF
11	Belize	21	F	29	Honduras	51	PF
12	Suriname	22	F	30	Colombia	57	PF
13	Grenada	23	F	31	Guatemala	59	PF
14	Trinidad & Tobago	24	F		Haiti	59	PF
15	Guyana	29	F	33	Paraguay	60	PF
16	Chile	30	F	34	Venezuela	74	NF
	Uruguay	30	F	35	Cuba	96	NF
18	Bolivia	37	PF				

Status	Number of Countries	Percent of Total
Free	17	48%
Partly Free	16	46%
Not Free	2	6%
TOTAL	35	100%

Middle East & North Africa

Rank	Country	Rating	Status	Rank	Country	Rating	Status
1	Israel	29	F	11	Bahrain	71	NF
2	Kuwait	56	PF		Oman	71	NF
3	Lebanon	59	PF	13	Yemen	80	NF
4	Jordan	61	NF	14	Saudi Arabia	82	NF
5	Algeria	62	NF	15	Syria	83	NF
	Egypt	62	NF		Tunisia	83	NF
	Morocco	62	NF	17	IOT /PA*	84	NF
8	Qatar	63	NF		Iran	84	NF
9	UAE	68	NF	19	Libya	96	NF
10	Iraq	70	NF				

*Israeli-Occupied Territories/Palestinian Authority

Status	Number of Countries	Percent of Total
Free	1	5%
Partly Free	2	11%
Not Free	16	84%
TOTAL	19	100%

Asia-Pacific

Rank	Country	Rating	Status	Rank	Country	Rating	Status
1	New Zealand	13	F	21	East Timor	42	PF
2	Palau	14	F	22	Philippines	46	PF
3	Marshall Islands	17	F	23	Indonesia	54	PF
4	Micronesia	20	F	24	Cambodia	58	PF
	Taiwan	20	F		Nepal	58	PF
6	Australia	21	F	26	Thailand	59	PF
	Japan	21	F	27	Bhutan	62	NF
8	Vanuatu	24	F	28	Pakistan	63	NF
9	Kiribati	26	F		Sri Lanka	63	NF
	Tuvalu	26	F	30	Bangladesh	66	NF
11	Nauru	28	F	31	Malaysia	68	NF
12	Hong Kong	30	F		Maldives	68	NF
	Papua New Guinea	30	F	33	Afghanistan	69	NF
	Samoa	30	F		Singapore	69	NF
	Solomon Islands	30	F	35	Brunei	76	NF
	South Korea	30	F	36	Vietnam	77	NF
17	Tonga	31	PF	37	Laos	81	NF
18	India	35	PF	38	China	84	NF
19	Mongolia	36	PF	39	Burma	96	NF
20	Fiji	39	PF	40	North Korea	97	NF

Status	Number of Countries	Percent of Total
Free	16	40%
Partly Free	10	25%
Not Free	14	35%
TOTAL	40	100%

Western Europe

Rank	Country	Rating	Status		Rank	Country	Rating	Status
1	Finland	9	F			Ireland	16	F
	Iceland	9	F			Monaco	16	F
3	Belgium	11	F		16	Malta	17	F
	Denmark	11	F			San Marino	17	F
	Norway	11	F		18	United Kingdom	19	F
	Sweden	11	F		19	Austria	21	F
7	Luxembourg	12	F			France	21	F
	Switzerland	12	F		21	Cyprus	22	F
9	Andorra	13	F			Spain	22	F
	Netherlands	13	F		23	Greece	25	F
11	Liechtenstein	14	F		24	Italy	29	F
	Portugal	14	F		25	Turkey	49	PF
13	Germany	16	F					

Status	Number of Countries	Percent of Total
Free	24	96%
Partly Free	1	4%
Not Free	0	0%
TOTAL	25	100%

Central and Eastern Europe / Former Soviet Union

Rank	Country	Rating	Status		Rank	Country	Rating	Status
1	Estonia	16	F			Macedonia	45	PF
2	Czech Republic	18	F		16	Albania	50	PF
	Lithuania	18	F		17	Ukraine	53	PF
4	Latvia	19	F		18	Georgia	57	PF
5	Slovakia	20	F		19	Armenia	64	NF
6	Hungary	21	F		20	Moldova	65	NF
	Slovenia	21	F		21	Kyrgyzstan	67	NF
8	Poland	22	F		22	Azerbaijan	75	NF
9	Bulgaria	34	PF			Russia	75	NF
10	Croatia	37	PF		24	Kazakhstan	76	NF
	Montenegro	37	PF			Tajikistan	76	NF
12	Serbia	39	PF		26	Belarus	89	NF
13	Romania	42	PF		27	Uzbekistan	91	NF
14	Bosnia	45	PF		28	Turkmenistan	96	NF

Status	Number of Countries	Percent of Total
Free	8	28%
Partly Free	10	36%
Not Free	10	36%
TOTAL	28	100%

Summary of Results

Regional Press Freedom Breakdown

Region	Free	Partly Free	Not Free	Number of Countries
Americas	17 (48%)	16 (46%)	2 (6%)	35
Asia-Pacific	16 (40%)	10 (25%)	14 (3.5%)	40
CEE/FSU	8 (28%)	10 (36%)	10 (36%)	28
Middle East & North Africa	1 (5%)	2 (11%)	16 (84%)	19
Sub-Saharan Africa	8 (14.5%)	19 (39%)	21 (44%)	48
Western Europe	24 (96%)	1 (4%)	0 (0%)	25
TOTAL	74 (38%)	58 (30%)	63 (32%)	195

Press Freedom by Population

Status	By Country	By Population (millions)
Free	74 (38%)	1,181 (18%)
Partly Free	58 (30%)	2,568 (39%)
Not Free	63 (32%)	2,799 (43%)
TOTAL	195 (100%)	6,548 (100%)

Muzzling the Media: The Return of Censorship in the Commonwealth Independent States

Christopher Walker

Overview

Only a decade and a half since the end of the cold war, freedom of the press for millions of people across the Commonwealth of Independent States (CIS) has come nearly full circle.

The media landscape across most of today's CIS in some aspects differs from that of the Soviet era but in important ways is imposing a no less repressive news media environment. Gone is all-encompassing ideological state media control. Russia—and most of the countries on its periphery— today features modern methods of information control that effectively shuts off the majority of people in these lands from news and information of political consequence.

This contemporary form of censorship is achieved through a mix of state-enabled oligarchic control, broadcast monopolies of presidential "families," judicial persecution, and subtle and overt forms of intimidation. Unlike during the Soviet era, some intrepid journalists now manage to report independently. The internet is a principal alternative and challenger to media hegemony in the CIS. Despite the best efforts of the authorities,

---

Christopher Walker is director of studies at Freedom House.

some degree of independent reporting persists in authoritarian CIS states owing to the commitment of enterprising and courageous journalists as well as the possibilities offered by new technologies. Bloggers and other new media practitioners continue to push the boundaries of 21st-century journalism. But while the internet remains relatively free in Russia and a number of other post-Soviet countries, it is fast becoming a target of greater interest for new regulatory intervention by the authorities.

Absent the rule of law and meaningful legal protections, however, the CIS is today one of the world's most dangerous places for journalists. Reporters willing to investigate issues such as political and corporate corruption are confronted by powerful vested interests striving to muzzle news professionals. Intimidation, physical violence, and even murder of reporters and editors have become commonplace. Journalists in virtually every CIS country have been victims of contract killings or otherwise met death under suspicious circumstances.

This brutal, efficiently repressive 21st-century media environment is made possible by a reconsolidated authoritarian model that has anchored itself from Belarus on the European Union's eastern border to Kazakhstan on China's western frontier. To ensure regime security and shield from public view rampant official corruption and rent seeking, post-Soviet authorities seek to limit scrutiny of their decisions and activities by silencing the independent press.

Russia has seen the most precipitous decline in recent years. Today, all of the major national television channels (Channel One, RTR, and NTV), from which most Russians get their news and information, have come under state control and are effectively censored. Control of national television news broadcasting is, however, only one piece of a broad and comprehensive campaign to bring independent media under the sway of the authorities.

Press freedom's trajectory in the CIS was not always so dire. In the period immediately preceding the Soviet collapse and in its immediate aftermath, the emergence of a nascent independent press suggested that a durable and institutionalized Fourth Estate might materialize. The Soviet era's waning days saw the exertion from below of significant pressure for greater freedom of expression and a diverse and independent reporting of news. In the former satellite countries of Central Europe—the Czech Republic, Hungary, Poland, Slovakia—and the Baltic states, censorship was cast aside and a free press rose from the ashes of the Soviet system.

For the 12 non-Baltic former Soviet republics, however, the promise of the opening in the late 1980s and early 1990s was short-lived.

The repressive media landscape in the CIS is illuminated by findings from *Freedom of the Press*, Freedom House's annual survey of global media independence. The survey's most recent findings show that 10 of the 12 post-Soviet states are ranked Not Free, indicating that these countries do not provide the basic guarantees and protections in the legal, political, and economic spheres to enable open and independent journalism.

Of particular concern is the sharp downward decline in many CIS countries in the last several years. Authoritarian regimes have implemented an increasingly brutal response to homegrown and foreign journalists who take an independent line, especially since the first "color" revolution, in Georgia, in 2003. During this time, four major press freedom trends have emerged.

❚ First, authoritarian regimes have intensified mass media control, with television serving as the favored tool in regime security efforts.

❚ Second, legislative screws have been tightened across the region to exert further control on the media and impede independent reporting. In countries such as Belarus, Kazakhstan, and Russia, restrictive laws have been adopted in the last three years to further curb media freedom.

❚ The third part of the broader crackdown pattern is increasing attention on international media, especially international broadcasting. The Russian authorities, for instance, have focused on the broadcasts of Radio Free Europe/Radio Liberty (RFE/RL). Since 2005, the Kremlin has undertaken a systematic intimidation campaign whereby RFE/RL's partners—Russian radio stations that rebroadcast their programs as part of their own formats—have been audited and subjected to harassment. Similar efforts to obstruct international broadcasting have been undertaken in other CIS countries, including Azerbaijan and Uzbekistan.

❚ The fourth element of the most recent phase of the press freedom crackdown has been refocused attention on the print media. The priority medium for post-Soviet authoritarian regimes to control typically has been television, which reaches the largest audiences and continues to exert the most influence in shaping views. Nevertheless, in the last several years independent newspapers have been in the crosshairs of authoritarian governments, with Russia taking a leading role. The recent attention paid by the Kremlin and other post-Soviet authorities to assert further control over newspapers may simply be a part of the broader press freedom crackdown or could be a recognition by authoritarian leadership that, in the internet age, politically consequential content produced by newspapers finds its way to much larger audiences via the web and therefore poses a greater threat.

Introduction

Winston Churchill's historic speech in March 1946 painted the indelibly stark image of an "iron curtain" descending across the European continent and set a clear marker for assessing global political developments in the second half of the 20th century. Churchill's remarks six decades ago[1] helped put into context a world that was evolving in distinctly different directions.

On the far side of the iron curtain, a closed and repressive system of governance was rapidly taking hold, in which dissent was ruthlessly suppressed, economic life rigidly managed by Communist authorities, and media used exclusively as an instrument of the state. This all-encompassing effort to control ideas, commerce, and media was a defining feature of the Soviet system. It took seven decades for the fatally flawed Soviet experiment to collapse under the weight of its own contradictions in an economic and political meltdown that ended the cold war and brought the promise of freer and more open systems to tens of millions of formerly captive peoples. Hopes ran high that these openings would enable all of the fundamental freedoms to emerge and flourish, including freedom of expression and freedom of the press.

In fact, in the period immediately preceding the Soviet collapse and in its immediate aftermath, the flowering of open expression and a nascent independent press suggested a durable and institutionalized Fourth

---

[1] Churchill's speech was titled "Sinews of Peace" and was delivered on March 5, 1946, at Westminster College in Fulton, Missouri.

Estate might materialize. The Soviet era's waning days saw the exertion from below of significant pressure for greater freedom of expression and a diverse and independent reporting of news. In the former satellite countries of Central Europe—the Czech Republic, Hungary, Poland, Slovakia, and the Baltic states—censorship was cast aside and a free press rose from the ashes of the Soviet system. For the 12 former Soviet republics, however, the promise of the opening in the late 1980s and early 1990s was short-lived.

Only a decade and a half since the end of the cold war, freedom of the press for millions of people across the CIS has come nearly full circle. For now, there seems little hope that the rights succinctly enshrined in Article 19 of the Universal Declaration of Human Rights will be enjoyed in these countries anytime soon.[2]

Drawing on findings from *Freedom of the Press,* Freedom House's annual survey of global media independence, this essay traces the press freedom environment through key points on the post-Soviet timeline, looking at the media situation in the immediate aftermath of the Soviet collapse, the period from the mid-1990s to the early 2000s when the "color" revolutions occurred, and then from the post–color revolution period to the present, where an authoritarian resurgence has consolidated media control.

The Return of Censorship

The media landscape across most of the former Soviet Union in some aspects differs from that of the Soviet era but in important ways is imposing a no less repressive news media environment. Gone is the smothering, all-encompassing ideological control across wide swaths of Europe and Eurasia. A more geographically circumscribed area—Russia and most of the countries on its periphery—confronts modern methods of information control that effectively shuts off the majority of people in these lands from news and information of political consequence. Today, methods for dominating news media are different, based on state-enabled oligarchic control, broadcast monopolies of presidential "families," and mass media manipulation to create a veneer of democratic practice without its substance.

---

[2] "Everyone has the right to freedom of opinion and expression; this right includes freedom to hold opinions without interference and to seek, receive and impart information and ideas through any media and regardless of frontiers."

Unlike during the Soviet era, some intrepid journalists now manage to report independently. However, absent the rule of law and meaningful legal protections, the former Soviet Union is today one of the world's most dangerous places for journalists. Reporters willing to investigate issues such as political and corporate corruption are confronted by powerful vested interests striving to muzzle news professionals. Intimidation, physical violence, and even murder of reporters and editors have become commonplace. Journalists in virtually every former Soviet country have been victims of contract killings or otherwise met death under suspicious circumstances. Russia, for example, has been a deadly place for journalists in both the Yeltsin and the Putin eras. Since President Vladimir Putin assumed office seven years ago, at least two dozen journalists have been killed, including the notable cases of Paul Klebnikov, editor of *Forbes Russia*, who was shot nine times with a semiautomatic weapon on the street outside his Moscow office in July 2004; Anna Politkovskaya, an investigative journalist who wrote for *Novaya Gazeta* and was executed in the elevator of her apartment building in October 2006; and Ivan Safronov, a defense correspondent for the *Kommersant* newspaper, who in very unclear circumstances plunged to his death from his apartment building in Moscow in March 2007. Rarely are serious investigations pursued or perpetrators brought to justice. Impunity is the standard.

This brutal, efficiently repressive 21st-century media environment is made possible by a reconsolidated authoritarian model that has anchored itself from Belarus on the European Union's eastern frontier all the way to Kazakhstan on China's western flank. To ensure regime security and shield from public view rent seeking and rampant official corruption, post-Soviet authorities seek to limit scrutiny of their decisions and activities by silencing the independent press.

This modern variant of media management is a far more sophisticated, distant cousin of the raw and overweening institutional media control of the Soviet era. The stodgy, Soviet-era broadcasting diet has in large measure been cast aside. With the exception of remaining retrograde former Soviet regimes such as those in Turkmenistan and Uzbekistan, the stiff, gray, cold war–era news broadcasters who parroted official bulletins and spewed turgid party propaganda have vanished from the news. Today, modern media fare, rich in entertainment, and news programming often of high technical quality and production values are staples, especially in Russia. While the contemporary media menu in Russia offers a wide assortment of entertainment options, it for the most part excludes alternative views and analysis on news and public affairs, particularly where it counts most, on national television broadcasts, from which most citizens continue to get their information. Russian media also play an important role in influencing perceptions in neighboring countries. Russian-language broadcasting delivers the Kremlin spin on regional and world events to millions of Russian speakers in countries on Russia's periphery.

The internet is a principal alternative and challenger to media hegemony in the former Soviet Union. But while the internet remains relatively free in Russia and a number of other post-Soviet countries, it is fast becoming a target of greater interest for new regulatory intervention by the authorities.

The repressive media landscape in the CIS is illuminated by findings from *Freedom of the Press*. The Russian authorities are not alone in forging a media environment that filters out critical voices and views, resulting in media systems that lack freedom. The survey's most recent findings show that 10 of the 12 post-Soviet states are ranked Not Free, indicating that these countries do not provide the basic guarantees and protections in the legal, political, and economic spheres to enable open and independent journalism.

The only 2 that enjoy Partly Free status, Georgia and Ukraine, have experienced recent political upheaval and democratic opening. Of the 10 Not Free countries, none is moving in the direction of more freedom and most have a decidedly downward trajectory. Of the 195 countries and territories examined in the survey, 3 of the 10 worst press freedom abusers—Belarus, Uzbekistan, and Turkmenistan—are found in the CIS. By contrast, today all of the countries of Central Europe and the Baltic states, which themselves needed to overcome a decades-long legacy of Soviet media culture and control, are assessed as Free in Freedom of the Press. Although they contend with challenges and imperfections that media in democratic systems invariably face, the news media from the Czech Republic to Estonia have achieved pluralistic and competitive news environments.

Some of this success can be attributed to economics. The Central European countries, now members of the European Union and NATO, have achieved solid levels of economic growth, developed diverse economies, and feature a range of political and economic voices in the media mix. But if economic wherewithal were the key determinant of levels of press freedom, then Azerbaijan, Kazakhstan, and Russia, which have also enjoyed considerable economic growth in recent years, should likewise be enjoying increased press freedom. Yet they are not. The pathologies associated with the "resource curse" in these resource-based economies could explain their poor performance, but this phenomenon would not then explain, for example, resource-poor but economically vibrant Armenia's consistently lackluster performance on press freedom.

History might provide some guide. Prior to World War II, the Central European states enjoyed a free press tradition that the republics of the former Soviet Union did not. Nevertheless, press freedom's steep plunge in the CIS into the depths of the Not Free ranks suggests something more profound is at work in this part of the world. The authorities have undertaken an orchestrated effort to arrogate to themselves greater control of media infrastructure and to limit public space for ideas and debate. The coercive and systematic reassertion of media control has strangled, at least for the time being, the nascent independent journalism that surfaced briefly in the immediate aftermath of the Soviet collapse.

The End of the Soviet Union and the Ephemera of Press Freedom

Mikhail Gorbachev's embrace of glasnost in the mid-1980s led to openings with vast and historic implications. Glasnost, which translates literally as "openness," did not produce freedom of speech and free media; it instead launched a process that loosened the smothering control of the Soviet system. From the time Gorbachev introduced this policy until the dissolution of the Soviet Union in 1991, journalists pushed then strict boundaries imposed on expression. Gorbachev, for his part, encouraged papers to publish criticism of the authorities and to continue a reevaluation of the Stalinist period in order to spur a change in policy direction.

Years later, the salutary impact of the forces unleashed by glasnost was apparent. In the post-Soviet period—nearly 10 years after Gorbachev's emergence on the political scene—half of the former Soviet republics had achieved Partly Free status in *Freedom of the Press*, indicating an increasing degree of openness in the media sector. While this progress on press freedom was unconsolidated, it was impressive, given decades of Soviet repression in settings with no real history of an open and free press. To be sure, this opening did not represent a fully free and mature media sector. It was, however, a period that saw unprecedented media freedoms and journalistic courage by newsmen and -women who had been accustomed to observing limits rather than testing them.

The same period also saw fierce resistance to the nascent press openings. By early 1991, Communist hard-liners were seeking to reassert control over a news media that had already established some autonomy and influence. The desire of the republics within the Soviet Union to pull away and declare independence was a source of tension between conservatives and reformers, a dynamic that had serious implications for the embryonic independent press.

An early test for media freedom was the independence movements in the Baltic countries. As part of a crackdown ordered by the authorities in Moscow, Soviet special Interior Ministry forces in January 1991 attacked and occupied the television broadcast facility in Vilnius, killing 14 people and wounding several hundred others. A week after the attack in Vilnius, Soviet troops attacked the Latvian Interior Ministry in Riga, killing five people, among them members of Juris Podnieks's film crew. Pre-glasnost reporting would have offered only carefully crafted, officially controlled characterizations of such events. By early 1991, however, autonomous media outlets were able to report on the violent and controversial conflict in the Baltics. Dueling accounts of what transpired in Lithuania and Latvia emerged. Soviet-controlled media, first and foremost the State Television and Radio Committee, provided a portrayal of events from the Soviet military's point of view, alleging that locals triggered the bloodshed. These claims were directly contradicted by eyewitness and foreign journalist accounts.

The unconstrained, non-official reporting on the violence in the Baltics elicited a reaction from Soviet hard-liners as well as Gorbachev, who responded by suggesting the suspension of the liberal Law on Freedom of the Press adopted in 1990. The Soviet authorities also dispatched censors to muzzle independent reports on events in Vilnius and Riga, including those from news programs such as the Television News Service (TSN) and Radio Russia, both of which had earned reputations for more open coverage. Following what amounted to the recensoring of these programs, Tatyana Mitkova, a commentator for TSN, delivered the news in February 1991 by winking and nodding to the audience and letting her viewers know that she was permitted to present only the official version of events relating to the attack on the television broadcast facility in Vilnius.[3]

These early episodes in the Baltics pitted the old habits of information control against the growing desire for independent, open reporting. This

---

[3] Jeff Sallot, "Censorship: In Moscow, the Government Is Tightening Controls on the Media—And It Is Meeting Considerable Opposition," Globe and Mail, February 4, 1991.

contest between journalistic values would play out over and over again in coming years. For independent news outlets, however, surviving in the post-Soviet economy was increasingly difficult. Meanwhile, powerful political and economic interests were reorganizing themselves in order to limit the development of an autonomous press.

Resurgent Authoritarianism: The Beginning of the End of Press Freedom

By 1994, 6 of 12 countries in the former Soviet Union had risen to the Partly Free category in *Freedom of the Press*. Over the course of the next decade, this number would drop to 1: Georgia. By 2004, 11 countries found themselves in the ranks of Not Free. Through a revitalized crackdown on press freedom, post-Soviet leadership managed to claw the media back under its control.

A stubborn authoritarian thread throughout the region was key to the reassertion of media control. The middle 1990s saw authoritarian leaders, many of whom earned their bona fides during the Soviet period, consolidate power in most of the post-Soviet states. Belarus's Aleksandr Lukashenka and Azerbaijan's Heidar Aliyev were among those who assumed leadership. Other leaders simply changed hats in 1991 to make the transition from chairman of the Supreme Soviet to president of a newly independent republic, as was the case throughout Central Asia. Kazakhstan's Nursultan Nazarbayev, for instance, used this pathway to power and, over the course of the 1990s, oversaw the reining in of his country's independent press.

Shortly after coming to power in July 1994, President Aleksandr Lukashenka made it clear that tightening control of the Belarusian news media would be a priority. A host of presidential edicts consolidated authority over the press within the president's office. An August 1994 decree brought the state printing house in Minsk under the direct control of the presidential administration. Printing facilities elsewhere in the country had to receive the authorization of the presidential administration to conclude printing contracts with nonstate media. In October 1995, a number of independent publications were denied the right to publish at the state printing house in Minsk. In order to continue publishing, those newspapers were then compelled to use printing facilities in Lithuania and transport back into Belarus for distribution.

In Kazakhstan, a steady monopolization of media was implemented. Dariga Nazarbayeva, the influential daughter of the president and onetime head of the state news agency, played a pivotal role in the effort to take control of that country's news media infrastructure. In Kazakhstan, as in a number of the former Soviet states, broadcast media have been taken into the hands of members of the presidential family or those with close ties to it. Meanwhile, the screws were tightened on journalists who took an independent line. A campaign to silence critics who reported on official corruption caught in its web journalists such as Sergei Duvanov and Nuri Muftakh. Muftakh died at the time he was following allegations that Kazakhstan's president had secretly transferred large amounts of money to foreign banks. In November 2002, he was run over by a bus in what authorities regarded as an accident but what many speculate was a politically motivated assassination. Duvanov, who also wrote on political corruption and was following the "Kazakhgate" scandal, was found guilty of what many believed to be trumped-up rape charges and sentenced to several years in prison in January 2003.

In Russia, "oligarchs" sought to establish their own media empires in order to exercise control over Russia's politics. Television became the medium of choice for intraoligarchic battles and for politically influential billionaires to advance their own interests. Media in the public interest was marginalized.

Ukraine, which today features the region's freest media, hit its press freedom nadir in 2003. A spate of journalists' deaths and increasing pressure on independent news outlets characterized the preceding years. Georgi Gongadze, who co-founded the independent news website *Ukrayinska Pravda*, was kidnapped and murdered in 2000. Under Leonid Kuchma, Ukraine's increasingly authoritarian president, *temnyky*—theme directives from the president's office that instruct editors on news coverage—had become a regular feature of the editorial process. Such editorial theme directives continue to be standard operating procedure in authoritarian governments throughout the region; it was only in the aftermath of Ukraine's political breakthrough in the winter of 2004 that *temnyky* were purged from Ukraine's news media.

Four Major Trends in the Media Crackdown

Three "color" revolutions—the "Rose" variety in Georgia, "Orange" in Ukraine, and "Tulip" in Kyrgyzstan—triggered a fierce response from authoritarian governments, which turned to the media to deliver stricter "message control" as part of a broader regime security effort.

In the period since the first color revolution in Georgia in November 2003, autocratic regimes have implemented an increasingly brutal response to homegrown and foreign journalists who take an independent line. This trend is borne out in *Freedom of the Press* data since that time. In this period, 9 of the 12 former Soviet states' press freedom ratings have deteriorated: Uzbekistan, Russia, Belarus, and Azerbaijan have registered especially notable declines.

Four major press freedom trends have emerged in the post–color revolution period. First, authoritarian regimes have intensified mass media control, with television serving as the favored tool in regime security efforts. State-controlled national television broadcasts have presented a barrage of claims designed to identify external threats and scapegoats for domestic ills. The 2006 *Freedom of the Press* report on Uzbekistan, for instance, cites the September 2005 trial of 15 men accused of involvement in the Andijan unrest, where "[Uzbek] prosecutors charged that the British Broadcasting Corporation, the Institute for War and Peace Reporting, and Radio Free Europe/Radio Liberty had advance knowledge that violence would break out in the city." State-controlled media in Uzbekistan gave prominent coverage to these charges, which fit a broader pattern of fact twisting and propagandizing. In the larger regional context, authoritarian governments have used state-controlled television to distort reporting and attack the legitimacy of political reform efforts in Ukraine and Georgia.

Legislative screws have been tightened across the region to exert further controls on the media and impede independent reporting. In Belarus, the autocratic government of Aleksandr Lukashenka intensified its control over the country's media. In 2005, among the measures taken by the Belarusian authorities was passage of broadly defined legislation that makes it a crime punishable by up to two years in jail to "discredit Belarus" in the eyes of international organizations and foreign governments. The same prison terms apply to those convicted of distributing "false information" about Belarus's political, economic, social, or international situation. In July 2006, President Putin signed a law that expanded the definition of extremist activity to include public slander of a government official related to his or her duties, using or threatening violence against a government official or his family, and publicly justifying or excusing terrorism. The definition of extremism in this new law is so broad that it allows the authorities to use unchecked power against their critics, including in the media. Also in 2006, Kazakh president Nursultan Nazarbayev signed into law media legislation that increased government control over news media by imposing costly registration fees for journalists, expanding criteria for denying registration to media outlets, and requiring news outlets to reregister in the event of a change of address.

The third part of the broader crackdown pattern is increasing attention on international media, especially international broadcasting. Not content to suppress and control domestic media, the Russian authorities, for instance, have focused on the broadcasts of the U.S. government–funded RFE/RL, whose radio programming has attracted dedicated listeners across Russia interested in an alternative voice. Since 2005, the Kremlin has orchestrated a systematic intimidation campaign whereby RFE/RL's partners—Russian radio stations that rebroadcast their programs as part of their own formats—have been audited and subjected to harassment. While the precise number of RL affiliates that have been driven off the air is unclear, apparently no more than 12 are now broadcasting regularly. Prior to the campaign to drive them from the airwaves, about 25 affiliates carried RL programs. Similar efforts to obstruct international broadcasting have been undertaken in other countries, including Azerbaijan and Uzbekistan.

The Kremlin has also sought to rein in domestic radio. The Russian News Service, Russia's largest independent radio network, is required by station management to work under a "50 percent rule" to ensure that at least half of all reporting by the network on Russia is "positive." This editorial guidance was put in place after new, Kremlin-friendly ownership took over the network and in early 2007 brought in new management from state-run Channel One. In May 2007, eight journalists who worked at the radio network resigned in protest of editorial direction that amounted to censorship.

The fourth element of the most recent phase of the press freedom crackdown has been refocused attention on the print media. The priority medium for post-Soviet authoritarian regimes to control has been television, which reaches the largest audiences and continues to exert the most influence in shaping views. Newspapers typically suffer from the unfriendly post-Soviet economic landscape and confront a range of bureaucratic and legal obstacles, including politicized tax inspections and frequent use of libel laws. Newspapers have tended to have small print runs and therefore have not captured the intensive attention of the authorities in the way broadcast media have. Nevertheless, the last several years have seen renewed interest in taking control of independent newspapers, with Russia taking the lead.

Gazprom-Media, an arm of the state-controlled gas behemoth, has acquired control of a number of previously independent news outlets and either closed their doors or drained them of independent reporting. While as early as 2001 Gazprom took control of *Segodnya*, the flagship paper of Vladimir Gusinsky's Media-Most group, more recent takeovers have included the June 2005 acquisition of *Izvestia* by Gazprom-Media. *Izvestia*, which had been recognized for sound and balanced coverage, has since joined the growing ranks of Kremlin-friendly news outlets. Other major dailies have come into the hands of government-friendly financial groups. The Kremlin recently orchestrated ownership takeovers at a number of newspapers, including *Nezavisimaya Gazeta*, which have functioned as alternative information lifelines to small but influential audiences in the country. The purchase of *Kommersant* in September 2006 by metals magnate Alisher Usmanov, a Kremlin-connected businessman, was another blow for the independent print media. *Kommersant* has been the most visible Russian newspaper to take a critical view of the country's politics.

The recent efforts made by the Kremlin and other post-Soviet authorities to assert further control over newspapers may simply be a part of the broader press freedom crackdown. It may be, however, a recognition by authoritarian leadership that in the internet age, politically consequential content produced by newspapers finds its way to much larger audiences via the web and therefore poses a greater threat.

The Internet and New Media: Permeating the Curtain?

The emergence of new technologies and media has afforded fresh opportunities for greater freedom of expression and for an independent press in the CIS that can evade official control.

Soviet-era controls meant that virtually all means of disseminating information were state controlled. Photocopying machines and typewriters, for example, were a tightly restricted privilege that needed to be registered with the authorities. And of course, infrastructure for mass media dissemination—printing presses, newspaper distribution channels, and broadcast facilities—were all under the control of the state. In comparison, the internet's diffuse structure opens the door to finding and sharing information in ways that were impossible during the cold war.

Most rulers in the former Soviet countries view the internet as a threat. Opposition websites or those otherwise of political consequence are often subject to interference. In Belarus and Tajikistan, to take just two examples, the authorities have taken measures to curb access to the internet, especially during election cycles. In Belarus, in advance of that country's presidential election in March 2006, the regime of Aleksandr Lukashenka used a range of measures, many of them subtle, to disrupt internet and cell phone access in the run-up to election day. A comprehensive report by the OpenNet Initiative assessed internet openness in Belarus in the period leading up to the election and found that a number of opposition and politically sensitive websites were inoperative. The report did not find "evidence of systematic and comprehensive interference" with the internet. The analysis suggested that any of the authorities' measures were "fairly subtle, causing disruptions to access, but never completely turning off the alternative information tap."

The OpenNet Initiative report, published in April 2006, added that "Belarus' regime has both the will and capability to clamp down on Internet openness, and that its capacities to do so are more pervasive and subtle than outright filtering and blocking." The analysis went on to say that the "openness of the Internet in Belarus is likely to come under increasing threat both from pending legislation that promises to legalize more active state monitoring, content regulation and blocking of the Net, as well as from increased pressures for self-censorship."

In Tajikistan, the authorities shut down five opposition websites one month in advance of presidential elections held in November 2006. Access to these websites was blocked by order of the Tajik Communications Ministry. Tajik officials said the decision was taken "to filter and block access to websites aimed at disrupting the state policy via information resources, and create all conditions for harmonious development of the republic's information infrastructure." In Kazakhstan, the internet is developing, but the authorities devote considerable attention and resources to blocking opposition websites and articles critical of the country's president and his family. Website content is frequently subject to civil and criminal libel suits.

Meanwhile, other governments, including in Azerbaijan, are viewing the internet more benignly and generally not interfering or otherwise disrupting its development and use. The authorities in Azerbaijan use economic, legal, and political interference to prevent traditional media from operating freely and independently, however. There are increasing exceptions to the generally hands-off approach to the internet. In 2006, the Azeri authorities blocked the website www.tinsohbeti.com, which offers satirical opposition views often critical of the Azerbaijani authorities. While the website is hosted abroad, access to it in Azerbaijan was blocked a number of times in 2006. More recently, www.susmayag.biz ("Let's Not Keep Silence"), an opposition website, was blocked in January 2007 after the site launched a signature collection campaign to protest a government decision to significantly increase prices for energy and utilities. One of the site's founders, Bakhtiyar Hajiyev, was sentenced to 12 days in prison for sending SMS messages calling on citizens to protest the authorities' utilities price hike.

In Russia, the internet remains relatively free and provides information on a wide range of issues. However, elections scheduled for 2007 and 2008 have triggered more intense attention from the authorities, including a number of proposed legislative and regulatory initiatives to extend control over the internet. In March 2007, President Vladimir Putin issued a presidential decree to set up a new agency to supervise both mass media and the internet, which has increased concerns that more comprehensive internet controls may be on the horizon.

Ukraine is perhaps the best example of a country where the internet is free to add significant information on political affairs and spur public discussion. New technologies were pivotal in the events of late 2004, when thousands of demonstrators coordinated their activities and took to the streets of Kyiv to contest the November 2004 election results. Mobile phone text messaging was critical to this effort. "Smart mobbing"—bulk text messaging to gather people at a specified location—has also been used to organize demonstrations in other post-Soviet countries, including Belarus.

Despite the authorities' best efforts to control it, the internet and other new media set today's CIS apart from its cold war ancestor. Blogs are enabling and stimulating debate and discussion, and domestic and foreign news websites offer an alternative to state-controlled or -influenced news outlets. However, while the internet holds further promise and connectivity is growing at an impressive rate, it remains a medium through which only a small fraction of news is obtained. As internet use grows, it will become critically important to safeguard its integrity from the increasingly frequent interventions of authorities intent on controlling it.

Media in the Commonwealth of Independent States: Back to the Future?

In 2002, a comprehensive report assessing needs for international journalism found that repressive trends were undoing progress in transition countries, threatening the development of a free press, and jeopardizing gains supported by international media assistance.

The report *The Media Missionaries: American Support for International Journalism* found that in "much of the former U.S.S.R., the millions of dollars spent [in international assistance to support independent journalism] have not yet produced a viable independent media sector. Politicians or oligarchs have taken over much of what was developed, diverting the media's mission from public to private ends." In the years since the report was published, the media environment in most of the former Soviet republics has worsened significantly, posing further challenges and raising new questions about how to effectively support media freedom in countries behind the new information curtain.

Despite the best efforts of the authorities, some degree of independent reporting persists owing to the commitment of enterprising and courageous journalists as well as the possibilities offered by new technologies. Bloggers and other new media practitioners continue to push the boundaries of 21st-century journalism.

Interestingly, neither the leadership in Russia nor other post-Soviet authoritarian regimes make the argument, at least publicly, that a Not Free media environment is desirable—a testament to the fact that a free press is now recognized as an international norm. By and large, the public line offered by the region's autocrats is that they already have free media, even if official repressive actions belie these declarations.

But the reality is that the denial of a wide range of views and critical voices is ensuring a political dead end for these societies. Without access to independent information and debate, citizens cannot accurately judge the performance of their leaders. Absent independent media that act as societal watchdogs and enable other essential institutions such as the judiciary, Parliament, and civil society to serve their roles in balancing executive power, there is no ameliorating, self-correcting mechanism that post-Soviet systems need as desperately as did their Soviet-era predecessors. In post-Soviet states that suffer from ill-conceived policies, entrenched corruption, and unaccountable governance, the denial of the indispensable role of the free press in allowing critical scrutiny is bound to consign these countries to an undemocratic future.

COUNTRY REPORTS AND RATINGS

Afghanistan

LEGAL ENVIRONMENT: 21
POLITICAL ENVIRONMENT: 28
ECONOMIC ENVIRONMENT: 20

Status: Not Free

TOTAL SCORE: 69

Survey Edition	2002	2003	2004	2005	2006
Total Score, Status	NA	74,NF	72,NF	68,NF	69,NF

The environment for Afghanistan's fledgling media remained fragile in 2006, as journalists faced harassment, threats, and attacks during the year. Article 34 of the new constitution, passed in January 2004, provides for freedom of the press and of expression. A revised Press Law passed in December 2005 guarantees the right of citizens to obtain information and prohibits censorship. However, it retains broad restrictions on content that is "contrary to the principles of Islam or offensive to other religions and sects" and "matters leading to dishonoring and defaming individuals." It also establishes five commissions intended to regulate media agencies and investigate complaints of misconduct; one of the commissions has the power to decide if journalists who contravene the law should face court prosecution or a fine. Critics of the law have alleged that its prohibition of "anti-Islamic" writings is overly vague and has led to considerable confusion within the journalistic community on what constitutes permissible content. During 2006, several stations were fined or given warnings for broadcasting "un-Islamic" material or offending local culture.

Although Ali Mohaqqiq Nasab, editor of the monthly women's rights magazine *Haqooq-i-Zan* who had been sentenced on blasphemy charges, was released from prison with a suspended sentence in December 2005, his case was considered to have had a chilling effect on press freedom, with an accompanying rise in self-censorship. Many journalists avoid writing about sensitive issues such as Islam, national unity, or crimes committed by specific warlords. In June 2006, intelligence officials at the National Security Directorate issued "guidelines" to a number of news media outlets to restrict their coverage of security issues, terrorist incidents or groups, the conduct of foreign troops, or other subjects perceived to harm the national interest or erode the people's morale. Although President Hamid Karzai initially distanced himself from the directive, other officials seem to favor more government control over the media, and at subsequent meetings with media representatives during the year, Karzai himself did indicate support for the guidelines. As a result, the initial atmosphere of official support for press freedom that emerged after the end of Taliban rule eroded slightly in 2006.

Media diversity and freedom are markedly higher in the capital, Kabul, and some warlords and provincial governors exercise authority over media in the areas under their control. A number of journalists were threatened or harassed by government ministers, politicians, police and security services, and others in positions of power as a result of their reporting. Other journalists have been arrested and detained, in one case for months. Staff of the outspoken Tolo network have been particularly targeted. Increasing violence during 2006 also took a toll on the media. In July, cameraman Abdul Qudoos was killed in a suicide bombing in Kandahar; on several occasions, reporters were assaulted when attempting to cover the news; two German freelancers were killed by unidentified gunmen in October; and an Italian journalist was kidnapped in southern Afghanistan in the same month and held for several weeks before being released. In August, gunmen set fire to a building housing an independent radio station, causing thousands of dollars' worth of damage. Reporters have also faced difficulties in covering proceedings at the newly established Parliament, with several being assaulted and many more denied access on various occasions. In general, according to the Committee to Protect Journalists, official information is not readily available to members of the press.

Although registration requirements remain in place, authorities have granted more than 400 publication licenses, and over 60 private radio stations and 8 television stations are now broadcasting, providing an expanding diversity of views. National and local governments own or control several dozen newspapers and many electronic media outlets. In the country's underdeveloped economic environment, the majority of media outlets remain dependent on the state, political parties, or international donors for financial support. One prominent exception is the popular and progressive Tolo network of television and radio stations, which provides dynamic coverage and scrutiny of current events and politics in a format that has proved to be financially viable. International radio broadcasts in Dari or Pashto, such as those from the BBC, Voice of America, Radio Liberty, and Radio Free Afghanistan, remain a key source of information for many Afghans. Access to the internet and to satellite TV dishes remains largely unrestricted, although their use is confined predominantly to Kabul and other major cities (only 1 percent of the total population was able to access the internet in 2006). The use of the internet and mobile phones continues to grow rapidly and has broadened the flow of news and other information, particularly for urban Afghans.

Albania

Status: Partly Free

LEGAL ENVIRONMENT: 17
POLITICAL ENVIRONMENT: 16
ECONOMIC ENVIRONMENT: 17
TOTAL SCORE: 50

Survey Edition	2002	2003	2004	2005	2006
Total Score, Status	48,PF	50,PF	49,PF	51,PF	50,PF

The legal system protects freedom of the press, and it is generally respected by the authorities. Press freedom advocates in 2006 continued to urge the government to decriminalize defamation, which could incur a maximum sentence of two years in prison under existing statutes. Although the Parliament failed to act on draft amendments introduced in 2005, Prime Minister Sali Berisha in October of that year ordered government officials to use the right of reply rather than civil or criminal defamation suits to address perceived bias or inaccuracy in the media. No major libel cases were reported in 2006. The prospects for legal reform improved in June, when Albania signed a Stabilization and Association Agreement with the European Union (EU). The pact, which capped more than two years of negotiations, was considered a key milestone on the path to EU membership, and EU officials said media freedom would be among their priorities as they pressed Albania to make additional structural improvements. The country's Parliament-appointed broadcast regulator, the National Council of Radio and Television, continued to face accusations of political influence and incompetence. However, Berisha and Tirana mayor Edi Rama, leader of the opposition Socialist Party, agreed in August to add two opposition appointees to the council's membership. The plan came as part of a deal allowing municipal elections to proceed in early 2007.

Independent media continued to be active and were generally able to criticize the government. Coverage by state-owned broadcasters had favored the incumbents in the run-up to July 2005 elections, and at least four cases of violence against journalists were reported that year, but the country largely avoided a repeat of such problems in 2006. The media played a prominent role in at least two new incidents that proved embarrassing to the government. In March, the Tirana-based television station Alsat broadcast a gaffe in which Foreign Minister Besnik Mustafaj predicted further regional border changes if Kosovo were partitioned between Serbs and ethnic Albanians. In September, an investigative television show aired recorded conversations in which a government official appeared to pressure two nephews of President Alfred Moisiu to convince their uncle to fire the attorney general, whom Berisha has accused of corruption in a politically charged standoff.

Albania has 66 private television stations, at least 45 private radio stations, and roughly 200 print publications in circulation. Many independent media outlets are hampered by a lack of revenue. Publishers and media owners tend to dictate editorial policy based on political and economic affiliations, which together with the employment insecurity journalists face nurtures a culture of self-censorship. The internet is a relatively unimportant source of information, since access is limited by a weak telecommunications infrastructure outside major urban areas. Despite the absence of government restrictions, barely 6 percent of the population is able to use the internet on a regular basis.

Algeria

Status: Not Free

LEGAL ENVIRONMENT: 22
POLITICAL ENVIRONMENT: 23
ECONOMIC ENVIRONMENT: 17
TOTAL SCORE: 62

Survey Edition	2002	2003	2004	2005	2006
Total Score, Status	62,NF	62,NF	63,NF	64,NF	61,NF

According to Algeria's constitution, press freedom is a guaranteed right, but this has not stopped authorities from using legal and extralegal methods to harass the independent press. The laws were amended in 2001 to criminalize defamation of the president, the Parliament, the judiciary, and the military. Algerian courts are subject to government pressure when adjudicating cases of libel and related offenses. Free expression was dealt another blow in 2006 as a result of President Abdelaziz Bouteflika's plan for national reconciliation after the civil conflict of the 1990s. In February, the cabinet passed a decree that granted immunity to perpetrators of violence during the conflict and authorized up to five years' imprisonment for "anyone who by speech, writing, or any other act uses or exploits the wounds of the National Tragedy...to weaken the state...or to tarnish the image of Algeria internationally," according to the Committee to Protect Journalists.

The pattern of harassment aimed at critical or partisan Algerian journalists over the past several years continued in 2006. Journalists were arrested and charged with criminal violations in February after their newspapers published controversial cartoons of the prophet Muhammad, which first appeared in a Danish newspaper and sparked riots and demonstrations across the Muslim world. As is often the case in Algeria, the journalists were soon released, but the arrests illustrated the unpredictable nature of the authorities. In January, reporter Bachir Larabi of the independent daily *El-Khabar* was imprisoned for a month in the southwestern town of El-Bayadh after he was found guilty of defaming a local mayor. In June, journalist Mohamed Benchicou was released from prison after completing his two-year sentence for violating Algerian currency transportation laws. Benchicou's case was politically motivated—his defunct newspaper, *Le Matin*, had published harsh criticism of the government, and Benchicou himself had written a book that pilloried the president. Bouteflika issued a pardon for journalists in July—although the pardon applied only to those who had been "definitively" convicted, leaving unpardoned the majority of journalists, who were in the process of appealing their convictions—but the laws used to punish them remained on the books, and several other journalists were charged and sentenced to jail terms for their writing in the months after the pardon. Despite such persistent government harassment, Algeria's newspapers remained feisty and assertive in their opinions. Columnists and editorial cartoonists skewer the authorities on a regular basis.

Radio and television, two of the main news sources, are largely under government direction and, for the most part, follow the government line. Popular Pan-Arab satellite television stations, like Qatar-based Al-Jazeera, as well as French-based channels provide an alternate source of information. Although the government dominates the broadcast industry, there are more than 100 private daily and weekly newspapers presenting a variety of political perspectives. However, the government uses its control over the country's printing presses and a state advertising agency to influence the independent print media. Authorities have on several occasions punished critical newspapers by suddenly demanding payment for debts owed to the state printer. Internet penetration is still quite low at only 5 percent of the population, but access is not restricted by the government.

LEGAL ENVIRONMENT: 1
POLITICAL ENVIRONMENT: 4

Andorra

ECONOMIC ENVIRONMENT: 8

Status: Free

TOTAL SCORE: 13

Survey Edition	2002	2003	2004	2005	2006
Total Score, Status	NA	8,F	13,F	14,F	14,F

Freedom of expression is protected under Article 12 of the Andorran constitution, which also allows for laws that regulate the right of reply, correction, and professional confidentiality. The Universal Declaration of Human Rights, which is binding in Andorra, also ensures media freedom. No major incidents relating to press freedom were reported in 2006. Owing to Andorra's size and its proximity to France and Spain, its media landscape is partially shaped by foreign outlets; the majority of television transmissions are provided through technical accords with the Spanish and French government networks. Domestically, there are two daily papers, *Diari d'Andorra* and *El Periodic*, as well as two major weekly newspapers, *Informacions* and *7 Dies*. There are approximately 15 radio and 6 television stations. The government also releases a daily news bulletin. Internet access is open and unrestricted, with approximately 30 percent of the population accessing this medium in 2006.

LEGAL ENVIRONMENT: 17
POLITICAL ENVIRONMENT: 24

Angola

ECONOMIC ENVIRONMENT: 21

Status: Not Free

TOTAL SCORE: 62

Survey Edition	2002	2003	2004	2005	2006
Total Score, Status	79,NF	72,NF	66,NF	66,NF	65,NF

Despite constitutional guarantees, freedom of the press is restricted in Angola. In May, the government enacted a new Press Law that marks an improvement over previous legislation. The law ends the state monopoly on television broadcasting, calls for the creation of a public broadcaster that ensures the "right of citizens to inform, seek information, and be informed," and allows journalists to use the truth defense in libel and defamation trials. However, the law includes several restrictive provisions and requires implementing legislation for the execution of some of the more positive reforms (including application for independent television and radio licenses). Libel of the president or his representatives is still a criminal offense, punishable by high fines and possibly imprisonment (the wording of the legislation is vague). Authorities can suspend a publication for up to a year if it has published three articles that lead to defamation convictions within a three-year period. Particularly in the interior of the country, the judicial system has little independence to enforce legislation guaranteeing press freedom. The Law on State Secrecy permits the government to classify information, at times unnecessarily, and those who publish classified information are prosecuted. Private media are often denied access to official information or events. The new Press Law authorizes the creation—pending legislation—of an independent National Council for Media Communication.

Although generally tolerant of criticism from private media, officials often pressure independent media to cover the government in a more favorable light. While less common than in previous years, arbitrary detention, harassment, and attacks on journalists continue to take place. For fear of reprisals, many journalists practice self-censorship. In July, Reporters Sans Frontieres condemned the murders of two Angolan journalists, though it was unclear whether their deaths were related to their media work. Foreign media are able to operate with fewer government restrictions. However, journalists must first secure work visas to enter the country and then must receive authorization from the Ministry of the Interior to meet government officials or travel within Angola.

The government continues to dominate both print and broadcast media. The largest media sources are state run and allow very little criticism of government officials. The official Radio Nacional de Angola is the only radio station with national coverage; the state also controls the only nonsatellite television station. While the new Press Law opens television broadcasting to the private sector and establishes principles prohibiting censorship and respecting freedom of the press and access to information sources, the effective promulgation and implementation of the law is another matter. Four private radio stations operate under government license from Luanda, the capital. As of 2006, authorities continued to prevent Radio Ecclesia, the outspoken Roman Catholic radio station, from broadcasting outside Luanda. The country's seven private weeklies have low circulation and face financial constraints as well as high costs of production and distribution. Few outside the capital can afford private newspapers. Internet access is unrestricted and is available in several provincial capitals, though less than 1 percent of the population was able to make use of this new medium in 2006.

Antigua and Barbuda

Status: Partly Free

LEGAL ENVIRONMENT: 10
POLITICAL ENVIRONMENT: 14
ECONOMIC ENVIRONMENT: 14
TOTAL SCORE: 38

Survey Edition	2002	2003	2004	2005	2006
Total Score, Status	44,PF	45,PF	43,PF	40,PF	38,PF

The constitution of Antigua and Barbuda explicitly protects freedom of speech and of the press, and freedom of information legislation was passed in 2005. A major source of concern for media freedom advocates remained the legal action initiated in 2005 by Gene Pestaina, director of public prosecutions, against Lennox Linton, manager of the popular station Observer Radio, who was accused of defamation for verbally ridiculing the director's office while on the air. In August 2006, a high court judge ruled against Linton's application to have the case thrown out, which subsequently opened the way for the issue to be heard in court.

Relations between the United Progressive Party government and the media continued to be tense. In April, the minister of information, broadcasting, and communications, Edmund Mansoor, publicly criticized what he called "special interests" in the media, stating that the content of commentaries, editorials, and talk shows "smack of…gutter journalism." In February, the opposition Antigua Labour Party complained to the Inter-American Commission on Human Rights' Special Rapporteur for Freedom of Expression about alleged government restrictions on access to state-owned media. In 2005, authorities arrested opposition ZDK radio announcer James "Tanny" Rose for misbehavior in public office, in a case that occurred when he was serving as chief information officer of the state-owned ABS Radio and Television Authority in 1994. In 2006, the prosecutor brought criminal charges against Rose, but he had not been tried by the year's end.

There are 2 daily newspapers, 1 weekly paper, and 10 radio stations, including the state-owned Antigua and Barbuda Network, which also runs the islands' only freely available television service; there is 1 cable television company. There are no government restrictions on the internet, which was accessed by 40 percent of the population in 2006.

Argentina

Status: Partly Free

LEGAL ENVIRONMENT: 13
POLITICAL ENVIRONMENT: 20
ECONOMIC ENVIRONMENT: 16
TOTAL SCORE: 49

Survey Edition	2002	2003	2004	2005	2006
Total Score, Status	37,PF	39,PF	35,PF	41,PF	45,PF

Local and national politicians followed President Nestor Kirchner's lead in 2006, showing little tolerance for press criticism. Tactics used against media critical of the administration included control of government advertising and access to information; termination of programs on private and state-owned broadcasters; and use of authoritarian press laws, threats, and physical assault to intimidate journalists.

While criminal insult and defamation laws no longer exist in Argentina, "crimes against honor" prohibit intentionally accusing someone of committing a crime and/or impugning their honor. Civil laws call for the accuser to pay fines for any material or "moral" damages caused, while criminal laws carry jail time of up to three years. Both laws were used against journalists in 2006. Investigative reporter Mariano Saravia received a grant from the World Press Freedom Committee to fight charges of civil crimes against honor filed by a retired military officer and a former policeman who appeared in his book, *La Sombra Azul*. The journalist's defense is that what he wrote was true. Prior to the charges, Saravia received death threats and was harassed. Although not used against Saravia, crimes against honor also exist in the federal penal code, to which truth is a defense if the accusation is made in the public interest. The minister of culture in Rio Negro province filed criminal charges against journalist Angel Ruiz in 2006 after his reports linked the official to fossil smuggling. Prior to the charges, the journalist received threatening calls. Other criminal laws were used against journalists during the year. In Cordoba province, radio journalists Nestor Pasquini and Hugo Francischelli were jailed in December on charges of inciting violence and arson during a riot they covered.

The press also faced various forms of political pressure. President Kirchner continued to criticize conservative journalists and publications for complicity with the 1976–1983 military dictatorship. These publications, especially the daily *La Nacion*, provide the most hard-hitting coverage of his government. First Lady and Senator Cristina Fernandez called journalists covering Congress "ignoramuses" and "dimwits." These comments seemed to have incited attacks on journalists, including threats made against *La*

Nacion columnist Joaquin Morales Sola and the publisher of the critical newsmagazine *Noticias,* Jorge Fontevecchia. On state-owned Channel 7 television, "irreverent" journalist Victor Hugo Morales's program, *Desayuno,* was canceled after a seven-year run. The order came following the station management's replacement and the unexplained dismissal of anchor Marcela Pacheca after she criticized a gathering that President Kirchner organized on the anniversary of his inauguration. Similarly, Radio Nacional discontinued host Jose Eliaschev's commentary program. Three current affairs programs on privately owned media suffered the same fate.

Reporters Sans Frontieres reported that 34 Argentine journalists were physically attacked in 2006, often by politicians, bureaucrats, or police. In Quilmes Town Hall in Buenos Aires province, a local leader of the Peronist Party beat radio journalist Pedro Navarro unconscious. The mayor of Quilmes convinced the Federal Broadcast Commission to revoke the licenses of two local radio stations, Navarro's Radio Quilmes 106.9 and Fan 103.9. The lower house of Congress unsuccessfully called upon the commission to restore their licenses. Furthermore, three well-known journalists' e-mail accounts were hacked into, giving perpetrators access to the names of confidential sources.

There are more than 150 daily newspapers, hundreds of radio stations, and dozens of television channels in Argentina. The country's print media are all privately owned, while the numerous privately owned radio and television stations are able to broadcast without restrictions. The use of state advertising to reward or punish media outlets is considered the biggest threat to press freedom nationally. According to the U.S. State Department, national government spending on advertising increased from 15.4 million pesos (approximately US$5 million) in 2002 to 127.5 million pesos (approximately US$47 million) in 2006. Shows were canceled on privately owned Radio Rio Gallegos in Santa Cruz province, on LT 24 radio in Buenos Aires province, and on TV 5 in Tucuman after local authorities threatened to withdraw advertising. In May, Grupo Editorial Perfil sued the national government for discrimination after the administration withheld official advertising from some of its publications. Legislation that would set market-based or program-oriented criteria for the distribution of state advertising was stalled in congressional committees. The media company Perfil, owner of *Noticias,* has sued over the government's refusal to award state advertising or grant the newspaper's reporters interviews with top officials. Foreign news broadcasts are available in Argentina, and the internet was unrestricted by the government and used by 34 percent of the population.

Armenia

LEGAL ENVIRONMENT: 20
POLITICAL ENVIRONMENT: 24
ECONOMIC ENVIRONMENT: 20

Status: Not Free

TOTAL SCORE: 64

Survey Edition	2002	2003	2004	2005	2006
Total Score, Status	60,PF	65,NF	64,NF	64,NF	64,NF

The constitution guarantees freedom of the press, although the government and those closely connected to the ruling party frequently fail to respect press freedom in practice. Libel remains a criminal offense. A coalition of nongovernmental organizations (NGOs)—including the Yerevan Press Club, the Journalists Union of Armenia, Internews Armenia, the Committee to Protect Freedom of Expression, and the Investigative Journalists Association—drafted a proposal to abolish Article 318 of the criminal code, which establishes criminal liability for insulting a public official. Armenia adopted freedom of information legislation in 2003, but the law has been poorly implemented.

In September, Armen Babajanian, editor of the opposition daily *Zhamanak Yerevan*, was sentenced to four years in prison for falsifying documents to avoid military service. Although he pleaded guilty, media organizations expressed concern that the trial was politically influenced, since the sentence was unusually harsh for such an offense. In July, editors from eight leading newspapers and several NGO directors issued a joint statement highlighting the ever-increasing pressure put on journalists who criticize the authorities. The president appoints all members of the National Commission for Television and Radio (NCTVR), the body that oversees the broadcast media. The commission's actions are government controlled and not transparent. During the year, A1+, once a vocal and politically independent television station, continued efforts to obtain a frequency license, but all 12 of its applications over the past four years have been denied by the NCTVR. In 2002, the NCTVR had revoked A1+'s license and subsequently gave it to a pro-government national television station. Since then, the station has remained vocal by producing television programs and internet publications. Each year, Armenian journalists organize protests on the anniversary of the station's license revocation. The Armenian National Academy of Sciences filed a lawsuit in March 2006 demanding that A1+ vacate the building it had occupied for the past 15 years. The academy owned the building and won the lawsuit, and the journalists were given 24 hours to leave. Separately, the government proposed a draft law that would have changed the composition of the NCTVR, with half the members appointed by the Parliament and the other half by the president. The legislation also sought to reduce television coverage of the Parliament. However, lawmakers rejected the bill in September.

While the government does not exert direct control or censorship over the media, it maintains a firm grip, particularly over broadcast media, through informal pressure on outlet owners. Print publications are typically free to report diverse views, partly because their low circulation and lack of presence in rural areas make them a less likely target for government pressure. The highest-circulation daily, *Haykakan Zhamanak*, sells fewer than 6,000 copies a day. Since A1+ was taken off the air, most television stations have grown more politically aligned with the government, remain selective in their reporting, and routinely ignore opposition members. Armenian Public Television, which has national reach, avoids criticizing the government amid the evident climate of self-censorship in the broadcast media. Toward the end of the year, as the campaign for the spring 2007 parliamentary elections intensified, opposition figures faced discriminatory coverage and high prices for campaign advertisements. There were reports throughout the year of physical violence inflicted against members of the press. In July, Gagik Shamshian, a freelancer writing for the opposition weekly *Chorrord Ishkhanutyun* and the independent daily *Aravot*, was allegedly assaulted by the local government leader's brother and other assailants, and *Chorrord Ishkhanutyun*'s offices were damaged by an arson attack. In September, Hovhannes Galajian, editor in chief of the opposition-sponsored *Iravunk* newspaper, was attacked and beaten.

The print media are privately owned, except for the government-subsidized *Hayastani Hanrapetutyun* and its Russian-language version. But print publications struggle with financial difficulties, and few newspapers are able to function independently of economic or political interest groups. The government has further restricted the print media's distribution ability with new legislation that requires delivery companies to apply for costly licenses. The legislation threatens to bankrupt smaller companies and force all print media to use either Armenia's postal service or the main kiosk vendor, both of which are government affiliated. In 2006, owing to the Russian transportation embargo on Georgia, Armenia faced a shortage of newsprint. Most television stations are also privately owned, but the owners are often pro-government politicians or government-affiliated business magnates. Internet access remains low at 5 percent of the population thanks to high connection costs, but there have been no reports of official restrictions imposed on its use.

LEGAL ENVIRONMENT: 6

POLITICAL ENVIRONMENT: 9

Australia
ECONOMIC ENVIRONMENT: 6

Status: Free
TOTAL SCORE: 21

Survey Edition	2002	2003	2004	2005	2006
Total Score, Status	10,F	14,F	14,F	18,F	19,F

Press freedom in Australia operates by convention rather than by constitutional guarantees. However, in July the state of Victoria introduced a Charter of Human Rights and Responsibilities that includes protection for freedom of expression. The Australian Press Council and the Media, Entertainment, and Arts Alliance (MEAA) monitor journalistic freedom and access to information. Both groups have expressed concern over a decline in press freedom in a number of areas in 2006.

In spite of recommendations by the Australian Law Reform Commission, the Antiterrorism Act of 2005, which imposes a blanket ban on reporting about people detained under antiterrorism legislation, has yet to be reformed. Journalists may be charged with sedition and face a seven-year jail sentence for reporting against the actions of the government, police, or judiciary. Additionally, the Telecommunications (Interception) Amendment Act of 2006 was passed, affording the right to police and other security agencies to monitor phone conversations as well as access the e-mail and text messages of people who have associated with those accused of crimes. The MEAA has expressed concern that this will lead to greater journalistic self-censorship and hesitancy of sources to reveal information to the press.

In 2006, a judge upheld the decision to hold two journalists from the *Herald Sun* in contempt for refusing to reveal a source before a judge in Melbourne in 2005. In an assault on freedom of information in late 2006, the high court of Australia voted 3–2 to deny access to documents requested by *The Australian* journalist Michael McKinnon. McKinnon requested documents on income tax and first-time home buyers grants but was denied by Treasurer Peter Costello, who stated that the documents were not "in the public interest." Lengthy delays and high costs already impede access to information. In a victory for press freedom, Australia introduced uniform defamation laws that cap maximum damages, restrict action to one year after publication, bar legal action from large corporations, and introduce truth as a complete defense.

Australia has a strong tradition of public broadcasting, though the Australian Broadcasting Corporation has faced dramatic funding cuts and in 2006 was stripped of its only staff-elected board position. Private media ownership is concentrated, with the majority of ownership by Rupert Murdoch's News Ltd. and Fairfax Group (negotiations are under way for a possible merger with Rural Press Ltd.). Media ownership laws were further relaxed in 2006 when the minimum number of "voices" in a city was reduced to five and in regions to four. The internet is a vibrant medium in Australia, accessed by 70 percent of the population. However, censorship concerns were raised when the prime minister's office closed down a website, 36 hours after its launch, for satirizing Prime Minister John Howard.

Austria

LEGAL ENVIRONMENT: 8
POLITICAL ENVIRONMENT: 8
ECONOMIC ENVIRONMENT: 5

Status: Free

TOTAL SCORE: 21

Survey Edition	2002	2003	2004	2005	2006
Total Score, Status	24,F	23,F	23,F	21,F	21,F

The federal constitution and the Media Law of 1981 provide the basis for free media in Austria. Freedom of information legislation is in place, and the government generally respects these provisions in practice. Libel and slander laws protect politicians and other government officials and in some cases lead to self-censorship. In November 2006, the European Court of Human Rights overturned decisions in three cases brought to trial by public figures on defamation charges related to articles published in the daily *Der Standard*. The Austrian courts' reasoning "had not been relevant or sufficient to justify the interference in the applicants' right to freedom of expression," which was judged a violation of Article 10 of the European Convention on Human Rights.

Any form of pro-Nazism or anti-Semitism is prohibited by law, as is Holocaust denial. In February, British author David Irving, who had been charged with violating the law banning neo-Nazi activities, was sentenced to three years in prison. In April, John Gudenus, a former member of the upper house of Parliament, was sentenced to probation for statements denying the events of the Holocaust.

Since 2004's Broadcasting Law amendments, Austria's public broadcaster, which operates two television stations and four radio channels, faces growing competition for audiences from private broadcasters. Cable and satellite are widely available and are often used to watch German stations, some of which tailor programming for the Austrian audience. Daily newspapers, both national and regional, are very popular and contest fiercely for readers. Foreign investors have a solid presence in the predominantly privately owned print market, and ownership concentration is high. Many radio stations have ties to print outlets, and additionally there is cross-ownership of daily and weekly newspapers. Press subsidies help newspapers survive and are designed to encourage pluralism. Internet access is unrestricted and was made use of by more than 50 percent of the population in 2006.

	LEGAL ENVIRONMENT: 24
	POLITICAL ENVIRONMENT: 29
Azerbaijan	ECONOMIC ENVIRONMENT: 22
Status: Not Free	TOTAL SCORE: 75

Survey Edition	2002	2003	2004	2005	2006
Total Score, Status	77,NF	73,NF	71,NF	72,NF	73,NF

Azerbaijan's constitution guarantees freedom of the press, but the government hardly respects it, and media freedom continues to decline in practice. Despite the completion of a draft Law on Defamation that would decriminalize libel, it remains a criminal offense punishable by large fines and up to three years' imprisonment. Defamation lawsuits are the most common method of government intimidation aimed at opposition and independent media. The minister of interior affairs alone filed five lawsuits in 2006. In one such case in September, Eynulla Fatullayev, founder and editor of the Russian-language newspaper *Realny Azerbaijan*, received a suspended two-year prison sentence and a fine of US$11,000 for libeling the minister. Fikret Faramazoglu, editor in chief of the weekly opposition newspaper *24 Saat*, was also sentenced to a suspended one-year prison term in August for libeling the minister. In August, Shakhin Agabeili, editor of the magazine *Milli Yol*, was sentenced to one year in prison for defaming a leader of the ruling Yeni Azerbaijan Party; he was pardoned by President Ilham Aliyev in October.

Azerbaijan passed a Freedom of Information Law in December 2005, but it has not been implemented effectively; government institutions continue to ban opposition and independent journalists from public hearings. The government wields significant control over the National

Radio and Television Council (NRTC), the broadcast watchdog and licenser. In November, the NRTC suspended transmission of the country's first independent television and radio station, ANS, citing a series of legal and regulatory violations. After harsh international criticism, the NRTC allowed ANS to resume broadcasts in December. However, the station remained vulnerable owing to outstanding problems with the regulator. The suspension disrupted local transmission of the British Broadcasting Corporation, Radio Free Europe/Radio Liberty, and Voice of America. On the same day as the action against ANS, a ruling by Baku's economic court on the 1992 lease of a city building forced the evictions of the newspapers *Azadliq* and *Bizim Yol* and the Turan information agency, as well as the headquarters of the main opposition party, the Popular Front. The news outlets were able to relocate and resume operations after about a week. Foreign broadcasts of Turkish and Russian media were suspended at the end of the year.

Harassment and violence against journalists remains a serious concern in Azerbaijan. In October, members of the Azadliq opposition political bloc began a hunger strike to protest the government's harassment of the media, and they were later joined by independent media representatives; it was the second time since 1999 that Azerbaijani journalists have gone on a collective hunger strike. In March, *Azadliq* journalist Fikret Huseynli was kidnapped and stabbed before being released. *Azadliq* was also evicted by police from its premises in November only 30 minutes after a court approved the case for eviction. In May, *Bizim Yol* editor Bakhaddin Khaziyev was kidnapped, beaten, and ordered to stop reporting on sensitive issues, including corruption. His assailants reportedly ran over his legs with a car. Eynulla Fatullayev ceased publishing both *Realny Azerbaijan* and its Azerbaijani-language sister publication in October, apparently to secure the release of his kidnapped father. *Realny Azerbaijan* resumed publishing in December. In June, authorities detained a prominent satirist for *Azadliq*, Mirza Sakit Zakhidov, on charges of narcotics trafficking and possession. Although he insisted the charges were fabricated, he was convicted of drug possession in October and sentenced to three years in prison. The 2005 murder of Elmar Huseynov, founder and editor of the opposition *Monitor* magazine, remained unresolved. The Institute for Reporter Freedom and Safety was established in 2006 for the protection of journalists who have been seriously injured at the hands of the authorities while attempting to carry out duties related to their work.

Although independent and opposition-affiliated media outlets exist in Azerbaijan, most private broadcast outlets are owned by ruling party supporters. The independent print media are generally able to express a wide variety of views but have minimal circulation outside Baku, unlike pro-government-subsidized newspapers. Most print media are typeset at government-owned publishing houses, and the owners of private printing presses also frequently have strong government connections. State-owned print and broadcast media, including a public television station established in 2005, toe the government line. The private and independent broadcast channels that are able to express diverse views are not available throughout the country. Independent and opposition media struggle financially because the government prohibits state-owned companies from purchasing advertising space from them and pressures private business to advertise in state-owned media. Internet access is generally unrestricted, although it is limited to less than 10 percent of the population (located primarily in larger cities). In July, local media reported that a popular blog had been blocked after it had parodied the president. Furthermore, the newspapers *Azadliq, Gundelik Azerbaijan,* and *Realny Azerbaijan* all claimed that their websites had been hacked into.

Bahamas

LEGAL ENVIRONMENT: 2
POLITICAL ENVIRONMENT: 9
ECONOMIC ENVIRONMENT: 6

Status: Free

TOTAL SCORE: 17

Survey Edition	2002	2003	2004	2005	2006
Total Score, Status	8,F	11,F	14,F	14,F	16,F

The constitution guarantees freedom of speech and of the press, and although there is no freedom of information legislation, the government does generally support the public's right to access to information. However, during 2006 there were indications that some members of the ruling Progressive Liberal Party (PLP) were exerting undue pressure on the media in response to less than flattering news coverage. In early May, PLP chairman Raynard Rigby publicly warned the publishers of the *Nassau Guardian* and the *Bahamas Tribune*—two of the four daily newspapers—that they should be careful to be objective when reporting news of political affairs. In June, the foreign minister, Fred Mitchell, publicly criticized the print media, accusing it of lacking "balance and fairness." The following month, managing editor of the *Tribune* and British citizen John Marquis was informed that his work permit would not be renewed. Marquis and other media freedom advocates claimed the move was a response to several critical articles. After protests, the authorities issued a one-year permit. In February, prison guards outside the Carmichael Detention Centre in Nassau attacked four journalists from Miami-based television stations. The state-owned Broadcasting Corporation of the Bahamas operates a television station and the ZNS Radio Bahamas network. There are also numerous privately owned radio stations. The internet was unrestricted and was accessed by 30 percent of the population.

Bahrain

LEGAL ENVIRONMENT: 23
POLITICAL ENVIRONMENT: 26
ECONOMIC ENVIRONMENT: 22

Status: Not Free   TOTAL SCORE: 71

Survey Edition	2002	2003	2004	2005	2006
Total Score, Status	75,NF	68,NF	70,NF	71,NF	72,NF

The government continues to restrict media reporting, including the internet, despite laws providing for freedom of the press and of expression. In spite of the government's claims to further the democratic process, media restrictions were tightened in 2006. Articles 23 and 24 of Bahrain's constitution guarantee freedom of expression and of the press. However, a suspended 2002 Press Law (No. 47) continues to enable the prosecution of journalists based on 17 categories of offenses. Offenses against Islam, the king, and "the unity of the people," as well as acts of inciting division or sectarianism, are punishable by six months to five years in prison. According to the Bahrain Journalists Association, 30 legal cases were brought against journalists in 2006 by individuals alleging defamation or insult. Conflicting conservative and liberal efforts to reform the 2002 Press Law continued in 2006, with two emergency sessions for debate called in April. Despite government commitments to a more democratic society, three laws were passed in 2006 that have the potential to undermine the rights to free expression. On July 20, amendments to the Association Law (No. 18/1973) were ratified that forbade any speech or discussion infringing on "public order or morals." A counterterrorism bill was signed into law on August 12 that contains excessively broad definitions of terrorism and terrorist acts and criminalizes advocating terrorist acts as well as the possession of documents promoting the same. An amendment to the penal code (Act No. 65/2006) in September made it a crime to publish the names or pictures of accused persons before a court verdict and without the permission of the public prosecutor.

News regarding international issues, local economic and commercial issues, and opposition politics is generally less restricted than news on issues concerning the royal family, the Saudi royal family, national security, and judges. Two reporters from local papers *Al-Mithak* and *Al-Wasat* received anonymous telephone threats in October for writing about the "Bandargate" scandal that centered on a report written by Sudanese-born British citizen Salah al-Bandar regarding alleged election fraud and involved members of the royal family and politicians. Despite governmental censorship and self-censorship among journalists, many local and foreign media outlets are able to cover a diversity of issues without restriction. Nevertheless, some subjects of local concern continue to be untouchable.

Print media are privately owned, and there are nearly 100 Bahraini newspapers and journals in circulation. A number of new Arabic daily newspapers have opened since the reforms of 2002, including *Al-Watan*, which debuted in December 2005, and *Al-Waqt*, which entered the market in 2006. Although they are privately owned, the government retains the right to control publishing policies, appoint the papers' officials, and dismiss journalists. All local radio and television stations are state run; however, satellite television is widely available, providing access to international broadcasts. The country's first private radio station, which began broadcasting from Manama in October 2005, was shut down in 2006 by the authorities, who alleged irregularities.

While the internet has provided journalists in Bahrain with greater freedom to report and access to more diverse and critical forms of information, it has also served as yet another medium for the government to censor and regulate. The only internet provider is the government-owned Batelco, which reported that 135,000 persons (about 21 percent of the population) used its service. Batelco prohibits user access to antigovernment, anti-Islamic, and human rights websites. In August, a government decree was issued to block access to Google Earth, Google Video, and Google Maps, but this was lifted days later following pressure from civil society. The media block on the "Bandargate" scandal extended beyond traditional media outlets to the internet, where blogs were forbidden to discuss the issue. In October, many websites and blogs were banned in the month leading up to the elections. On November 16, Dr. Mohammed Saeed Al-Sahlawi and Husain Abdulaziz Al-Hebshi were arrested for possessing publications downloaded from the internet calling for the boycott of the November elections. The two activists were charged with promoting an illegal change of the state and spreading false news and rumors that would disrupt public security and damage public interest. The two remained in prison at the end of 2006. By year's end, almost two dozen websites had been blocked.

Bangladesh

LEGAL ENVIRONMENT: 20
POLITICAL ENVIRONMENT: 30
ECONOMIC ENVIRONMENT: 16

Status: Not Free

TOTAL SCORE: 66

Survey Edition	2002	2003	2004	2005	2006
Total Score, Status	63,NF	65,NF	68,NF	68,NF	68,NF

While an expanding number of privately owned broadcast outlets provide greater diversity, media continued to face myriad pressures in 2006, the most striking of which is the high level of violence directed against journalists and the impunity enjoyed by those who attack them. Although the constitution provides for freedom of expression subject to "reasonable restrictions," the press is constrained by national security legislation as well as sedition and criminal libel laws. Journalists continue to be slapped with contempt of court and defamation charges or arrested under the 1974 Special Powers Act (which allows detentions of up to 90 days without trial) in reprisal for filing stories critical of government officials or policies. Cases of criminal defamation suits against private newspapers by ruling party politicians reportedly increased in 2006. The case of journalist and writer Salah Uddin Shoaib Choudhury—who was arrested in 2003 and prevented from traveling to a conference in Israel, charged with sedition, and spent 17 months in jail before being released on bail in 2005—remained open throughout 2006 as he awaited trial. Choudhury also received death threats from Islamist groups, and in July the offices of his magazine were bombed.

Authorities limit official access to journalists from certain publications. The government remained sensitive to international scrutiny; foreign publications are subject to censorship, while foreign journalists and press freedom advocates have encountered increasing difficulties in obtaining visas to enter Bangladesh and are put under surveillance while in the country. In an effort to tighten censorship laws, the government passed legislation in September that would enable officials to suspend the broadcast of any private satellite television channel "for the public interest."

Journalists are regularly harassed and violently attacked by a range of actors, including organized crime groups, political parties and their supporters, government authorities, and leftist and Islamist militant groups. Most commonly, they are subjected to such attacks as a result of their coverage of corruption, criminal activity, political violence, the rise of Islamic fundamentalism, or human rights abuses. Police brutality toward photographers attempting to document protests or other political events also remained a concern. Reporter Bellal Hossain Dafadar was murdered in September 2006, and several hundred others received death threats or were physically assaulted and injured. In several instances, the offices of news outlets were attacked by unknown assailants. Harassment of journalists intensified alongside the rise in political tension preceding the November handover to the caretaker government. Impunity for those who perpetrate crimes against journalists is the norm, and investigations into the cases of reporters killed in previous years generally proceed slowly, if at all. However, in March a fast-track tribunal sentenced 1 person to death and 11 others to life imprisonment for the 2004 killing of journalist Kamal Hossain. The fear of violent reprisals causes many journalists to practice some level of self-censorship when covering sensitive topics.

With hundreds of daily and weekly publications, the privately owned print media continue to present an array of views, although political coverage at a number of newspapers is highly partisan. The state owns or influences several broadcast media outlets, whose coverage sometimes favors the ruling party but generally provided more balanced coverage in 2006 than previously. Private broadcasting has expanded in recent years, with six satellite television stations now broadcasting. Private outlets are required to air selected government-produced news segments as a condition of their operation, and the new broadcast licenses issued in 2005 were allegedly given to those with close political connections, according to the U.S. State Department. Political considerations influence the distribution of government advertising revenue and subsidized newsprint, upon which many publications depend. Access to the internet, although generally unrestricted, is limited to less than 1 percent of the population, and some journalists' e-mail is reportedly monitored by police.

LEGAL ENVIRONMENT: 3
POLITICAL ENVIRONMENT: 8

Barbados

ECONOMIC ENVIRONMENT: 6

Status: Free

TOTAL SCORE: 17

Survey Edition	2002	2003	2004	2005	2006
Total Score, Status	16,F	14,F	17,F	17,F	17,F

Freedom of the press is constitutionally guaranteed, and media are generally able to operate without restrictions; however, Barbados does not have freedom of information legislation. Representatives of the ruling Barbados Labour Party (BLP) occasionally criticized the media for spreading what they said was ill-informed criticism of the government. In February, Prime Minister and BLP leader Owen Arthur publicly criticized Harold Hoyte, president of the Nation Publishing Company Ltd. and editor in chief of *The Nation*. Arthur said that *The Nation* newspaper—one of the country's two dailies—ran articles that were driven by Hoyte's "political agenda." Of the 11 radio frequencies, 3 are run by the state-owned Caribbean Broadcasting Corporation, which also operates a television station. In August, the Barbados-based Caribbean Media Corporation launched CaribVision, a new 24-hour Caribbean television channel. CaribVision is beamed to over 10 Caribbean countries and to North America. There are no government restrictions on use of the internet, which was accessed by nearly 60 percent of the population in 2006.

LEGAL ENVIRONMENT: 27
POLITICAL ENVIRONMENT: 34

Belarus

ECONOMIC ENVIRONMENT: 28

Status: Not Free

TOTAL SCORE: 89

Survey Edition	2002	2003	2004	2005	2006
Total Score, Status	82,NF	82,NF	84,NF	86,NF	88,NF

Belarus's limited level of press freedom deteriorated further in 2006 as President Aleksandr Lukashenko's government suppressed independent media during the March presidential election and ensuing protests against election fraud. Despite constitutional provisions for freedom of the press, criticism of the president and his government is considered a criminal offense, and libel convictions can result in prison sentences or high fines. During the 2006 election period, the courts halted the publication of numerous independent newspapers. The weekly *Zgoda* was shuttered for republishing contentious Danish cartoons of the prophet Muhammad, although it had also reportedly drawn officials' attention by covering an opposition presidential candidate. Another weekly, *Nasha Niva*—the first Belarusian newspaper, founded in 1906—was informed that it could no longer be registered in Minsk after its editor in chief brought food to protesters in the capital's main square and was temporarily detained on charges of hooliganism. Nevertheless, the paper reportedly continued to publish.

The government subjected the independent media to systematic political intimidation. Police blockaded the print runs of such opposition newspapers as *Narodnaja Volya* and the Communist Party's *Tovarishch,* confiscating hundreds of thousands of copies. State media, focusing coverage on Lukashenko, issued propaganda warning Belarusians about violence at the polls. Meanwhile, police assaulted presidential candidate Aleksandr Kozulin when he tried to enter a meeting to hear the incumbent speak, and reporters attempting to cover the attack were similarly mistreated. The authorities also arrested and detained more than 30 Belarusian journalists and 12 foreign correspondents from countries like Canada, Georgia, Poland, Russia, and Ukraine for covering the elections and round-the-clock opposition demonstrations. In April, the authorities also prevented two groups of Polish journalists from entering Belarus to cover the twentieth anniversary of the Chernobyl nuclear disaster. Also that month, a court sentenced 16-year-old Anton Filimonov, the son of murdered journalist Veronika Cherkasova, to a suspended prison term of two and a half years for creating counterfeit currency. He had been arrested in late 2005 and then released in March, and critics had accused the government of using the counterfeiting case to force him to confess to his mother's 2004 murder, which remained unsolved.

The state, which maintains a monopoly over the broadcast media and controls the content of television programming, uses a range of economic pressures to weaken independent media. Much of Belarus's independent press has been run out of business and forced to close because authorities routinely pressure managers of state enterprises to advertise only in state media, banks to refuse deposits from readers into independent newspapers' accounts, and distributors and printing presses to deny nonstate media contracts. Opposition newspapers such as the aforementioned *Narodnaja Volya* and *Tovarishch* had little choice but to use printing houses outside of Belarus, such as in Smolensk, Russia, until those printing contracts were terminated in 2006 as well. Many independent papers are also banned from sale at newsstands, forcing them to resort to underground distribution methods like selling directly from the newsroom and using volunteers to deliver copies. Because the internet is widely used (accessed by 35 percent of the population in 2006) and Belarusian websites are not yet obliged to register with the authorities, many print publications have moved online. However, the state-owned telecommunications company (Beltelecom), which controls all Belarusian servers, can still block access, and legislators have been considering a new law to regulate the internet. The government reportedly monitored internet communications and attempted to deny access to opposition or independent websites during the presidential election period.

Belgium

Status: Free

LEGAL ENVIRONMENT: 2
POLITICAL ENVIRONMENT: 4
ECONOMIC ENVIRONMENT: 5
TOTAL SCORE: 11

Survey Edition	2002	2003	2004	2005	2006
Total Score, Status	9,F	9,F	9,F	11,F	11,F

The constitution guarantees freedom of speech and of the press, which are generally respected by the government. The Belgian Chamber of Deputies voted unanimously in March 2005 to approve a law that protects journalists' sources. The vote came after police raids in 2004 on the home and office of a Brussels-based reporter, Hans Martin Tillack, which shocked the community of international journalists. The new law protects reporters from home searches and seizures and gives them the right to silence if called as a witness. Journalists can only be forced to reveal sources to "prevent crimes that represent a serious attack on the physical integrity of one or several third parties." In October 2006, Tillack brought his case before the European court of first instance, where he argued that the action against him by Belgian police violated his rights. Although the court recognized that his complaints of mistreatment were legitimate, in the end it ruled that the case was out of its jurisdiction.

Newspaper ownership concentration has increased since the 1960s as corporations have steadily been buying up papers. As a result, today a handful of corporations run most of the country's newspapers. As for the broadcasting sector, unlike most other European nations, Belgium has two separate public broadcasting organizations (one operating in French and the other in Flemish), each with its own domestic and international broadcasting network. The government does not limit access to the internet, which was used by just under 50 percent of the population in 2006.

Belize

LEGAL ENVIRONMENT: 8
POLITICAL ENVIRONMENT: 8
ECONOMIC ENVIRONMENT: 5

Status: Free

TOTAL SCORE: 21

Survey Edition	2002	2003	2004	2005	2006
Total Score, Status	24,F	23,F	22,F	20,F	21,F

The constitution of Belize protects the right to freedom of expression, although there are several legal limitations to that right. The government may fine up to US$2,500 and imprison up to three years those who question the financial disclosures of public officials, though there were no reports of this law being exercised in 2006. Newspapers are subject to libel laws; furthermore, the Belize Broadcasting Authority (BBA) holds the right to preview broadcasts with political content and remove libelous material, but this right was not exercised during the year. In June, Prime Minister Said Wilbert Musa stated that media freedom may have gone too far. Although not calling for direct restrictions, he encouraged the BBA to act on curbing abuses to press freedom such as instilling violence, hate, and devious behavior.

There are 8 television and 33 licensed radio stations, including 1 affiliated directly with the United Democratic Party. There are no daily newspapers in Belize, though there is a vibrant market for weeklies. Papers are privately owned, with two weeklies directly affiliated with political parties. In general, reporting covers a wide range of opinions. Belize has close to 40,000 registered internet users (approximately 12 percent of the population), and the internet is unrestricted by the government.

Benin

Status: Free

LEGAL ENVIRONMENT: 10
POLITICAL ENVIRONMENT: 10
ECONOMIC ENVIRONMENT: 10
TOTAL SCORE: 30

Survey Edition	2002	2003	2004	2005	2006
Total Score, Status	30,F	28,F	30,F	30,F	30,F

Freedom of speech and of the press are protected by the constitution, and the government has developed a reputation for respecting these rights in practice. However, in 2006 a number of worrying developments occurred that, if continued, could threaten Benin's status as one of the freest environments for the media in Africa. In December, a 1997 Press Law that criminalizes libel was implemented for the first time in two years. A court bailiff, Maxime Bankole, pressed charges against the private newspaper *L'Informateur* for refusing to retract a story accusing him of rape. The courts sentenced both the editor and a journalist at *L'Informateur* to six months in prison and a US$1,000 fine. During 2005, in preparation for the March 2006 presidential election, the High Council for Audiovisual Media and Communications (HAAC) passed provisions mandating fair and balanced coverage of all presidential candidates. The provisions also restricted the amount of time a media outlet could devote to a particular presidential candidate and forbade opinion pieces on the election that might jeopardize "national unity." At year's end, as part of the new government's effort to "clean up the journalism sector," the HAAC instituted a requirement that all working journalists obtain a new press card; the conditions for obtaining one of these cards are strict and were intended to apply to less than 40 percent of those journalists in order to weed out the nonprofessionals.

During its final days in power leading up to the March election, Mathieu Kerekou's regime made a number of direct attempts to limit critical content in the media industry. In February, the managing editor of a private daily newspaper, *Panorama*, was temporarily detained and charged with high treason after publishing an article describing an alleged coup attempt intended to keep Kerekou in power. Also, in early March Kerekou's communications minister fired two top officials at the state-run broadcast office (Office de Radiodiffusion et de Television du Benin—ORTB) after they refused to broadcast a government videotape that allegedly proved the presence of electoral fraud, citing doubts about the tape's authenticity. After the election, the new president, Boni Yayi, appointed a minister of communications who immediately reinstated the fired ORTB officials.

However, threats against the press did not disappear entirely with the resignation of Kerekou; in September, three journalists with two separate privately run newspapers were arrested and temporarily detained for articles critical of the police and the new president's family.

Benin's numerous established media outlets have a history of providing aggressive reporting and robust scrutiny of both government and opposition leaders. However, the media market has recently become saturated by a number of publications that emerged for the first time in the month preceding the election, many of which receive direct political funding. The inability of most of Benin's media operators to garner a consistent profit further limits accuracy and fairness in reporting by making poorly paid reporters susceptible to bribery and blackmail. Internet access is available primarily through dial-up internet cafés that remain unhindered by government censorship, and at 425,000 users (just over 5 percent of the population), Benin had one of West Africa's highest rates of access to this new medium in 2006.

Bhutan

Status: Not Free

LEGAL ENVIRONMENT: 19
POLITICAL ENVIRONMENT: 23 .
ECONOMIC ENVIRONMENT: 20
TOTAL SCORE: 62

Survey Edition	2002	2003	2004	2005	2006
Total Score, Status	72,NF	70,NF	68,NF	66,NF	65,NF

Freedom of expression and of the press, as well as media diversity, continue to be limited in Bhutan despite some improvements in 2006. The Bhutan Information, Communications, and Media Act, passed in July, is designed to regulate the information, communications, and media industries. However, many observers have expressed concern that the law, which is concerned primarily with technological specifics, licensing, and ownership, provides no specific protections for journalists and does not guarantee freedom of information, although it does contain general provisions for freedom of expression and of the press. Under the 1992 National Security Act, any criticism of King Jigme Singye Wangchuk and Bhutan's political system is prohibited.

Physical attacks on the press in Bhutan are rare, and there were no reported cases of this occurring in 2006. Bhutan's main print publication, the state-owned biweekly *Kuensel*—now funded entirely by advertising and subscription revenues—generally reports news that puts the kingdom in a favorable light but has increasingly been highlighting societal problems and carrying stories critical of the government. In 2005, *Kuensel* announced plans to open another printing press in Tashingang so that it could improve its distribution network. Two new private weekly newspapers, the *Bhutan Times* and *Bhutan Observer*, were launched in April and June, respectively. Although the papers have published mainly pro-government articles, with the *Times* particularly supportive of the government stance toward refugees in Nepal, both have occasionally been critical of the government. A monthly periodical, *Bhutan Now*, started publishing in November.

State-owned broadcast media, which consist of a radio and a television station operated by the Bhutan Broadcasting Service, carry broadly pro-government programming and do not air opposition positions and statements. In September, Kuzoo FM 90, Bhutan's first private radio station, began operations. There are no private television broadcasters, but cable television services carry uncensored foreign programming. In 2005, in response to concerns voiced by authorities as well as by members of the public, the Association of Private Cable Operators resolved to limit cable access to 30 channels, with a complete ban on 12 music and other channels that provided "controversial" content such as wrestling. Internet access is growing and is unrestricted—two new internet service providers were licensed during 2005—and the daily online editions of several print publications provide somewhat livelier forums for discussion and debate. Nonetheless, owing to infrastructure and financial limitations, less than 4 percent of the population is able to access this new medium.

Bolivia

LEGAL ENVIRONMENT: 10
POLITICAL ENVIRONMENT: 16
ECONOMIC ENVIRONMENT: 11

Status: Partly Free

TOTAL SCORE: 37

Survey Edition	2002	2003	2004	2005	2006
Total Score, Status	25,F	30,F	37,PF	35,PF	33,PF

Heightened political tensions in 2006 resulted in a climate of increased hostility toward the press among both government and opposition supporters. Freedom of the press remains compromised by inadequate legal guarantees. The constitution provides for freedom of speech and of the press, but Bolivia's penal code stipulates that journalists can be jailed for one month to two years if found guilty of slandering, insulting, or defaming public officials. When the infractions involve the president, vice president, or a minister, the sentence may be increased by half. In May 2006, in the face of increasing discussion regarding potential changes to the 1925 Printing Law that still governs Bolivian media, several journalists groups combined to form a National Ethics Council. The council's goal is to act as a self-regulator, establishing a code of ethics and journalistic standards and issuing resolutions regarding violations of these guidelines.

Bolivia's journalists continued to face the challenges of reporting on their country's volatile politics. President Evo Morales, who took office January 2006, used his inaugural address to criticize opposition media outlets, a perspective that he repeated on several occasions throughout the year. As political conflict between Bolivia's eastern and western regions mounted throughout the year, attacks on journalists increased as well. The state-owned television channel, Canal 7, was attacked on both September 8 and December 6 in Santa Cruz, an opposition stronghold. Meanwhile, opposition-aligned television channel Unitel, whose owner was declared an enemy of the state by President Morales, was attacked in La Paz on October 12 and December 8. In November, police officers assaulted Martin Alipaz, a reporter from the Spanish news agency EFE, while he was covering a protest in Konani. The year's protests peaked in mid-December with rallies throughout the country; in incidents on December 12 and December 15, nearly a dozen journalists—both government and opposition supporters—were assaulted in Cochabamba and Santa Cruz. According to the U.S. State Department, the newspaper *El Nuevo Dia*, with the support of the national press association and human rights groups, filed a complaint against Interior Vice Minister Ruben Gamarra after its journalist Jose Antonio Quisbert was arrested while investigating allegations of corruption in the immigration service.

Print media are privately owned and diverse in their editorial views. The television industry is privately owned except for one government-run TV network. Broadcast outlets express a variety of political views, but stations have been criticized for their overt partisanship in news coverage, with outlets from the eastern department of Santa Cruz among the most hostile to the new president. With the exception of one government-run outlet, radio stations are also privately owned. Radio is the major news disseminator to the countryside, with an estimated 800 stations nationwide. With Venezuelan financial support, the government embarked on an effort to establish a new set of community radio networks. One of the largest is Radio Erbol, operated by a consortium of 70 churches. Conflict between newspaper vendors and the newspaper *La Razon* resulted in violence when the daily's employees attempted to distribute the paper themselves. In recent years, Bolivia has experienced a growth in alternative media that includes radio along with new internet news operations. The internet is not restricted by the government, but barely 5 percent of the population was able to access it in 2006.

Bosnia and Herzegovina

LEGAL ENVIRONMENT: 8
POLITICAL ENVIRONMENT: 21
ECONOMIC ENVIRONMENT: 16

Status: Partly Free

TOTAL SCORE: 45

Survey Edition	2002	2003	2004	2005	2006
Total Score, Status	53,PF	49,PF	48,PF	45,PF	45,PF

Freedom of the press in Bosnia and Herzegovina (BiH) is guaranteed by the constitution as well as the human rights annex to the Dayton Peace Accords, which ended the country's 1992–1995 civil war. Bosnia has one of the most liberal legal environments in the world for media freedom, but effective enforcement of these laws is largely absent owing to an overburdened judiciary. Libel and defamation were decriminalized in 2003, but individuals and institutions can still bring civil suits for such claims. Government officials often file lawsuits against journalists, but instances of journalists suing their colleagues are also common. New legislation that would reorganize and unify the country's public broadcasting system—the first element of which had passed the BiH Parliament in October 2005—was blocked by the Federation Constitutional Court in July 2006 amid complaints that the new system would violate Croats' vital interests.

Journalism in both of the country's state entities—the Federation, made up of Bosniak (Muslim) and Croat cantons; and the Serb-dominated Republika Srpska—continues to be plagued by a relatively low standard of professionalism and the fact that most media outlets appeal only to narrow ethnic constituencies. During the 2006 general election campaigns, the media respected legal requirements guaranteeing candidates free airtime on public broadcasters. However, according to the October 2006 election-monitoring report published by the Organization for Security and Cooperation in Europe, most of the media devoted a disproportionately large amount of time to the activities of the authorities, thus creating an environment more favorable to incumbents.

Journalists throughout BiH remain subject to violent threats and political pressure, and there is growing concern over the influence of organized crime on the media. From January through June 2006, the Free Media Help Line documented 41 reported violations of journalists' freedoms, including instances of pressure by politicians and law enforcement officials. A journalist from the public broadcaster BH1-TV received over 100 intimidating telephone calls in November after airing an investigative report about an alleged prostitution ring involving a number of public officials whose names were not revealed. Some media analysts argue that the current prime minister of Republika Srpska, Milorad Dodik, has tightened control over the media in the entity, citing in part his government's July 2006 decision to replace the managing director of the state news agency, the SRNA, with one of Dodik's party colleagues.

Numerous independent electronic and print media organizations operate in BiH, but most are closely aligned to either economic or political interests. Some media owners perceive that their economic well-being depends on their good relationships with various political figures, and the government also strongly influences media coverage through its advertising subsidies. This most likely explains the lack of editorials critical of influential politicians among certain media holdings. Overtly critical media outlets tend to have difficulty attracting advertising revenue, which has led to self-censorship. Many journalists are inadequately paid and face challenging economic conditions. Managers at privately owned media outlets were responsible for the bulk of violations of journalists' employee rights in 2006; a number of journalists reported working without legally mandated contracts and health benefits. Internet access is unrestricted, and although the number of users in BiH has increased dramatically in recent years, it remains low for the region at 17 percent of the population.

	LEGAL ENVIRONMENT: 8
	POLITICAL ENVIRONMENT: 16
Botswana	ECONOMIC ENVIRONMENT: 11
Status: Partly Free	TOTAL SCORE: 35

Survey Edition	2002	2003	2004	2005	2006
Total Score, Status	30,F	30,F	30,F	30,F	35,PF

Freedom of speech and of the press are provided for in the constitution, and the government generally respects these rights in practice. However, recent years have seen deterioration in freedom of expression in Botswana. Libel is a civil offense, and in past years publications have been charged with defamation and have had to pay large amounts of money in court-ordered damages or as part of a settlement. The National Security Act (NSA), enacted in 1986 during Botswana's conflict with apartheid South Africa, remains on the books and has been used to restrict reporting on government activities. In August, the government presented Parliament with a draft version of the Botswana Broadcasting bill. The bill included plans to establish a new community broadcasting sector—though the number of licenses available to community radio and television stations was not specified—as well as a public entity to monitor the quality and objectivity of state-owned media. Botswana does not have a freedom of information law, and critics accuse the government of excessive secrecy.

Journalists are occasionally threatened, harassed, or attacked in retaliation for their reporting. This was a particularly acute problem in 2005 when the government employed immigration legislation to deport two Zimbabwean journalists, Rodrick Mukumbira and Charles Chirinda, who had criticized state policies; both were not given specific reasons for their expulsion. Also in 2005, Kenneth Good, an Australian-born academic who criticized as undemocratic certain elements of Botswana's political system, was charged under the NSA and deported; he has not yet been able to return. No cases of journalists being deported for the content of their work were reported in 2006; however, in May a photographer with the weekly newspaper *Echo* was assaulted by a businessman on trial for rape while he was covering the case's proceedings in court. The government sometimes censors or otherwise restricts news sources or stories that it finds undesirable, and editorial interference in the state-owned media from the Ministry of Communication, Science, and Technology has increased in recent years. In September, press freedom advocates and opposition political parties condemned a government warning to state-owned media to exercise "maximum patriotic solidarity, collective responsibility, [and] allegiance to country and nation" in reporting about the Central Kalahari Game Reserve. Radio Botswana's popular call-in segment of the morning show *Masa-a-sele*, suspended in 2003, began broadcasting again in 2006.

Independent print media and radio stations provide vigorous scrutiny of the government and air a wide range of opinions, mostly without government interference. Several independent newspapers and magazines are published in the capital, Gaborone. However, the state-owned Botswana Press Agency dominates the media landscape via its *Daily News* newspaper and two nationally broadcast FM radio stations; radio remains the chief source of news for the majority of the population. Botswana Television, also owned by the state, is the country's only source of local television news. Government-controlled media outlets generally confine themselves to coverage that is supportive of official policies and do not adequately cover the activities or viewpoints of opposition parties and other critics. Privately owned radio stations and the sole private television station have a limited reach, particularly within the rural districts; however, Botswana can easily receive broadcasts from neighboring South Africa. The financial viability of Botswana's independent newspapers is undermined by the fact that the *Daily News* is distributed nationwide at no cost. Internet access is unrestricted, albeit limited to approximately 3 percent of the population because of poverty and infrastructural constraints.

Brazil

LEGAL ENVIRONMENT: 15
POLITICAL ENVIRONMENT: 16
ECONOMIC ENVIRONMENT: 11

Status: Partly Free

TOTAL SCORE: 42

Survey Edition	2002	2003	2004	2005	2006
Total Score, Status	32,PF	38,PF	36,PF	40,PF	39,PF

Freedom of speech and of the press are protected by the 1988 constitution, and Brazil's media are both diverse and vigorous. Nevertheless, press freedom was affected by negative developments in 2006. Lower courts and electoral tribunals have issued rulings that continued to criminalize defamation, and the intensification of criminal activities by drug-trafficking gangs has imposed a number of new constraints on the press.

Articles 5 and 220 of the constitution guarantee freedom from "restriction" of thought, process, or medium; however, journalists faced some difficulties when reporting on the general elections of October 2006. Although the elections were free and fair, they were marked by several political scandals involving President Luis Inacio Lula da Silva's administration and his political party, the Workers Party (PT). For example, two weeks before the election, federal police detained two PT members carrying about US$790,000. According to investigations, the money was going to be used to purchase a "dossier" with photographs and videos that linked two leaders of the main opposition party, the Brazilian Social Democracy Party, to a corruption scheme. On October 31, three reporters of the country's leading weekly newsmagazine, *Veja*, were threatened by federal police officers while the reporters were giving a deposition about the dossier scandal. Later, it was revealed that one of the telephones of the leading newspaper, *Folha de S. Paulo*, in the press committee of the Chamber of Deputies was tapped during federal police investigations of the same scandal. Although the judiciary had authorized the tapping, the contacts of the reporters were exposed, violating individual privacy rights as well as the right of journalists to protect the anonymity of their sources. Also in late October, *Correio do Estado* editor Fausto Brites was found guilty of defamation, sentenced to 10 months in prison, and fined approximately US$875.

Civil and electoral judges have also limited the ability of journalists to report on the activities of politicians and candidates. On May 8, the civil court of Campo Grande granted an injunction to a candidate for the governorship of the Mato Grosso do Sul state against the newspaper *Correio do Estado*. On May 17, the regional electoral court in the northern state of Amapa ordered the weekly *Folha do Amapa* to remove its May 12 online edition, following a petition by the party of the state's governor. The two cases involved the reporting of irregularities by public officials or candidates.

The rise of criminal organizations and the general intensification of violence have also affected the news media. In May, the criminal gang First Capital Command (PCC) organized a wave of attacks in the state of Sao Paulo, which included prison rebellions, bank robberies, and attacks on police stations and government buildings. According to some sources, more than 400 people died in the conflicts. On May 18, three heavily armed men invaded the daily *Imprensa Livre* in Sao Sebastiao, in the state of Sao Paulo. The assailants set the building on fire and hit five employees, telling them to stop reporting on the PCC. A few months later, in August, reporter Guilherme Portanova and technician Alexandre Calado, both from the country's main television network, TV Globo, were abducted in Sao Paulo by PCC members. Calado was freed the next day with a recorded message demanding improved conditions for prisoners in Brazilian jails. The kidnappers announced they would kill Portanova if TV Globo did not broadcast the three-minute tape. The journalist was freed only after the network ran the criminals' message. Among other cases of attacks on the press, Reporters Sans Frontieres (RSF) reported the assassination of journalist Ajuricaba Monassa de Paula in the city of Guapirimim (Rio de Janeiro state) on July 24. According to RSF, he was beaten to death by town councillor Osvaldo Vivas after reporting on financial irregularities in the local government.

As South America's largest media market, Brazil boasts dynamic and diverse media able to provide a lively array of views, including investigative reporting published through privately owned newspapers, magazines, and online periodicals. However, despite the pluralism of Brazil's media, ownership is highly concentrated, particularly within the broadcast sector. Globo Organizations, a large media conglomerate, continues to enjoy a dominant position, maintaining ownership of Brazil's primary television network, radio stations, print media, and cable television distribution. Several new community radio stations requested broadcast licenses during the year. There are no restrictions on the internet, which is accessible to 17 percent of the population; Brazil has the largest number of internet users in South America.

Brunei

Status: Not Free

LEGAL ENVIRONMENT: 28
POLITICAL ENVIRONMENT: 26
ECONOMIC ENVIRONMENT: 22
TOTAL SCORE: 76

Survey Edition	2002	2003	2004	2005	2006
Total Score, Status	78,NF	76,NF	74,NF	75,NF	77,NF

The absolute monarchy of Sultan Hassanal Bolkiah and emergency laws—in effect for nearly half a century—continue to restrict journalists and limit the diversity of media content in Brunei. Since 2001, harsh press legislation has required that newspapers apply for annual publishing permits and that noncitizens obtain government approval to work as journalists. The government has the authority to arbitrarily shut down media outlets and to bar distribution of foreign publications. Journalists can be jailed for up to three years for reporting "false and malicious" news. The May 2005 Sedition Act further restricted press freedom by expanding the list of punishable offenses to include criticism of the sultan, the royal family, or the prominence of the national philosophy, the Malay Islamic monarchy concept. Under the amended law, persons convicted of such crimes, or any publishers, editors, or proprietors of a newspaper publishing matters with seditious intention, face fines of up to B$5,000 (US$2,965).

Media are not able to convey a diversity of viewpoints and opinions, and criticism of the government is rare. The private press is either owned or controlled by the sultan's family or practices self-censorship on political and religious matters. The country's main English-language daily newspaper, the

Borneo Bulletin, is controlled by the sultan's family and generally practices self-censorship to avoid angering the government, though it does publish letters to the editor that criticize government policies. A second English-language daily, the *Brunei Times,* was launched in July by a media company run by a group of prominent businessmen, after receiving permission from the sultan. While the paper is run out of an office away from the city center and covers a wider range of international news, its global focus is intended to help foster international investment in light of the country's depleting oil and gas reserves, thus falling in line with current government priorities. A smaller Malay newspaper and several Chinese newspapers are also published within Brunei. The only local broadcast outlets, including the country's one television station, are operated by the government-controlled Radio Television Brunei, but residents can also receive Malaysian broadcasts, and international news is available via satellite channels. No incidents of attacks on or harassment of the press were reported in 2006.

With roughly 33 percent of the population accessing the internet, usage is growing and access is reportedly unrestricted. Yet the primary internet service provider is state owned, and the country's internet practice code stipulates that content must not be subversive, promote illegitimate reform efforts, incite disharmony or instability, or fall out of line with "Brunei Darussalam's religious values, social and societal mores." It also requires all sites that carry content or discuss issues of a religious or political nature to register with the Broadcasting Authority and makes failure to register punishable on conviction by imprisonment for up to three years and/or a fine of up to US$200,000. The government stepped up internet monitoring efforts in 2006, for the 33 percent of the population with online access, by calling on internet cafés to install firewalls to prevent users from viewing immoral content and, according to the U.S. State Department, to monitor private e-mail and internet chat-room exchanges of citizens believed to be subversive.

Bulgaria

Status: Partly Free

LEGAL ENVIRONMENT: 10
POLITICAL ENVIRONMENT: 12
ECONOMIC ENVIRONMENT: 12
TOTAL SCORE: 34

Survey Edition	2002	2003	2004	2005	2006
Total Score, Status	29,F	30,F	35,PF	35,PF	34,PF

The law provides for freedom of speech and of the press, and the government generally respects these rights in practice. However, the government's manipulation of media and the judiciary's lack of independence are causes for concern. Defamation is punishable by high fines, and many suits are filed in response to published reports detailing corruption of high-level officials. Although the courts usually decline to impose fines, the threat of legal action has led to some self-censorship. The government in 2006 moved to increase public access to the Communist-era archives of the state security service, which contain files identifying past informants and collaborators. Under the new policy, agreed to by the main political parties in October and passed by the Parliament in December, an independent commission would control the archives, which had previously been at the disposal of the interior minister. Except during a period of openness from 1997 to 2001, the government had often selectively leaked information on politicians and other public figures, including journalists. Critics of the new arrangement said the ruling Bulgarian Socialist Party, the political heirs of the Communists, had agreed to open the archives only because the most damaging files had long since been destroyed. Others noted that current prime minister Sergei Stanishev was too young to fear exposure of any personal wrongdoing.

Media outlets express a diverse range of public and political views, in most cases without government interference. Although the state-owned media are often critical of the government's actions, they remain vulnerable to political influence. Bulgarian National Television (BNT) was drawn into the October 2006 presidential campaign when the ultimately unsuccessful candidate of the nationalist Ataka party, Volen Siderov, pledged to eliminate content for the ethnic Turkish minority. The country's journalists continue to face pressure and intimidation aimed at protecting economic, political, and criminal interests. In April 2006, a bomb exploded outside the apartment of Vasil Ivanov, an investigative reporter for the private Nova TV station. The blast caused serious property damage but no injuries. Ivanov had previously received death threats linked to his work, which involved organized crime, prison abuse, and other topics.

There are a large number of private media outlets as well as publications disseminated by political parties and interest groups. However, state broadcasters BNT and Bulgarian National Radio continue to dominate their respective markets and have yet to be fully transformed into public service broadcasters. At the end of 2005, the Parliament included provisions in the budget that allowed the two broadcasters to air as much advertising as private stations, even though they would still receive state subsidies. The measure potentially violated European Union competition rules as Bulgaria prepared to join the bloc in January 2007. It also threatened the fragile economic prospects of private outlets, since commercial sponsors would likely shift ad funding to the larger stations. The government does not restrict use of the internet, which is accessed by almost 30 percent of the population.

Burkina Faso

LEGAL ENVIRONMENT: 12
POLITICAL ENVIRONMENT: 14
ECONOMIC ENVIRONMENT: 13

Status: Partly Free

TOTAL SCORE: 39

Survey Edition	2002	2003	2004	2005	2006
Total Score, Status	39,PF	39,PF	39,PF	40,PF	38,PF

Freedom of speech is protected by the constitution under Article 8, and this right is usually respected by the government in practice. However, under the 1993 information code, media outlets may be summarily banned if they are accused of distributing false information or endangering national security. Libel laws are also unfavorable to the press and put the burden of proof on the defendant. No law exists to guarantee equal access to information. The Supreme Council of Communication—which operates within the presidential office with limited independence—acts as the regulatory body for the media.

The most significant event for freedom of the press in Burkina Faso in 2006 involved the high-profile investigation of the 1998 murder of prominent journalist Norbert Zongo. In July, the presiding judge dismissed the case against a presidential guard, the only person ever formally charged in the murder. A month later, the appeal made by Zongo's family was also dismissed. This effectively closed the case until new evidence could be submitted that might strengthen existing charges found to be insufficient. An attempt in October by Reporters Sans Frontieres to submit such evidence and reopen the case also proved unsuccessful. In another example of judicial disinterest in protecting the principles of press freedom, the policemen who beat a journalist covering the Hajj pilgrimage in February 2005 have yet to be formally accused by a court. In addition, Burkinabe journalists experienced occasional instances of harassment in 2006. During a January 16 demonstration, police confiscated the camera of a reporter with *L'Independent* and held it for the duration of the demonstration; and in April, security forces detained and questioned a journalist for the private

Le Pays following an interview he conducted with former soldiers accused of attempting to stage a coup.

The media operate without restriction and report freely on the activities of the executive branch, and criticism of government action or inaction is regularly voiced. Although the state-operated media function with a noticeable pro-government bias, the media are generally free of overt censorship, and several newspapers were openly antigovernment. The state-run television station, TNB, accepted funding for remodeling the station headquarters from a number of major private sources, including the wealthy entrepreneur Oumarou Kanazoe, whom many consider to be a suspect in the Zongo case. TNB denies that this funding will influence coverage. Access to international print and broadcast media and the internet remains unrestricted by the government, but infrastructure limitations and poverty have held the percentage of the population able to access the internet at less than 1 percent.

Burma (Myanmar)

LEGAL ENVIRONMENT: 30
POLITICAL ENVIRONMENT: 38
ECONOMIC ENVIRONMENT: 28

Status: Not Free

TOTAL SCORE: 96

Survey Edition	2002	2003	2004	2005	2006
Total Score, Status	96,NF	94,NF	95,NF	96,NF	96,NF

The Burmese media environment remained among the most tightly restricted in the world in 2006. The ruling military junta zealously implements a 1996 decree banning speech or statements that "undermine national stability," and those who publicly express or disseminate views critical of the regime are subject to strict penalties, including lengthy prison terms. A number of journalists and writers continued to serve long sentences as a result of expressing dissident views. Other laws require private publications to apply for annual licenses and criminalize the use of unregistered telecommunications equipment, satellite dishes, computers, and software.

Private periodicals are subject to prepublication censorship under the 1962 Printers and Publishers Registration Act, which requires that all content be approved by the authorities. As a result, coverage is limited to a small range of permissible topics, publications are sometimes required to carry government-produced articles, and most publications are forced to appear as weeklies or monthlies. A new Press Scrutiny and Registration Division (PSRD), under the control of the Ministry of Information, was established in April 2005, at which time all publications were required to reregister with the PSRD and provide detailed information about staff, ownership, and financial backing. Under new censorship rules that came into effect in July 2005, media are ostensibly allowed to offer criticism of government projects as long as it is deemed "constructive" and are allowed to report on natural disasters and poverty as long as it does not affect the national interest. Several favored publications were able to take advantage of this greater leniency during the year, although others that aroused the ire of censorship authorities were banned from distributing editions or carrying stories by certain writers.

Both local and foreign journalists' ability to cover the news is restricted. Two Burmese photojournalists who photographed buildings in the new capital were arrested in March and sentenced to three-year prison terms. A few foreign reporters are allowed to enter Burma only on special visas; they are generally subjected to intense scrutiny while in the country and in past years have occasionally been deported. However, some foreign correspondents were invited to cover the October session of the National Convention. A number of Burmese journalists remain in exile; many work for Burma-focused media outlets based in the neighboring countries of India, Bangladesh, and Thailand. The Burma Media Association reported in February that the government had launched a campaign to track down and imprison people who gave information to international and exile-run media outlets. Several journalists, businessmen, and civil servants have reportedly been interrogated in relation to the program.

The government owns all broadcast media and daily newspapers and exercises tight control over a growing number of privately owned weekly and monthly publications. While official media outlets serve solely as mouthpieces of the state, private media generally avoid covering domestic political news, and the vast majority of journalists practice extensive self-censorship. Many nominally private outlets are owned either by government agents or supporters. A stagnant economy, increased prices for newsprint, and a limited market for advertising revenue (following a 2002 ban on advertising Thai products) continue to threaten the financial viability of the private press. Authorities restrict the importation of foreign news periodicals, and although some people have access to international shortwave radio or satellite television, those caught accessing foreign broadcasts can be arrested, according to the Committee to Protect Journalists. Nevertheless, as the only source of uncensored information, foreign radio programs produced by the Voice of America, Radio Free Asia, and Democratic Voice of Burma are very popular.

The internet, which operates in a limited fashion in cities accessible to less than 1 percent of the population, is expensive, tightly regulated, and censored, with the government controlling all of the several dozen domestic internet service providers. Authorities have upgraded filtering and surveillance technologies and actively engage in blocking access to websites run by Burmese exile groups and to international e-mail services such as Yahoo!, Hotmail, and Gmail.

Burundi

Status: Not Free

LEGAL ENVIRONMENT: 22
POLITICAL ENVIRONMENT: 31
ECONOMIC ENVIRONMENT: 24
TOTAL SCORE: 77

Survey Edition	2002	2003	2004	2005	2006
Total Score, Status	77,NF	76,NF	75,NF	74,NF	74,NF

Burundi has missed a unique opportunity to improve its press freedom status following the 2005 democratic election—the first since 1993—and the September 2006 signing of a cease-fire agreement with the last remaining rebel organization. Instead, the government abused its consolidated power and began a targeted crackdown on media outlets critical of government policy. The transitional constitution does provide for freedom of expression, but most media legislation is vague about the offenses for which a journalist may be charged. For example, the 1997 Press Law forbids the dissemination of "information inciting civil disobedience or serving as propaganda for enemies of the Burundian nation during a time of war." The November 2003 Media Law also provides for harsh fines and prison terms of up to five years for the dissemination of information that insults the president or is defamatory toward other individuals. However, according to the International Crisis Group, a new law is being drafted that would more accurately define the responsibilities and duties of the media.

With the control that the Hutu-dominated ruling party has over government institutions and the disunity of the rival political parties, much of this year's opposition originated from within the media and civil society. This fact, along with the alleged Tutsi dominance of the media elite, has propelled the government's harassment and detention of media personnel in 2006. After the exposure of an alleged coup attempt and the subsequent arrest and torture of several prominent opposition leaders, the government directly targeted a number of media outlets that questioned the veracity of the supposed coup attempt. In November, two journalists with the privately owned Radio Publique Africaine (RPA)—a frequent government target in recent years—and the director of Radio Isanganiro—a station backed by the American nongovernmental organization Search for Common Ground—were all charged with "violating state secrecy" and sentenced to prison for publishing information about the alleged coup; all three journalists remained incarcerated at year's end. In September, following three months of illegal pretrial detention, Aloys Kabura, a reporter with the state-run Agence Burundaise de Presse, was also sentenced to prison for five months for making critical comments about the police's temporary detention of 30 journalists at a news conference in mid-April. According to the Committee to Protect Journalists, this made Burundi Africa's third leading jailer of journalists for 2006.

Burundi's only daily newspaper, *Le Renouveau*, is controlled by the government along with the nation's sole television station and the only nationally broadcast radio station. Six private publications operate on a weekly basis, while private radio stations broadcast only irregularly and most are restricted to the capital city of Bujumbura. Private ownership tends to be highly concentrated, but outlets do represent a wide range of opinions, and some, like RPA, manage to present diverse and balanced coverage. No government restrictions on internet access are apparent, though the National Communication Council bans websites from "posting documents or other statements by political organizations that disseminate hate or violence," and owing to economic and infrastructure limitations, less than 1 percent of the population was able to access this new media in 2006.

Cambodia

Status: Partly Free

LEGAL ENVIRONMENT: 18
POLITICAL ENVIRONMENT: 21
ECONOMIC ENVIRONMENT: 19
TOTAL SCORE: 58

Survey Edition	2002	2003	2004	2005	2006
Total Score, Status	68,NF	64,NF	63,NF	62,NF	61, NF

Status change explanation: Cambodia's status improved from Not Free to Partly Free to reflect the decriminalization of defamation in May 2006, as well as a reduction in harassment of journalists.

The Cambodian media environment improved in 2006 as a result of changes to the Defamation Law and a continued decline in harassment and attacks on the press. The constitution guarantees the right to free expression and a free press, and while the 1995 Press Law also theoretically protects press freedom, the government has used it to censor stories deemed to undermine political stability. Under Article 12, the employer, editor, or author of an article may be subject to a fine of 5 million to 15 million riels (US$1,282 to US$3,846). The law also gives the Ministries of Information and the Interior the right to confiscate or suspend a publication for 30 days and transfer the case to court. Article 13 states that the press shall not publish or reproduce false information that humiliates or is in contempt of national institutions. In May, the National Assembly dropped criminal charges for defamation, though civil suits with potentially onerous fines remain in law and in use by political figures. The law represents a significant step forward for the Cambodian press, as criminal defamation charges had been used frequently to harass reporters who published articles critical of public figures. The ruling should allow journalists greater freedom to report on sensitive issues without fear of reprisal.

Press coverage is vigorous, and journalists regularly expose official corruption and scrutinize the government. Attacks against the press have declined significantly in recent years, although several cases of harassment and threats were reported in 2006. In January, two journalists and one journalist/activist who had been imprisoned in October 2005 on charges of defamation—for criticizing the government over a border agreement with Vietnam—were released on bail. Although the courts initially refused to drop the charges against them, they were later withdrawn. In July, the deputy prime minister filed defamation charges against the publisher of the Khmer-language newspaper *Meneaskseka*, following a June 13 article accusing the government of corruption. Another reporter for the occasional newspaper *Samrek Yutekthor* was arrested while covering the eviction of squatters in a property dispute. The editor of the biweekly *Sralanh Khmer*, which had published an article criticizing the prime minister's nephew for corrupt land seizures in Cambodia's northeast Mondolkiri province, faced death threats in July, according to the Committee to Protect Journalists. In August, the Cambodian Television Network was forced to pull a current affairs program, Cambodia Today, after the prime minister accused the program of damaging the nation's reputation.

Journalists from more than 20 publications aligned with or subsidized by various political factions are unbridled in criticizing their adversaries and public officials but generally do not criticize the king. The ruling

Cambodian People's Party, its coalition partner the royalist party Funcinpec, and the opposition Sam Rainsy Party each has its own newspaper. Overall, approximately 20 Khmer-language newspapers are published on a regular basis. However, the government dominates both radio and television, the main media sources for the two-thirds of the population that are functionally illiterate, and broadcast programming generally reflects official viewpoints. Independent broadcast outlets' operations are constrained by the refusal to allocate radio and television frequencies to stations that are aligned with the opposition. In addition, the economy is not strong enough to generate sufficient advertising revenues to support truly neutral or independent media. Access to foreign broadcasts and to the internet is generally unrestricted, although owing to infrastructure and economic constraints, less than 0.5 percent of the population was able to access the internet in 2006.

Cameroon

LEGAL ENVIRONMENT: 20
POLITICAL ENVIRONMENT: 25
ECONOMIC ENVIRONMENT: 22

Status: Not Free

TOTAL SCORE: 67

Survey Edition	2002	2003	2004	2005	2006
Total Score, Status	68,NF	65,NF	67,NF	68,NF	65,NF

The constitution provides for freedom of the press and of speech, but the government restricts these rights in practice. Criminal libel laws are used regularly to silence criticisms of the state and government officials. Although much of the independent press did persist in reporting critically about the government in 2006, a number of critics were prosecuted under the libel laws, and the threat of prosecution led many, particularly within the broadcast media, to self-censor their material. The most high-profile instance of such criminal libel convictions was when a number of newspapers published a list of supposed "secret homosexuals" within the government in January and February. Although this list was potentially offensive and insulting, the punishments of imprisonment and exorbitant fines that were handed out were disproportionate to the crimes committed. In March, Jean-Pierre Amougou Belinga, publisher of *L'Anecdote,* was sentenced to four months in prison and a US$2,000 fine, while Ayissi Biloa, publisher of *Nouvelle Afrique,* was sentenced to six months in prison and ordered to pay a total of US$6,000 in damages to two separate plaintiffs. Separately, many other journalists were convicted of libel by the courts; most received suspended prison sentences. These included Dieudonne Mveng, publisher of *La Meteo;* Socrate Dipanda, publisher of *Le Constat;* Peter William Mandio, publisher of *Le Front;* Henriette Ekwe, a *Le Front* columnist; and Georges Gilbert Baongla, publisher of *Le Dementi.*

Journalists were arbitrarily arrested, detained, harassed, intimidated, and physically abused in 2006, while some publications were confiscated by the state. In January, unidentified assailants set fire to Freedom FM, a private radio station that had yet to begin operations. In 2003, the government had originally forced the station to close before it ever began operating and refused to lift the ban until 2005. In November, after receiving numerous threats leading up to a radio show asking listeners to offer their opinion about the Paul Biya regime, Agnes Taile, host of the popular program on the local Sweet FM, was abducted from her home, beaten, and left for dead. Other instances of harassment of journalists included the illegal five-day detention of Duke Atangana Etotogo, managing editor of *L'Afrique Centrale,* by the military security services in September after he published articles addressing corruption and incompetence within the army.

There are about 25 regularly published newspapers; among them are the privately operating *Mutations, La Nouvelle Expression,* and *Le Messager,* as well as the state's *Cameroon Tribune,* which toes the government line in the majority of its coverage. Many of the private papers freely criticize government policies and report on controversial issues, including corruption, human rights abuses, homosexuality, and economic policies. Distribution problems and high government tariffs on production ensure that newspapers remain a uniquely urban phenomenon. There are about 20 privately owned broadcast stations; among them, 5 are television stations. The state-owned CRTV broadcasts on both television and radio and was the only officially recognized and fully licensed broadcaster in the country. In general, the broadcast media are tightly controlled by the government, and discussion or advocacy of secession is strictly prohibited. Several rural community radio stations were established by UNESCO in 2006, though they are all limited in the range of their broadcast capacity and prohibited from discussing politics at all. Foreign broadcasters, including the British Broadcasting Corporation and Radio France Internationale, are permitted to operate within Cameroon, but they must partner with the state-owned CRTV. Despite the signing into law of the National Anticorruption Commission, corruption is rampant in numerous sectors of the media; many journalists expect and accept payment from politicians for writing articles containing unsubstantiated allegations against their opponents. Access to the internet is not limited by the government, although slow connections and high fees at cybercafés serve to restrict access to only 1.5 percent of the population.

Canada

Status: Free

LEGAL ENVIRONMENT: 3
POLITICAL ENVIRONMENT: 8
ECONOMIC ENVIRONMENT: 6
TOTAL SCORE: 17

Survey Edition	2002	2003	2004	2005	2006
Total Score, Status	16,F	17,F	15,F	17,F	18,F

Canada's constitution of 1982 provides protection for freedom of expression, including freedom of the press. Defamatory or blasphemous libel remains a criminal offense under the federal criminal code. Legislation on access to information guarantees journalists' right to information, but in practice access can be hindered by bureaucratic delays, government interference, and numerous exemptions allowing government officials to reject requests. Although a 2006 accountability bill has expanded the number of government entities covered by information laws, the bill has been criticized for including several loopholes that will allow officials to decline information requests. In October 2006, a superior court judge struck down aspects of the Security and Information Act. The act had prohibited unauthorized communication and possession of sensitive government documents; anyone found guilty of providing, receiving, or hearing "secret" information could be punished with up to 14 years in prison. The court deemed that the law was "vague, overbroad, and open to misuse" and in violation of the press freedom guarantee in the Charter of Rights and Freedoms.

Journalists in Canada are generally free from violence or harassment. The only murder of a journalist as a result of their work occurred in 1998, when Tara Singh Hayer was shot and killed, most likely as a result of his investigative work into the 1985 Air India bombing. His murder remains unsolved. Under a 2004 law reporters can be forced to present documents to the police if deemed vital for a criminal case. In February 2006, *Hamilton Spectator* journalist Bill Dunphy was ordered to hand over notes of an interview related to a murder case. Dunphy appealed the order, however, and the Superior Court of Justice found in his favor. In 2004, another reporter for the *Hamilton Spectator*, Ken Peters, refused to comply with a police order to give up a confidential source. Although the source came forward independently, Peters was found to be in contempt of court and fined C$31,600. His case is currently under appeal. Derek Finkle, the author of a 1998 book relating to the recently re-opened Robert Baltovich murder case, was also ordered to turn over his research materials in 2006. In February, two writers for the *Canadian Medical Journal* were fired after publishing a controversial article regarding the emergency contraceptive drug known as Plan B. The majority of the editorial board resigned shortly after, alleging editorial interference by the journal's owners, the Canadian Medical Association.

Both print and broadcast media, which include the public Canadian Broadcasting Corporation (CBC), are generally free to express diverse views. The CBC was initially established in the 1930s to counter the growing influence of American radio. Now it broadcasts in French and English and provides television and radio services for indigenous peoples in the north. Broadcasting rules stipulate that 30–35 percent of material must be Canadian. Nonetheless, the extent of media concentration and the influence of powerful media conglomerates such as CanWest Global Communications continue to limit media pluralism. The internet is generally unrestricted and is used by roughly 22 million Canadians. In a positive move, in 2006 the Supreme Court refused to hear the case of Cheickh Bangoura, who had brought a libel case against the U.S.-based *Washington Post* for a report published on the internet accusing Bangoura of improprieties while serving with the UN in Kenya.

Cape Verde

Status: Free

LEGAL ENVIRONMENT: 5
POLITICAL ENVIRONMENT: 10
ECONOMIC ENVIRONMENT: 14
TOTAL SCORE: 29

Survey Edition	2002	2003	2004	2005	2006
Total Score, Status	30,F	30,F	36,PF	32,PF	32,PF

Status change explanation: Cape Verde's rating improved from Partly Free to Free as a result of the continued consolidation of democratic trends leading to greater opening in the media environment and a decrease in the number of cases of legal harassment of, and attacks on, journalists.

The constitution directly provides for freedom of the press, as well as confidentiality of sources, access to information, and freedom from arbitrary arrest. In recent years, the government has consistently demonstrated its ability to respect and protect these rights in practice, making Cape Verde an exemplary country in Africa. A 1999 constitutional amendment still excludes the use of freedom of expression as a defense in defamation cases; however, there have been no such libel cases since 2002. While the law requires a formal licensing mechanism for mass media, there have been no reports of the government refusing such licenses for political reasons, and no government authorization at all is needed for the establishment of a print publication. There were also no reported cases of intimidation or violence against journalists in 2006.

Much of the media is state operated, although there are a growing number of private publications and broadcast outlets. There are three privately owned newspapers and one run by the state. While there are six independent radio stations that broadcast regularly in Cape Verde, the government owns a national radio station as well as the only national television station. The government does not generally restrict access to the media that it controls; nonetheless, a number of opposition political candidates reported having trouble accessing airtime on the state broadcasters for the February presidential election. Self-censorship is also widely practiced among journalists and has been one of the largest obstacles in Cape Verde to the creation of a truly free press. Geographic barriers and harsh terrain in a country made up of several islands also constitute impediments to the distribution of newspapers and other media products. Access to the internet is not restricted by the government, and e-mail messages and foreign broadcasts are uncensored.

Central African Republic

LEGAL ENVIRONMENT: 18
POLITICAL ENVIRONMENT: 21
ECONOMIC ENVIRONMENT: 19

Status: Partly Free

TOTAL SCORE: 58

Survey Edition	2002	2003	2004	2005	2006
Total Score, Status	69,NF	67,NF	64,NF	63,NF	61,NF

Status change explanation: Central African Republic's rating improved from Not Free to Partly Free as a result of positive change in the environment for the media following the government's adherence to, and enforcement of, the new Press Law and constitution passed in 2005 respecting freedom of expression and decriminalizing libel.

The 2005 constitution provides for freedom of the press, though authorities have used intimidation and legal harassment to limit reporting, particularly on sensitive topics such as official corruption. In December 2005, an overwhelming majority of voters approved this new constitution, which recognizes the freedom to inform and express opinions as fundamental rights of the country's citizens. In addition, the new Press Law decriminalizing many press offenses, including defamation and slander, was approved by President Francois Bozize in early 2005; criminal penalties remain for incitement to ethnic or religious hatred and for the publication or broadcast of false information that could "disturb the peace." In 2006, the government generally respected these new laws—a noticeable improvement from the previous year, when the security forces arrested, detained, and threatened journalists.

Maka Gbossokotto, one of the Central African Republic's most prominent journalists and a correspondent for Reporters Sans Frontieres, led the struggle to decriminalize press offenses after his own imprisonment for defamation in 2004. No journalist was imprisoned in 2006, but Gbossokotto, who edits the independent daily *Le Citoyen*, received threats in January from a former member of the presidential guard after *Le Citoyen* reported on an outbreak of violence between factions of the military police in the capital, Bangui. The same month, President Bozize dissolved the executive board of the newly created High Communications Council in what appeared to be an attempt to strengthen the government's control of the media regulatory body. However, in July the president agreed to pass a new decree mandating parity between representatives of the private and public media within the council, a move supported by local journalists' organizations. In November, in response to politically motivated death threats against the heads of publications, a newspaper strike prevented a single newspaper from appearing on the streets of Bangui.

More than 30 newspapers published, with varying degrees of regularity, in 2006. Many of these were privately owned, including at least 3 independent dailies, and most were able to report on political issues such as government corruption and economic policies. Nonetheless, meager salaries and real or self-imposed censorship in a less than dynamic media market continue to hamper the editorial freedom of news organizations. The private press is restricted almost entirely to the capital, the result of financial constraints as well as the danger of working in the countryside, where anti-Bozize rebels as well as militias connected to the ongoing conflicts in neighboring Sudan and Chad operate with impunity. The state remains dominant in the broadcast sector, and private radio stations, reined in by legal and financial restrictions, are often intimidated by the powerful. A prominent exception is Radio Ndeke Luka, a joint initiative of the UN and the Switzerland-based Fondation Hirondelle, which broadcasts on FM in the capital and on shortwave in the rest of the country. Internet access is open and unrestricted, though the communications infrastructure is almost nonexistent outside of Bangui and less than 0.5 percent of the population was able to make use of this medium in 2006.

Chad

Status: Not Free

LEGAL ENVIRONMENT: 23
POLITICAL ENVIRONMENT: 30
ECONOMIC ENVIRONMENT: 21
TOTAL SCORE: 74

Survey Edition	2002	2003	2004	2005	2006
Total Score, Status	74,NF	67,NF	74,NF	73,NF	73,NF

The constitution allows for freedom of expression, but authorities have routinely used threats and legal provisions criminalizing defamation and vaguely defined "incitement" to imprison journalists and censor critical reporting. In Chad's conservative, ethnically polarized society, many subjects are considered off-limits to the press, including the armed rebellion on the border with Sudan and recurring tensions among tribal clans. The High Council of Communication (HCC), the official media regulatory body, has the authority to suspend publications and broadcast outlets for defamation or excessive criticism of the government, particularly President Idriss Deby. On November 13, 2006, amid worsening violence in the volatile east, which borders Darfur, the government instituted a state of emergency in six regions of Chad, as well as the capital, N'Djamena. The state of emergency included a ban on newspaper and radio coverage of issues and events "likely to threaten public order, national unity, territorial integrity, and respect for the republican institutions" and required radio stations to submit their recorded material to government censors. To protest the censorship regulations, many newspapers carried out a two-week hiatus on publishing and several radio stations initiated a 72-hour news strike. In late November, the National Assembly announced that they would extend the 10-day-old state of emergency for six months, granting the government the power to maintain prior censorship of the print media and permanent monitoring of radio stations. At the end of the year, the restrictions were still in place, depriving Chadians of vital sources of information at a time when conflict is sweeping the country.

In the lead-up to presidential elections held on May 3, the government arrested Tchanguis Vatankah, president of the Chadian Union of Private Radios and director of an independent radio station in the remote southern town of Moissala, over a radio union press release criticizing HCC restrictions against broadcasting live political debates (Deby was reelected in a poll boycotted by the opposition). Vatankah was held for three weeks and released only after he pledged to stay out of politics and to step down as head of the radio union. An Iranian national who has resided in Chad for decades, Vatankah has been a frequent target of government ire in the past in connection with his work for Radio Brakos in Moissala. Also in April, a journalist working for FM Liberté in central Chad was briefly held by rebels as they advanced toward N'Djamena. In the months that followed, government censorship increased amid heightened civil conflict. Journalists in Chad are restricted from discussing Darfur or Chad's confrontations with the Sudanese government. In October, a journalist for the private weekly *Notre Temps* was detained for four days over an editorial critical of the government's conduct in the war.

Private newspapers, many of which were critical of the government before the state of emergency was imposed, circulate freely in N'Djamena, but they have little impact on the largely rural and illiterate population; radio is the primary means of mass communication. The only television station, Teletchad, is state owned, and its coverage favors the government. Despite high licensing fees for commercial radio stations, there are over a dozen private and community-run stations on the air, some operated by nonprofit groups (including human rights groups and the Roman Catholic Church). These broadcasters are subject to close official scrutiny, and those that fail to pay annual fees to the state are threatened with closure. Access to the internet is limited by the high level of poverty in Chad to less than 0.5 percent of the population, but the government refrains from restricting access to those who can afford it. Nonetheless, according to the U.S. State Department, the government does occasionally engage in monitoring e-mail through the main post office server.

Chile

		LEGAL ENVIRONMENT: 10
		POLITICAL ENVIRONMENT: 12
		ECONOMIC ENVIRONMENT: 8
Status: Free		TOTAL SCORE: 30

Survey Edition	2002	2003	2004	2005	2006
Total Score, Status	22,F	22,F	23,F	24,F	26,F

Chilean law provides for freedom of speech and of the press. Although laws in the penal code and code of military justice and the State Security Law prohibit insulting state institutions such as the presidency, the legislature, and judicial bodies, there was at least one legal improvement during the year. Post-Pinochet governments have generally respected the constitutional right to freedom of expression, but definitive reform of the legal code has been more problematic. *Desacato* (disrespect) laws, which impede reporting on the government and military authorities, were eliminated from the penal code in 2005, and the same year Congress also reformed the constitution to eliminate defamation as an offense against public persons. However, *desacato* remains in the code of military justice and can be applied against civilians. In addition, the ambiguously worded criminal prohibition of threats against public officials allows the law to be interpreted in much the same way as *desacato*, according to the Inter-American Court of Human Rights (IACHR). While constitutional provisions allowing censorship have been eliminated, at least two books remain banned under judicial order since 1993: Humberto Palamara's *Etica y Servicios de Inteligencia* and Francisco Martorell's *Impunidad Diplomatica*. Supreme Court rulings have never equated judicial bans with censorship. The government did not act on a 2005 IACHR ruling calling for the state to end the Palamara ban and modify prohibitive laws. On a brighter note, for the first time, the IACHR ruled that access to information is a fundamental human right. The Court ruled in September in favor of Chilean activists who were denied government information about Trillium Ltd., a U.S. company backing a controversial logging project. The Court ordered Chile to release the information and adopt legal and other measures to guarantee effective access. Again, government compliance has yet to occur.

Investigative reporting and the expression of leftist viewpoints in the mass press continued to be difficult because of the concentration of state and private advertising in just two center-right newspaper companies. The newspaper *Diario Siete*, whose editor, Monica Gonzalez, won the 2005 Fundacion Nuevo Periodismo prize, and the literary-political criticism magazine *Rocinante* both closed for financial reasons. Some demanded state support for alternative publications, but the proposition is controversial. Chilean reporters, in part because of their experiences during the dictatorship and the narrow choice of viable employment, are considered among the hemisphere's most passive. Chile is generally a safe place to practice journalism. However, police or violent crowds injured several reporters last year. Six journalists were injured or detained by police during a student strike in August. President Michelle Bachelet called the attacks "unacceptable" and dismissed the head of the force responsible. In May, two photographers were wounded and four media vehicles destroyed during a union march. Police arrested 70 suspects related to the attacks. In December, pro-Pinochet crowds insulted, beat, or threw objects at reporters around the time of the former dictator's funeral.

Press ownership is highly concentrated in the hands of two companies that received preferential treatment during the conservative military dictatorship that left power in 1989. Left-oriented, investigative publications have trouble surviving financially and receive little or no government advertising. Chile maintains a mixed public-private system that is considered among the Americas' most diverse; even those stations owned by the state are considered to be independent of government influence. However, indigenous voices are not fairly represented in the mainstream press. Following an incident at the beginning of the year in which Jorge Molina, a reporter for the online daily *El Mostrador*, was forced from his job after posting the names of former torturers, there were no further reported government restrictions on the internet in 2006. More than 40 percent of Chileans accessed the internet during the year.

China

Status: Not Free

LEGAL ENVIRONMENT: 28
POLITICAL ENVIRONMENT: 34
ECONOMIC ENVIRONMENT: 22
TOTAL SCORE: 84

Survey Edition	2002	2003	2004	2005	2006
Total Score, Status	80,NF	80,NF	80,NF	82,NF	83,NF

The year 2006 was marked by an increased crackdown on press freedom in China. President Hu Jintao's administration effectively silenced the press by introducing new media regulations, jailing outspoken journalists, and restricting coverage of breaking news. Article 35 of the constitution guarantees freedom of speech, assembly, association, and publication. However, other articles subordinate these rights to the national interest, which is defined by party-appointed courts. The Communist Party maintains direct control over the news media through the Central Propaganda Department (CPD), especially with respect to topics deemed by the party to be politically sensitive. This control is reinforced by an elaborate web of regulations and laws, which are worded vaguely and interpreted according to the wishes of the party leadership. Press freedom was further undermined in 2006 by two new regulations aimed at controlling the distribution of foreign news and media coverage of unforeseen events. In July, the government proposed fines of up to US$12,500 for domestic and foreign news organizations that report "sudden events" (such as protests, disease outbreaks, or natural disasters) without government authorization. Two months later, the official Xinhua News Agency announced in a surprise move that all foreign news would be distributed solely through a Xinhua agent. The new measures allow Xinhua to censor news products from international news agencies if they "undermine national unity" or disrupt China's "economic and social order." While the distribution of news by foreign agencies in China was already tightly restricted, these new regulations extend the government's control over the distribution of economic and financial news by major foreign news providers such as Reuters and Bloomberg.

Throughout 2006, the government increased pressure on the media to ensure compliance with the propaganda standards of the Communist Party. The efforts to control the domestic press reflected a rising number of public protests, the growing importance and availability of independent online news, and the nation's march toward a market economy that forces the Chinese media to become profitable. In January, the CPD shut down *Bing Dian*, a weekly news supplement of the *China Youth Daily* known for its investigative reports and critical opinion pieces. While *Bing Dian* reopened in March, the weekly's editor and his deputy were removed from their posts and demoted. In April, the General Administration of Press and Publication, China's publishing authority, decided to step up controls over "illegal" foreign publications and to freeze the granting of publication licenses to joint ventures.

According to international media freedom watchdogs, 32 journalists and 59 internet-based "cyberdissidents" were in prison in China at year's end. Two journalists, Wu Xianghu and Xiao Guopeng, died owing to police violence in 2006. Wu was attacked in October 2005 by traffic police who were angry over a recently published exposé. He died in February 2006 following several months of hospitalization. Xiao was attacked and killed by a police officer in July 2006; press freedom groups said the attack might have been linked to a recent article that was critical of local police.

The convictions of two Chinese journalists working for foreign publications in China increased concern that the government was attempting to intimidate foreign correspondents and newspapers. According to Reporters Sans Frontieres, there were at least 25 incidents of arrests, threats, or assaults against members of the foreign press in 2006. The most prominent victim was Zhao Yan, a researcher working for the Beijing bureau of *The New York Times* who had been jailed in 2004 on a charge of leaking state secrets. While Zhao was acquitted of that charge in early 2006, he was convicted and sentenced to three years in prison in August on a lesser fraud charge related to his work as an investigative reporter for a Chinese magazine in 2001, a charge that was brought six months after he was originally jailed. In a similar case, Ching Cheong, a resident of Hong Kong who worked as a correspondent for Singapore's *Straits Times* in China, was convicted of espionage and sentenced in August to five years in prison. Ching had been detained during a visit to the southern city of Guangzhou in 2005 and accused of gathering information for an academic organization in Taiwan that China said was a front for the Taiwanese intelligence agency.

Encouraged by the nationwide crackdown on journalists in 2006, local authorities also responded to embarrassing news stories by arresting and imprisoning independent-minded journalists. In January, Zhu Wanxiang and Wu Zhengyou, editors of the magazine *Zhonghua Xin Qingnian*, were jailed for 10 and 6 years, respectively, for reporting on protesting villagers and a violent demonstration in the city of Lishui. Similarly, Yang Xiaoqing, a reporter for *China Industrial Economy News* in Sichuan province, was sentenced in June to one year in jail after reporting on alleged corruption among officials in his home county of Longhui.

In an attempt to quell possible concerns over censorship during the 2008 Olympic Games in Beijing, the Chinese government announced in December that it would not impose travel restrictions on the foreign media. Foreign journalists would be free to travel around China during the 2008 games and to interview organizations and individuals without prior government consent. The new regulations, effective through mid-October 2008, include Hong Kong, Macau, and Taiwan reporters but do not apply to mainland citizens. Ironically, the former editor of the popular but now closed news website *Aegean Sea*, Zhang Jianhong, had been arrested in September and charged with "inciting subversion" for posting an essay criticizing China's human rights record and the poor treatment of journalists ahead of the Olympic Games.

Media reforms have allowed for the commercialization of media outlets without the privatization of ownership. All Chinese media are owned by the state, but the majority no longer receive state subsidies and now rely on income from advertisement revenue, which some argue has shifted the media's loyalty from the party to the consumer. The CPD disseminates directives to media nationwide concerning mandatory use of state propaganda and indicating topics to be barred from reports. To avoid running afoul of the CPD, journalists often engage in self-censorship, a practice that is reinforced by frequent ideological indoctrination and a salary scheme that pays journalists only after their reports are published or broadcast. When a journalist writes a report that is considered too controversial, payment is withheld, and in some cases the journalist must pay for the cost of news gathering out of pocket. A small number of elite media outlets combat such deterrents to aggressive reporting by paying journalists for reports that are subject to censorship. This has resulted in a few outlets championing popular causes and printing embarrassing exposures of official malfeasance. Nevertheless, media personnel who engage in such journalism are often fired or arrested.

China has the world's second largest population of internet users after the United States, with an estimated 137 million people online (just over 10 percent of the population) by the end of 2006. The government employs an extensive surveillance and filtering system to prevent Chinese users from accessing material that is considered obscene or politically subversive. Internet censorship increased sharply after the government introduced new regulations in 2005. The so-called "11 Commandments of the Chinese Internet" bar websites from distributing information that, among other offenses, violates the Chinese constitution, endangers national security, encourages illegal strikes, contains pornographic or violent content, or promotes religious sects. Foreign internet companies have largely cooperated with the Chinese government on censorship enforcement. In January, U.S.-based Microsoft closed the site of a well-known Chinese blogger who used its MSN online service in China to discuss a high-profile newspaper strike at the *Beijing News.* The Chinese-language search engines of the U.S. firms Yahoo!, MSN, and Google filter search results and restrict access to information about controversial topics such as the Falun Gong, Tibetan independence, and human rights. Yahoo!, in at least four separate cases, cooperated with Chinese police, leading to the jailing of dissidents who had posted subversive information and opinions on the internet. In a positive development for internet freedom, Chinese authorities in November unblocked the Chinese-language version of the online encyclopedia Wikipedia, which had been blocked for about a year.

The government, in its desperate attempt to keep control over the dissemination of information through new technologies such as the internet, email, cellular phones and digital recording engines, has been passing a number of regulations such as those which force bloggers to register with their real names or forbid distribution on the internet of any information prohibited in the traditional media. A large number of reporters and activists were convicted for using the internet to protest human rights abuses or call for greater democracy in China. In January, Li Changqing, a journalist for the *Fuzhou Daily*, was sentenced to three years in prison for "spreading false and alarmist information" with a report about a 2004 dengue fever outbreak for the U.S.-based online news service Boxun News. Four other online journalists were charged with "inciting subversion to state authority" and sentenced to lengthy prison terms. In March, high school teacher Ren Zhiyuan was sentenced to 10 years in prison for an internet article holding that people could rightfully overthrow tyrannical governments by violent means. In May, internet essayist Yang Tongyan (also known as Yang Tianshui) was sentenced to 12 years in prison for posting articles on overseas websites in which he called for the release of Chinese dissidents. In July, Li Yuanlong, a reporter for the *Bijie Daily*, was sentenced to two years in prison after he posted essays on foreign websites in which he discussed the harsh living conditions of peasants in Guizhou province. In October, Guo Qizhen and Li Jianping were sentenced to four and two years in prison, respectively, for writing essays on foreign websites that criticized the Communist Party leadership and expressed concerns about China's human rights situation.

Colombia

Status: Partly Free

LEGAL ENVIRONMENT: 13
POLITICAL ENVIRONMENT: 29
ECONOMIC ENVIRONMENT: 15
TOTAL SCORE: 57

Survey Edition	2002	2003	2004	2005	2006
Total Score, Status	60,PF	63,NF	63,NF	63,NF	61,NF

Status change explanation: Colombia's status improved from Not Free to Partly Free owing to the increased willingness of journalists to report critically on political issues such as high-level corruption scandals, as well as a gradually improving security situation.

Freedom of the press is guaranteed by the 1991 constitution, but journalists have trouble exercising their rights in a country racked by a complex armed conflict involving left-wing guerrilla organizations, drug traffickers, paramilitary groups, and government security forces. Human rights organizations expressed concern about comments made by high-ranking government officials, including President Alvaro Uribe, who have chastised journalists for their reporting on the war. Journalists believe that such commentary stigmatizes them and puts them at risk for retribution. Though legal actions against journalists declined in 2006, occasional criminal complaints and civil lawsuits continue to be filed against media outlets and reporters. Colombia's penal code does not contain provisions allowing journalists to be charged with contempt, but it does allow for slander and libel to be filed as criminal charges. The criminal procedure code also allows prosecutors to execute searches in advance of securing a warrant; this provision could make it easier for prosecutors to seize notes or information kept by journalists. In a positive development—reported by the Inter American Press Association (IAPA)—the Senate's First Commission set aside a legislative bill that would have expanded the definition of insult and defamation offenses.

Colombia remains the most dangerous country for journalists in South America, and violence and harassment of journalists by state and nonstate actors are the primary impediments to a free media. The Bogota-based watchdog Fundacion para la Libertad de Prensa (FLIP) reported a significant (37 percent) increase in violations of press freedom in 2006, with the greatest number of incidents occurring during March and May, months in which Colombia held elections for Congress and the presidency, respectively. Three journalists were killed during the year. In Cordoba, radio host Gustavo Rojas Gabaldo was shot and killed on February 4 in an incident that the IAPA attributed to demobilized paramilitaries angered by his criticism of links between local government and the *paras*. Community radio host Milton Fabian Sanchez was killed in August in Valle del Cauca after denouncing local-level drug trafficking. Atilano Segundo Perez Barrios was killed later the same month in Bolivar; the motive for the slaying remains undetermined. Numerous threats against journalists occurred throughout the country, forcing many journalists to go into hiding or exile. The Committee to Protect Journalists (CPJ) reported that at least seven journalists were forced to flee their homes owing to threats and intimidation. Journalist Olga Cecilia

Vega, who survived two brutal attacks on her life in 2002, was forced to flee into exile in 2006 after receiving numerous death threats. Since 2000, the Ministries of Justice and the Interior have operated the Journalist Protection Program to assist with security, transportation, financial aid, and assistance to leave the country if necessary for those journalists who become targets; this program covered 94 media representatives during the year, compared with 46 in the previous year. Additionally, the journalists' group Media for Peace, along with several dozen other nongovernmental organizations, received a series of e-mails during the summer and fall threatening physical attacks against organizations deemed to be pro-Revolutionary Armed Forces of Colombia (FARC).

Security forces were implicated in over 20 violations of press freedom, often in the context of protests against state policies, including a free trade agreement with the United States. Government investigations and prosecutions for crimes against journalists have been slow and inconclusive, contributing to an atmosphere of impunity. According to CPJ, none of the 39 cases of journalists murdered since 1992 have been fully resolved. In 2005, the government established a special unit in the Office of the Public Prosecutor to deal specifically with cases involving the assassination of journalists, but the unit has been hamstrung by insufficient personnel and budgetary resources. However, according to the U.S. State Department, in the case of threats against Daniel Coronell, well-known director of a television news show, a Bogota court found Luis Fernandez Uribe Botero guilty of making the threats and sentenced him to 16 months in prison and a fine of 8.16 million pesos (US$3,520).

Politicians, especially at the local level, frequently denounce members of the press as enemies. In 2006, President Uribe mixed firm rhetoric regarding the need to protect provincial journalists' right to report with a display of anger toward national press outlets, notably the weekly magazine *Semana*, regarding reports on the burgeoning *"parapolitica"* scandal concerning links between paramilitaries and the government. Generally, however, Colombian reporting on the *parapolitica* scandal was persistent, demonstrating that the security improvements of the last five years opened space for journalists to report on high-level scandals involving dangerous and powerful actors.

Most of the country's media outlets are controlled by groups of private investors. The government operates 1 educational and 2 commercial television stations along with a national radio network. Although the Ministry of Communications has been active in promoting the development of community radio station, and over 400 stations are currently in operation, the process was paralyzed in several cities, including the capital city, Bogota. After pressure from civil society groups, in October the government announced that frequencies would be issued for community radio stations in cities across the country. Separately, in October, the transmission of Senate hearings regarding the *parapolitica* scandal was temporarily blocked in two northern departments. Government advertising is an important source of revenue since local media depend heavily on advertising by provincial and municipal agencies in order to stay in business. This financial dependence creates a powerful incentive for collusion among media owners, journalists, and officials that affects editorial views and news coverage. There is a widespread perception that journalists accept bribes in exchange for biased coverage. There were no reported cases of government monitoring or censoring the internet, though internet usage remained fairly low, at around 13 percent of the population, in 2006.

LEGAL ENVIRONMENT: 12
POLITICAL ENVIRONMENT: 21

Comoros

ECONOMIC ENVIRONMENT: 15

Status: Partly Free

TOTAL: 48

Survey Edition	2002	2003	2004	2005	2006
Total Score, Status	41,PF	43,PF	45,PF	44,PF	47,PF

Freedom of speech and of the press are protected under the preamble to the 2001 constitution. These rights are generally respected by the government, but journalists are subject to harassment and harsh defamation laws. In March, paramilitary police detained Aboubacar M'changama, editor of the private weekly *L'Archipel*, for printing two articles concerning discontent within the military. M'changama, who also heads the Comorian Print Media Organization, was held for 54 hours, exceeding the legal 48-hour maximum detention limit. Several radio stations were targeted prior to the May 2006 presidential elections. Radio Ngazidja, the official government station of Grand Comore, and private station Moroni FM were ransacked and temporarily forced off the air by armed assailants. Equipment was confiscated from Radio Moheli by the local military commander. Several journalists claimed that the Radio Moheli censorship was the result of having aired protests against the director of a state-owned agency.

Comoros has several independent newspapers and one state-owned weekly, *Al-Watan*. Of the two national radio stations, one (Radio Comoros) is run by the government, and the other (Radio Tropique) is run by the opposition. Private local radio and television stations have proliferated in the last few years and are funded predominantly by donations from locals as well as from citizens living abroad. Although available and unrestricted by the government, poverty, illiteracy, and poor telecommunications infrastructure severely limited access to the internet, which was used by only 3 percent of the population in 2006.

Congo, Republic of (Brazzaville)

LEGAL ENVIRONMENT: 17
POLITICAL ENVIRONMENT: 17
ECONOMIC ENVIRONMENT: 17

Status: Partly Free

TOTAL SCORE: 51

Survey Edition	2002	2003	2004	2005	2006
Total Score, Status	53,PF	55,PF	54,PF	51,PF	51,PF

The constitution provides for freedom of the press, but several types of expression are considered to be criminal offenses, including incitement to ethnic hatred and violence. Following legal reforms in 2001, many press offenses are punishable by fines rather than imprisonment, including libel and publishing "false news." Nonetheless, these fines are often excessive and quickly handed down to publications critical of the government. Local stringers for international media outlets, as well as those employed by the state-run media, have in the past had their accreditation revoked if their reporting was perceived to portray the government in a bad light.

In April, authorities detained the director of a private newspaper, *Thalassa*, overnight and charged him with defamation, insulting the president, and publishing false news, after the paper published a report accusing the president of poisoning a retired general. A judge later imposed a six-month ban on *Thalassa*. Also in April, two prominent local anticorruption campaigners were arrested and detained for three weeks after they contributed to a Global Witness report criticizing the government's misuse of oil revenues. In a subsequent trial condemned by the World Bank and others, the two were given suspended prison sentences and fines of US$600 each.

In 2006, over 15 private weekly newspapers published in the capital, Brazzaville, and provided some scrutiny of the government, though few were readily available in rural areas. Officially, the state does not publish its own newspapers, but a number of publications are believed to be allied with the regime of President Denis Sassou-Nguesso. Radio remains the best means of reaching large audiences nationwide. The government has been slow to loosen its grip on the broadcast sector and continues to run three radio stations and one television station. Political parties are not permitted to own radio stations or television channels; and although several private radio and television stations have won permission to broadcast in recent years, they rarely criticize the government. In 2006, little more than 1 percent of the population was able to access the internet, amounting to 50,000 people, few of whom resided outside of urban areas; the government is not known to restrict online traffic or content.

Congo, Democratic Republic of (Kinshasa)

LEGAL ENVIRONMENT: 24
POLITICAL ENVIRONMENT: 32
ECONOMIC ENVIRONMENT: 24

Status: Not Free

TOTAL SCORE: 80

Survey Edition	2002	2003	2004	2005	2006
Total Score, Status	86,NF	82,NF	80,NF	81,NF	81,NF

The law provides for freedom of speech and of the press, but these rights are limited in practice by President Joseph Kabila's government and various nonstate actors. Officials used an array of prohibitive licensing and criminal libel laws to restrict free speech and suppress political criticism by imprisoning journalists under the country's repressive defamation laws, shutting down broadcast operations, and seizing copies of newspapers critical of the authorities. Several Congolese journalists spent time in jail in 2006, including a newspaper publisher in the capital, Kinshasa, who was arrested in November 2005 and held for nine months on charges of publishing "false rumors," insulting the head of state, and "insulting the government." Patrice Booto was finally freed after being sentenced to six months in jail and a fine, but many such cases never go to court. Local media outlets are also subject to regulation by the High Authority on Media (HAM), a public agency created under the 2002 peace accords that formally ended the civil war within the Democratic Republic of the Congo (DRC). The agency's mandate is to ensure freedom of expression, but it has the authority to temporarily suspend media outlets for hate speech and other serious ethical transgressions. The HAM targeted several media outlets owned by politicians opposed to Kabila in 2006, prompting allegations that the sanctions were politically motivated.

Multiparty presidential elections were held on July 30, 2006, for the first time since independence from Belgium in 1960. Kabila, who had led the country's transitional government since 2002, won in an October runoff against his main rival, former rebel leader Jean-Pierre Bemba. During the preelectoral period, journalists faced physical abuse, imprisonment, and threats from all parties to the country's debilitating internal strife. Instances of harassment and physical intimidation of journalists were particularly severe in the eastern Ituri, Kivu, and Kasai provinces, where the central government exercises little control and armed groups continue to terrorize journalists and the civilian population. On July 8, unidentified gunmen killed Bapuwa Mwamba, a Congolese journalist who worked for several local publications, in his home in Kinshasa. Authorities charged a soldier and two civilians in connection with the murder, saying that Mwamba was killed in an attempted robbery; however, the local press freedom group Journaliste en Danger (JED) ruled out robbery as a motive based on their own investigation. In July, the government expelled a respected Radio France Internationale correspondent after repeatedly denying her accreditation to cover the elections. In a earlier sign of pressure on the media ahead of the elections, on 16 April, 40 men entered a station owned by the Congo National Radio and Television (RTNC) in Butembo province and destroyed its capacity to broadcast. The trial of three soldiers accused of murdering another prominent journalist in November 2005 began in July but remained unresolved at year's end, and members of JED reported that they had received threats in connection with their inquiry into the incident.

The people of the DRC are largely illiterate and depend upon radio broadcasts for the news. Nonetheless, many private newspapers exist, and although not always objective, they are often able to be highly critical of the government. Multiple privately owned radio and television stations also operate in tandem with two state-owned radio stations as well as a state-owned television station. The state-owned broadcasters operate with a pro-government bias but permit other major political parties represented in the transitional government to gain access to airtime. Together with the Swiss-funded Fondation Hirondelle, MONUC operates an independent countrywide radio network, Radio Okapi, which has set new standards for reporting and media objectivity in a volatile political scene. Journalists in all major media outlets are usually poorly paid and lack sufficient training, making them vulnerable to bribery and political manipulation. The government refrains from any overt internet censorship. However, only a tiny portion of the population (less than 0.5 percent) was able to access the internet owing to financial constraints and the volatile political situation.

Costa Rica

LEGAL ENVIRONMENT: 7
POLITICAL ENVIRONMENT: 7
ECONOMIC ENVIRONMENT: 6

Status: Free

TOTAL SCORE: 20

Survey Edition	2002	2003	2004	2005	2006
Total Score, Status	17,F	14,F	19,F	19,F	18,F

Costa Rica's press environment is considered to be among the freest in Latin America. Freedom of communication is guaranteed under Article 24 of the constitution, which also reserves the government's right to seize private documents. However, strict libel laws provide for penalties of up to three years' imprisonment in cases of insult of a public official, though these have been under review since 2004.

On May 3, the Constitutional Court upheld press legislation declaring libel and slander to be crimes. Article 7 of the 1902 statute known as Ley de Imprenta imposes a prison sentence of up to 120 days for defamation in print media. A petition to strike down the law was filed in February 2004 by the lawyer of the San Jose–based daily *Extra*, after three of its journalists were convicted under Article 7 and given suspended prison sentences. The Court rejected the appeal. Also in May, a bill was introduced in Congress seeking to regulate journalism. The same bill would limit press freedom by introducing the notion of "truthful information." But the government has shown support for a bill in Congress that would ban all these restrictive press laws. Access to official information remains a challenge for journalists.

While violence against journalists is not common in Costa Rica, in February Jose Alberto Gatgens, a correspondent with *La Nacion*, was fired upon by security guards as he left a shopping mall in the town of Guapiles. Gatgens, who was not hurt in the attack, was preparing a report on alleged irregularities in the licensing of casinos. In November, human rights groups and press freedom advocates expressed concern over the impunity surrounding the murders of journalists Parmenio Medina and Ivannia Mora, both killed in 2003. Also in November, judges in the Mora case dropped the charges against all of the six alleged suspects, saying "essential" evidence for the case was inadmissible in court.

Costa Rica has a vibrant media scene, although private media ownership is highly concentrated and generally conservative. Radio is the most popular outlet for news dissemination, though several daily newspapers are widely circulated. Access to the internet is unrestricted, and more than 20 percent of the population made use of this medium in 2006.

Cote d'Ivoire

LEGAL ENVIRONMENT: 19
POLITICAL ENVIRONMENT: 30
ECONOMIC ENVIRONMENT: 19

Status: Not Free

TOTAL SCORE: 68

Survey Edition	2002	2003	2004	2005	2006
Total Score, Status	66,NF	68,NF	65,NF	69,NF	65,NF

The constitution provides for freedom of the press, but since the 2002 rebellion that divided the country into government and rebel-held portions, the government has reduced media freedoms in the name of patriotism and national unity. Parliament scrapped criminal libel and other punitive laws for press offenses in December 2004. However, these legal improvements were disregarded in June 2006 when the editor and publications director at the opposition daily *Le Font* were sentenced to three months in prison and large fines on charges of defamation. The journalists had not yet served their time in prison by year's end, hoping to overturn the ruling in the appeals court.

Journalists remain vulnerable to physical and other abuse by police and extralegal militias, and many journalists, particularly those involved in media outlets expressing dissenting views, were subject to direct attacks and intimidation throughout the year. However, the primary threat to the media in 2006 came from the blatant attempts made by President Laurent Gbagbo and pro-government militias to control media content, particularly that of the state-run media. In January, following the UN's announcement that the mandate of the National Assembly did not extend beyond 2005, hundreds of members of the militant pro-government group the Young Patriots and other government supporters rallied in front of the offices of the state-run media outlet, Radiotelevision Ivoirienne (RTI), eventually using force to gain access to the station and broadcast messages inciting violence and instructing protesters to target specific buildings, including the UN headquarters and the French embassy. This incident has intensified international concern about xenophobia and hate language in the Ivorian media. During the occupation of the outlet, which was aided by state security personnel and a number of senior broadcast officials, demonstrators threatened to kill or rape journalists who were unwilling to cooperate. Many other journalists were harassed, attacked, and threatened amid the wider violence that month, and a number of media outlets were intimidated into temporarily closing their offices.

As a further direct assault on the independence of the state media in general, and RTI in particular, in November President Gbagbo dissolved the entire board of directors and fired the director general of RTI, replacing him with Pierre Brou Amessan, who had served as the government's news anchor during the Young Patriots takeover in January. This move came during a period of heightened tension between Gbagbo and his prime minister after RTI aired one of the prime minister's press releases, which condemned Gbagbo's actions following the dumping of toxic waste in the capital, Abidjan, and called for state institutions to refuse to enforce decrees signed by the president. In the same move, the director of the state-owned daily *Fraternite Matin* was also replaced with someone more favorable to the administration.

Little changed in 2006 for media practitioners in the northern rebel-held territory. Only one incident of media harassment was reported in which an independent journalist was allegedly beaten by security forces while leaving an interview with a rebel spokesman. The rebels operate at least one television and two radio stations in their zone and continue to allow the circulation of pro-government newspapers and the broadcasting of government television and radio programs.

The government controls two major radio stations, one of which is the only national station and a key source of news in the country. Private print and community radio stations do present diverse views and frequently scrutinize the government, but they are regularly harassed for these reports. Since 2002, pro-government media have led an ultranationalistic campaign against France, which they accuse of backing the rebellion; this campaign, supported by President Gbagbo, has increasingly included calls for the removal of the UN mission and its peacekeeping troops stationed in Cote d'Ivoire. Following a 10-month ban on its FM radio transmissions, in May 2006 French government–owned Radio France Internationale (RFI) was allowed to resume its broadcasting in return for a US$18,000 fine and the reappointment of a permanent RFI correspondent in Abidjan. Internet access, though severely constrained by poverty and infrastructure limitations (only 1 percent of the population was able to access the internet in 2006), is unrestricted by the government.

LEGAL ENVIRONMENT: 9

POLITICAL ENVIRONMENT: 14

Croatia

ECONOMIC ENVIRONMENT: 14

Status: Partly Free

TOTAL SCORE: 37

Survey Edition	2002	2003	2004	2005	2006
Total Score, Status	33,PF	33,PF	37,PF	37,PF	39,PF

Freedom of the press is enshrined in the constitution, but media outlets are still influenced by various political and economic interests. Amendments to the criminal code that were passed in June 2006 and took effect in October eliminated imprisonment as a punishment for libel, leaving fines as the only sanction. If a person convicted of libel does not pay the fine, the court is authorized to seize his or her assets, and in the absence of adequate assets the individual is obliged to perform community service. Government officials occasionally use libel laws against the media. In August, Croatian president Stjepan Mesic sued the daily *Vecernji List* for running a reprint of an article claiming that Mesic had a supervisory role in the secret service of the former Yugoslavia. Although the paper also printed the president's response to the claims, Mesic proceeded with the suit, arguing that the paper had attacked him for political reasons.

Political interference and undue pressure on the media persist. In July, the Croatian Journalists Association protested the government's appointments to the advisory board for the state news agency Hina, alleging that the new appointees—who included a veterinarian, a recent law school graduate, and an owner of a political marketing firm—lacked qualifications and were essentially political lackeys. However, the government in October asked Parliament to dismiss the board after a disagreement over its selection of a general manager, and lawmakers complied with the request in December. Also in December, two journalists from the state-owned Croatian Radio and Television (HRT) were temporarily suspended for broadcasting a speech from the early 1990s in which Mesic appeared to speak favorably about Croatia's Fascist past. Following the incident, Mesic publicly condemned the journalists' suspension. The two journalists were later reinstated following a decision by HRT's Ethics Council that they had not violated the HRT code of conduct. Journalists remain exposed to physical threats and violence. In particular, the issue of war crimes remains a sensitive topic, and journalists face pressure and intimidation if their reporting challenges the virtue of Croatia's role in the 1991–1995 Balkans conflict. At least in some instances, these attacks are instigated by local officials. Drago Hedl, a journalist for the weekly *Feral Tribune*, received death threats in May linked to an article accusing local officials of committing war crimes. In response, police granted Hedl protection and later arrested two individuals, one of whom was a local politician. In another incident, a reporter from Nova Television was allegedly attacked both physically and verbally in July by the mayor of Novalja, who sought to prevent her from reporting on water shortages on the island of Pag.

Approximately 140 radio stations and 15 television channels operate in Croatia, and 2 out of 3 national television stations are privately owned. Many Croats also have access to various European channels via satellite. HRT is the market leader at the national level, and the state remains the single largest media owner. The press has increasingly been used as a tool by media owners to promote their business and political interests. Several prominent journalists expressed concerns in 2006 that the media were becoming subverted to the interests of powerful advertisers, who were able to control content by threatening to redirect their sponsorship. The state does not restrict the foreign press or internet use, and more than 30 percent of the population accessed the internet in 2006.

Cuba

Status: Not Free

LEGAL ENVIRONMENT: 30
POLITICAL ENVIRONMENT: 39
ECONOMIC ENVIRONMENT: 27
TOTAL SCORE: 96

Survey Edition	2002	2003	2004	2005	2006
Total Score, Status	96,NF	94,NF	96,NF	96,NF	96,NF

Cuba has the most restrictive laws on free speech and press freedom in the hemisphere. The constitution prohibits private ownership of media and allows free speech and press only if they "conform to the aims of a socialist society." Cuba's legal and institutional structures are firmly under the control of the executive. The country's criminal code provides the legal basis for the repression of dissent, and under the guise of protecting state security, laws criminalizing "enemy propaganda" and the dissemination of "unauthorized news" are used to restrict freedom of speech. Insult laws carry penalties of three months to one year in prison, with sentences of up to three years if the president or members of the Council of State or National Assembly are the objects of criticism. The 1997 Law of National Dignity, which provides for jail sentences of 3 to 10 years for "anyone who, in a direct or indirect form, collaborates with the enemy's media," is aimed at the independent news agencies, serving primarily as moral support for local journalists, that send their material abroad.

The few journalists who do work for independent news agencies, write articles for foreign websites, or publish underground newsletters are routinely monitored, harassed, detained, interrogated, or imprisoned. At best they are accused of giving the Cuban revolution a "bad name," at worst of working as counterrevolutionaries for the United States government or Cuban exiles. During the year, three journalists were released from prison, but two more were imprisoned, leaving several dozen journalists in long-term detention. One of those released, Lamasiel Gutierrez Romero, correspondent for the website *Nueva Prensa Cubana*, was freed on March 22 after serving a seven-month sentence for "civil disobedience and resistance." She returned to her home on the Isle of Youth under heavy police surveillance and was forbidden to leave the island, but in October was transferred to a women's prison in Mantonegro because she had continued her journalistic activities in defiance of the terms of her house arrest. The three journalists who received lengthy prison sentences in 2006 were Armando Betancourt Reina, Raymundo Perdigon Brito, and Guillermo Espinosa Rodriguez. Reina, a freelance journalist and editor of a small underground magazine, was arrested while covering evictions in the city of Camaguey, but formal charges have yet to be filed. At the conclusion of 2006, Raymundo Perdigon Brito—who together with his sister had recently established a small news agency—was arrested and sentenced to four years' imprisonment for attempting to set up an independent media outlet. Rodriguez, a reporter for *Agencia de Prensa Libre Oriental*, was sentenced to two years' house arrest on charges of "social dangerousness" for his coverage of an outbreak of dengue fever in Santiago de Cuba that authorities were trying to downplay. At the beginning of August, six foreign journalists hoping to enter the country to cover reactions to the temporary transfer of power from President Fidel Castro to his brother, Raul, were interrogated by agents of the Ministry of the Interior and required to return to their country of departure. They were told that they did not have the work visa needed to practice journalism in Cuba.

The Communist Party controls all national media, including all print and electronic media outlets, apart from one or two unauthorized Catholic Church newsletters. Cubans do not have access to foreign media, although some international papers are for sale in hotels. The government continues to jam transmissions of the U.S. government–sponsored Radio and Television Marti. Although Telecommunications Minister Ignacio

Gonzalez Planas has repeatedly stated that the internet is essential for the country's development, the government does its best to restrict access, and less than 2 percent of the population was online in 2006. An investigation carried out by Reporters Sans Frontieres revealed that the government has banned most private internet connections and has installed software in all internet cafés and leading hotels that triggers an alert message whenever "subversive" keywords are entered. This strict control is backed by the threat of 5 years in prison for connecting to the internet illegally and 20 years for writing "counterrevolutionary" articles for foreign websites.

Cyprus

LEGAL ENVIRONMENT: 5
POLITICAL ENVIRONMENT: 9
ECONOMIC ENVIRONMENT: 8

Status: Free

TOTAL SCORE: 22

Survey Edition	2002	2003	2004	2005	2006
Total Score, Status	18,F	18,F	18,F	22,F	22,F

Freedom of speech and of expression are guaranteed under Article 19 of the constitution, and these rights are generally respected in practice in the Greek part of Cyprus, where the independent press is vibrant and frequently criticizes authorities. In August, Cypriot media imposed a 15-day blanket ban on covering the Turkish-controlled north of the island, protesting the frequent number of arrests there of Greek Cypriot journalists.

Some laws are in place for freedom of the press in the northern, Turkish part of Cyprus, but authorities are overtly hostile to the independent press, and journalists can be arrested, put on trial, and sentenced under the "unjust actions" section of the criminal code. Although Turkish Cypriot journalists can enter the south, Turkish journalists based in the north are often denied entry across the border. Harassment of Turkish Cypriot journalists by Greek Cypriot border guards and ultranationalist Greek Cypriot groups has been reported by the U.S. State Department. Several local daily newspapers are available, but the broadcasting service is controlled exclusively by the Turkish Cypriot administration. In November, two French journalists were arrested and accused of filming at a restricted military site while working in the city of Varosha. They were later freed and fined 300 Cyprus pounds (US$665). Independent newspapers have frequently been targeted by the government; in December, the editor of the *Kibrisli* paper was charged with defamation of the attorney general following the publication of a critical article. The case was pending at year's end. The newspaper with the most legal cases in the territory controlled by the Turkish authorities is the daily *Afrika* newspaper. If successfully applied, cases against *Afrika*'s editor, Sener Levent, brought by the regime in the past years would amass to more than 2,000 years of imprisonment.

Cypriots have access to Greek and Turkish broadcasts. There are seven major dailies, two weekly newspapers, and six major magazines. However, most daily newspapers belong or are linked to political parties or other groups. A few private television and radio stations compete effectively with government-controlled stations, but only the state broadcaster has sufficient funds to produce its own programming. Ownership is highly concentrated. Approximately 33 percent of Cypriots are able to access the internet on a regular basis and are not subject to any known government restrictions on internet use.

[The numerical rating for Cyprus is based on conditions on the Greek side of the island.]

Czech Republic

LEGAL ENVIRONMENT: 4
POLITICAL ENVIRONMENT: 7
ECONOMIC ENVIRONMENT: 7

Status: Free

TOTAL SCORE: 18

Survey Edition	2002	2003	2004	2005	2006
Total Score, Status	25,F	23,F	23,F	22,F	20,F

Freedom of the press is constitutionally guaranteed, though the Charter of Fundamental Rights and Freedoms prohibits speech that might infringe on national security, individual rights, public health, or morality or that may evoke hatred based on race, ethnicity, or national origin. Libel remains a criminal offense, but prosecutions were rare. The Press Law provides a sound basis for independent journalism, and media protections were bolstered by a 2005 Constitutional Court ruling that journalists do not have to disclose their sources. However, a 2006 wiretapping scandal revealed that police had monitored the telephone conversations of two reporters in order to identify their sources on a story linking civil servants and politicians to organized crime. Media freedom advocates have also warned against recent legislative efforts to restrict the use of hidden cameras.

Press freedom has long been secure in the Czech Republic, but observers have raised concerns over the quality and depth of reporting, as well as weak accountability and increasing cross-ownership of media outlets. The news media are occasionally accused of political or economic bias, and such allegations were renewed in the context of the 2006 parliamentary elections. In February, Tomas Nemecek, a journalist with Czech Radio, was fired after a commentary about the amendment of a church bill. The editor who broadcast this commentary also left the station. Most major media outlets are privately owned, and they are generally able to represent diverse views without fear of government or partisan pressure. Public broadcasters supplement private media and have the confidence of a large majority of society. The internet continues to develop rapidly, with just over 50 percent of the population enjoying regular and unrestricted access.

Denmark

Legal Environment: 2
Political Environment: 4
Economic Environment: 5

Status: Free

Total Score: 11

Survey Edition	2002	2003	2004	2005	2006
Total Score, Status	9,F	11,F	8,F	10,F	10,F

Freedom of speech and of expression are protected in Section 77 of the constitution, and the government generally respects these rights in practice. Nevertheless, certain legal restrictions for libel, blasphemy, and racism were at the center of a number of incidents in 2006. Press freedom was put to the test when international furor continued over 12 cartoons of the prophet Muhammad that were published in the Copenhagen daily *Jyllands-Posten* in September 2005. Several Muslim countries boycotted Danish goods, and Danish embassies came under attack. The cartoonists received death threats, bomb threats were made against the newspaper's headquarters, and hackers attempted to shut down the daily's online site. Prime Minister Anders Fogh Rasmussen refused to intervene in the matter, stating that it was an issue of free speech. In February, *Jyllands-Posten* apologized publicly for any offense caused to Muslims. However, anger flared again in October when two Danish television channels aired a video of political activists drawing cartoons of the prophet.

In 2006, two journalists were indicted for the first time in the country's history on account of leaking state secrets. In 2004, Michael Bjerre and Jesper Larsen of *Berlingske Tidende* published a series of articles based on leaked reports from the Danish Defense Intelligence Service questioning the existence of weapons of mass destruction in Iraq. The two journalists, along with editor in chief Niels Lunde, were brought to trial in November 2006, and all three were acquitted in December. According to the U.S. State Department, radio announcer Kaj Wilhelmsen was given a suspended two-week prison sentence for violating the country's Antiracism Law. Similarly, in November Radio Hoger's license was suspended for refusing to supply the Radio and Television Board with a copy of an August broadcast that allegedly contained racist programming. Both Wilhelmsen and Radio Hoger continued to broadcast via the internet, for which a license is not needed.

The private print press is vibrant, though many papers have political affiliations. Government subsidies are available to the press, as are low-interest loans for struggling newspapers. State-run television and radio broadcasting is financed by an annual license fee. TV2 is a privately run television network, and satellite and cable television is also available. The government does not restrict use of the internet, which was accessed by 70 percent of the population in 2006.

Djibouti

LEGAL ENVIRONMENT: 23
POLITICAL ENVIRONMENT: 25
ECONOMIC ENVIRONMENT: 21

Status: Not Free

TOTAL SCORE: 69

Survey Edition	2002	2003	2004	2005	2006
Total Score, Status	67,NF	65,NF	66,NF	67,NF	69,NF

Although Article 15 of the constitution affords the right to express and disseminate "opinions by word, pen, or image," the government imposes restrictions on the independent press. Free speech is limited by prohibitions on slander and the dissemination of "false information" as well as difficulties in obtaining broadcasting licenses, arrest and detention of journalists, seizure of newspapers, and high court fines for "offensive" reporting, according to the British Broadcasting Corporation (BBC). The U.S. military presence in Djibouti creates additional pressure for self-censorship, as journalists are encouraged not to report on soldiers' activities. On May 30, a journalist for the government broadcast operator Radiodiffusion-Television de Djibouti was suspended for three months for broadcasting a story on a child who reportedly had avian influenza and whose mother denied the illness, accusing the Ministry of Health of creating the story to try to obtain foreign assistance.

Because of extreme poverty, radio is the most popular news medium, as few can afford newspapers or TV sets. Television and radio broadcasts are controlled by the government and report favorably on government activities; however, the BBC World Service, Radio France Internationale, and Voice of America are also accessible. The largest newspaper is the biweekly government-owned *La Nation*, though opposition parties also print two weekly papers—*Le Renouveau* and *Le Republique*. The only internet service provider is government owned. In January, the website of the Association for Respect of Human Rights in Djibouti (ARDHD) was blocked. The ARDHD is often critical of the government, which denied involvement in the blocking. Just over 1 percent of the population was able to access the internet in 2006.

Dominica

LEGAL ENVIRONMENT: 4
POLITICAL ENVIRONMENT: 10
ECONOMIC ENVIRONMENT: 6

Status: Free

TOTAL SCORE: 20

Survey Edition	2002	2003	2004	2005	2006
Total Score, Status	16,F	14,F	17,F	17,F	19,F

The constitution guarantees freedom of the press. The media are often critical of the government, and as a result, relations with the ruling Dominica Labor Party continued to be strained. Representatives of the government issued forthright criticisms of unfavorable coverage. In August, a dispute arose over media coverage of Prime Minister Roosevelt Skerrit's relationship with a Bahamian businessman with an allegedly dubious past, causing Skerrit to denounce sections of the media for their "sensationalist" reporting. In September, the printing house of the *Sun* newspaper refused to publish an issue containing an article about the controversy. The owner took the decision to stop the print run after receiving a warning from a lawyer claiming to represent the prime minister. The Media Workers Association of Dominica expressed its concern that the incident would increase media fears of the application of existing libel and defamation legislation. In November, following the expulsion from Parliament of a journalist with the *Chronicle* newspaper, the leader of the opposition United Workers Party called for the publication of clear guidelines on the rules regarding reporting procedures at the National Assembly. There is no daily newspaper, but there are several weekly publications. Dominica has four radio stations, including the state-owned Dominica Broadcasting Corporation, and two television stations. The internet, used by approximately 36 percent of the population, is neither restricted nor censored by the government.

Dominican Republic

Status: Partly Free

LEGAL ENVIRONMENT: 8
POLITICAL ENVIRONMENT: 18
ECONOMIC ENVIRONMENT: 14

TOTAL SCORE: 40

Survey Edition	2002	2003	2004	2005	2006
Total Score, Status	30,F	33,PF	39,PF	38,PF	37,PF

The law provides for freedom of speech and of the press, and the government generally respects these rights in practice. Official attempts to impose legal restrictions on media coverage have been vociferously opposed by journalists. However, during 2006 there was a troubling deterioration in the media environment. Three journalists were murdered, one was kidnapped, and another was the target of an alleged assassination plot. Although there is no incontrovertible evidence that these attacks were linked directly to the victims' work, there are indications that some of the attacks were connected to their profession. In April, Johnny Martinez, director of *Equilibrio* magazine and producer of a television program by the same name, was found stabbed to death near his hometown, San Cristobal. Two men—both former policemen—were later found guilty of the murder. In late August, Domingo Disla "Diaz" Florentino, a radio and television commentator, was shot dead in Boca Chica. On September 25, Facundo Labata "Lavatta" Ramirez, a correspondent for Radio Comercial and several other radio stations, was shot dead in Los Alcarrizos. He had recently been reporting on crime and drug trafficking in the area where he lived, and his daughter told the media that he had received threatening letters. In March, Roberto Sandoval, host of critical opinion programs on Radio Comercial and Telecable Nacional's Canal 10, was abducted by gunmen and wounded as he escaped from a moving vehicle. In late December, veteran journalist Julio Martinez Pozo denounced an alleged plot against his life orchestrated by a senior government official. Martinez Pozo, who hosts a popular radio program on Z-101, claimed that Jose Venegas, a man rumored to have been involved in the disappearance and presumed murder of journalist Narciso Gonzalez in 1994, had been hired to kill him. Investigations into the case continued through the year's end.

There were numerous other reports of journalists being threatened and intimidated, and the Inter American Press Association denounced an increase in wiretapping and other forms of spying on journalists and executives at various media outlets. Little progress was made on judicial investigations into attacks on journalists from previous years. Media generally avoid serious reportage on some subjects, such as the army and the Catholic Church, as well as on topics that might adversely affect the economic or political interests of a particular outlet's owners. In November, popular journalist Adolfo Salomon was fired from news agency Color Vision after complaints were filed by high-level officials in the Catholic Church and the armed forces that Salomon had asked inappropriate questions.

There are five national daily newspapers and numerous local publications. The state-owned Radio Television Dominicana operates radio and television services. Private owners operate over 300 AM and FM radio stations and more than 40 television stations, most of them small, regional broadcasters. Overall, media remain subject to some government influence, particularly through the denial of advertising revenues for controversial publications and the implementation of taxes on imported newsprint. No government restrictions on internet access were reported in 2006, though only 16 percent of the population was able to take advantage of this owing to the high costs.

East Timor

LEGAL ENVIRONMENT: 12
POLITICAL ENVIRONMENT: 17
ECONOMIC ENVIRONMENT: 13

Status: Partly Free

TOTAL SCORE: 42

Survey Edition	2002	2003	2004	2005	2006
Total Score, Status	21,F	22,F	29,F	30,F	39, PF

Political violence led to a continued deterioration of the press environment in 2006, as widespread unrest hampered the media's ability to disseminate news. Although the 2002 constitution guarantees that the state shall protect "the freedom and independence of the public mass media from political and economic powers," Section 40 states that the rights to freedom of speech and of information "shall be regulated by law," thereby opening the door to criminal penalties for defamation. In December 2005, Prime Minister Mari Alkatiri signed an executive decree approving a new penal code that contains severe penalties for defamation of public figures. Under Article

173, anyone can be jailed for up to three years and fined for publishing comments seen as defaming public officials. Article 176 doubles the terms of imprisonment when defamation is made through the media. The code sets no limits on fines or other penalties for defamation. President Xanana Gusmao neither signed nor vetoed the bill and in February 2006 sent it back to the Ministry of Justice for reconsideration, where it remains. A 2004 court of appeals ruling suggested that until a new Timorese penal code is passed, the Indonesian law (which contains criminal penalties for defamation) still applies.

A power struggle between Prime Minister Alkatiri and his political opponents in April resulted in civil unrest, gang violence, the deaths of at least 37 people, and the internal displacement of 15 percent of the population. Many journalists were among the displaced, and for a period of several weeks each of three newspapers based in the capital city of Dili was temporarily unable to publish. Although the political crisis lessened after Alkatiri resigned on June 26, Jose Ramos Horta, the new Prime Minister, has not eliminated criminal penalties for defamation.

A small number of privately owned daily and weekly newspapers publish in a variety of languages and provide some diversity of views. The Public Broadcast Service owns and operates a radio station that reaches most of the population, as well as a television station that has a limited geographic range. However, severe economic pressures on the press continued to hamper the free flow of information. A majority of the community radio stations established after independence failed to function during the crisis. Owing to the technical limitations of public radio and television broadcaster Radio and Televisao de Timor Leste (RTTL), those Timorese who were outside Dili had almost no access to news. Moreover, although RTTL is supposed to be an independent institution governed by an independent board of directors, the public broadcaster was reportedly under political pressure from the Fretilin ruling party-appointed president of the board not to broadcast reports critical of the government. Infrastructure limitations and poverty severely restricted access to the internet in 2006 (less than 0.1 percent of the population was able to make use of this new medium during the year); nonetheless, the government does not censor websites or limit users' access to diverse content.

LEGAL ENVIRONMENT: 13
POLITICAL ENVIRONMENT: 18

Ecuador

ECONOMIC ENVIRONMENT: 10

Status: Partly Free

TOTAL SCORE: 41

Survey Edition	2002	2003	2004	2005	2006
Total Score, Status	40,PF	41,PF	42,PF	41,PF	41,PF

The constitution guarantees freedom of the press. However, given that defamation and slander remain criminal offenses punishable by up to three years in prison, these guarantees are often weak in practice. Concern about the implementation of such restrictive libel laws often results in self-censorship, affecting reporting on public officials and the armed forces. In October, the Inter American Press Association faulted the level of compliance with the 2004 Law on Transparency and Freedom of Information.

Ecuadorian journalists were subject to occasional government harassment and other types of extralegal intimidation in 2006, though the level of attacks was low compared with the regional average. In February, two journalists were killed in 24 hours in the Guayaquil area; no arrests were made, though the police described the murders as unrelated to the journalists' work. Under President Alfredo Palacio, a state of emergency was declared in March in six provinces experiencing fierce social protests. In the following weeks, several journalists were detained briefly, and one radio station was temporarily censored. On August 13, the building of the publisher of two Guayaquil dailies was sprayed with bullets, causing damage but no injuries. The presidential candidacy of banana magnate Alvaro Noboa caused serious tensions with the press. Noboa avoided the media and several times accused specific outlets of "dishonoring" journalism and being "accomplices to the destruction of the country." One critical journalist received a death threat and had the transmission of his television program interrupted, acts he ascribed to Noboa backers.

Except for one government-owned radio station, broadcast and print media outlets are privately owned and express a broad range of editorial viewpoints. However, owing to self-censorship regarding sensitive issues such as the military, the British Broadcasting Corporation reported that the media are generally nonconfrontational. Most media outlets are heavily influenced by their financiers and often reflect the political perspectives of their sponsors. This proved to be a particularly volatile situation in the context of the 2006 elections; during the campaign, many commentators were accused of crossing the line between analysis and partisanship. The broadcast media are required to give the government free airtime; thus stations can be forced to show programs featuring the president and other officials. In 2006, airtime was granted to presidential candidates as well. Access to the internet is not restricted by the government, but the medium is used by only 8 percent of the population.

LEGAL ENVIRONMENT: 22
POLITICAL ENVIRONMENT: 22

Egypt

ECONOMIC ENVIRONMENT: 18

Status: Not Free

TOTAL SCORE: 62

Survey Edition	2002	2003	2004	2005	2006
Total Score, Status	77,NF	79,NF	76,NF	68,NF	61,NF

Though journalists increasingly cross the "red lines" that previously constrained the media, press freedom continues to suffer from repressive laws and extralegal intimidation of journalists. The Emergency Law, the Press Law, and provisions of the penal code regulate the press, despite constitutional guarantees of press freedom. Much anticipated amendments to the Press Law were enacted in July 2006, but they did not alter provisions that criminalized the publication of "false news" and criticism of the president and foreign leaders. Publishing material that constitutes "an attack against the dignity and honor of individuals" or an "outrage of the reputation of families" also remains a criminal offense—albeit an offense that is rarely but opportunistically prosecuted by the authorities. In June, Ibrahim Issa, editor of the weekly *Al-Dustur*, and Sahar Zaki, a journalist at the same paper, were sentenced to one year in prison for "insulting the president" and "spreading false or tendentious rumors" after reporting on an antigovernment lawsuit. At year's end, Issa and Zaki were free on bail bonds of 10,000 Egyptian pounds (US$1,700), pending an appeal. Shahenda Mekled, author of *From the Papers of Shahenda Mekled*; Shirin Abu al-Naga, the book's editor; and award-winning publisher Muhammad Hashim all faced criminal charges at the end of the year because of the book's portrayal of a prominent landowning family.

Journalists continued to face harassment and violence in 2006. Over the course of the year, police detained over a dozen journalists and assaulted many more. Hussein Abd al-Ghani, the Cairo bureau chief of the Qatar-based satellite television channel Al-Jazeera, was detained in April while reporting on bombings in southern Sinai. He was accused of disseminating "inaccurate news harmful to the country's reputation" after mistakenly reporting violence between security forces and terrorists elsewhere in Egypt that had apparently never occurred; several other news outlets made the same error. Although he was freed, Abd al-Ghani was still barred from leaving Egypt at the end of the year. In May, riot police attacked more than a dozen local and foreign journalists at peaceful demonstrations in support of judicial independence.

While there are more than 500 newspapers, magazines, journals, and other periodicals in Egypt, this apparent diversity disguises the government's role as a media owner and sponsor. The government is at least a partial owner of all of Egypt's three largest newspapers, whose editors are appointed by the president. Opposition parties may form their own newspapers, and in recent years the Shura Council—one-third of whose members are appointed by the president—has granted licenses to the Ghad and Karama parties to publish eponymous weekly newspapers. The Ministry of Information controls content in the state-owned broadcast media. Privately owned domestic broadcasters are not allowed to air news bulletins and focus instead on music and entertainment. However, Egypt permits the establishment of locally based private satellite television stations, and the government does not block foreign satellite channels.

Thanks in large part to government efforts to aggressively promote internet use, the number of Egyptians with access to the internet has more than quadrupled over the past several years, but the number of regular users rarely exceeds seven percent of the population. The Egyptian government does not engage in widespread online censorship, but in June the Supreme Administrative Court ruled that the Ministry of Information and Ministry of Communications had the authority to block, suspend, or shut down websites considered a threat to "national security." In November, blogger Abd al-Karim Nabil Suleiman, better known as Karim Amer, was detained for insulting Islam, the authorities at Al-Azhar University, and President Hosni Mubarak. He remained in pretrial detention at year's end and was set to become the first blogger in Egypt to be prosecuted for his online writings, though others had been detained without charge.

El Salvador

LEGAL ENVIRONMENT: 10
POLITICAL ENVIRONMENT: 18
ECONOMIC ENVIRONMENT: 14

Status: Partly Free

TOTAL SCORE: 42

Survey Edition	2002	2003	2004	2005	2006
Total Score, Status	35,PF	38,PF	42,PF	41,PF	43,PF

Freedom of the press is protected through the constitution, and Salvadoran journalists are generally able to report freely on the news, including reports critical of the government and opposition parties. At the same time, press freedom is hindered by a lack of public transparency, reflected in the absence of freedom of information legislation. Judges have the right to restrict media access to legal proceedings for cases they deem to be in the public interest or of national security. Another provision in the criminal code that allows judges to close court proceedings if they determine that the publicity will prejudice a case is considered by some media groups to limit press freedom, according to the U.S. State Department. Despite reforms made in 2004 to the code of criminal procedure, defamation remains a criminal offense.

Although El Salvador is generally a safe place to practice journalism, 2006 saw an increase in the number of journalists who suffered physical attacks because of their work. More than 20 journalists were assaulted by politicians, protesters, or the national civil police while covering political unrest or riots on the streets. On February 27, cameraman Joel Martinez from the Telemundo newsmagazine *Al Rojo Vivo* was shot with a rubber bullet fired by the police, who were trying to break up a protest against a proposed free trade agreement with the United States. For three days in July, journalists were harassed and attacked with stones, sticks, and pepper spray during violent street protests against increases in electric and public transportation fees in San Salvador. Protesters wearing red shirts identifying them as supporters of the Farabundo Marti National Liberation Front, or FMLN, were seen attacking journalists. Journalists were being targeted as alleged supporters of the "right-wing" Salvadoran government, according to protesters. On July 5, reporter Ernesto Landos and cameraman Carlos Duran of the San Salvador–based television station TeleDos suffered bruises and cuts when they were attacked with sticks and stones. The same day, journalist Ivan Perez of Radio YSUCA was threatened near the University of El Salvador, while Carlos Henriquez from the private daily *La Prensa Grafica* was attacked by a group of high school students participating in the street violence. During the same incident, protesters took away a memory card with pictures belonging to photojournalist Felipe Ayala from *El Diario de Hoy*. Employees of *La Prensa Grafica* were also targets of violent attacks on a number of other occasions throughout the year.

There are five daily newspapers that each have a circulation of approximately 250,000, but most of the country depends on privately-owned television and radio networks for the news. Limited resources prevent many media outlets from producing to their full capacity, and self-censorship is often exercised to avoid offending media owners, editors, and government officials. There were no reported government restrictions on the internet in 2006, and access has grown by more than 1,000 percent in the last five years to just under 10 percent of the population.

Equatorial Guinea

Status: Not Free

LEGAL ENVIRONMENT: 27
POLITICAL ENVIRONMENT: 35
ECONOMIC ENVIRONMENT: 27
TOTAL SCORE: 89

Survey Edition	2002	2003	2004	2005	2006
Total Score, Status	80,NF	81,NF	89,NF	88,NF	88,NF

Freedom of expression and of the press are legally guaranteed, but these rights are severely restricted in practice. The 1992 Press Law gives the government unusually extensive authority to restrict press activities through official prepublication censorship. All domestic journalists are required to register with the Ministry of Information, and equally strict accreditation procedures are in place for foreign correspondents. In 2006, the Committee to Protect Journalists listed Equatorial Guinea as one of the world's most censored countries, noting that almost all local coverage is orchestrated or tightly controlled by the government.

Local journalists, including the few who work for foreign news outlets, were subject to systematic harassment and surveillance. However, in 2006 there were no reported cases of physical abuse or deportation. Mild criticism of infrastructure and public institutions is allowed, but nothing disparaging about the president or security forces is tolerated. In the past, foreign journalists have been monitored closely and occasionally deported if their coverage is deemed to be sensitive.

Equatorial Guinea is one of the few African countries to have virtually no independent media. Given the high level of poverty and illiteracy throughout the country, the most influential form of media is radio, but all domestic radio and television stations are owned directly by the government or by the president's family. State-owned media are dominated by sycophantic coverage of the government and the president. Applications to open private radio stations have been pending for several years but have thus far not been approved. One opposition newspaper continued to appear occasionally throughout the year but practiced self-censorship because of government intimidation. A dozen other private newspapers are licensed to publish but function primarily as opposition mouthpieces and are therefore tied to the political fortunes of their sponsors. According to the U.S. State Department, foreign celebrity and sports publications were available for sale, but there were no foreign newspapers, bookstores, or even newsstands in the country. Foreign broadcasts are allowed, including those of Radio France Internationale and Radio Exterior, an international shortwave service from Spain. Through its interviews with opposition politicians, Radio Exterior operates as the only means by which opposition voices can reach rural populations. Internet access is limited to just over 0.5 percent of the population by the level of poverty in Equatorial Guinea but is not directly restricted by the government. Nonetheless, government operatives are believed to monitor citizens' e-mail and internet use.

Eritrea

LEGAL ENVIRONMENT: 30
POLITICAL ENVIRONMENT: 40
ECONOMIC ENVIRONMENT: 24

Status: Not Free

TOTAL SCORE: 94

Survey Edition	2002	2003	2004	2005	2006
Total Score, Status	79,NF	83,NF	89,NF	91,NF	91,NF

In an already inhibiting media environment, the situation for the Eritrean press deteriorated further in 2006 as the government tightened restrictions for foreign reporters traveling within the country. Eritrean law guarantees freedom of speech and of the press. However, the 1996 Press Law prohibits the establishment of private broadcast media outlets and foreign ownership of media and requires all newspapers and journalists to be licensed. It also stipulates that publications be submitted for government approval prior to release and prohibits reprinting articles from banned publications. Since a government ban on all privately owned media was imposed in September 2001, Eritrea remains one of the harshest environments worldwide for the press and is a leading jailer of journalists in Africa. Following the official ban, an unknown number of government critics were detained, including many journalists. According to the Committee to Protect Journalists (CPJ), at least 13 journalists remained behind bars in 2006, with 2 more enduring prolonged forced labor euphemistically called "national service." Many of the jailed journalists are being held incommunicado in undisclosed locations, without access to their families or the Red Cross. Most have been incarcerated since the crackdown in 2001, and despite Eritrean legal guarantees, they were never formally charged. In response to queries from a number of press freedom organizations, the president and senior government officials have accused the journalists of espionage and threatening national security, but they have declined to provide details or evidence in support of these accusations.

The tiny handful of local and foreign independent journalists who continue to operate in the country on behalf of international media are constantly harassed, detained, and threatened. In June 2006, the government tightened restrictions on foreigners seeking to travel inside the country. According to CPJ, the new restrictions were intended partly as a means of preventing foreign journalists from reporting outside the capital. The restrictions were imposed after Eritrea expelled several international aid groups that had provided food assistance in the countryside. An article in *The Economist* noted that the expulsions may be one way of "muzzling reports of any impending humanitarian disaster."

There is currently no independent or privately owned press. Only three newspapers, one television station, and one radio station operate, and they all remain under state control. Journalists working for the state-owned media operate under strict surveillance and severe pressure to report positively on government programs. The importation of foreign periodicals is forbidden. The government requires all internet service providers (ISPs) to use government-controlled internet infrastructure and owns a large percentage of them; in addition, according to the U.S. State Department, the government restricts the bandwidth available to ISPs, thus hindering their ability to provide services. Internet use is extremely limited (just under 2 percent of the population was able to access it in 2006), and authorities are believed to monitor private e-mail communication.

LEGAL ENVIRONMENT: 5
POLITICAL ENVIRONMENT: 5

Estonia

ECONOMIC ENVIRONMENT: 6

Status: Free

TOTAL SCORE: 16

Survey Edition	2002	2003	2004	2005	2006
Total Score, Status	18,F	17,F	17,F	17,F	16,F

The constitution provides for and the government respects freedom of speech and of the press. Numerous media outlets operate in Estonia, and legal protections for press freedom are enforced. Libel has been removed from the penal code, but it is still treated as a criminal offense. There are no legal penalties for "irresponsible journalism." The independent media express a wide variety of views without government interference. However, in August Mart Soidro, a longtime journalist and state official, was told privately by his boss, the director general of the Citizenship and Migration Board, that he should resign because of his earlier article criticizing the Centre Party's behavior during the presidential elections.

The two main commercial television stations, which have nationwide reach, are owned by Scandinavian companies. The country's public broadcasters are Eesti Televisioon and Eesti Raadio. Residents have access to a number of private radio stations and regional television channels, as well as cable and satellite services. Various public and private media outlets provide Russian-language news to the country's sizable Russian-speaking population. There are dozens of newspapers in the country, most of them financed not by advertising revenues, but by readers or owners. However, according to the Tallinn-based marketing research and consulting company TNS Emor, Estonia's advertising market grew by nearly 18 percent from 2005 to 2006; the largest measure of growth occurred in newspapers, followed by television, magazines, and radio. The government allows unrestricted access to the internet, and the country has an unusually high rate of internet usage, with about 52 percent of the population active online.

Ethiopia

Status: Not Free

LEGAL ENVIRONMENT: 27
POLITICAL ENVIRONMENT: 30
ECONOMIC ENVIRONMENT: 20
TOTAL SCORE: 77

Survey Edition	2002	2003	2004	2005	2006
Total Score, Status	61,NF	64,NF	66,NF	68,NF	75,NF

Following a November 2005 crackdown on opposition political parties as well as on the civil society groups and media outlets that were perceived to support them, press freedom in Ethiopia remained extremely limited during 2006. The constitution guarantees freedom of the press, but this right is often restricted in practice. Authorities frequently invoke the 1992 Press Law regarding publication of false and offensive information, incitement of ethnic hatred, or libel in order to justify the arrest and detainment of journalists. Court cases can drag on for years, and journalists often have multiple charges pending against them; at the end of 2006, three reporters who had been sentenced under the Press Law remained in jail. A 2003 draft Press Law, which has been widely criticized by the private press and by press freedom groups, remained under consideration in 2006, although certain provisions of the law were included in the new penal code that took effect in May 2005. Issues of concern include restrictions on who may practice journalism; government-controlled licensing and registration systems; restrictions on print and broadcast cross-ownership; harsh sanctions for violations of the law, including up to five years' imprisonment; excessively broad exceptions to the right of access to information held by public authorities; and the establishment of a government-controlled press council with powers to engage in pre-publication censorship. The Ethiopian Free Press Journalists Association (EFJA), one of the most vocal opponents of the draft Press Law, continued to face harassment from the government, and EFJA president Kifle Mulat remained in exile at year's end. The administration has traditionally denied access to the independent press, limiting coverage of official events to state-owned media outlets, although these restrictions were loosened on several occasions during 2006 for the first time in more than a dozen years.

The broader political crackdown that began in November 2005 continued to have extremely negative implications for the media. Of several dozen journalists arrested alongside civil society activists and politicians, a number were charged with treason, genocide, and attempts to subvert the constitution, all charges that carry prison terms and the possibility of the death penalty. However, according to a report by the Committee to Protect Journalists, the government has not yet produced any evidence demonstrating convincingly that the work of these journalists was intended to incite violence or encourage ethnic tension or genocide. While the charges against some, such as a group of reporters who work for the U.S.-based Voice of America (VOA) service, were dropped in early 2006, at least 15 journalists remained jailed on these charges at year's end. Their trial began in February and could last for months or years, and meanwhile the accused are incarcerated, some in harsh conditions. Numerous other journalists fled the country to avoid arrest in late 2005 and remained in exile throughout 2006. Foreign journalists have generally operated with fewer restrictions than their local counterparts. However, they also faced official pressure during the year: In January, AP correspondent Anthony Mitchell was expelled for his reporting; and in February, another foreign reporter was denied accreditation. As a result of the crackdown, those journalists still able to work are increasingly practicing self-censorship on sensitive topics and face regular threats and harassment from authorities.

The state controls all broadcast media and operates the only television station. A 1999 law permits private radio stations, and although licenses were finally awarded to two private FM stations in the capital, Addis Ababa, in February, neither was operational by year's end. Dozens of print outlets publish regularly and offer diverse views, although many are firmly aligned with either the government or the opposition and provide slanted news coverage. Following the November 2005 crackdown, only a limited number of newspapers, including those English-language papers that are viewed as being relatively unbiased such as the *Reporter* and *Fortune*, were allowed to continue publishing without interruption. Authorities targeted the Amharic-language private press, banning or shuttering more than a dozen opposition-inclined papers that together accounted for more than 80 percent of total Amharic circulation. Fewer than 10 papers, most Amharic- or English-language weeklies with relatively small circulation figures, are now publishing in Addis Ababa compared with more than 20 in 2005. Most private newspapers struggle to remain financially viable and to meet Ministry of Information requirements that newspapers have a minimum bank balance in order to renew their annual publishing licenses. Printing presses are all government owned and frequently refuse to print some private publications, citing the fact that they are held accountable for the content of what they publish.

Access to foreign broadcasts is sometimes restricted, with VOA signals being sporadically jammed. Owing to an extremely poor telecommunications infrastructure, internet access is limited primarily to the major urban areas (less than 0.5 percent of the population) but is growing in popularity with the proliferation of internet cafés. As more citizens, faced with an increasingly restricted print and broadcast media environment, turned to the internet to get information, the government responded accordingly. Starting in 2006, access to some blogs and websites was blocked, including news websites run by members of the Ethiopian diaspora who were critical of the government. Internet journalist Frezer Negash was detained but not charged. Negash worked for the website Ethiopian Review and had previously been threatened by officials for her critical writing. By year's end, the state telecommunications agency distributed regulations requiring that internet cafés register their users and threatened to jail owners of cafés that served unregistered users.

Fiji

LEGAL ENVIRONMENT: 12
POLITICAL ENVIRONMENT: 19
ECONOMIC ENVIRONMENT: 8
Status: Partly Free   TOTAL SCORE: 39

Survey Edition	2002	2003	2004	2005	2006
Total Score, Status	33,PF	29,F	29,F	30,F	28,F

Status change explanation: Fiji's press freedom rating dropped from Free to Partly Free in 2006 owing to a government crackdown on the media following the military coup, during which time the bill of rights protecting press freedom was suspended.

Press freedom in the Fiji Islands suffered a major reversal in 2006. The country endured its fourth coup in almost two decades when military chief Commodore Voreqe Bainimarama formalized his "creeping putsch" on December 5, 2006, and ousted the democratically elected government of Laisenia Qarase's Soqosoqo Duavata ni Lewenivanua (SDL) party. While Bainimarama promoted an image of a bloodless and benign coup, the military commander had zero tolerance for media criticism.

The legal framework generally gives journalists considerable freedom as guaranteed by the 1997 constitution; however, the judiciary was in disarray and the status of the constitution unclear at the end of 2006. The bill of rights provisions under Section 187 (3) were suspended, including Section 30, which guarantees freedom of speech. Earlier, in August 2006 news media had condemned a draft broadcast licensing bill, saying it was an attempt to control news organizations. The bill provided for a government-appointed six-member Broadcasting Licensing Authority with powers related to programming and content. The authority would be empowered to fine broadcast companies FJ$500,000 (US$310,000) for "breaching" their licensing agreement or to revoke licenses.

Claiming his coup was a "cleanup" campaign against corruption and on behalf of all citizens in the multiracial Pacific country, Bainimarama quickly clamped down on media and other critics of his regime. On the day after the coup, December 6, he declared a state of emergency, and international press freedom organizations protested against this overt form of censorship. The leading national daily newspaper, the *Fiji Times,* as well as the smaller *Fiji Daily Post* temporarily closed publishing operations in the face of threats. The editor in chief of the *Daily Post,* Dr. Robert Wolfgramm, an Australian citizen, a Fijian native, and previously a strong critic of the military, was threatened with deportation when his paper refused to publish material in keeping with the demands of the coup leaders. Separately, after receiving instructions to broadcast only pro-coup material, Fiji 1, the national state-owned broadcaster, chose to temporarily shut down its transmission instead of comply with such orders. Throughout the coup, the news media continued to defy political pressures to censor their material.

In spite of the coup, the economic climate for independently owned media continued to prosper. The state-run Fiji Broadcasting Corporation operates three main radio stations in English, Fijian, and Hindustani; the state also runs three national newspapers. These compete with two private national newspapers, the *Fiji Times* and the *Fiji Sun,* as well as a privately owned FM broadcaster, Communications Fiji Ltd. The Fijian investment group Yasana Holdings holds a controlling 51 percent stake in Fiji TV, while the government owns 14 percent but plans to sell its stake. According to the U.S. State Department, the government has been known to direct advertising to media outlets in which it has a stake. In 2006, approximately 8 percent of the population was able to access the internet, which was not restricted during the coup.

LEGAL ENVIRONMENT: 2
POLITICAL ENVIRONMENT: 3

Finland

ECONOMIC ENVIRONMENT: 4

Status: Free

TOTAL SCORE: 9

Survey Edition	2002	2003	2004	2005	2006
Total Score, Status	10,F	10,F	9,F	9,F	9,F

Finland maintained its position as one of the most democratic countries in the world, with a government that generally respects freedom of the press in practice. Freedom of expression and access to information are guaranteed under Article 12 of the revised constitution, adopted in March 2000. There were no cases of defamation suits filed against journalists or media outlets during the year, nor were there any attacks on the press.

Finland has an impressive newspaper readership, ranking third in the world for circulation in relation to population. Two hundred newspapers are published, including 31 dailies, according to the Finnish Newspaper Association. The government provided grants for 15 Finnish newspapers and an additional 8 million euros (US$10.75 million) for political party presses in the autonomous territory of Aland. The majority of advertising subsidies was spent on print media in 2006. Media ownership is concentrated, with Alma Media and SanomaWSOY controlling most newspaper distribution. Broadcasting was once dominated by the public broadcaster Yleisradio OY and commercial MTV, but 2 new broadcasters have since emerged. Included in the 67 commercial radio stations are 3 national public stations in Finnish, 2 in Swedish, and 1 in the Sami (Lapp) language. The internet is open and unrestricted, and more than 62 percent of all citizens have regular access. However, web publications must name a responsible editor in chief and archive published materials for at least 21 days. In addition, Finnish law, which gives every citizen the right of reply and to have false published information corrected, includes internet publications.

LEGAL ENVIRONMENT: 5
POLITICAL ENVIRONMENT: 9

France

ECONOMIC ENVIRONMENT: 7

Status: Free

TOTAL SCORE: 21

Survey Edition	2002	2003	2004	2005	2006
Total Score, Status	17,F	17,F	19,F	20,F	21,F

The media environment remained free, but France continued to struggle to define the rights of journalists concerning confidential sources and court documents, as well as dealing with freedom of expression issues surrounding the country's growing Muslim population. The constitution and governing institutions support an open press environment. The law provides for freedom of speech and of the press, although a law adopted in October makes it a crime to deny the Armenian genocide. Freedom of information legislation exists, but it can be restricted to protect the reputation or rights of a third party, and the majority of requests are regularly denied.

Cases of formal questioning of journalists, searches of media premises, and the courts' tendency to put pressure on journalists to reveal their sources all continued to be prominent issues in 2006. In June, the minister of justice proposed that the protection of journalistic sources be written into the country's Press Law. However, less than a month later police raided the daily *Midi Libre* in order to obtain confidential information about a regional council; an official investigation was launched into the incident, but it remained open at year's end. Also in contravention of the government's promises to amend the Press Law, two reporters with the independent daily *L'Equipe* were formally placed under investigation for "helping to violate the confidentiality of a judicial investigation." The two journalists had originally published an investigative report concerning the alleged doping of a cycling team that the courts had been investigating in 2005. In addition, in late October the Office of the Public Prosecutor announced its intention to investigate Denis Robert, a former journalist with *Liberation*, for the "possession of confidential material" and libel of the finance house Clearstream. Robert, who is also the author of two investigative-reporting books on Clearstream implicating a number of high-ranking government officials of fraud, was found guilty of libel in December.

French courts have increasingly been applying Article 10 of the European Convention on Human Rights, which protects freedom of expression. In November, for example, charges were dropped against both a lawyer accused of revealing details of a judicial investigation into alleged corruption in school meal contracts and the journalist who had been accused of abetting him. In this case, the court disregarded Article 38 of the domestic Press Law, which states that "it is forbidden to publish indictments or any other criminal procedural document," and chose instead to refer to Article 10 of the convention. In July, also citing the convention, the Supreme Court struck down a judgment that convicted *Le Monde* journalists of racial defamation for a 2002 article criticizing Israel.

Cases of physical threats or harassment are rare. However, in February, after the daily *France-Soir* republished the Danish Muhammad cartoons that sparked an international furor, the paper became the victim of a bomb hoax and the editor in chief was forced to resign. Also, a high school philosophy teacher went into hiding after receiving death threats from radical Islamists because of an opinion piece he wrote in *Le Figaro* criticizing the prophet Muhammad.

Most of France's over 100 newspapers are privately owned and not linked to political parties; however, newspaper circulation continued to decline in 2006. After 2004's consolidation of the newspaper market, ownership is becoming more concentrated. Many media outlets are owned by companies with close ties to prominent politicians and the defense establishment, leading some to question potential conflicts of interest. In May, the prime minister called for increased investment in newspapers to maintain their financial viability as well as tax reductions for newspaper producers, also intended to help ease the financial burden. The government controls many of the firms that provide advertising revenue to media groups; it also provides direct and indirect subsidies, particularly to regional papers. The French broadcasting market continues to be dominated by TF1, although the growth of satellite and cable and the launch of digital terrestrial television in March 2005 have led to a proliferation of channels. This trend has been accentuated by the approval of the merger between two of the biggest satellite pay-TV operators, CanalSatellite and TPS. France abides by a European Union law that requires 60 percent of broadcast content to be of European origin. The internet is generally unrestricted and used by approximately 50 percent of the population. However, in 2006 a court decided to open an investigation against the editor of a left-wing website in response to a libel suit over a controversial union press release that he had posted. The case was unresolved at year's end, but if the court rules against the editor, the website may be forced to close.

Gabon

Status: Not Free

LEGAL ENVIRONMENT: 24
POLITICAL ENVIRONMENT: 23
ECONOMIC ENVIRONMENT: 22
TOTAL SCORE: 69

Survey Edition	2002	2003	2004	2005	2006
Total Score, Status	52,PF	58,PF	62,NF	66,NF	67,NF

The media environment remained restricted as the government continues to force journalists to choose between self-censorship and risking a ban in reprisal for being critical of government policies. The constitution guarantees freedom of expression and of the press, but authorities used legal harassment, threats, and financial pressure to curb critical reporting. While the imprisonment of journalists by the state is relatively rare, local media professionals face repressive press laws that allow for prison penalties for defamation—including a minimum sentence of three months for a repeat offense—particularly with regard to the president, his relatives, or members of his cabinet. In May, the independent website Gabonews commented that many journalists resort to self-censorship, as coverage of corruption or mismanagement within the government is seen as incitement to political upheaval.

A government agency charged with upholding journalistic standards, the National Communications Council (CNC), has a history of using intimidation tactics against the independent press and has forcibly shut down more than half a dozen publications in the last three years. At least three news outlets remain banned since 2003 for allegedly defaming the president and "attacking the dignity of the institutions of the Republic," among other charges. In June, the CNC lifted a ban imposed in December 2003 on the private bimonthly *L'Autre Journal*, though no reason was given publicly for the decision. However, in September the CNC banned the private weekly *Les Echos du Nord* for three months over an article criticizing the pro-government press for reports that several government officials had tried to sell a disputed offshore island to neighboring Equatorial Guinea. In October, the government arrested Norbert Mezui, director of the independent weekly *Nku'u Le Messager*, and held him for 21 days on the pretext of a three-year-old defamation verdict that was pending appeal. The arrest, which appeared to violate Gabonese procedural law, occurred after Mezui's newspaper ran a similar article criticizing the pro-government press over the scandal.

Gabon has over a dozen private radio stations and 4 private television stations, while as many as 20 private weeklies and monthlies circulate in the capital, Libreville. However, the state-affiliated *L'Union* is the country's only daily newspaper, and local journalists complain that many nominally private publications are controlled by political factions. Much of the private press appears irregularly because of financial constraints and frequent government censorship. Almost all Gabonese private newspapers are printed in Cameroon because of the high cost at the only local printing company, and publications printed outside the country are subject to review before distribution. The government owns two radio stations and two television stations that are able to broadcast nationwide. Private broadcasting tends to be nonpolitical. The government does not restrict access to, or use of, the internet for the 4.6 percent of the population wealthy enough to have access, and foreign publications and broadcasts are widely available.

The Gambia

LEGAL ENVIRONMENT: 24
POLITICAL ENVIRONMENT: 33
ECONOMIC ENVIRONMENT: 20

Status: Not Free

TOTAL SCORE: 77

Survey Edition	2002	2003	2004	2005	2006
Total Score, Status	65,NF	65,NF	63,NF	72,NF	73,NF

Conditions for media practice in The Gambia worsened in 2006 as President Yahya Jammeh swept into office for a third consecutive five-year term following elections in September 2006. Media practitioners were already operating under severe constraints ahead of national elections as Jammeh maintained an iron grip on the media despite a 1997 constitution that, in theory, guarantees freedom of expression. At the end of 2004, the Parliament passed two bills intended to impose harsh penalties on the media, including mandatory prison sentences of at least six months, for media owners or journalists convicted of publishing or broadcasting defamatory or seditious material or "false news." Jammeh signed these bills into law at the end of 2005. Following dissolution of a government-controlled media commission by Parliament in 2005, additional oppressive gag laws were passed making all press offenses punishable by imprisonment.

Jammeh's electoral victory did not signal the likelihood that he was willing to make any concessions for relaxing the restrictive media environment, his inauguration taking place on the second anniversary of the still unsolved murder of journalist Deyda Hydara. At the time of his murder, Hydara was managing editor of the private weekly *The Point* and a correspondent for both Reporters Sans Frontieres and Agence France-Presse. Asked about press freedom at a news conference following his election victory, Jammeh responded that the whole world could "go to hell," that he could ban any newspaper he wished to "with good reason," and that he wanted to rule The Gambia for at least three more decades. Jammeh showed in 2006 that his disdain for press freedom was backed by continuing intimidation, imprisonment, and exile of journalists and political opponents. Ten journalists were arrested in 2006, and many others fled into exile, joining those such as editor Alagi Yorrow Jallow, who, fearing reprisals, remained abroad. Prominent cases include those of Malick Mbob, a journalist of the pro-government *Daily Observer* who was detained illegally by the National Intelligence Agency for 139 days and then fired from his job after his release. He was one of five journalists arrested for sending damaging information to a U.S.-based online publication, *Freedom Newspaper*. Another reporter employed by the state-owned Gambia Radio Television Services, Doudou Sanneh, was freed and then fired after one week's detention by the National Intelligence Agency.

The government owns a daily newspaper, a national radio station, and the only national television station. Political news coverage at these outlets favors the official line. In the period leading up to the presidential election, the government did provide time slots for opposition candidates on the national television station, although the ruling Alliance for Patriotic Reorientation and Construction party received the most coverage. The Gambia has three private newspapers that publish biweekly or thrice weekly and four private FM radio stations. These outlets are subject to considerable pressure from the government, and faced considerable difficulty operating in 2006, but provide occasional critical coverage of the administration. A premium television network operates as a satellite station. The internet is not as tightly regulated, and over 3 percent of the population was able to access this growing medium in 2006, representing one of the highest rates of internet access in West Africa.

Georgia

Status: Partly Free

LEGAL ENVIRONMENT: 13
POLITICAL ENVIRONMENT: 27
ECONOMIC ENVIRONMENT: 17
TOTAL SCORE: 57

Survey Edition	2002	2003	2004	2005	2006
Total Score, Status	53,PF	54,PF	54,PF	56,PF	57,PF

The constitution and the Law on Freedom of Speech and Expression guarantee press freedom, but these rights were increasingly restricted by the government throughout 2006. The restrictions rarely took the form of direct pressure, although there were some reports of harassment and physical abuse of journalists by government officials. Instead, the government has failed to properly implement legislation, including freedom of information laws. The Georgian National Communications Commission in 2006 prepared a controversial draft broadcasting bill that in its original form would have made ethical standards, including a dress code and use of language, legally binding on journalists. The draft bill also required journalists to receive formal permission before airing live footage and limited journalists' ability to use anonymous sources. The vote on the bill was postponed until April 2007. If adopted, it would pose a serious threat to press freedom in Georgia.

While there is still a diverse range of media outlets in Georgia, including a number that criticize the government openly, media owners and managers continue to exert pressure on journalists in an effort to maintain amicable ties with the authorities. As a result, journalists frequently practice self-censorship. The government in turn remains particularly critical and intolerant of the media, leading to an overall decrease in media independence since the 2003 Rose Revolution. For example, Rustavi-2, formerly known as an independent and investigative television station, has become less critical and cut back its political programming. A Rustavi-2 talk-show host, Eka Khoperia, resigned on the air in July, citing government attempts to influence her treatment of a story concerning the implication of Ministry of the Interior employees in the murder of a bank official. In August, other Rustavi-2 staff staged a boycott and a strike to protest the reportedly political dismissal of the station's general director and the appointment of a government ally to replace him; several journalists resigned in September.

Separately, the Ministry of Defense continued its practice of banning critical journalists from public events. There were reports of harassment and violence against journalists, and a sense of impunity prevailed in the country, particularly with regard to crimes committed against journalists. Media freedom is legally guaranteed in the separatist regions of Abkhazia and South Ossetia, but the separatist authorities in both areas restricted media outlets and journalists.

The low profitability of media outlets, as well as their lack of economic independence, left them vulnerable to economic and political pressure in 2006; print publications were particularly at risk. Government officials have attempted to channel advertising away from critical independent outlets. Very few independent newspapers were commercially viable, and most papers depended on subsidies and patronage, but print media on the whole presented a diverse range of views. U.S.-based News Corporation became a majority owner of Imedi television in 2006, which was expected to increase the station's independence. The independent television station

202 suspended broadcasting in October after a 2005 extortion scandal damaged its reputation and income. There were no restrictions on internet usage, but the percentage of the population accessing this medium was low at 4 percent.

Germany

Status: Free

LEGAL ENVIRONMENT: 6
POLITICAL ENVIRONMENT: 6
ECONOMIC ENVIRONMENT: 4
TOTAL SCORE: 16

Survey Edition	2002	2003	2004	2005	2006
Total Score, Status	15,F	15,F	16,F	16,F	16,F

Germany's media remained free and vibrant in 2006, even as the country continued to battle over issues concerning access to information. The constitution guarantees freedom of expression and of the press, although there are exceptions for hate speech, Holocaust denial, and Nazi propaganda. Freedom of information legislation finally went into force in January 2006, containing numerous exemptions and requiring the payment of high fees in advance of every request. The press was critical of the government throughout the year and extensively covered Germany's alleged participation in or knowledge of the U.S. Central Intelligence Agency's detention and transfer of terrorist suspects. In October, the private newspaper *Bild* widely circulated pictures that appear to show German soldiers in Afghanistan posing with a skull, which initiated investigations into the incidents.

In March, journalist Bruno Schirra and the head of the foreign section of the Swiss weekly *SonntagsBlick*, Johannes von Dohnanyi, were charged with "complicity in divulging a state secret"; but their case has yet to go to trial. Schirra is alleged to have divulged information about the al-Qaeda network contained in a confidential German police report that was passed to him by von Dohnanyi. In 2005, the newsroom of *Cicero* magazine and Schirra's home were raided under the authorization of Interior Minister Otto Schily, who again cited "betraying state secrets" as the rationale. German journalists protested widely against the raid and there has not been a similar case in 2006.

In May, the German Parliament posted on its website part of a report revealing that the country's external intelligence service had been spying on journalists. The post was in reaction to the 2005 scandal involving journalists who were paid by the federal intelligence agency to spy on their colleagues. After singer Robbie Williams imposed restrictions on photographers while on tour, German media boycotted his concerts. In 2005, journalists were concerned about proposed restrictions on media coverage of the 2006 World Cup that included mandatory clearance checks on journalists before they could be accredited to report on matches from the stadium. But all of these restrictions were eventually lifted prior to the event. There were no attacks on the press in Germany in 2006.

The private media are diverse and independent. Each of the 16 regional governments is in charge of its own public radio and television broadcasters, and there are many private stations as well. The print press is dominated by numerous regional papers. Only a handful of national papers are published. A small number of centralized editorial offices control most content, and only a few commercial groups, which are some of the largest in the world, dominate the media market. The internet is open and largely unrestricted and was accessed regularly by over 60 percent of the population in 2006. However, German law bans internet access to the aforementioned prohibited material. Many search engines in Germany have subscribed to the Voluntary Self-Control for Multimedia Service Providers association, filtering websites based on a list created by Germany's Federal Department for Media Harmful to Young Persons.

Ghana

Status: Free

LEGAL ENVIRONMENT: 8
POLITICAL ENVIRONMENT: 9
ECONOMIC ENVIRONMENT: 9
TOTAL SCORE: 26

Survey Edition	2002	2003	2004	2005	2006
Total Score, Status	27,F	30,F	28,F	26,F	28,F

Ghana's press continued to be one of the freest in Africa in 2006. Freedom of the press is guaranteed by law, and the government has a reputation within the region for respecting it in practice. In recent years, President John Kufuor's administration has demonstrated its desire to expand freedom of expression by repealing criminal libel legislation. A subsequent spate of civil libel cases brought by former public officials and private citizens against media outlets with cripplingly high fines—often in excess of US$100,000—took the place of criminal defamation charges. Nonetheless, despite a number of new libel suits during the year, this trend abated slightly in 2006 as no new convictions were reported.

A proposal in Parliament for the establishment of a presidential commission for reforms that would strengthen the editorial independence and guarantee the funding of the Ghana Broadcasting Corporation (GBC) under an act of Parliament was unlikely to gain much traction. The proposal was made by Member of Parliament Haruna Idrissu, who argued that access to information leads to greater public transparency, accountability, and good governance. But the minister in charge of government sector reform responded that although reform was necessary at the GBC, there was no need for a presidential commission to do so and that such reforms could be addressed under the Subvented Agencies Law, which covers the GBC. Ghana has yet to pass legislation protecting freedom of information. A civil society initiative in 1997 brought the need for such a bill to the nation's attention, but neither the president nor the Parliament has taken any action as yet.

The press is generally free to function independently, with private newspapers and broadcasters operating without any significant restrictions. The environment includes a lively private press that often carries criticisms of the government. Animated phone-ins on local radio broadcasts are also a staple of daily life in Ghana. However, the Media Foundation of West Africa did report an increase in the number of cases of harassment against journalists by nonstate actors; 18 such cases were reported by the foundation in 2006. In particular, several journalists were targeted by supporters of drug barons on trial for large cocaine scandals, and a few other journalists were the victims of violent harassment at the hands of police officers while covering the news.

More than 135 newspapers, including 2 state-owned dailies, publish in Ghana, and approximately 110 FM radio stations function nationwide, 11 of which are state run; 27 television stations operate in Ghana. Opponents of the government complain of biased coverage in the state-owned press, but independent and critical reporting is pervasive in the private sector. Radio remains the most popular medium. Poor pay and unprofessional conduct, including newspapers that invent highly sensationalist news stories, remain problematic. The ethical lapses are condemned by professional media bodies because they undermine media credibility. Limited revenue from advertising and reader subscriptions threatens the financial viability of private media outlets. Foreign media presence is highly visible, most notably through broadcasts from the British Broadcasting Corporation, Radio France Internationale, and Voice of America. Access to the internet is available to less than 2 percent of the population, primarily through internet cafés, and remains unrestricted by the government.

Legal Environment: 8
Political Environment: 12
Greece
Economic Environment: 5

Status: Free   Total Score: 25

Survey Edition	2002	2003	2004	2005	2006
Total Score, Status	30,F	28,F	28,F	28,F	28,F

The media environment remained relatively free, although the details of the law leave holes in the protection of free speech. While the constitution purports to protect freedom of speech, there are some restrictions, including limits to speech that incites fear, violence, and disharmony among the population, as well as publications that offend religious beliefs, are obscene, or advocate the violent overthrow of the political system. Under a new Press Law, media companies are required to have registered shares held by individuals. The law, which also limits foreign ownership of Greek media, has been cited by the European Union for possible incompatibility with the provisions of the European Community Treaty dealing with the free movement of capital and freedom of establishment. Defamation remains a criminal offense under Greek law, but defendants have typically been released on bail and have not served time in jail. However, a number of journalists faced defamation charges throughout the year, including a journalist and cameraman with the private television channel Super B who were both sentenced to eight months in prison and a US$37,000 fine for interviewing an Albanian immigrant who was facing trial for drunk driving in a stolen vehicle. Unlike in previous years, there were no physical attacks on journalists during 2006.

There are many independent newspapers and magazines, including those that are critical of the government, and many broadcasters are privately owned. Greek law places limits on ownership of broadcast frequencies. The media, both public and private, are largely free from government restrictions, but state-owned stations tend to report along the official line. However, politically sensitive issues—such as the status of Macedonians and other ethnic minorities in the country—still provoke government pressure and lead to self-censorship. Broadcasting is largely unregulated, and many broadcast stations are not licensed. In June 2006, journalists working for the Greek public broadcasting service went on strike, demanding job security for colleagues working with short-term contracts. Internet access is not restricted by the government, but the proportion of the population that used this medium in 2006 (33 percent) was one of the lowest in

Western Europe. In February 2006, an internet artist who had created a satirical website about corruption in civil service hiring was arrested for internet fraud.

Grenada

LEGAL ENVIRONMENT: 8
POLITICAL ENVIRONMENT: 9
ECONOMIC ENVIRONMENT: 6

Status: Free

TOTAL SCORE: 23

Survey Edition	2002	2003	2004	2005	2006
Total Score, Status	16,F	14,F	16,F	20,F	23,F

Grenada's media situation remained free but legally fragile in 2006. Although freedom of the press is guaranteed by law, the government is accused of using both the threat of libel laws and its right to grant broadcast licenses to apply pressure on the media. One incident of particular concern during 2006 involved George Worme, editor of the *Grenada Today* newspaper. Worme—who has clashed with the authorities over libel issues in the past—was detained by police for several hours on March 14 in relation to a possibly libelous article published the previous month. No charges were made against him, but media freedom advocates claimed it was another indication of the ruling New National Party's efforts to limit media criticism. According to the U.S. State Department, in June the prime minister won a libel case he brought against the editor of a newspaper, and the editor was ordered to pay approximately US$37,000. On several occasions, members of the government publicly criticized the print media for running critical articles. At a meeting of the Media Workers Association of Grenada in June, the organization's president, Michael Bascombe, again complained that authorities' selection for granting radio licenses was guided by political considerations. Grenada has 5 television stations, 11 radio stations, 4 newspapers, and 5 periodicals. The government does not place restrictions on the internet, which was accessed by nearly 20 percent of the population in 2006.

LEGAL ENVIRONMENT: 17
POLITICAL ENVIRONMENT: 26
Guatemala
ECONOMIC ENVIRONMENT: 16
Status: Partly Free   TOTAL SCORE: 59

Survey Edition	2002	2003	2004	2005	2006
Total Score, Status	49,PF	58,PF	62,NF	58,PF	58,PF

Guatemalan journalists work under difficult conditions, threatened by rising violence from basic and organized crime as well as premeditated attacks on human rights workers and other critical voices, including independent journalists. In a positive step, in 2006 the government decriminalized press offenses, while the Constitutional Court declared that Articles 411 and 412 of the press code were unconstitutional. In its decision, the Court noted that those articles of the press code contradicted Article 35 of the Constitution, which ensures freedom of expression. However, reporters say that obtaining access to government information is difficult. Nine community radio stations were closed in 2006 for reportedly having no licenses, and some of the directors were arrested and detained briefly. According to Reporters Sans Frontieres, the closures were ordered by the Prosecutor's Office for Crimes Against Journalists and Unionists with the support of the Telecommunications Authority and the National Broadcast Commission.

While the situation is far better than during the country's protracted civil war, several attacks on journalists this year drew concern from international press advocates. The U.S. State Department reported that 67 incidents of intimidation of journalists were recorded in 2006, a significant rise over the reported 26 incidents in 2005. This included the murder of one journalist as well as the attempted assassination of another. The murder occurred in September when Eduardo Maas Bol, who worked for three different newspapers and radio stations, was shot outside the city of Coban. One possible suspect has been arrested in connection with the crime, and Maas Bol's journalism is still believed to be a possible motive. Separately, in August Vinicio Aguilar Mancilla, a presenter on Radio 10, survived an assassination attempt by two gunmen. Two other journalists received death threats, one during a live call-in radio show. Moreover, the Prosecutor's Office for Crimes Against Journalists and Unionists has solved only one case involving the killing of a journalist since it was created in 2001, adding to an atmosphere of impunity. These attacks seem linked to the general lack of guarantees for those denouncing abuses of all kinds. However, work linking police to extrajudicial killings reminiscent of the death squad era was especially dangerous. Advocates report that the psychological effect is taking its toll, leading to self-censorship.

Newspaper ownership is concentrated in the hands of business elites with centrist or conservative editorial stances, with one company—Prensa Libre—dominating the newspaper market, although facing two weaker national competitors. Electronic media ownership remained concentrated in the hands of Mexican Angel Gonzalez, a politically connected entrepreneur who favors conservative perspectives and holds a monopoly on national television. Only one cable newscast, with a professional (if somewhat cautious) staff, offers a contrasting viewpoint to this on-air news monopoly. In a nation where only 60 percent of the population can speak Spanish, the paucity of indigenous language programming is a severe constraint on freedom of expression and of the press. Indigenous languages are rarely heard in national media, and the government continued to repress independent community broadcasters in 2006. The resolution of their legal status was part of the 1996 peace accords but has not been addressed. There are no reports of government limitations on internet usage, although the internet is accessed by only approximately 8 percent of the population.

Guinea

Status: Not Free

LEGAL ENVIRONMENT: 22
POLITICAL ENVIRONMENT: 29
ECONOMIC ENVIRONMENT: 16
TOTAL SCORE: 67

Survey Edition	2002	2003	2004	2005	2006
Total Score, Status	74,NF	74,NF	71,NF	73,NF	67,NF

Overall, press freedom in Guinea remained largely unchanged in 2006, primarily because the aging regime of President Lansana Conte frequently resorted to old habits in launching reprisals against the press. But important qualitative changes did take place during the year. The constitution guarantees freedom of the press, but this right is not respected in practice and has been widely abused in the past, including through the enforcement of restrictive press legislation that considers defamation and slander criminal offenses and permits the authorities to censor publications. Although there were fewer arrests and detentions than in previous years, the government did suspend a number of publications. In 2005, President Conte signed a media liberalization decree that finally permitted the establishment of private radio and television broadcasting. The decree limited ownership by political parties and religious institutions but did not restrict programming on these subjects.

The number of attacks on the press diminished during the year, in large part because of the 2005 media liberalization decree. However, this concession to the press did not come without cost. Four separate newspapers were suspended by the Conseil National de la Communication (CNC) in 2006 for publishing excessively critical or contentious information. In February, the private bimonthly *Les Echos* was banned for two months for publishing allegedly false information about a government minister; in April, the biweekly independent *L'Enqueteur* was also suspended for two months for an article highlighting government corruption; and in October, the managing director of the state-owned and -published *Horoya* received an indefinite suspension after he refused to publish a picture of the president. Finally, in November the *Kalum Express*, a private weekly based in the capital, Conakry, also received a two-month suspension for publishing an editorial accusing the government of dishonesty in its dealings with a prominent businessman. The paper was accused of "damaging the reputation of the state"; the editor was forced into hiding and was later recalled and demoted to the rank of reporter. The independent journalist and respected newspaper editor Boubacar Yaccine Diallo now serves as chairman of the CNC. Following his appointment, Diallo initiated programs to increase professionalism in the practice of journalism and implemented a requirement that journalists must meet higher professional standards to obtain press credentials.

State-owned media provide extensive, mostly favorable coverage of the government but also criticize local-level officials and increasingly report on opposition activities. The liberalization of the airwaves in August 2005 has led to the emergence of privately owned radio broadcasters, with four private stations broadcasting alongside state-owned Radio Television Guinea (RTG). However, RTG is still the only television broadcaster. Within the private print media, newspapers openly criticize the president and the government. Ten private weekly newspapers publish in Conakry, while a dozen others publish sporadically. Last year, the government gave financial subsidies of around US$100,000 to private newspapers through the Guinea Association of Independent Editors, which divided the money among various press organizations. The government does not directly restrict access to the internet, although there was a previous case of reprisals against a journalist in response to an article he had published online about economic corruption. Less than 1 percent of the population had the financial means to access this new medium in 2006.

Guinea-Bissau

LEGAL ENVIRONMENT: 14
POLITICAL ENVIRONMENT: 19
ECONOMIC ENVIRONMENT: 15

Status: Partly Free

TOTAL SCORE: 48

Survey Edition	2002	2003	2004	2005	2006
Total Score, Status	56,PF	60,PF	63,NF	55,PF	47,PF

Recent gains in the legal and political environments for the media in Guinea-Bissau, following a 2005 law that provided for freedom of speech and of the press, appeared to be holding fast by the end of 2006. But the return to power of President Joao Bernado "Nino" Vieira, the former military ruler in exile, has been accompanied by economic and political crises that have both fractured the governing coalition and led to a number of troubling cases of press intimidation. The law currently provides for freedom of speech and of the press, but incidents in 2006 have hinted at an overall weakening in governmental respect for those rights.

Media practitioners have also occasionally been caught in the crossfire of partisan political wrangling. In November, the Media Foundation of West Africa reported that sympathizers of President Vieira besieged the privately owned radio station Bombolom FM and forced a reporter, Antonio Iaia Seidi, to disclose a source of information used in a report he had filed earlier. The angry group also forcibly broadcast a rejoinder to the story. In June, another Bombolom FM journalist was detained and severely beaten in custody after being accused of broadcasting "false news" for accusing a police officer of violence against a woman in one of his reports.

While the country's only television station remains state run, three private radio stations—Bombolom FM, Radio Pindjiguiti, and Voice of Quelele—compete with the state-run radio broadcaster, Radio Nacional, and the Portuguese-owned public broadcaster, RTP Africa. Three privately run newspapers operate alongside the state-owned weekly *No Pintcha*. Owing to considerable financial constraints and government control of the sole functioning printing house, newspapers publish only sporadically. The impact of such financial constraints has been particularly severe for the state-owned media because of a lack of government ability to earmark adequate operational funding, as well as the fact that private advertising funds are directed primarily toward the private media sector. No government interference with or attempts to censor the internet were reported in 2006, and the rate of access to this new medium was estimated to be just over 2 percent of the population.

LEGAL ENVIRONMENT: 7
POLITICAL ENVIRONMENT: 13
Guyana
ECONOMIC ENVIRONMENT: 9
Status: Free
TOTAL SCORE: 29

Survey Edition	2002	2003	2004	2005	2006
Total Score, Status	23,F	21,F	20,F	23,F	27,F

Guyana's media situation remained relatively open this year, despite several violent incidents involving media workers. The constitution provides for freedom of speech and of the press, and the media are generally allowed to operate without interference. Legislation to facilitate the distribution of private radio licenses has been promised but has not yet been introduced. Private media outlets experience great difficulty in persuading government officials to comment on issues, and instead of being granted interviews, journalists are referred to press releases issued by the Government Information Agency. There is no freedom of information legislation. An electoral campaign that culminated in the August reelection of the People's Progressive Party, led by President Bharrat Jagdeo, was free of the violence that has marred previous elections. Credit for this may in part be due to the creation and reasonably successful application of a code of conduct for media organizations covering the election campaign. The code was agreed upon by 14 media organizations at the start of the year.

However, two serious and deadly attacks on media workers during the year cast a cloud over the media scene. On January 30, Ronald Waddell, the 57-year-old host of a recently canceled television program, was shot dead at his home in a suburb of the capital, Georgetown. An active member of the opposition People's National Congress and a well-known campaigner for the rights of Guyanese of African descent, Waddell often criticized the government on his talk show on HBTV Channel 9. On August 8, five pressroom workers at the *Kaieteur News* printing plant were shot dead by a group of unidentified masked men. Following the arrests of some of the alleged attackers, it was suggested that the aim was to take guns from the plant's security guards. While the killings seem not to have been related to the newspaper's work, it created an environment of fear among media workers in the country. Representatives of media organizations called for heightened security for the press.

The government maintains a long-established radio monopoly and operates the country's only 2 radio stations. There are 23 television stations, 6 national newspapers (including the government-owned daily, the *Chronicle*), and 6 periodicals, all of which are allowed to operate freely. According to the U.S. State Department, in the month before elections, the government-run television and radio stations tripled the cost for political advertisements, effectively denying access to less well-funded opposition parties. There are 160,000 internet users in Guyana (18 percent of the population), and the government does not place any restrictions on its access.

Haiti

Status: Partly Free

LEGAL ENVIRONMENT: 16
POLITICAL ENVIRONMENT: 24
ECONOMIC ENVIRONMENT: 19
TOTAL SCORE: 59

Survey Edition	2002	2003	2004	2005	2006
Total Score, Status	72,NF	79,NF	79,NF	66,NF	68,NF

Status change explanation: Haiti's press freedom rating improved from Not Free to Partly Free as a result of improvements in the legal and political environments in which journalists operate, resulting from a new, more media-tolerant government elected in April and a reduction in overall political tensions.

After several years during which media freedom was severely compromised by the actions—often violent—of both state and nonstate actors, there was a welcome improvement in the media environment during 2006. Following elections in February and April, a new coalition government was formed, led by President Rene Preval and Prime Minister Jacques-Edouard Alexis. A subsequent reduction in political tensions and the new government's tolerance towards independent media were significant changes. Freedom of expression is safeguarded in Section C of the 1987 constitution, including protections against censorship and the right not to reveal sources. However, the persistence of a climate of impunity—particularly in the context of several murders of journalists—remains a serious obstacle to further improvement in the media environment. For example, there has been no progress with ongoing judicial investigations into the cases of Jean Dominique or Brignol Lindor, two journalists murdered in recent years. Throughout 2006, a new media rights organization, SOS Journalistes, was active in support of media workers and in trying to improve the quality of media coverage. The relaunch in August of the previously moribund

Syndicat National des Travailleurs de la Presse d'Haiti was another sign of an improving media situation.

Unlike in the previous six years, no journalists were killed in 2006 and there were few attacks on the media. However, many reporters remained too afraid to venture into certain parts of the capital, Port-au-Prince, where, after a lull of several months following the presidential election in February, armed clashes between gunmen and the authorities resumed. Simultaneously, a wave of kidnappings for ransom in and around Port-au-Prince posed a serious problem affecting all social sectors. A number of journalists were kidnapped, but there were no indications that they had been targeted specifically because of their profession. In September, a gang leader in the Solino neighborhood of the capital and one of the suspected murderers of journalist Jacques Roche, kidnapped and killed in July 2005, was handed over to the Haitian police after he turned himself in to UN troops and requested participation in a national disarmament and reinsertion campaign. However, no information about a trial or charges against him has been released.

Some of the main Port-au-Prince-based media houses—members of the Association Nationale des Medias Haitiens—continued to take a hostile editorial position with regard to the residents of certain shantytowns where support for the exiled Lavalas Family party leader Jean-Bertrand Aristide was believed to remain strong. However, the previously stark political divisions within the media community began to diminish during the year, and news coverage and analysis took on a more neutral tone. With the new government making notable efforts to provide greater access to information—particularly regarding the economy and development issues—the media as a whole, and the print media especially, were able to provide more detailed and informative news.

There are two newspapers published several times a week and four weeklies, all privately owned. Television Nationale d'Haiti is government owned, and there are several private stations, including Telemax, purchased by the Haitian-American music star Wyclef Jean in November 2005. The illiteracy rate is over 50 percent, making radio by far the most popular medium. More than 30 stations broadcast to the capital and surrounding areas, and scores more operate in the provinces. News coverage is heavily reliant on the output of foreign news agencies and a handful of the more powerful Port-au-Prince-based media outlets. There were no government restrictions on internet access, and usage has increased to just over 7 percent of the population. However, the illiteracy rate and the extent of poverty prevent the internet from being a widespread source of information.

Honduras

Status: Partly Free

LEGAL ENVIRONMENT: 15
POLITICAL ENVIRONMENT: 22
ECONOMIC ENVIRONMENT: 14
TOTAL SCORE: 51

Survey Edition	2002	2003	2004	2005	2006
Total Score, Status	43,PF	51,PF	52,PF	51,PF	52,PF

Freedom of speech and of the press are constitutionally protected; however, the government generally does not respect these rights in practice. Despite the fact that Honduras banned *desacato* (disrespect) or criminal defamation legislation aimed at protecting the honor of public officials, restrictive press laws are still often used to subpoena journalists for reporting on official corruption, drug trafficking, and human rights abuses. In a positive step, the Transparency and Access to Public Information Law was approved by Congress, but it will take effect only in 2008, when a new regulatory institution will be created. Local press freedom advocacy groups are still concerned about the effectiveness of the new law because it leaves open to interpretation the terms "national security" and "confidential information." The law also adds another ambiguous term, "secret information," and does not specify when such information can be made public. Nonetheless, for the first time in Honduras the new law also protects journalists from having to reveal their sources.

President Manuel Zelaya usually criticizes the media when he perceives news reports as being unfriendly to his government. He has accused journalists of exaggerating the government's mistakes and minimizing its accomplishments. During the year, journalists faced a number of legal prosecutions from political figures. On September 4, Ernesto Rojas, a reporter for Radio San Pedro, was sued by city council member Guillermo Villatoro Hall, while Francisco Romero, a reporter on the program "Hablemos de Noche de Honduras," was sued by Yansen Juarez, the national coordinator of programs and projects in the Ministry of Public Education. Both suits were considered to be on charges of harassment.

The number of threats and physical attacks against journalists diminished in 2006, but some incidents did occur, particularly following the publication of articles on organized crime or corruption. Among a number of other incidents, journalists Roberto Marin Garcia and Dina Meza of the website Revistazo.com, an online publication of the Association for a Fairer Society, were followed and hounded after revealing fraud and labor violations at security firm Delta Segurity. Liberal Party representative Romualdo Bueso

Melghem tried to strangle community journalist Martha Vasquez during a public meeting in April. Vasquez is a contributor for the website Indymedia. com. Separately in April, Wendy Guerra, host of the Santa Rosa de Copan city–based Channel 49 news program "Denuncias 49," was fired following political pressure felt by the station's manager, who is a member of the Liberal Party. In May, Guerra was rehired after a public outcry.

Honduras has around nine daily papers, including the popular *El Heraldo* and *El Tiempo*. There are six private television stations and five nationally broadcasting radio stations—one state owned and four independent. Although both print and broadcast outlets are predominantly privately owned, media ownership is concentrated in the hands of a few powerful business conglomerates with intersecting political and economic ties; this has led to self-censorship. Corruption among journalists also has an unfavorable impact on reporting. In addition, the government influences media coverage through bribes, the granting or denial of access to government officials, and selective placement of official advertisements. The government did not restrict access to the internet; however, less than 5 percent of the population used the internet in 2006.

Hong Kong

Status: Free

LEGAL ENVIRONMENT: 11
POLITICAL ENVIRONMENT: 11
ECONOMIC ENVIRONMENT: 8
TOTAL SCORE: 30

Survey Edition	2002	2003	2004	2005	2006
Total Score, Status	NA	NA	NA	28,F	29,F

Although freedom of expression is provided for under the law, press freedom continued to deteriorate in 2006 owing to legislative pressures and a perceived increase in self-censorship in the mass media. In March, the government introduced new regulations for covert surveillance in Hong Kong that would make it a criminal offense to trespass on private premises with the intention of obtaining personal information of individuals or to employ any sense-enhancing or recording devices in order to do so. The Hong Kong Journalists Association warned that these regulations could turn journalists into criminals and damage Hong Kong's reputation of a free press.

Outright attacks on the press are rare. In March, however, four men armed with hammers broke into the office of the *Epoch Times*, a newspaper known for criticizing the Chinese Communist Party and reporting on China's persecution of the outlawed Falun Gong movement. The intruders damaged computer and printing equipment but left without attacking the staff. In November, local journalists came under increased pressure to self-censor their reports from China after a Chinese court upheld a five-year jail term given to Hong Kong journalist Ching Cheong on charges of spying for Taiwan. Ching, the chief China correspondent for Singapore's *Straits Times* newspaper, was arrested in April 2005 during a visit to China's Guangdong province and charged with taking payoffs in exchange for gathering information for Taiwan. The Hong Kong government said it was concerned about the case but could not comment on the judgment handed down by the Beijing court under the "one country, two systems" policy that outlines China's relationship with Hong Kong. A survey conducted among local journalists found that about 58 percent think that press freedom in Hong Kong has deteriorated since the end of British rule in 1997 and that self-censorship is more prevalent now. About a third of the interviewed journalists also admitted to self-censorship in their work.

Despite widespread self-censorship, media remain outspoken, and political debate can be vigorous in the extremely diverse and partisan press. Hong Kong has 49 daily newspapers (including 23 in Chinese and 13 in English); 4 of them are funded by pro-Beijing interests and follow the Chinese Communist Party's lead on political and social issues. International media organizations operate freely in Hong Kong, and foreign reporters do not need government-issued identification to operate. In April, a government review of the public service broadcaster Radio Television Hong Kong (RTHK) prompted fears that RTHK could be turned into a government propaganda channel. The review highlighted RTHK's poor financial controls, management problems, and failure to comply with government rules and procedures. In the past, RTHK has come under pressure on several occasions for not defending or promoting government policies and for its coverage of Taiwan. The internet in Hong Kong remains free of censorship and is used by about 68 percent of the population, which represents a slight increase compared with 2005.

LEGAL ENVIRONMENT: 5
POLITICAL ENVIRONMENT: 8
Hungary
ECONOMIC ENVIRONMENT: 8
Status: Free
TOTAL SCORE: 21

Survey Edition	2002	2003	2004	2005	2006
Total Score, Status	23,F	23,F	20,F	21,F	21,F

Hungary's constitution protects freedom of speech and of the press, and a wide selection of competitive media outlets generally operate without interference from the state. However, the Media Law of 1996 has been widely criticized, partly because it has not facilitated the much-needed transformation of the public service media. Instead, it has reinforced entrenched interests and institutionalized political interference, including in political and civic appointments to oversight bodies. In one step forward in August 2006, the board of Hungarian public radio elected a new president, filling a position that had been in dispute for about two years. Libel remains a criminal offense, and the criminal code holds journalists responsible not only for their own words, but for publicizing libelous statements made by others. State secrecy legislation has also raised press freedom concerns. Rita Csik, a journalist for the daily *Nepszava*, had been acquitted of state secrecy violations in 2005. The government appealed, but a higher court upheld the verdict in May 2006.

Attacks on the press in Hungary are rare, but in September 2006, after several nights of heated protests calling for the resignation of Prime Minister Ferenc Gyurcsany over his admission that he had lied for more than a year about Hungary's economic state, protesters broke into public broadcaster Magyar Televizio and forced it off the air. It was reported that the protesters were trying to broadcast their own message.

The media landscape is dominated by private companies, with high levels of foreign investment in both national and local newspapers. Independent news outlets operate freely in Hungary, though they clearly reflect the divisions of the national political scene. Diversity is on the rise in both print and electronic media. The internet is widely accessible, was used by over 30 percent of the population in 2006, and has been governed by a voluntary code of conduct introduced by a professional association of internet content and service providers.

LEGAL ENVIRONMENT: 1
POLITICAL ENVIRONMENT: 4

Iceland

ECONOMIC ENVIRONMENT: 4

Status: Free

TOTAL SCORE: 9

Survey Edition	2002	2003	2004	2005	2006
Total Score, Status	8,F	8,F	8,F	9,F	9,F

Freedom of the press and of expression are protected under Article 72 of the constitution, and the government generally does not interfere in the independent media's expression of a wide variety of views. There are limitations to these rights, including fines or imprisonment for people who belittle the doctrines of officially recognized religious groups. Additionally, people may face fines and up to two years' imprisonment for assaults against race, religion, nationality, or sexual orientation.

In January 2006, Gisli Hjartarson took his own life after *DV*, an Icelandic tabloid paper, printed a photograph and ran a cover story accusing him of sexually abusing teenage boys. As a direct result, members of Parliament proposed a bill to increase damages in libel cases. Public outrage and certain shareholders have pushed for the tabloid's closure, and in April its circulation was reduced to weekends only.

A wide range of publications includes both independent and party-affiliated newspapers. An autonomous board of directors oversees the Icelandic National Broadcasting Service (RUV), which runs radio and television stations funded by both a license fee and advertising revenue. According to the British Broadcasting Corporation, RUV is obliged to promote Icelandic history, culture, and language. In 2006, RUV switched from being a state-owned institution to a public limited company in an attempt to strengthen its autonomy. Media concentration is a concern in Iceland, with the company 365 controlling much of television and radio broadcasting as well as one of the major national newspapers and several magazines. A media concentration bill, reintroduced during the summer of 2006 (though still pending at year's end), caps ownership at 25 percent for individuals who own shares in companies that control more than one-third of media markets. In 2006, 87 percent of the country's population was reported to use the internet, which is unrestricted by the government.

India
Status: Partly Free

LEGAL ENVIRONMENT: 9
POLITICAL ENVIRONMENT: 16
ECONOMIC ENVIRONMENT: 10
TOTAL SCORE: 35

Survey Edition	2002	2003	2004	2005	2006
Total Score, Status	42,PF	45,PF	41,PF	38,PF	37,PF

India's media continue to be vigorous and are by far the freest in South Asia, although journalists face a number of constraints. The constitution provides for freedom of speech and of expression, and although there are some legal limitations, these rights are generally upheld. In recent years, the government has occasionally used its power under the Official Secrets Act to censor security-related articles or prosecute members of the press, but no cases were reported during 2006. State and national governments have also on occasion used other security laws, contempt of court charges, and criminal defamation legislation to curb the media and other critical voices. A Right to Information Law was passed in May 2005. The Press Council of India, an independent body composed of journalists, publishers, and politicians, serves as a self-regulatory mechanism for the print press through its investigations of complaints of misconduct or irresponsible reporting. In June, the International Federation of Journalists expressed concern regarding a proposed broadcasting services regulation bill that would give the government greater power over the media, restrict media cross-ownership, and introduce greater content regulation for news channels.

Intimidation of journalists by a variety of actors continues; on a number of occasions during 2006, reporters were attacked by police or others while attempting to cover the news, and others were abducted or threatened by right-wing groups, insurgents, local-level officials, or criminals. Members of the press are particularly vulnerable in rural areas and insurgency-racked states such as Chhattisgarh, Kashmir, Assam, and Manipur. Two journalists were killed, including Prahlad Goala, a young journalist apparently murdered in Assam after writing a series of articles accusing a forest warden of misconduct and corruption. Conditions are particularly difficult in the state of Jammu and Kashmir, where the fact that militants routinely issue death threats against local media personnel has led to significant levels of self-censorship. In May, the main cable TV operator withdrew some programming after threats from insurgents. Pressure to self-censor has also been reported at smaller media outlets that rely on state government advertising for the majority of their revenue. In late November, a journalist and his wife were arrested and detained, accused of harboring insurgents; police refused to release his wife even when ordered to by a judge. Photojournalist Maqbool Sahil has been detained since September 2004 under the Public Safety Act despite October 2005 and August 2006 high court decisions calling for his release.

Most print media, particularly the national and English-language press, are privately owned, provide diverse coverage, and frequently scrutinize the government. The broadcast media are predominantly in private hands, but the state retains a monopoly on AM radio broadcasting, and private FM radio stations are not allowed to broadcast news content. In November, the government announced a new policy designed to legitimize community radio and enable nonprofit groups and others to apply for station licenses. Doordarshan, the state-controlled television station, has been accused of manipulating the news to favor the government, and some private satellite TV channels also provide slanted coverage that reflects the political affiliation of their owners, according to the U.S. State Department. Foreign media are allowed to operate freely. Internet access is unrestricted, although some states have proposed legislation that would require the registration of customers at internet cafés, and the government retains the right to censor the internet, particularly on the grounds of morality or national security. Following the Mumbai train bombings of July 2006, an official attempt to block several controversial web pages led inadvertently to a temporary ban on access to thousands of blogs. The internet was accessed by only 3.5 percent of the population during the year.

Indonesia

Status: Partly Free

LEGAL ENVIRONMENT: 17
POLITICAL ENVIRONMENT: 22
ECONOMIC ENVIRONMENT: 15
TOTAL SCORE: 54

Survey Edition	2002	2003	2004	2005	2006
Total Score, Status	53,PF	56,PF	55,PF	58,PF	58,PF

The media landscape saw both positive and negative turns in 2006, with certain gains in the legal environment and setbacks in the rising number of attacks against journalists. The legal environment for the press improved owing to several important court decisions that signaled what the *Jakarta Post* daily called "a seismic shift in the Indonesian judiciary." On February 9, the Supreme Court unanimously overturned the criminal defamation conviction and one-year prison sentence of *Tempo* magazine chief editor Bambang Harymurti, stating that the 1999 Press Law rather than the penal code should be used in defamation cases. The editor had been convicted of defaming Tomy Winata in a March 2003 article that linked the business tycoon to a suspicious fire in the Tanah Abang textile market. In September, a south Jakarta district court similarly agreed to use the Press Law when *Rakyat Merdeka* editor Teguh Santosa was charged with insulting Islam and the prophet Muhammad. Later, presiding Judge Wahyono dismissed charges against the editor, who had posted three of the controversial Danish cartoons on the newspaper's website. The judge stated that "what the defendant did was not based on disrespect. The pictures only appeared as background to the news." Despite these developments, the question of whether the 1999 Press Law should be used as a special law, or *lex specialis,* in cases involving the press remained up in the air, with outcomes seeming to depend largely upon the educational background of the presiding judge. At the end of 2006, at least four defamation cases were still being tried under the penal code. On December 6, 2006, the Indonesian Constitutional Court made a landmark ruling that declared as unconstitutional the articles of the penal code (134, 136, and 137) that criminalize the dissemination of insults against the president and vice president of Indonesia. The Court ruled that these articles violated Indonesia's 1945 constitution, which guarantees freedom of "verbal and written expression." Nevertheless, a new draft penal code now under consideration contains 49 articles pertaining to defamation, including criminal penalties for libel, insulting public authorities and state institutions, disseminating news that could lead to social disorder, leaking state secrets, and spreading Communism or Marxism-Leninism.

New regulations came into effect in February that prevent the direct relay of foreign broadcast content by local private radio and television stations, confining them to shortwave radio and cable television networks. The regulations were greeted with considerable protest from those who argued that Indonesians' access to news and information would be severely limited. An article that transferred the power to issue broadcasting licenses from the independent National Broadcasting Commission to the Ministry of Communications and Information likewise raised concerns that the process of obtaining licenses would become politicized.

Violence against journalists continued to be an issue in 2006. In April, supporters of the political party Golkar attacked striking *Timika Pos* journalists in West Papua. That same month, freelance journalist Herliyanto was found dead of stab wounds in East Java, his camera and notebook stolen. Local police officials said that Herliyanto's murder was directly related to a newspaper report concerning official corruption in a nearby bridge project. The April launch of the Indonesian version of *Playboy* magazine sparked intimidation and threats of physical violence against the magazine's Jakarta office, as well as acts of vigilantism in other Indonesian cities. Rightist Islamic elements demanded the banning of the magazine. Although the magazine contains no nudity, the magazine's editor, Erwin Arnada, was charged with indecency. If convicted, he could face 32 months in prison.

The Indonesian government continued to ban foreign journalists from entering West Papua. Defense Minister Juwono Sudarsono explained that their presence would "encourage Papuans to campaign on issues of human rights." In September, five Australian television journalists were expelled from Papua for traveling on tourist visas. In April, U.S. journalist William Nesson, who had written about the war in Aceh from the rebels' perspective, was denied entry into Indonesia on the grounds that his reports were "hostile to Indonesia."

Indonesia is home to a large independent media generally able to provide a wide variety of opinions and perspectives. The broadcast market includes some 60 private radio stations in the Jakarta area alone and 10 private television networks nationwide that operate in competition with the public Televisi Republik Indonesia. Strict licensing laws have created more than 2,000 illegal television and radio stations that operate on a regular basis without a license. In a countrywide survey, half of the journalists questioned revealed that their salaries were too low to cover basic living costs, as more than 60 percent of journalists earn less than US$200 a month. Internet access is on the rise, used by over 8 percent of the population, and there are no reported government restrictions on its access.

LEGAL ENVIRONMENT: 29
POLITICAL ENVIRONMENT: 34

Iran

ECONOMIC ENVIRONMENT: 21

Status: Not Free

TOTAL SCORE: 84

Survey Edition	2002	2003	2004	2005	2006
Total Score, Status	75,NF	76,NF	79,NF	80,NF	84,NF

Press freedom continued to deteriorate in 2006 as the regime's conservative leaders cracked down on critical publications and journalists through arrests, detentions, closures, and the establishment of new restrictions on internet media. At the same time, a striking contrast has emerged between government efforts to restrict information and the public's efforts and ability to access it, particularly through satellite and other foreign broadcasts that remain beyond government control.

The constitution provides for limited freedom of opinion and of the press. While it protects individuals from punishment for holding a certain belief, Article 24 of the charter, along with the vaguely worded 2000 Press Law, forbids the publication of ideas that are contrary to Islamic principles or detrimental to public rights. The government regularly invokes vaguely worded legislation to criminalize critical opinions, and punishments for violations are harsh. Article 500 of the penal code states that "anyone who undertakes any form of propaganda against the state...will be sentenced to between three months and one year in prison"; the code leaves "propaganda" undefined. Under Article 513, offenses deemed to be an "insult to religion" can be punished by death or by prison terms of one to five years for lesser offences, with "insult" similarly undefined. Other articles provide sentences of up to two years in prison, up to 74 lashes, or a fine for those convicted of intentionally creating "anxiety and unease in the public's mind," spreading "false rumors," writing about "acts that are not true," or criticizing state officials. Iran's judiciary frequently denies accused journalists due process by referring their cases to the Islamic Revolutionary Court, an emergency venue intended for those suspected of seeking to overthrow the regime. The Preventive Restraint Act is used regularly to temporarily ban publications without legal proceedings.

Critical journalists are deterred by a range of obstacles in the legal system. Charges against journalists, bloggers, editors, and publications are often arbitrary; prosecutions, trial dates, and sentences are delayed; and bail sums for provisional release while awaiting trial are substantial. Although fewer journalists are imprisoned today than in the past, laws prohibit editors and publishers from hiring journalists who have previously been sentenced, and imprisoned journalists have complained of solitary confinement and torture.

In 2006, many of those targeted by the Office of the Supreme Leader and the Iranian judiciary, led by Tehran prosecutor general Saeed Mortazavi, were well-known for their critical stance toward the government or advocacy of human rights and freedom of expression. In one of the year's more prominent cases, reformist intellectual and journalist Ramin Jahanbeglo was arrested in April, presumably in response to an article in which he challenged President Mahmoud Ahmadinejad's denial of the Holocaust. Jahanbeglo was held in Tehran's Evin prison without charge until his release in August. In July, the minister of intelligence accused Jahanbeglo of "taking part in a U.S. attempt to carry out a velvet revolution in Iran," prompting rights groups to view the case as the beginning of an intensified crackdown. Later that month, Hassan Hadad, a judge with a record of prosecuting journalists and personally torturing prisoners at Evin prison, was made deputy prosecutor for security issues. He was assigned the task of "forcefully cracking down on threats to overthrow the regime." In a more positive development, Akbar Ganji, a well-known writer sentenced in 2001 to six years in prison for "spreading propaganda" and "collecting confidential state documents to jeopardize state security," was released in March.

The government has forcibly closed or banned more than 100 publications since 2000. This trend continued in 2006, with a particular focus on critical media outlets. The most significant closure of the year occurred in September, when the *Sharq* daily, Iran's most prominent and last remaining reformist newspaper, was shuttered for failing to heed Ministry of Islamic Culture and Guidance (MICG) orders to replace its managing director. The director had been charged with more than 70 wide-ranging violations immediately after the paper ran a satirical report on the president. *Sharq* had previously come under pressure from the authorities for its editorial stance and particularly for criticizing the rulings of the Supreme National Security Council, which oversaw Iran's nuclear negotiations with the international community. Another daily, *Rouzegar*, was banned in October after taking in many former *Sharq* staff members.

The government continued to intimidate and harass journalists who covered ethnic minority issues in the country, where the dominant Persian ethnic group make up just over half of the population of roughly 70 million. In May, the MICG invoked Article 12 of the Press Law to close *Iran Friday*, a state paper, and arrest an editor and a cartoonist for "fomenting discord" by publishing a cartoon deemed insulting to the Azeri minority; Azeris make up about a quarter of the population. The editor was ultimately acquitted and the cartoonist fined, and the ban on the paper was lifted in September; it has since published under a largely new staff. In December, one of Iran's leading ayatollahs, Fazel Lankarani, issued a fatwa calling for the death of an Azeri journalist and his editor after the publication of an article claiming that European values were superior to those of Muslim countries.

The country's numerous legal restrictions and successive closings and arrests make self-censorship common. However, critical reporting was particularly prevalent in 2006 before and after the elections for the

Assembly of Experts and municipal governments in December. Criticism of the government among the hard-line and conservative press increased notably following the poor electoral performance of Ahmadinejad's allies, with some publications questioning the president's stance on the nuclear issue. Some observers attribute this development to a growing rift between Ahmadinejad and Supreme Leader Ali Khamenei.

Iran is home to more than 20 daily newspapers, though most Iranians do not read newspapers on a regular basis. The most widely distributed paper is the government-supported *Keyhan*, with a circulation of 350,000. More than 80 percent of residents receive their news from television, and the government directly maintains a monopoly over all domestic broadcast media, which present only official political and religious viewpoints. The Islamic Republic News Agency is the chief supplier of news to radio, television, print, and internet media. It falls under the authority of the MICG, headed by Mohammed-Hossein Saffar-Harandi, a former *Keyhan* employee with a long history of cracking down on the reformist press.

Although satellite dishes that receive foreign broadcasts are forbidden, an increasing number of people own them, allowing many of Iran's more prosperous city dwellers to access international news sources. Satellite radio allows a larger portion of the population to hear international broadcasts. Radio Farda, a joint initiative of Radio Free Europe/Radio Liberty and Voice of America, broadcasts news twice an hour, seven days a week, along with popular Persian and Western music, in an effort to reach Iran's growing youth population. According to *The Washington Post*, a survey conducted in 2006 found that roughly 13.6 percent of the adult population listened to Radio Farda each week.

Internet usage continues to increase, with more than seven million Iranians able to access the internet in 2006, but the press freedom watchdog Article 19 maintains that the government's heightened online censorship campaign has left fewer citizens willing to challenge the status quo. Still, websites continue to express opinions that the country's print media would never carry. Moreover, the internet provides a forum for political debate, with both conservatives and reform advocates using it to promote their political agendas. The internet has also provided a key platform for international initiatives—such as Article 19's Persianimpediment.org, Freedom House's *Gozaar*, and *Rooz Online*—to promote freedom of expression and inform the Iranian public on human rights issues.

Iran has roughly 100,000 bloggers, most of whom oppose the regime and publish anonymously to avoid detection, reflecting the extent to which journalists and dissidents have turned to the internet in the last several years in an effort to circumvent official control. The judiciary began targeting online journalists, bloggers, and technical support staff in 2004, and all of those detained in 2004 and 2005 were held in solitary confinement at a secret detention center, subjected to torture, and denied access to lawyers and medical care. Most of those imprisoned in 2004 were released in 2005. In January 2006, Arash Sigarchi, a blogger who campaigned actively for the promotion of diverse viewpoints through internet journalism, was sentenced to three years in prison for "insulting the Supreme Guide" and publishing "propaganda against the regime." A number of other online activists received jail sentences for critical writings during the year.

There was a hike in internet filtering in the name of morality over the summer, followed by a series of new restrictions aimed at preserving Islamic culture, especially for Iran's younger generation, according to Great Britain's *Guardian* newspaper. Sites dealing with the condition of women were targeted in particular. According to Information and Technology, the company responsible for internet filtering, 90 percent of filtered sites are proscribed owing to immoral character, and 1,000 new online publications are added to the blacklist each month. Public use of high-speed internet connections was banned in October, and a cabinet decision in November ordered all websites dealing with Iran to register with the authorities. The decision also officially outlawed all sites that insulted Islam and monotheism in general, disseminated separatist ideologies, published false information, or threatened individual privacy. While the registration of the country's tens of thousands of websites would be difficult to implement, the new edict established an ominous legal pretext for arbitrarily banning more sites. YouTube, *The New York Times* website, and the English version of Wikipedia were all blacklisted in December.

Iraq
Status: Not Free

LEGAL ENVIRONMENT: 22
POLITICAL ENVIRONMENT: 32
ECONOMIC ENVIRONMENT: 16
TOTAL SCORE: 70

Survey Edition	2002	2003	2004	2005	2006
Total Score, Status	96,NF	95,NF	66,NF	70,NF	71,NF

Restrictions on the press took fresh forms in 2006 as the new Iraqi government for the first time took action against reporters. The 2005 constitution outlines a legal framework concerning the activities of the press, including provisions guaranteeing freedom of the press and of expression "in a way that does not violate public order or morality," according to Article 38. In addition, Articles 101 and 102 outline a financially and administratively independent National Communications and Media Commission. However, like many other articles in the constitution, they do not specify the commission's mandate or define the implementation of regulations and legislation. Legal analysts have noted that some archaic laws dating from Saddam Hussein's rule remain on the books, including restrictive insult, antidefamation, and state secrecy legislation.

In 2006, authorities imposed restrictions on the media that could endanger news diversity. Iraqi security forces detained at least 30 journalists over the course of the year, with 4 still held without charge at year's end. Moreover, the U.S. military arrested 8 media workers; 4 were still in custody at the end of the year. Prime Minister Nuri al-Maliki's government threatened to close media outlets for "inciting violence," and television stations were banned from showing violent footage of events within Iraq. In November, the government shut down two television stations, Al-Zawra and Salah al-Din, for showing footage of Iraqis protesting Saddam Hussein's death sentence. Neither had been allowed back on the air at year's end. The Ministry of the Interior established a monitoring unit tasked with requesting that journalists broadcast corrections of "false news." Local and regional officials have been particularly aggressive in bringing charges against critical journalists. In January, the Kurdish regional government upheld a 30-year prison sentence for Kamal Sayid Qadir, who was charged with defaming public institutions. Two editors and a journalist for the Kurdish weekly *Hawlati* were also charged with defamation in May following an article critical of Kurdish political parties. The government placed restrictions on foreign media as well; in October, authorities briefly closed the Baghdad bureau of satellite news channel Al-Arabiya for inciting "sectarianism" and "violence," and Al-Jazeera's Baghdad bureau remained shuttered after it was forced to close in 2004. In 2005, it was revealed that the U.S. Department of Defense (DOD) had hired a public relations firm to place stories with media outlets in Iraq that were written by U.S. military officers and depicted conditions in the country in a favorable light. In December 2006, during an internal investigation, the DOD concluded that the program had been legal under the rules of psychological warfare. However, the United States faced criticism from international watchdog groups for trying to manipulate press coverage and spread propaganda in the Iraqi media.

Ongoing instability and violence remain the biggest threats to press freedom, with Iraqi insurgent groups conducting targeted kidnappings and attacks on the media. According to the International Press Institute, 46 journalists and media workers were confirmed killed in 2006; 44 of them were Iraqi nationals, and many were killed in deliberate attacks. Reporters Sans Frontieres reported that armed groups kidnapped 20 media workers and executed 7. Gunmen in the Adil neighborhood of Baghdad kidnapped U.S. journalist Jill Carroll on January 7 and released her three months later. The fate of two Iraqi reporters, Reem Zaid and her colleague Marwan Khazal of Al-Somariyah TV, was still unknown at the end of 2006. Armed groups have targeted local journalists who work with foreign media and have accused them of being spies. Self-censorship increased as a result of intimidation from violent groups, including sectarian militias. Much of the violence against journalists in 2006 occurred during the last months of the year, as hostilities among insurgent groups increased significantly. In the deadliest incident of 2006, gunmen raided the offices of the radio station Al-Shaabiya in October, killing six journalists and four guards. The station, owned by the National and Justice Party, was created in July but had yet to broadcast.

Iraq has more than 100 daily and weekly publications, and dozens of new private television and radio channels have emerged throughout the country. The financial viability of these outlets is severely threatened by the security situation. Nearly all media outlets are privately owned and operated, but most of them are affiliated with ethnic, sectarian, or partisan groups. Access to foreign satellite television, previously banned in all of Iraq under Saddam Hussein (except in the northern Kurdish regions since 1991), grew in 2006. Satellite stations are watched by around 70 percent of Iraqi viewers; the Pan-Arab news stations Al-Arabiya and Al-Jazeera are especially popular. Iran's Alalam TV, which broadcasts in Arabic, can be received in Baghdad without a satellite dish. Internet usage also increased during the year to 36,000 users (less than 1 percent of the population), with many internet cafés opening up in Iraqi cities and no direct government restriction on access to, or operation of, the internet.

Ireland

LEGAL ENVIRONMENT: 4
POLITICAL ENVIRONMENT: 7
ECONOMIC ENVIRONMENT: 5

Status: Free

TOTAL SCORE: 16

Survey Edition	2002	2003	2004	2005	2006
Total Score, Status	16,F	16,F	16,F	15,F	15,F

Press freedom is constitutionally guaranteed and generally respected in practice. Archaic defamation laws are still in place under which journalists remain guilty until proven innocent, but a new defamation bill was introduced at the end of 2006, following a growing movement to enact new media legislation. The bill decriminalizes most forms of defamation and will bring Irish laws into closer conformance with international standards. However, the bill has drawn criticism for a clause criminalizing the publication of "gravely harmful sentiments" and allowing summary convictions for "minor" transgressions. The proposed law incorporates a proposal for a press ombudsman and a press council—an independent watchdog that will deal with public complaints and regulate the media under a new code of conduct covering areas such as accuracy, fairness, privacy, and incitement to hatred. The bill further introduces the defense of "reasonable publication," under which journalists will not be held liable for a statement—even if it is subsequently proven to be false—if they acted in accordance with professional ethics and public interest justified publication. A new privacy bill was introduced alongside the defamation legislation but was met with less enthusiasm by both the press and the government. Journalists argued that overly broad clauses in the proposed law could allow everyday journalistic activity, such as telephone calls, e-mails, and approaches to sources, to lead to allegations of harassment and trespass. Some speculated that the law was proposed to counterbalance the more liberal defamation bill. Both bills were under discussion at year's end.

In late 2006, *Irish Times* editor Geraldine Kennedy and senior correspondent Colm Keena were accused of publishing classified information in an article disclosing details of the investigation of Bertie Ahern by the Mahon tribunal, a government anticorruption body. Following their indictment, the journalists destroyed all relevant documents in order to protect their source. In November, the tribunal announced plans to obtain an order from the high court forcing Kennedy and Keena to reveal their sources or face up to two years in prison or a US$300,000 fine. In November, multimillionaire Denis O'Brien was awarded US$990,000 in damages from the Mirror Newspaper Group, the highest award in Irish history for a defamation suit. In 1998, the *Irish Mirror* had alleged that O'Brien had paid former minister of communications Ray Burke US$60,000 to secure a radio broadcasting license for 98FM radio station— an allegation the newspaper later admitted was false.

The national public broadcaster, Radio Telefis Eireann, dominates the radio and television sectors, but the growth of cable and satellite has begun to weaken the state broadcaster's monopoly over the industry.

According to the U.S. State Department, there were 54 independent radio stations and 2 independent television stations operating during the year. British public and private television offers the main competition to Irish programming. According to the British Broadcasting Corporation, cross-media ownership is permitted within limits—press groups may own no more than 25 percent of local television and radio. Newspapers were dominated by the Independent News and Media Group, though diversity in views and political affiliations were seen across the multitude of dailies and weeklies produced in 2006. Internet access is unrestricted by the government, and 50 percent of Irish citizens use the internet regularly.

Israel

LEGAL ENVIRONMENT: 6
POLITICAL ENVIRONMENT: 13
ECONOMIC ENVIRONMENT: 10

Status: Free

TOTAL SCORE: 29

Survey Edition	2002	2003	2004	2005	2006
Total Score, Status	30,F	27,F	28,F	28,F	28,F

Press freedom is generally respected in Israel, and the country features a vibrant media landscape. Journalists are occasionally subject to official restrictions, but an independent judiciary and an active civil society adequately protect the free media. Hate speech and publishing praise of violence are prohibited, and the 1948 Prevention of Terrorism Ordinance prohibits expressions of support for terrorist organizations or groups that call for the destruction of Israel. In 2004, the Supreme Court denied a government appeal seeking to uphold a ban on granting press credentials to Palestinians. Israel's Government Press Office (GPO) had earlier ceased issuing press cards to Palestinians on security grounds, claiming that some Palestinians posing as journalists used the cards to enter Israel and carry out or abet terrorist attacks. Israeli press freedom organizations have since accused the GPO of continuing to restrict press credentials for Palestinians.

While newspaper and magazine articles on security matters are subject to a military censor, the scope of permissible reporting is wide and there is a broad range of published material. Editors may appeal a censorship decision to a three-member tribunal that includes two civilians, and publications cannot be shuttered because of censorship violations. Arabic-language publications are censored more frequently than those in Hebrew, and Arab-Israeli journalists are subject to greater restrictions than their Jewish counterparts. In 2005, the daily *Haaretz*, Channel 2 television station, and British Broadcasting Corporation News were made to apologize to the government for failing to submit for review stories containing "sensitive" information. In July 2006, Al-Jazeera reporters Walid Al-Omari and Elias Karram were detained briefly by Israeli security forces while covering Hezbollah rocket attacks in northern Israel; Israeli officials claimed that the reporters were assisting Hezbollah by revealing the locations of rocket hits. The 2004 release of Mordechai Vanunu, an Israeli citizen imprisoned for 18 years for espionage and disclosing information about Israel's nuclear weapons program, was conditioned on a series of restrictions on his speech and movement; these restrictions have been condemned by the International Federation of Journalists.

A wide variety of newspapers, reflecting a broad range of political viewpoints and religious outlooks, is available in Israel. All newspapers are privately owned and freely criticize government policy. Newspapers must be licensed by the locality in which they are published. A diverse selection of broadcast media is also available. The Israel Broadcasting Authority operates public radio and television services, including the popular Kol Israel radio station. There are also commercial television networks and radio stations, and most Israelis subscribe to cable or satellite television. Internet access is widespread and available to approximately 50 percent of the population, and it is not restricted by the government.

[This rating and report reflect the state of press freedom within Israel proper, not in the West Bank and Gaza Strip, which are covered in the following report on the Israeli-Occupied Territories and Palestinian Authority.]

Israel Occupied Territories/ Palestinian Authority

LEGAL ENVIRONMENT: 28
POLITICAL ENVIRONMENT: 34
ECONOMIC ENVIRONMENT: 22

Status: Not Free

TOTAL SCORE: 84

Survey Edition	2002	2003	2004	2005	2006
Total Score, Status	84,NF	86,NF	86,NF	84,NF	86,NF

Events in the West Bank and Gaza Strip are covered extensively by international media, but both Israel and the Palestinian Authority (PA) severely restrict press freedom and often impede journalists' ability to report safely and accurately. The Palestinian Basic Law provides for freedom of the press, and a 1995 Press Law calls for free and independent media, but the latter statute also stipulates that journalists may be punished and newspapers closed for publishing material deemed harmful to national unity or likely to incite violence. The Palestinian Legislative Council's 2005 deliberations on a draft bill on access to information were stalled after legislative elections in January 2006 resulted in an upset victory for the Islamist party Hamas.

Israel's army and security services continued to commit a range of press abuses in 2006. Journalists were subject to gunfire, physical abuse, arrest, and substantial limits on their freedom of movement. In April, Israeli soldiers were accused on two separate occasions of firing at journalists covering unrest in the West Bank city of Nablus. During a major Israeli military incursion into the Gaza Strip that began in June, several journalists were wounded by Israeli Defense Forces (IDF) gunfire: In early July, two photographers, Hamid al-Khur and Mohammad Az Zanoun, were shot and wounded; later that month, Palestinian television cameraman Ibrahim al-Atlah was seriously wounded by Israeli tank fire; in August, an Israeli tank fired on a marked Reuters press vehicle in Gaza. In December, Reporters Sans Frontieres released a report accusing the IDF of attacking or threatening 16 journalists and destroying the facilities of three news outlets during the year. In April, a British coroner's court declared the 2003 death of British journalist James Miller an unlawful killing on the part of the IDF, to which Israel responded with a promise to further examine the incident. Israel denies that it deliberately targets journalists and maintains that reporters covering the conflict bear responsibility for placing themselves in danger.

Journalists reporting from the Israeli-occupied territories are required to carry Israeli-issued press cards; for Palestinian journalists and Arab journalists more generally, these cards are very difficult to obtain. In December 2005, Al-Arabiya reporter Bassem El-Jamal was denied entry to the West Bank for the third time that year by Israeli authorities, who cited his "contacts with hostile groups." For one day after an attack on Israeli troops in southern Israel by Gaza-based militants, the IDF closed the Erez crossing to Gaza to the media; while protests from foreign journalists led Israel to reopen the border, the IDF prohibited Israeli passport holders from entering Gaza for several days afterward.

The Palestinian media have also faced pressure from the PA to provide positive coverage or forgo reporting on certain stories, and journalists who have filed stories considered unfavorable to the PA have been harassed.

Threats, arrests, and abuse of journalists deemed critical of the PA, the president's Fatah party, and now Hamas have become routine. With the legislative victory of Hamas in January, Palestinian media outlets have become targets of factional violence between Hamas and Fatah. In June, about 50 members of Hamas's military wing (Ezzedine al-Qassam Brigades) attacked Palestinian national television installations in Khan Yunis, destroying equipment and beating journalists. A Fatah-linked radio station in northern Gaza was attacked with light arms and destroyed in October by gunmen allegedly associated with Hamas. In November, a radio station associated with the militant Popular Front for the Liberation of Palestine (PFLP) was attacked during a live broadcast; the attack was believed to have been spurred by an incorrect news report about a PA cabinet shuffle. In its December report, Reporters Sans Frontieres cited attacks on seven news outlets in 2006 by various Palestinian factions.

The political instability that followed Israel's 2005 withdrawal from Gaza, greater internecine conflict between Hamas and Fatah, and the existence of renegade political factions all created dangerous conditions for journalists in the territories. Six foreign journalists were kidnapped by Palestinian militants in 2006. In March, reporter Caroline Laurent and photographers Yong Tae-young and Alfred Yaghobzadeh were briefly abducted by PFLP members in Gaza. In August, Fox News journalist Steve Centanni and cameraman Olaf Wiig were kidnapped and held for nearly two weeks by a group called the Holy Jihad Brigades; they were released unharmed. Associated Press photojournalist Emilio Morenatti was kidnapped and held for a few hours in October, while French journalist Didier Francois was shot and wounded while covering clashes between Hamas and Fatah gunmen in December.

There are 3 Palestinian dailies in addition to several weekly and monthly periodicals, and the territories host roughly 30 independently owned television stations and 25 radio stations. The single television station and radio station run by the PA function as government mouthpieces, though control of these outlets is being contested by Hamas and Fatah. Most independent media outlets exercise cautious self-censorship, particularly on the issue of internal Palestinian politics. Israeli checkpoints often prevent newspaper distribution in the territories. Access to satellite television is increasing, and unrestricted internet access is available to just under 10 percent of the population.

Italy

Status: Free

LEGAL ENVIRONMENT: 9
POLITICAL ENVIRONMENT: 11
ECONOMIC ENVIRONMENT: 9
TOTAL SCORE: 29

Survey Edition	2002	2003	2004	2005	2006
Total Score, Status	27,F	28,F	33,PF	35,PF	35,PF

Status change explanation: Italy's rating improved from Partly Free to Free primarily as a result of Silvio Berlusconi's exit as prime minister. Although private broadcast media in Italy are still concentrated in the hands of the Berlusconi-dominated Mediaset, the public broadcaster, RAI, is no longer under his control.

In April 2006, Romano Prodi's center-left Union bloc narrowly won parliamentary elections, putting an end to Silvio Berlusconi's long premiership. Under Berlusconi's rule, Italy suffered from a concentration of media power in the hands of the former prime minister, who, through his private media holdings and political power over the state television networks, controlled almost 90 percent of the country's broadcast media.

Freedom of speech and of the press are constitutionally guaranteed in Italy. In April 2004, the Senate adopted the Gasparri Law on Broadcasting, which ostensibly introduced a number of reforms, like the preparation for the switch-over from analog to digital broadcasting; however, the law was heavily criticized for providing measures that served the interests of then prime minister Berlusconi's extensive media holdings. For example, the law removed a previous restriction on one person owning more than two national broadcasting stations, allowing Retequattro, one of three television stations owned by Mediaset, to continue terrestrial broadcasting. In July 2006, the European Union (EU) Commission sent Italy a formal complaint that the law, because of its concessions to Mediaset, is not compatible with EU rules on competition in the markets for electronic communications networks and services and the new EU Regulatory Framework for Electronic Communications.

In April, Mario Spezi, a journalist working on a book about a series of murders in Florence from 1968 to 1985, was arrested and jailed for 22 days for allegedly obstructing the investigation of the murders. Spezi, who had his hard disk, notebooks, and other materials seized by the police in 2004, has criticized the judiciary a number of times over the past several years for their handling of the case. In August 2006, police searched the homes and offices of newspaper reporters in connection with the investigation of the supposed kidnapping and extradition of an imam by Central Intelligence Agency agents in Italy in 2002. In February 2006, the Italian broadcast regulatory authority fined Mediaset for giving Berlusconi extra time on the air to promote his campaign for prime minister. Berlusconi was also criticized for appearing alone for a debate on the show *Liberi Tutti*. Two additional fines were levied against two Mediaset stations for the same offense just a few days before the election.

Despite Berlusconi's resignation from the premiership, the broadcast media in Italy remain concentrated, with the state-owned RAI and Berlusconi's Mediaset controlling 87.5 percent of the market share. Nonetheless, a Council of Europe report released in February 2006 demonstrated that despite the concentration of broadcast media ownership in Italy, there is considerable diversity of content in the country's news and other media. In fact, the print media, which consist of several national newspapers (two of which are controlled by the Berlusconi family), continue to provide diverse political opinions, including those critical of the government. The government generally does not restrict access to the internet, and roughly 50 percent of the population accessed this new medium in 2006. However, the government can block foreign-based internet sites if they contravene national law. After the 2005 London bombings by Islamist extremists, Italy's Parliament approved a new Antiterror Law that includes surveillance of the internet and requires one to have a license to operate an internet café.

Jamaica

LEGAL ENVIRONMENT: 3
POLITICAL ENVIRONMENT: 6
ECONOMIC ENVIRONMENT: 6

Status: Free

TOTAL SCORE: 15

Survey Edition	2002	2003	2004	2005	2006
Total Score, Status	17,F	20,F	17,F	15,F	17,F

Jamaica continued to uphold its free media environment in 2006, while still considering further legal protection for the press. The constitution protects freedom of expression but does not explicitly mention the press. A process has begun to overhaul the constitution and replace it with a comprehensive charter of rights that the Inter American Press Association believes will better protect human rights. The Media Association of Jamaica, representing media owners and managers, lobbied to include separate protection for press freedom in the charter. Following full application of the Access to Information Act in the previous year, in June the information minister, Senator Colin Campbell, announced the launch of a public education campaign to make people aware of how the legislation will work in practice. Some media freedom advocates continue to complain that existing libel and defamation laws are hindering freedom of expression. It is thought that media owners, wary of the possibility of facing financially damaging libel suits, are less inclined to encourage journalists to investigate corruption and other sensitive issues. Nonetheless, there were no physical attacks on the press in Jamaica in 2006.

The country has two national daily newspapers and a daily afternoon tabloid. There are a number of national and regional periodicals serving a variety of sectors and interests. The state broadcasting service was largely privatized in 1997, although the Kool FM radio station is still government owned. At the end of March, the Public Broadcasting Corporation of Jamaica (PBCJ) was launched as a radio and television service to replace the state-run Jamaica Broadcasting Corporation. The PBCJ—funded by state and private sector contributions—will provide public education, information, and entertainment on radio and on television through cable transmission. There are over one million internet users in Jamaica (40 percent of the population), and access is unrestricted by the government.

	Legal Environment: 2
	Political Environment: 13
Japan	Economic Environment: 6
Status: Free	Total Score: 21

Survey Edition	2002	2003	2004	2005	2006
Total Score, Status	17,F	17,F	18,F	20,F	20,F

Japan's prolific media garners one of the highest readerships in the world, despite criticism about a lack of viewpoint diversity as a result of exclusive press clubs. Press freedom is constitutionally guaranteed and generally respected in practice. In 2005, the Niigata District Court upheld the right of journalists to refuse to reveal anonymous sources in a case in which a U.S. health food company asserted that inflammatory news reports dating from 1997 were based on a leak about the company's investigation for tax evasion. In March 2006, and again in June, a Tokyo high court upheld the ruling of the lower court that protection of news sources served the public interest and the public's right to know and that journalists could protect the identity of their sources, even if the source was a public official.

Concerns continue regarding the lack of diversity and independence in reporting, especially in political news. This is facilitated in part by a system of *kisha kurabu,* or journalist clubs, in which major media outlets have cozy relationships with bureaucrats and politicians. Exposés by media outlets that belong to such clubs are frowned upon and can result in the banning of members from press club briefings. Smaller media organizations and foreigners are excluded from journalist clubs altogether. The *kisha kurabu* have been criticized by Reporters Sans Frontieres and the European Union because the government gives club members exclusive access to political information. In return, journalists tend to avoid writing critical stories about the government, thereby reducing the media's ability to pressure politicians for greater transparency and accountability. Most of Japan's investigative journalism is conducted by reporters outside the press club system. In recent years, the rising number of journalists who do not participate in press clubs has slightly eroded their power to act as gatekeepers for news concerning government ministries and political parties.

Physical attacks against the media are rare. However, on July 21, an unidentified man hurled a Molotov cocktail into the headquarters of Japan's largest business daily, *Nihon Keizai Shimbun.* No one was hurt in the attack, but the office suffered minor damage. Police are investigating possible motives, including the newspaper's exclusive story about the late emperor Hirohito's refusal to visit the war memorial, known as the Yasukuni Shrine, after it began honoring 14 convicted war criminals in 1978.

Japan has a vigorous and free media and boasts the second highest daily newspaper circulation per capita in the world (after Norway). Many national dailies have circulations topping one million and often produce afternoon and evening editions as well. More than half of the national newspaper market share is controlled by "the big three": the *Yomiuri Shimbun,* the *Asahi Shimbun,* and the *Mainichi Shimbun.* There is considerable homogeneity in reports, which relate the news in a factual and neutral manner. Television news content, once dominated by the public station Nippon Hoso Kyokai, has diversified considerably with the rising popularity of TV Asahi, Fuji TV, the Tokyo Broadcasting System, and satellite television. Japan boasts over 47 million registered internet users, representing almost 70 percent of the population. No government restrictions on access to the internet were reported in 2006.

LEGAL ENVIRONMENT: 21
POLITICAL ENVIRONMENT: 22

Jordan

ECONOMIC ENVIRONMENT: 18

Status: Not Free

TOTAL SCORE: 61

Survey Edition	2002	2003	2004	2005	2006
Total Score, Status	60,PF	65,NF	63,NF	62,NF	61,NF

Jordan's media has not seen any of the reforms promised by the government and still operates under the thumb of both oppressive media legislation and politically motivated advertisers and printers. While the constitution guarantees citizens the right to freedom of expression and of the press, articles of the penal and press codes restrict criticism of the royal family, the National Assembly, public officials, and the armed forces, as well as speech that might harm Jordan's foreign relations. In practice, limited criticism of the government and its allies is tolerated, as is speech in favor of Islamist movements, but criticism of the royal family is still taboo. Journalists must be members of the Jordan Press Association (JPA) to work legally. In the past, critical journalists have been excluded from the JPA and prevented from practicing their profession. Although King Abdullah II has repeatedly pledged reform, the government in 2006 again failed to enact a long-awaited new press bill. The draft before the Parliament at the end of the year did not eliminate jail sentences for journalists in connection with their work and allowed for the enforcement of statutes such as Article 150 of the penal code, which bans all writing and speech that is "intended to, or results in, stirring up sectarian or racial tension or strife among different elements of the nation."

Intelligence agencies watch journalists closely, and the government of Prime Minister Ma'ruf al-Bakhit has given free rein to these agencies, the police, and prosecutors to clamp down on legitimate speech. Editors and journalists report that they have received official warnings to refrain from publishing certain articles or to avoid certain topics and that security officials have pressured printers to hold publications until editors agree to remove sensitive stories. Several journalists were arrested in 2006 for articles criticizing the government or detailing sensitive political information. In January and February, the Jordanian weeklies *Al-Mehwar* and *Shihan* published caricatures of the prophet Muhammad that had first appeared in Denmark's *Jyllands-Posten* in September 2005. The two papers' respective editors, Hisham al-Khalidi and Jihad Mu'mini, were charged with "offending religious feelings" and given two-month prison sentences in May; they were released pending their appeal. The death of Abu Musab al-Zarqawi, a Jordanian-born terrorist leader in Iraq, also proved contentious, as Jordanian authorities interrupted a June interview with his brother-in-law on the Qatar-based satellite television station Al-Jazeera and briefly detained the station's Amman bureau chief, Yassir Abu Hilala. Several members of Parliament were arrested for consoling members of al-Zarqawi's family and charged under Article 150 of the penal code. A state security court in August sentenced two of the lawmakers to prison terms and fines, but they were pardoned by the king in September. In December, three photojournalists were assaulted in Parliament after taking photos of an altercation between two legislators.

The government owns substantial shares in Jordan's two leading daily newspapers, and all publications must obtain licenses from the state. There are high taxes on the media industry and tariffs on paper, and the government has been criticized for advertising primarily in newspapers in which it owns a stake. In 2003, the government officially gave up its monopoly on domestic television and radio broadcasting by creating the Audiovisual Licensing Authority, which in 2004 began to license and regulate private radio and television outlets. No restrictions are placed on satellite broadcasts, and satellite dishes continue to proliferate. The Jordanian government is actively seeking to promote access to the internet and says it places no restrictions on the 11 percent of the population who use the internet.

		LEGAL ENVIRONMENT: 26
		POLITICAL ENVIRONMENT: 28
Kazakhstan		ECONOMIC ENVIRONMENT: 22
Status: Not Free		TOTAL SCORE: 76

Survey Edition	2002	2003	2004	2005	2006
Total Score, Status	69,NF	73,NF	74,NF	75,NF	75,NF

The media situation continues to suffer from an oppressive environment where legal restrictions, self-censorship, and the risk of retribution hamper independent reporting. Kazakhstan's constitution guarantees freedom of the press but also provides special protection for the president. The authorities allow limited press freedom but safeguard the existing power structure against the dangers that truly independent media might pose. There were fewer examples of government pressure against independent media in 2006 than in 2005, when the country held a presidential election, but new legislative restrictions were passed during the year. Amendments to media legislation signed into law by President Nursultan Nazarbayev in July imposed costly registration fees for journalists, broadened criteria for denying media outlets registration, required news outlets to submit the names of editors with their registration applications, and necessitated reregistration in the event of an address change. The amendments drew widespread condemnation from nongovernmental organizations and media watchdog groups.

Journalists continued to face obstacles in the form of criminal and civil libel suits and occasional physical assaults. Kazis Toguzbayev, a journalist and activist in the unregistered opposition party Alga, faced criminal charges under Article 318 of Kazakhstan's criminal code, which imposes penalties for "undermining the reputation and dignity of the country's president and hindering his activities." Toguzbayev had published two articles on the internet in April and May criticizing Nazarbayev's actions in the context of the February murder of opposition leader Altynbek Sarsenbayev. The cases against Toguzbayev, still pending at year's end, underscored the special protections Kazakh legislation extends to the country's leader. In April, Kenzhegali Aytbakiyev, an editor for the opposition newspaper *Ayna-Plus*, which had reported on corruption allegations against Nazarbayev, was badly beaten by unknown assailants. Despite calls from Parliament for an investigation, prosecutors failed to take any substantive action after the assault. *Ayna-Plus* had begun publication after a court in February shut it down under its old name, *Zhuma Times*.

As in previous years, prominent broadcast media were either state run or controlled by members or associates of the president's family. For example, Nazarbayev's daughter ran several television channels and controlled two of the nation's leading newspapers. Nominally independent media often had ties to the state through subsidies or holding companies. This had several deleterious effects. Media outlets avoided aggressive coverage of sensitive issues, in particular allegations of improper conduct by the president and his family, and provided tendentious coverage according to the interests of the groups that controlled them. This was evident after Sarsenbayev's murder, when various factions within the country's elite used media they controlled to leak compromising information of dubious veracity. Against this backdrop, Culture and Information Minister Yermukhamet Yertysbayev said in May that the state would restore full control over the Khabar Media Holding Company, controlled by Nazarbayev's daughter. The state had not followed through on the move by year's end. Independent print publications were hampered by low circulation and government influence over printing and distribution facilities. In January, the printing company Dauir—directed by the president's sister-in-law—briefly refused to print seven Almaty-based opposition newspapers. The internet provided a refuge of sorts for Kazakhstan's beleaguered independent press, although there were reports of government interference in the form of monitoring and blocking of opposition websites. Moreover, less than 3 percent of the Kazakh population had internet access, and as the Toguzbayev case indicated, the authors of internet publications were as vulnerable to the country's strict libel laws as other journalists.

Kenya

Status: Partly Free

LEGAL ENVIRONMENT: 20
POLITICAL ENVIRONMENT: 21
ECONOMIC ENVIRONMENT: 18
TOTAL SCORE: 59

Survey Edition	2002	2003	2004	2005	2006
Total Score, Status	67,NF	68,NF	60,PF	61,NF	58,PF

Although Kenya's media continued to be vibrant in 2006, legal restrictions and the threat of violence restricted the country's press freedom. The constitution does not explicitly guarantee press freedom. As such, media operations are governed by Section 79 of the constitution, which, while not providing for freedom of speech, does guarantee citizens the broader right to freedom of expression. Nevertheless, the government routinely restricts this right by widely interpreting several laws, including the Official Secrets Act, the penal code, and criminal libel legislation. The Miscellaneous Amendment Act of 2002, which raised publishers' mandatory insurance bond to one million Kenyan shillings (about US$13,100), has had a negative impact on numerous independent newspapers that cannot afford to pay the increased fees. Although defamation remains criminalized in Kenyan law, in a 2005 defamation case the attorney general declared that the archaic law would no longer be used to suppress freedom of expression, and no journalists were prosecuted for criminal libel in 2006. A freedom of information bill is still pending before the Parliament.

Although the media scene in Kenya remained vibrant, there were continued instances of extralegal intimidation of private media outlets during the year. In February, the premises of the privately owned *Weekly Citizen* and the *Independent* were raided by police after the papers carried articles about power struggles within the ruling coalition. Also in February, an editorial cartoonist with the *Daily Nation*, Godfrey Mwapembwa (Gado), was threatened with legal action after featuring the minister of justice and constitutional affairs in a cartoon about the Anglo-Leasing corruption scandal. In an unprecedented move, in March the offices of the independent daily the *Standard*—one of the oldest and most well-respected papers in Kenya—were raided, and three journalists were arrested for questioning in connection with a story of political intrigue within the government. Approximately 20,000 copies of the March 2 issue were seized and burned, printing equipment was vandalized, and computers were confiscated. A similar raid resulted in the closure of the national broadcasting station, Kenya Television Network, which is also owned by the Standard Group. The police action provoked local and international outrage and came two days after Information and Communication Minister Mutahi Kagwe issued a warning against media abusing press freedom. National Security Minister John Michuki told journalists that the raid was carried out to protect state security, commenting that "if you rattle a snake, you must be prepared to be bitten by it." The charges against the three journalists were later dropped.

Although the number of private media outlets is rising, the government-controlled public broadcaster, Kenya Broadcasting Corporation, remains dominant outside the major urban centers, and its coverage still favors the ruling party. Private media are generally outspoken and critical of government policies. There has been a significant expansion of FM radio, particularly ethnic FM radio stations, increasing public participation as well as commentary unfavorable to the government through call-in shows. Individual journalists continue to practice self-censorship because of either political pressure or bribes. Foreign media are widely available, including FM radio broadcasts of the British Broadcasting Corporation, Voice of America, and Radio France Internationale. Use of the internet is unrestricted; however, only 3 percent of Kenyans were able to access the internet in 2006 owing to the high costs involved.

Kiribati

LEGAL ENVIRONMENT: 5
POLITICAL ENVIRONMENT: 8
ECONOMIC ENVIRONMENT: 13

Status: Free

TOTAL SCORE: 26

Survey Edition	2002	2003	2004	2005	2006
Total Score, Status	21,F	26,F	27,F	26,F	28,F

The tiny island nation of Kiribati has a free and open media system, despite the government's registration requirements. Freedom of expression is safeguarded under Article 12 of the constitution; however, there are some restrictions. Newspapers are required to register with the government under the Newspaper Registration Act. Additionally, the Newspaper Registration (Amendment) Act of 2004 gives the government the power to stop publication of newspapers that face complaints. There is no official censorship, although in August local media were accused of self-censorship by not reporting on the government's controversial university scholarship allocations, even though the story was covered by the foreign press. While there were no physical attacks on the press in 2006, in March former state radio journalist Taberannang Korauaba lost his appeal against the government for wrongful dismissal. Korauaba was relieved of his position at Radio Kiribati in December 2005 after refusing to reveal his sources for a report on corruption involving Kiribati's auditor general.

The state-run newspaper, *Te Uekera*, and the nation's only privately owned newspaper, *Kiribati New Star,* both operate on a weekly basis and offer diverse viewpoints. Newsletters from Catholic and Protestant churches provide additional sources of information. There is one state AM and FM radio station and one private broadcaster in Tarawa. In 2006, the government hired Powercom, a Tasmanian company, to set up the country's first radio contact between the coral islands. The internet is unrestricted; however, with a single provider access is among the most expensive in the world, and only 2 percent of the country's population was able to make use of the internet on a regular basis during the year.

Kuwait

LEGAL ENVIRONMENT: 19
POLITICAL ENVIRONMENT: 21
ECONOMIC ENVIRONMENT: 16

Status: Partly Free

TOTAL SCORE: 56

Survey Edition	2002	2003	2004	2005	2006
Total Score, Status	49,PF	54,PF	57,PF	58,PF	56,PF

Despite some positive revisions in press legislation, the country's media still operate under a restrictive legal and political environment. Articles 36 and 37 of the constitution provide for freedom of speech and of the press, and Kuwait is frequently considered to be among the best performers in the region, but there are numerous limitations to these rights. A new law passed in 2006 was met with mixed reactions. On March 6, after 20 years of debate, the country passed a new Press and Publications Law. While this legislation ends the government's monopoly on licensing new media outlets, it retains many of the repressive measures used to prosecute journalists in the past. Journalists can no longer be detained without a court order, but they may still be prosecuted under the penal code for a number of offenses. Those found guilty of criticizing Islam may be imprisoned for up to one year and fined up to US$70,000. The new law also criminalizes the publication of material that criticizes, among other things, the constitution, the emir, or Islam or incites acts that will offend public morality or religious sensibilities. Such transgressions are no longer punishable by jail terms but may be subject to staggeringly high fines. A number of journalists were arrested under the new legislation during the rest of the year. For example, Amid Buyabis was jailed on May 15 for directly quoting criticism of the emir; he was released the next day. Separately, Kuwaiti journalist Khaled Obaysan al-Mutairi was arrested for an article published in the Kuwaiti daily *Al-Seyassah* that praised Saddam Hussein and called upon the Arab League to support the Iraqi resistance. The information minister stated that the paper had been charged with "publishing reports that negatively impact Kuwaiti society," but the charges were dropped and al-Mutairi was released the next day. Finally, on November 18 journalist Aziza al-Mufarig of the daily *Al-Watan* was fined 1,000 dinars (US$3,500) and given a three-month suspended sentence and three years' probation for an article she had written that questioned the independence of a Kuwaiti judge.

Despite these instances of journalists being arrested, there were no direct physical attacks on the press in 2006. In general, the Ministry of Information (MOI) does not actively interfere or restrict access to local or international news, and the Kuwaiti media are known to provide more critical and outspoken coverage of the government and politics than the rest of the region. Nevertheless, given the ongoing restrictions in the new Press and Publications Law, journalists continued to practice self-censorship. The MOI can also censor all books, films, and periodicals it deems morally offensive.

Although there are five Arabic and two English daily newspapers, all privately owned, the last government-issued license was in 1976. The old Press Law of 1963 had limited the press to five dailies. While all publishers are required to obtain an operating license from the MOI in order to launch a daily under the new 2006 Press and Publications Law, the MOI must now issue the license or provide an explanation for its refusal within 90 days of application, and those denied licenses may appeal such action in court.

Nevertheless, 250,000 dinars (US$950,000) is the required minimum capital to establish a paper under the new law, limiting the number of individuals capable of doing so. There are nine state-owned radio stations and television stations, and the government has finally granted licenses to a few private television and radio stations, such as satellite television channel Al-Rai and Marina FM radio. However, the content of these private stations tends more toward entertainment than critical news. The government tried to shut down a number of satellite stations that were broadcasting programs related to the June parliamentary elections. Twenty-five percent of the population accessed the internet in 2006, although the government has blocked websites considered to promote terrorism and political instability; several websites were blocked during the year. The U.S. State Department reported that internet café owners are required to obtain the names and identification of internet users and must submit the information if required by the Ministry of Communication.

Kyrgyzstan

LEGAL ENVIRONMENT: 22
POLITICAL ENVIRONMENT: 25
ECONOMIC ENVIRONMENT: 20

Status: Not Free

TOTAL SCORE: 67

Survey Edition	2002	2003	2004	2005	2006
Total Score, Status	68,PF	71,NF	71,NF	71,NF	64,NF

Kyrgyzstan's inability to make full use of the democratic opportunity afforded by the fall of President Askar Akayev in 2005 was compounded in 2006 by increasing government attempts to exert control over the country's media environment. The political situation remained unstable, leading the government to curb media outlets that threatened to undermine its position. While Kyrgyz law protects freedom of speech and prohibits censorship, it is ineffectively and unevenly applied. Libel is considered a criminal offense, although the practice of filing libel suits against obstreperous media outlets has become less common since Akayev's ouster.

Throughout 2006, media outlets that provided coverage deemed undesirable by the authorities experienced a variety of difficulties, particularly in early November, when the opposition staged a large demonstration in the capital, Bishkek. At that time, the authorities blocked opposition leaders from appearing on state television, privately owned New Television Network (NTS) lost power to its antennae in Bishkek and Osh, and hacker attacks rendered the independent news websites akipress.org and 24.kg inaccessible for several days. In addition, a number of journalists—particularly those covering the demonstration—also fell victim to violent attacks and harassment.

Other efforts to exert control were more overt. In January, Prime Minister Felix Kulov signed a decree dismissing Bakyt Orunbekov as editor in chief of the state-run Kyrgyz-language newspaper *Kyrgyz Tuusu*. Orunbekov, a critic of Akayev who had ascended to his post after the long-ruling president's departure, charged that his firing was retaliation for articles critical of Kulov. Also in January, journalists at the state-run Kyrgyz National Television and Radio Corporation (KTR) staged a protest over the appointment of an ally of President Kurmanbek Bakiyev as deputy director. A concerted campaign targeted privately owned Pyramid TV, which had been the object of a forcible takeover attempt in late 2005 amid allegations that current and former officials were behind the bid. In September, four men broke into Pyramid's offices and started a fire, causing US$200,000 in damage, according to Pyramid producer Turat Bektenov. Authorities did not actively pursue an investigation of the attack. Pyramid, which provided critical coverage of Bakiyev, encountered harassment in a number of other forms, including an assault on Bektenov in November. The station managed to resume VHF broadcasts by the end of the year, however.

Overall, the authorities, led by the presidential administration, seemed intent in 2006 on retaining a significant level of control over the broadcast media, which remain the primary source of news for most Kyrgyz citizens. After the fall of President Akayev, the opposition forces that came to power advanced plans to transform KTR into a public broadcaster. However, Bakiyev vetoed a bill passed by Parliament in September that would have implemented that proposal. The government ended privately-run NTS's transmissions in a number of regions in May, citing the need to use the frequency for a new state channel, El TV, which is frequently subject to government controls. Kyrgyzstan has 40 to 50 regularly printed newspapers and magazines, most of them private but not all independent. Uchkun, the state-owned printing house, controls the primary means of publication in the country, but a U.S.-sponsored printing house (operated by Freedom House) established in 2004 provides publishers with an alternative. Foreign media are allowed to operate freely within the country, but foreign ownership of domestic media outlets is prohibited. The internet is available in just a few places in the country, and only 5 percent of the population accesses the internet on a regular basis. Nevertheless, Kyrgyzstan has a lively and growing selection of internet news sites, blogs, and forums for political discussion.

Laos

Status: Not Free

LEGAL ENVIRONMENT: 26
POLITICAL ENVIRONMENT: 31
ECONOMIC ENVIRONMENT: 24
TOTAL SCORE: 81

Survey Edition	2002	2003	2004	2005	2006
Total Score, Status	82,NF	80,NF	82,NF	83,NF	81,NF

Media remained tightly controlled by the authoritarian, one-party state in 2006. Article 6 of the 1991 constitution guarantees press freedom and civil liberties, but only in theory. Few citizens actually feel free to exercise these rights because there are no legal safeguards for voicing dissent in public. Article 7 requires the mass media, particularly Lao-language papers such as *Vientiane Mai* and *Pasason* and the national news agency, Khaosan Pathet Lao, to "unite and mobilize" the diverse ethnic groups to support the ruling Lao People's Revolutionary Party. The criminal code provides for up to one year in prison for those found to be reporting on news that weakens the state.

Although central censorship is no longer imposed directly on the press, the Ministry of Information and Culture continues to oversee media coverage and academic publishing, and self-censorship is commonplace. Editors are government appointees assigned to ensure that media function as links between the party and the people. All editors are members of the Lao Journalists Association, presided over by the minister of information and culture. Thus, journalists whose salaries are paid by the government are guided by the editors' promulgation of the media as an instrument of the government. The media's role is to link the people to the party, deliver party policy messages, and disseminate political ideology. Military abuses against the Lao-Hmong people, as well as arrests of Christians for practicing their faith, go unreported in the Lao-language papers. To date, there are no international media agencies in Laos. Foreign journalists must apply for a special visa to enter the country and are accompanied by official escorts throughout their stay. Nonetheless, there were no reports of physical attacks on the media in 2006.

The majority of print and electronic media are state owned. The French weekly *Le Renovateur* and the English daily *Vientiane Times*, which are subsidized by the Ministry of Information and Culture, occasionally report on social and economic problems, framing their content primarily to attract tourists, expatriates, and investors to the country. Thai television stations can be accessed in border areas. Tourism has led to the proliferation of internet kiosks with unrestricted access to foreign news sites. However, language barriers and high monthly connection fees (approximately US$300–US$400 compared with the average monthly salary of US$20–US$30) limit regular internet use to only 0.4 percent of the population or exclusively wealthy individuals, expatriates, and business organizations. Internet service providers must submit quarterly reports to the government to facilitate monitoring.

Latvia

Status: Free

LEGAL ENVIRONMENT: 6
POLITICAL ENVIRONMENT: 6
ECONOMIC ENVIRONMENT: 7
TOTAL SCORE: 19

Survey Edition	2002	2003	2004	2005	2006
Total Score, Status	19,F	18,F	17,F	17,F	19,F

Latvia's press continued to operate in a free and open environment in 2006. The constitution protects freedom of speech and of the press, and the government upholds these rights in practice. However, libel remains a criminal offense. In a high-profile case, the daily newspaper *Neatkariga Rita Avize* published transcripts in September 2006 of a television journalist's private mobile telephone conversations. An investigation by the prosecutor's office revealed that a judge had given permission for the wiretapping to the financial police as part of an organized crime probe, and the police had then leaked the transcripts. The judge received a disciplinary sanction, and the investigation continued at year's end. *Neatkariga Rita Avize* is widely believed to be controlled by Ventspils mayor Aivars Lembergs, who is under criminal investigation for corruption. In another case, LTV received a court order in September to reveal its sources for a story about the Lembergs investigation. LTV refused, and an appeal in the case was pending at year's end. There were no attacks on the press in 2006.

Latvian media are diverse and competitive, offering a wide range of political viewpoints. The print media are independent and privately owned. There are four national terrestrial television channels: two public channels, LTV 1 and LTV 7, and two private stations, LNT and TV3. Primary broadcast media are required to use Latvian, while secondary broadcasters may reserve up to 20 percent of their airtime for Russian-language programming; these requirements apply to terrestrial services only.

Foreign companies, including Swedish and Polish firms, own or control a substantial portion of Latvia's print and broadcast media, as well as media distribution and printing facilities. According to the World Association of Newspapers, newspaper advertising revenues in Latvia increased by nearly 10 percent in 2005 and more than 43 percent from 2001 to 2005. The government does not restrict access to the internet, which was used by an estimated 45 percent of the population during the year.

Lebanon

Status: Partly Free

LEGAL ENVIRONMENT: 19
POLITICAL ENVIRONMENT: 25
ECONOMIC ENVIRONMENT: 15
TOTAL SCORE: 59

Survey Edition	2002	2003	2004	2005	2006
Total Score, Status	74,NF	71,NF	66,NF	60,PF	60,PF

While the media have more freedom in Lebanon than in other countries in the region, they still face political and judicial obstacles. The constitution provides for freedom of the press, and although the press does not face direct interference from the government, recent political developments have resulted in an increase in self-censorship among journalists. Under law, pornography or political and religious material deemed a threat to national security can be censored by the government. Security services are authorized to censor all foreign magazines, books, and films before they are distributed in Lebanon. Journalists and publications accused of press offenses may be prosecuted in a special publications court. In March, criminal libel charges were brought against two journalists accused of insulting and defaming the president. However, in general government efforts to limit journalists are much less effective than previously, as the diversity of media outlets and the momentum of political events have made it increasingly difficult to restrict press coverage.

The most significant development of 2006 was the July military conflict between Israel and Lebanon. Israeli strikes killed 2 journalists and injured 10. Israeli warplanes bombed Al-Manar television, which is funded and operated by Hezbollah, and destroyed the Fiah transmission tower of the Lebanese Broadcasting Corporation (LBC), temporarily taking the station off the air, killing LBC technician Sleiman Chidiac, and injuring two other employees. Press photographer Layal Najib was killed while covering Israeli attacks in southern Lebanon when a missile exploded near her car in Qana.

Significant damage to roads and bridges limited journalists' ability to travel within the country throughout the conflict. Increased tension as a result of the violence also led to greater dangers for journalists covering the news; there were several cases late in the year in which journalists covering Hezbollah demonstrations were attacked and injured.

No significant progress was made in the investigations of the 2005 attacks on media workers who spoke out against Syria's role in Lebanon. All victims of car bombs, Samir Kassir and Gibran Tueni were both killed, while May Chidiac survived but lost an arm and a leg as a result of the attack. On June 17, a prosecuting judge was assigned to pursue the murder case of Gibran Tueni, managing editor of the daily paper *Al-Nahar*. French judge Jean-Louis Bruguiere, known for his prosecution of high-profile terrorism cases, went to Beirut in July to investigate the death of Franco-Lebanese journalist Samir Kassir, who was killed in June 2005. Those responsible for all three attacks have yet to be identified or prosecuted.

Lebanon features dozens of newspapers and hundreds of periodicals, many of which publish criticism of the government. Because almost a dozen daily newspapers are published in Lebanon, competition for readers is quite stiff. Newspapers have experienced a dramatic drop in advertising revenues since the beginning of the conflict with Israel over the summer. All national daily newspapers are privately owned, as are most television and radio stations, including six independent television and satellite stations and nearly three dozen independent radio stations. However, many media outlets are linked to political and/or sectarian interests that exert significant influence over content. Access to satellite television has grown substantially over the last decade, and 15.4 percent of Lebanese are now able to use the internet on a regular basis.

Lesotho

Status: Partly Free

LEGAL ENVIRONMENT: 13
POLITICAL ENVIRONMENT: 15
ECONOMIC ENVIRONMENT: 14
TOTAL SCORE: 42

Survey Edition	2002	2003	2004	2005	2006
Total Score, Status	46,PF	42,PF	40,PF	42,PF	42,PF

The media environment remained hampered in 2006 owing to the perpetuation of legal harassment, government secrecy, and economic constraints. The government generally respects freedom of speech and of the press, both of which are provided for in the constitution. However, a 1938 proclamation prohibits criticism of the government and provides penalties for seditious libel. In recent years, extremely high fines have been handed down by the courts in libel cases against publications and radio stations known for criticizing the government, forcing some to the verge of closure. In August, the editor in chief of the Lesotho Police Service tabloid *Leseli Ka Sepolesa*, Clifford Molefe, received a US$422,000 defamation claim issued by the Lesotho Football Association's former PR agent, Mohau Thakaso. In 2005, the English-language weekly *Public Eye* was ordered to pay a private businessman, Lebohang Thotanyana, 1.5 million maloti (about US$220,000) for alleged defamation. Journalism groups have urged the government to create a media council or other regulatory body empowered to mediate such defamation disputes before they end up in court.

The government periodically attempts to pressure the independent press, and journalists have suffered occasional harassment or attack. Beginning in October, Thabo Thakalekoala—a prominent journalist and president of the Media Institute of Southern Africa—received daily death threats aimed at both him and his family. The threats are believed to be motivated by Thakalekoala's coverage of the October split in the ruling Lesotho Congress for Democracy for international news agencies, as well as his advocacy for a more independent state broadcasting sector.

Several independent newspapers operate freely and routinely criticize the government, while state-owned print and broadcast media mostly reflect the views of the ruling party. There are four private radio stations, and extensive South African radio and television broadcasts reach Lesotho. Journalists reportedly have trouble gaining free access to official information, and media development is constrained by inadequate funding and resources. In 2006, less than 2 percent of the population accessed the internet, which remains unrestricted by the government.

Liberia
Status: Not Free

LEGAL ENVIRONMENT: 19
POLITICAL ENVIRONMENT: 24
ECONOMIC ENVIRONMENT: 22
TOTAL SCORE: 65

Survey Edition	2002	2003	2004	2005	2006
Total Score, Status	77,NF	79,NF	75,NF	73,NF	64,NF

Despite a small improvement in press-government relations brought about by the election of President Ellen Johnson-Sirleaf, the relationship between the press and the government soured in 2006 amid a series of incidents in which authorities accused the press of writing intentionally misleading stories, while the press complained about a lack of government transparency. Liberia's 1986 constitution guarantees that citizens enjoy freedom of expression, "being fully responsible for the abuse thereof." This opaque clause helped the Charles Taylor regime harass the media with a semblance of legitimacy during his presidency. Under the transitional government and the newly elected administration of Johnson-Sirleaf, respect for freedom of the press has improved noticeably. Nonetheless, strict libel laws are still in place, and in March 2006 the private biweekly *Independent* newspaper was banned for two days by the government in response to the publication of compromising photos of the ex–presidential affairs minister. In April, the directors of three separate newspapers were required to appear before the Senate on accusations of publishing "false and misleading" information in response to allegedly defamatory articles claiming that senators received exorbitant salaries. Constitutional guarantees for access to information are vague; access to budgetary and financial information, in particular, remains difficult owing to bureaucratic inefficiencies and frequent requests for additional payment from civil servants involved. Decades of civil war and mismanagement also mean that there are very few public records to access. A media reform bill and a more progressive freedom of information bill are currently being debated in the legislature; although this is a promising improvement from years past, in the last year little progress has been made in passing or implementing these bills.

Journalists frequently reported unfavorably on government behavior, and 2006 saw a noticeable deterioration in the relationship between the government and the media from the improvements made in 2005. A number of journalists were harassed, beaten, or detained while covering the news. Upon returning from a trip in June, President Johnson-Sirleaf announced that she would talk to only three reporters of her choosing. The rest of the press corps became angry, and a number of journalists were harassed by the president's security personnel. A week later, four journalists were hassled and briefly detained by security personnel at the president's executive mansion while attempting to authenticate reports of the dismissal of five senior security officers. Nevertheless, for these and other incidents the government has often made visible efforts to investigate the perpetrators; even so, many journalists claim that these investigations are often more image than substance. On a number of occasions, government representatives accused the media of acting unprofessionally. The most high-profile of these instances was when, while speaking at a university graduation, President Johnson-Sirleaf accused many journalists of sensationalizing the news and often replacing accuracy and truth with lies and exaggerations.

There are now approximately a dozen newspapers publishing in Monrovia with varying degrees of regularity. However, newspaper distribution is limited to the capital, and most Liberians rely on radio broadcasts to receive news owing to low literacy rates. There are now 15 different independent radio stations in Monrovia, 24 local radio stations outside of the capital, 1 radio station run by the government, and 1 run by the United Nations Mission in Liberia—all of which generally operate without excessive government influence. However, in May 2006 the Liberian Broadcasting System announced that all journalists working for state-run outlets would be required to obtain clearance before publishing articles accusing government officials of corruption. The independent media have grown significantly since the removal of Taylor, though the number of outlets has decreased over the last year, typically because of financial difficulties. Such financial constraints, inevitable in the operation of a news outlet in such a poor country recovering from war, cause some of the largest impediments to unbiased accurate journalism. Reporters commonly accept payment from individuals they file stories about, and even the placement of a story in a paper or a radio show can often be bought and influenced by outside interests. Access to foreign broadcasts and the internet is unrestricted by the government but is severely limited by the dire financial situation of most Liberians to less than 0.5 percent of the population.

Libya

LEGAL ENVIRONMENT: 29
POLITICAL ENVIRONMENT: 38
ECONOMIC ENVIRONMENT: 29

Status: Not Free

TOTAL SCORE: 96

Survey Edition	2002	2003	2004	2005	2006
Total Score, Status	88,NF	89,NF	94,NF	95,NF	96,NF

The press remains tightly controlled despite the regime's continued efforts to curry favor with the West by presenting Libya as a changed nation. Libyan law provides for freedom of speech and of the press within the confines of the "principles of the Revolution." Authorities strictly control these freedoms, especially criticism of the government. The press laws are draconian, and regime opponents face punishments as harsh as death for crossing the government. All unsanctioned political acts are illegal, so many forms of expression are illegal as well. Foreign publications are censored and occasionally outlawed. Any criticism of Colonel Muammar Qaddafi can lead to time in prison.

Challenging the regime in any meaningful way is not part of public discourse in Libya. A vast network of secret police and informers exists to ensure that state critics are known to the regime. Most critics of the government are political activists of Libyan origin living outside the country. These critics publish information about human rights abuses and other domestic events on the internet. But the government is well aware of these activities, and emigrés who take public positions critical of the regime can be imprisoned if they travel to Libya. Cyberdissident Abdel Razek al-Mansouri, arrested in January 2005 for publishing critical articles on a London-based website, was released in March 2006. However, another cyberdissident, Idrees Mohammed Boufayed, has not been heard from since November, when he was required to attend a meeting with the Internal Security Agency. In fact, the Libyan government has even exerted pressure on other governments, particularly those in neighboring countries, to crack down on critics of the regime. For example, in October 2006 Libya's diplomatic mission to Algeria filed a complaint against the independent paper *Ech-Chourouk* after the paper suggested that Qaddafi should negotiate with the Touareg tribes regarding the creation of an independent state. Less than a month later, Algerian courts suspended the paper for two months, ordered it to pay 500,000 dinars (US$7,150) in damages directly to Qaddafi, and sentenced the paper's editor, Ali Fadil, and the article's author, Naila Berrahal, to six months each in prison. The only person allowed to offer harsh criticism about the lack of democracy is Qaddafi's son, Saif al-Islam, who in August admitted that there is "no press" and "no democracy" in Libya and recognized that this fact was known by all.

Much of Libya's local press is moribund, and pro-government party newspapers publish Soviet-era regime praises daily. Editors and journalists who want to keep their jobs are close to the regime. There is no independent press. The General Press Institute (GPI), a branch of the Information Ministry, owns three of the major newspapers, while the fourth is owned by the Movement of Revolutionary Committees, a state-supported ideological organization. The same is true of broadcast media. Television and radio are state controlled, and popular Pan-Arab satellite TV stations like Al-Jazeera and Al-Arabiya do not have local correspondents covering Libya. Internet use is reported at only 3 percent of the population, and access is monitored carefully. Few have recourse to news and information from outside the country, but more people are turning to the internet for information, to which authorities have responded by cracking down on online dissent. The GPI reportedly imposed web-proxy blocking architecture on certain websites, severely restricting the ability of journalists from GPI–financed newspapers to access papers from outside Libya.

Liechtenstein

LEGAL ENVIRONMENT: 1
POLITICAL ENVIRONMENT: 5
ECONOMIC ENVIRONMENT: 8

Status: Free

TOTAL SCORE: 14

Survey Edition	2002	2003	2004	2005	2006
Total Score, Status	NA	11,F	12,F	14,F	13,F

Liechtenstein's press continued to be one of the freest in the world. Freedom of expression is guaranteed under Article 40 of the 1921 constitution, and no major press freedom violations were reported in 2006. When posters put up under a government-organized antidiscrimination campaign were disfigured, the government recognized the right to free expression but noted that it should not be used in this way. Laws currently being prepared by the government concerning press freedom include one on electronic communication to foster media and to promote smaller media outlets. There were no attacks on the press in 2006.

Liechtenstein has two publicly owned daily newspapers, *Liechtensteiner Vaterland* and *Liechtensteiner Volksblatt;* one Sunday paper, *Liewo;* and the monthly *Der Monat.* Since it encountered financial troubles in 2004, the former private radio station Radio Liechtenstein is now owned by the government and funded by some commercial revenue. The local TV-Channel Landeskanal broadcasts official information over the cable network. Anyone can submit a request to broadcast material of national relevance. All content has to be authorized by the government. Satellite television is widely viewed. Because of its small size and shared language, Liechtenstein relies heavily on media from neighboring Austria, Germany, and Switzerland. The internet is open and unrestricted, and more than 60 percent of the population accessed this medium on a regular basis in 2006. The government has started to publish information online and has established feedback mechanisms.

LEGAL ENVIRONMENT: 5
POLITICAL ENVIRONMENT: 7

Lithuania
ECONOMIC ENVIRONMENT: 6

Status: Free
TOTAL SCORE: 18

Survey Edition	2002	2003	2004	2005	2006
Total Score, Status	19,F	18,F	18,F	18,F	18,F

Lithuania's media environment continued to remain free in 2006 despite an incident of government seizure of printed materials. The constitution provides for freedom of speech and of the press, and those guarantees are respected by the government in practice. According to the criminal code, libel or defamation is punishable by a fine or imprisonment, though few journalists have been convicted of such crimes in recent years. In September 2006, agents from the State Security Department briefly detained the editor of the *Laisvas Laikrastis* newspaper, seized all 15,000 copies of the latest issue, and confiscated computers from the newsroom and the editor's home. Government agents maintained that the issue in question, which included a story about alleged political corruption, contained information classified as a state secret. President Valdas Adamkus, the Lithuanian Journalists Union, and press advocacy groups condemned the action. Even while this incident occurred, Lithuanian journalists were generally free to practice and were not subject to physical attacks or harassment attempts throughout the year.

The media freely criticize the government and express a wide variety of views. There are a large number of privately owned newspapers, and several independent and public television and radio stations broadcast throughout the country. However, media ownership has undergone increased concentration over the last few years, leading to concerns about the possible effects on media independence and quality. Investors in the country's media market include both domestic firms and foreign companies, mainly from Scandinavia. Lithuania saw a decline in newspaper advertising revenues of about 7 percent in 2005, according to the World Association of Newspapers. The government does not limit access to the internet; nonetheless, only 36 percent of Lithuanians made use of the internet in 2006—the lowest percentage among the three Baltic countries.

Luxembourg

LEGAL ENVIRONMENT: 2
POLITICAL ENVIRONMENT: 3
ECONOMIC ENVIRONMENT: 7

Status: Free   TOTAL SCORE: 12

Survey Edition	2002	2003	2004	2005	2006
Total Score, Status	14,F	14,F	12,F	11,F	11,F

Luxembourg, one of the world's richest countries, retained its open media environment in 2006. Freedom of speech and of the press are safeguarded under Article 24 of the constitution and are respected in practice, although no freedom of information legislation is currently in place. An independent press council deals with press complaints and ethical questions. Owing to an extremely liberal media policy and a long tradition of providing television and radio services to European audiences, Luxembourg has a rich and diverse media whose influence goes beyond its borders. Exemplary of the free and open press environment that exists in Luxembourg, no journalists were subject to violent attacks or harassment in 2006.

Dailies are printed in Luxembourgish, German, and French, and one weekly publishes in Portuguese. Newspapers represent diverse viewpoints and are privately owned, though state subsidies protect presses from closing. Broadcast media are highly concentrated, dominated by the local group RTL. Luxembourg is also home to the largest European satellite operator. There is only one public broadcasting station, CLT. Many broadcasters operate only a few hours a day. There are two national and four regional broadcasters as well as several local radio stations. The internet is open and unrestricted, with an estimated 300,000 users, or 68 percent of the population.

Macedonia

LEGAL ENVIRONMENT: 11
POLITICAL ENVIRONMENT: 18
ECONOMIC ENVIRONMENT: 16

Status: Partly Free   TOTAL SCORE: 45

Survey Edition	2002	2003	2004	2005	2006
Total Score, Status	46,PF	50,PF	53,PF	51,PF	49,PF

The legal framework contains most of the basic laws protecting freedom of the press and of expression, and government representatives generally respect these rights. In January 2006, Parliament approved the Law on

Freedom of Information, which requires government agencies to release information as long as the public interest is greater than any harm that might result. The law gives some protection to whistle-blowers, limiting punishments for public employees who reported corruption or a significant threat to human health or the environment. A special commission will hear disputes related to the law, but appeals of its decisions will be processed through the normal court system. In May, Parliament passed legislation that eliminates imprisonment as a penalty for libel and defamation. Nevertheless, investigative journalist Zoran Bozinovski was sentenced to one to three months in jail for defamation in a December 2003 newspaper article. He spent several days behind bars in November before being released, reportedly as a result of intervention by the European Union. Bozinovski, who still faced the possibility of a retrial as well as numerous other pending libel cases, had been physically attacked in the past for his reporting.

While the number of libel and defamation cases are of particular concern to press freedom advocates, Macedonian journalists have been relatively free from physical harassment and abuse since 2001. However, on September 23 two employees from the television station ALSAT M were attacked while reporting on a story in Lazec. The attackers threatened to decapitate the reporters if they broadcast their story concerning the construction of a mosque. Most of the country's numerous and diverse private media outlets are tied to political or business interests that influence their content, and the state-owned media tend to support government positions. In early 2006, the independent newspaper *Vreme* reported that a number of journalists at major news outlets were moonlighting for a public relations firm, working on speeches and talking points for government ministers. Most other outlets failed to cover the ethics scandal, which added to widespread distrust of the media.

Macedonia has a high density of media outlets for its population, including 5 private nationwide television broadcasters, more than 50 local stations, some 160 radio stations, and nearly 20 newspapers. The resulting competition for advertising revenue and audiences has led to low pay, small staffs, and a general lack of professionalism. Observers have noted the prevalence of speculative reporting and anonymous sources. Financial constraints hindered pluralism in 2005, when the closure of two publications left only one Albanian-language newspaper, the daily *Fakti,* to serve the ethnic Albanian minority. Minority-language media have relied primarily on foreign aid, which has not proven to be sustainable. There are no major state-controlled print media, but private ownership is concentrated, with the German group WAZ owning the three major dailies. The government tried unsuccessfully to take over the private newspaper *Nova Makedonija*, which would have been a breach of the constitutional pledge regarding freedom of entrepreneurship, according to the International Press Institute. Even though the government does not place any restrictions on access to the internet, its usage remains relatively low, at just under 20 percent of the population, owing to lack of access and high prices.

Madagascar

Status: Partly Free

Legal Environment: 14
Political Environment: 21
Economic Environment: 15
Total Score: 50

Survey Edition	2002	2003	2004	2005	2006
Total Score, Status	31,PF	38,PF	41,PF	50,PF	49,PF

Although freedom of speech and of the press are protected by the constitution, strict libel laws and other restrictions are occasionally used to muzzle the media. In June, the government media regulatory body, the Direction de l'Information, de la Regulation, et des Media, proposed a measure to regulate guests invited to appear on radio and television broadcasts. In November, higher fines and maximum prison sentences of up to five years were proposed for journalists convicted of libel or "disturbing the peace."

Unlike in the previous year, in 2006 no journalists were convicted of libel. However, several attempts to restrict government criticism occurred prior to the December presidential elections. In October, a journalist from the daily *L'Objectif Malaza* was arrested for covering protests in Toamasina. Days later, a female journalist was harassed by security forces, and reporter Eloi Ravelonjato was arrested at a welcoming rally for a presidential candidate, Pierrot Rajaonarivelo. Radio Don Bosco and TV Plus were warned by government officials to cease reporting on the failed coup attempt by General Fidy in November. President Marc Ravalomanana additionally issued a public warning following the coup for journalists not to publish unchecked news or face action against them, according to the U.S. State Department. The government continued to refuse to renew a work permit for the Radio France Internationale (RFI) correspondent Olivier Peguy; RFI subsequently assigned a new correspondent to cover Madagascar.

There are 14 major privately owned dailies and several weeklies and monthlies; however, because of the low literacy rate, print media are aimed primarily at the French-educated urban elite. The majority of the population receives news through the broadcast media, which the government continues to monopolize nationwide. There were nonetheless over 200 radio stations, 137 of which were licensed, and 20 licensed television stations. Owing to low pay, journalists are subject to bribery. Occasionally, the government also employs strong-arm tactics to pressure private media outlets to curb their coverage of political issues, causing many journalists to practice self-censorship. The internet is unrestricted by the government but was accessed by less than 1 percent of the population in 2006.

Malawi

Status: Partly Free

LEGAL ENVIRONMENT: 16
POLITICAL ENVIRONMENT: 20
ECONOMIC ENVIRONMENT: 17
TOTAL SCORE: 53

Survey Edition	2002	2003	2004	2005	2006
Total Score, Status	54,PF	57,PF	52,PF	54,PF	55,PF

Freedom of speech and of the press are constitutionally guaranteed, although these rights are occasionally restricted in practice. The government does not exercise overt censorship, but freedom of expression is threatened in more subtle ways, resulting in some self-censorship. The Protected Emblems and Names Act prohibits insulting the president, which may result in fines and prison terms. A case was filed by Capitol Radio to declare the act unconstitutional; however, the case has been pending since September 2005. Journalists are also subject to occasional restrictions and harassment.

In May 2006, President Bingu wa Mutharika fired his attorney general, Ralph Kasambara, two days after the Media Institute of Southern Africa (MISA)–Malawi asked Mutharika to protect the good relations he has with the media. Earlier, Kasambara had made headlines after he ordered police to arrest three journalists at the *Chronicle* for defaming him. The journalists had published a story exposing MISA–Malawi's suspended national director, Charles Simango, as having tried to sell a laptop previously stolen from a Reuters photojournalist. Throughout the year, a number of other journalists faced harassment at the hands of security personnel, often after they had criticized public officials. A number of unofficial attempts at censorship occurred surrounding the visit of Zimbabwean president Robert Mugabe in May. Reporters from the *Chronicle* were barred from attending Mugabe's arrival ceremony for fear their coverage would reflect badly on the administration.

The print media represent a broad spectrum of opinion; 10 independent newspapers are available, 6 of which are privately owned and not politically affiliated. The state-owned Malawi Broadcasting Corporation (MBC) operates the country's 2 largest radio stations, and there are approximately 15 private radio stations with limited coverage. State-owned Television Malawi (TVM) is the country's only television station. State-run media generally adhere to a pro-government editorial line and grant opposition parties limited access. In 2006, the Malawi Parliament approved only half of the funding for the MBC and TVM, accusing the two state broadcasters of bias toward the government and the Democratic Progressive Party. The National Assembly said the rest of the funding for the two institutions will be approved only if they improve their coverage. Independent radio broadcasters receive no support from the state in terms of advertising revenue, and all equipment must be imported and paid for in U.S. dollars. There are no restrictions on the internet, although with access at less than 1 percent of the population, it is not a major source for news.

Malaysia

LEGAL ENVIRONMENT: 24
POLITICAL ENVIRONMENT: 25
ECONOMIC ENVIRONMENT: 19

Status: Not Free

TOTAL SCORE: 68

Survey Edition	2002	2003	2004	2005	2006
Total Score, Status	71,NF	71,NF	69,NF	69,NF	65,NF

Malaysian media—traditionally constrained by significant legal restrictions and intimidation—were further restricted in 2006 as a by-product of government attempts to suppress public discussion of divisive and potentially explosive issues. The constitution provides each citizen with "the right to freedom of speech and expression" but allows for limitations on this right. The 1984 Printing Presses and Publications Act (PPPA) requires all publishers and printing firms to obtain an annual operations permit and gives the prime minister the authority to revoke licenses at any time without judicial review. The PPPA has been used by authorities to shut down or otherwise circumscribe the distribution of pro-opposition media outlets and was invoked in early 2006 to indefinitely suspend the *Sarawak Tribune* and temporarily suspend the *Guang Ming Daily* for reproducing the Danish cartoons of the prophet Muhammad. Prime Minister Abdullah Badawi invoked the act again in mid-February to prohibit the publication, distribution, or possession of any materials relating to the Danish caricatures. The government's handling of the cartoon issue and use of the PPPA fostered fear of a selective crackdown on the press and resulted in media self-censorship.

Among other legal restrictions is the 1988 Broadcasting Act, which allows the information minister to decide who can own a broadcast station and the type of television service suitable for the Malaysian public. The Official Secrets Act, Sedition Act, and harsh criminal defamation legislation are also used to impose restrictions on the press and other critics. The country has no access to information legislation, and officials are reluctant to share controversial data. In October, government leaders refused to publicize the data and analysis behind the official Bumiputera corporate equity calculations used to uphold the country's affirmative action quotas after forcing the withdrawal of a study that challenged them.

The threat of expensive defamation suits, sackings, media closures, media bans, and unannounced interrogation by the Ministry of Internal Security for any "mishandling" of information generally inhibit investigative reporting. Moreover, self-censorship has been entrenched by a history of political interference in media coverage of issues considered by the government to be against the national interest or "sensitive." This trend culminated in mid-July 2006, when heightened tensions related to the perceived "Islamization" of Malaysia led the prime minister to ban all reporting on the issues of race and religion. A few days later, in violation of the 1998 Communications and Multimedia Act, which guarantees that the internet will not be censored, the prime minister threatened to detain those who "spread untruths and slander" on the internet and in text messages. The government directly censors books and films for profanity, nudity, and violence as well as certain political and religious material. The Ministry of Internal Security banned 18 books from mid-June to early July under the PPPA on the grounds they might "disrupt peace and harmony." Television stations censor programming according to government guidelines. A weekend newspaper, the *Weekend Mail*, and its editor were suspended for publishing a spread in November on what Malaysians think about sex.

Also in 2006, while they have traditionally owned all eight major daily newspapers, a business deal between the Malaysian Chinese Association and media tycoon Tiong Hiew King in October solidified the monopolization of the Chinese press, with all top four Chinese dailies now concentrated in the hands of a firm political-business alliance. Despite a call for media law reform launched by 47 civil society organizations in response to the October merger, newspaper reports in late November indicated plans for a subsequent merger in the Malay print industry that would grant UMNO, the ruling party, direct ownership of most local media through a new partnership with the Media Prima company. Both the print and broadcast media's news coverage and editorials already generally support the government line. There has been somewhat greater criticism of official policy in the mainstream print press in recent years, however. Foreign publications are subject to censorship, and the distribution of issues containing critical articles is frequently delayed.

With nearly 48 percent of the population accessing the internet, online media have helped minimize the government's monopoly of information in the past few years and bolstered the average Malaysian's access to alternative information sources. However, bloggers continue to be subject to repeated instances of harassment at the hands of authorities. The year's debate over Islam and minority rights prompted some government ministers to call for extending the PPPA to online media in 2006 and, in December, Science and Technology Minister Kong Cho Ha announced that the government planned to impose restrictions on the internet to prevent bloggers from disrupting social harmony. Prime Minister Abdullah proposed the launch of an internet exchange for Malaysia toward the end of the year that would make such controls easier to impose.

Maldives

Status: Not Free

LEGAL ENVIRONMENT: 23
POLITICAL ENVIRONMENT: 27
ECONOMIC ENVIRONMENT: 18
TOTAL SCORE: 68

Survey Edition	2002	2003	2004	2005	2006
Total Score, Status	61,NF	64,NF	64,NF	68,NF	70,NF

Over the past several years, a modest expansion of media diversity has been met by official crackdowns and harassment of journalists. Freedom of expression and of the press are not provided for in the constitution and are generally not respected by the government in practice. The legal environment remains harsh: The penal code bans speech or actions that could "arouse people against the government"; a 1968 law prohibits speech considered libelous, inimical to Islam, or a threat to national security; regulations make editors responsible for the content of material they publish; and authorities are empowered by law to shut newspapers and sanction journalists for articles containing unfounded criticism of the government. The Press Council, which is composed of lawyers, media representatives, and government officials, is mandated with reviewing lapses of journalistic conduct. In a positive move, legislation passed in July 2005 liberalized the registration process for newspapers, and since then, 6 daily newspapers and 11 other publications, some with an oppositionist slant, have been registered. The Information Ministry, which is spearheading reform efforts, submitted four media-related bills to Parliament in February 2006, including bills on freedom of information, press freedom, a proposed Media Council, and registration of print media. However, the government announced in November that it was retracting previously announced plans to allow private broadcasting.

Journalists, particularly those who cover political events or demonstrations or who write critical stories, continue to be subject to arrest or other forms of harassment, including death threats, from government officials and allies of President Maumoon Abdul Gayoom. On May 3, international press freedom monitors were assaulted by riot police and local journalists were arrested during celebrations to mark World Press Freedom Day. In November, foreign journalists covering the arrests of opposition Maldivian Democratic Party (MDP) activists were forced to leave the country, while cartoonist and MDP official Ahmed Abbas was arrested after being charged with criticizing police brutality in a cartoon. Abbas claimed that he never received a summons to attend his trial and was not allowed to present a defense. Owing to *Minivan News*'s overtly oppositionist stance, its management and employees have faced the brunt of official intimidation. A number of staff have been detained or subject to house arrest for extended periods, and others face criminal charges; journalist Abdullah Saeed was convicted of alleged drug possession and trafficking in May and was sentenced to life imprisonment, while his colleague Mohamed Yushau was held on terrorism charges from May to July. Ahmed Didi, the founder and one of four employees of the internet magazine *Sandhaanu* who were arrested in 2002 and sentenced to lengthy prison terms, was released from house arrest and pardoned in February. In this environment, many journalists practice self-censorship and remain reluctant to overtly criticize official policies.

All broadcast media continue to be government owned and operated, and while these outlets have recently provided more diverse coverage, they continue to reflect pro-government views. Most major print outlets are also owned by those connected to the government, but some publications, such as the weekly *Adduvas* and the newly registered *Jazeera* and *Hamma*, have generally adopted a more critical, balanced tone. The pro-opposition *Minivan News*, which started as an online publication, began publishing a print version in the Maldives in July 2005, but after the August protests, the printing house refused to continue publishing it under pressure from the authorities.

Groups of Maldivian exiles run independent news outlets in the United Kingdom and Sri Lanka and attempt to transmit news into the Maldives via shortwave radio stations and websites. Although the country's sole internet service provider is state owned, the internet is generally not restricted and was accessed by less than 7 percent of the population in 2006. However, the websites of the MDP and other pro-opposition news websites have been blocked by the government and are inaccessible from internet cafés in the capital, Male, and internet connectivity has occasionally been suspended altogether in the wake of political disturbances.

Mali

LEGAL ENVIRONMENT: 7
POLITICAL ENVIRONMENT: 9
ECONOMIC ENVIRONMENT: 8

Status: Free

TOTAL SCORE: 24

Survey Edition	2002	2003	2004	2005	2006
Total Score, Status	23,F	24,F	27,F	23,F	24,F

Mali is home to one of the freest media environments in Africa, with a constitution that protects the right to free speech and a government that generally respects this right in practice. Nevertheless, severe punishments for libel still exist under a 1993 law that criminalizes slander. Legislation passed in 2000 reduced the maximum penalty for those convicted, but the accused still remain guilty until proven innocent. These libel laws, though rarely implemented, were enforced in April 2006 when a weekly independent newspaper, *L'Inter de Bamako*, was ordered to pay Diacounda Traore, chairman of an opposition political party, a US$580 fine in response to an article published in February accusing Traore and fellow party leaders of corruption and mismanagement. In addition, two of the paper's editors were each fined US$135 and ordered to publish the court's ruling in three local newspapers at their own expense.

In 2005, a journalist with Radio Keledou was abducted and severely beaten by a group of unknown assailants. Although investigations into the identity of the perpetrators continue, no charges had yet been filed at the end of 2006. In August 2006, the government chose to inflict a disproportionate punishment on a radio network when it was found to be operating one of its stations without a license. Police shut down the broadcasting capabilities of Radio Kayira's station in southern Mali and arrested a number of station staff, including the managing director, two station hosts, and a station coordinator. Less than a week after their arrest, all were charged with "opposition to the authority of the State" and sentenced to, and served, a month in prison. Radio Kayira's defense claimed that they had submitted a license application as early as September 2005 but failed to receive a response from the authorities. The radio station is run by the opposition party African Solidarity for Democracy and Independence, which caused some to believe that the prosecution was politically motivated.

Today, there are more than 100 private radio stations and over 50 independent newspapers, many of which openly criticize the government. The country's only national television station remains under state control but provides balanced political coverage. Access to foreign media and to the internet is unrestricted by the government, though the internet was accessed by less than 1 percent of the population, mostly the very wealthy or well connected.

Malta

LEGAL ENVIRONMENT: 2
POLITICAL ENVIRONMENT: 6
ECONOMIC ENVIRONMENT: 9

Status: Free

TOTAL SCORE: 17

Survey Edition	2002	2003	2004	2005	2006
Total Score, Status	13,F	13,F	15,F	18,F	18,F

The constitution guarantees freedom of speech and of the press but also restricts these rights under a variety of circumstances. Malta bases its laws on the European model but is one of only three European Union members not to have freedom of information legislation. According to a recent survey conducted in June 2006 by Ernst & Young, television broadcasting suffers from a lack of quality with "too much teleshopping and not enough education," as well as "mediocre copying" of foreign programs. Alarmed at the low quality of children's programming on television, the government allocated 240,000 euros (US$327,824) to improve the local production of children's programs. In addition, the Ministry of Culture issued directives aimed at increasing "program quality and offering better service to the public." In December 2006, Lou Bondi, a television journalist for the country's Public Broadcasting Services (PBS), complained to the Institute of Maltese Journalists that PBS forced him to change the subject of one of his shows. The subject of the show was former finance and foreign affairs minister John Dalli, who stepped down in 2004 over his alleged involvement in a scandal involving irregularities in the allocation of a hospital tender. The arrest of another individual in 2006 cleared the former minister's name in this matter.

There are at least five daily and two weekly newspapers operating in both Maltese and English. Political parties, private investors, and the Catholic Church all have direct investments in broadcasting and print media that openly express partisan views. The only national television broadcaster is TVM, though the island also has access to Italian television, which many Maltese watch. Several domestic radio stations are regulated through the Broadcasting Authority of Malta. The government does not block the internet, which was accessed by 30 percent of the population in 2006.

Marshall Islands

LEGAL ENVIRONMENT: 2
POLITICAL ENVIRONMENT: 6
ECONOMIC ENVIRONMENT: 9

Status: Free

TOTAL SCORE: 17

Survey Edition	2002	2003	2004	2005	2006
Total Score, Status	10,F	10,F	12,F	13,F	15,F

Freedom of speech and of the press are safeguarded in Article 2 of the Marshallese constitution, and the government generally respects these rights. There is no freedom of information legislation and no immediate plans to draft such legislation in spite of recommendations made by the Pacific Islands Forum Secretariat in August 2006. During the year, the government launched an investigation into "dissenting comments" made by members of the local Chamber of Commerce concerning a trip to the People's Republic of China by members of the Marshallese Parliament. The Chamber of Commerce wrote a letter condemning the trip which was then published by the local press. Some fear the investigation will aggravate self-censorship, which is practiced on occasion over politically sensitive issues. After broadcasting on a state-owned radio station in September, Women United Together in the Marshall Islands was later denied further air time by the government. The Marshallese people receive most of their news from the independent weekly *Marshall Islands Journal* and the state-run V7AB radio. The government also releases a monthly newspaper, the

Marshall Islands Gazette, and broadcasts MBC TV. American broadcasts are available via satellite. Blackouts occasionally interfere with radio and television broadcasts. The internet is unrestricted, although accessed by less than 4 percent of the population. The government launched a new website in October 2006 to facilitate online communication with its citizens.

Mauritania

Status: Partly Free

LEGAL ENVIRONMENT: 18
POLITICAL ENVIRONMENT: 20
ECONOMIC ENVIRONMENT: 17
TOTAL SCORE: 55

Survey Edition	2002	2003	2004	2005	2006
Total Score, Status	61,NF	61,NF	64,NF	65,NF	57,PF

Significant progress has been made in opening Mauritania's media environment since a bloodless coup in 2005 overthrew the existing authoritarian regime. The transitional military government has since followed through on a number of promises to reform archaic press laws; however, the government still maintains a monopoly over the radio and television broadcast sectors. In 2005, the Military Council established the National Commission in Charge of the Reform of the Press and Broadcasting, which in March 2006 submitted a report on the reforms the government should design and implement in order to democratize the media. An ordinance based on the commission's report was adopted in June, eliminating the previous requirement for prepublication government approval of all newspapers while still requiring publishers to submit a copy of each issue to the government prior to its distribution, even though its approval was no longer required. The new law also transfers responsibility for journalists' registration from the Ministry of the Interior to the Ministry of Justice and gives journalists the legal right to protection of sources. In addition, in October 2006 the government created the High Authority for the Press and Broadcasting (HAPA), the first nominally independent media regulatory body in Mauritania. Nonetheless, the HAPA's independence is far from certain, as the president is responsible for appointing three of the body's six members, including the chair. The HAPA has been tasked with monitoring public communications and ensuring equal access to the state-run media outlets. It is also intended to lead the process of creating independent, private television and radio stations; in 2006, it began accepting applications, though no new television or radio outlet had been created by year's end.

Although no journalists were formally arrested or charged in 2006, a few reporters, including international correspondents, spent time in temporary detention. In one instance, security authorities detained a correspondent for the Iranian satellite channel Al-Alam who was also the chief editor for Mauritanian TV, after a guest on the state-run television station accused the government of neighboring Mali of carrying out extrajudicial killings against opposition Tuareg activists. After being accused of "aiding someone hostile to a friendly nation," the correspondent was fired from his position on Mauritanian TV. Separately, in April two journalists for the weekly newspaper *Ahira* complained that they were treated harshly by police while covering the president's visit to a local town. In February, armed men raided the daily *Al Akbar* in search of editor in chief Khalil Ould Jdoud, who had sanctioned a story the day before about investigations into an embezzlement of bank BACIM. Police later arrested Mohamed Mahmoud Ould Deh, who is indirectly affiliated with the bank.

The government owns 2 daily newspapers, and approximately 40 privately owned newspapers operate on a regular basis—nearly double the figure from the previous year. In the new press law passed in 2006, privately owned newspaper operators and book publishers are exempt from all taxes on material used in their production. Nevertheless, a large and persistent impediment to a genuinely free media environment is the government's monopoly of all broadcast media. Internet access is available and has been unrestricted by the transition government, but less than 0.5 percent of the population has the means to access it.

Mauritius

LEGAL ENVIRONMENT: 6
POLITICAL ENVIRONMENT: 8
ECONOMIC ENVIRONMENT: 12
Status: Free
TOTAL SCORE: 26

Survey Edition	2002	2003	2004	2005	2006
Total Score, Status	17,F	24,F	26,F	28,F	26,F

Freedom of expression is safeguarded by the constitution, and this right was respected in practice in 2006. In August, the government proposed a plan to diffuse the Independent Broadcasting Authority (IBA), the media regulatory body, and replace it with a media commission that would have the power to sanction the press and impose stronger punishments for libel and sedition. Penalties for libel could reach 2 million MUR (US$65,000) along with a prison term of up to two years. An additional Broadcasting Compliance Committee would be established to respond to complaints against broadcasters and would have the power to suspend or revoke licenses. These acts were pending at year's end. Also pending is a proposed freedom of information bill, which would increase government transparency by giving journalists access to official documents. In September, 106 members of the press convened to establish the Mauritius Journalists Association to safeguard their rights. In December, the IBA sanctioned state-owned MBC-TV for biased political coverage. The sanctions were sparked by complaints by the Mauritian Militant Movement claiming that MBC-TV allowed the Republican Movement greater airtime. Mauritians receive the majority of their news from television, which is monopolized by the government. Radio broadcasts are dominated by the government's Mauritius Broadcasting Corporation, which is funded predominantly through a television license fee, though private stations also operate. The private press is vibrant, with 12 daily and weekly independent papers, but ownership is concentrated in two main media houses, Le Mauricien Ltd. and La Sentinelle Ltd. The internet is unrestricted by the government and usage is wide compared with other African nations, at 14 percent of the population.

Mexico

LEGAL ENVIRONMENT: 12
POLITICAL ENVIRONMENT: 23
ECONOMIC ENVIRONMENT: 13

Status: Partly Free

TOTAL SCORE: 48

Survey Edition	2002	2003	2004	2005	2006
Total Score, Status	40,PF	38,PF	36,PF	42,PF	48,PF

The law provides for press freedom, and improvements were made in the legal sector in 2006, but violence against journalists, impunity for such crimes, and subsequent self-censorship overshadowed gains. A new federal law gave journalists the right to protect confidential sources, and the Mexico City Assembly passed the first state-level shield law. The assembly also became the first state-level authority to eliminate criminal defamation. The lower house of Congress passed a similar proposal, and some expect a Senate vote to end federal criminal defamation in 2007; however, state-level defamation laws continued to pose problems for the press. A journalist was jailed in Chiapas under its criminal defamation statute, and two lawmakers in Michoacan filed charges against a journalist. The 2005 case against journalist and author Lydia Cacho was thrown out by the courts on a technicality. Based on recorded conversations between Puebla businessman Kamel Nacif Borge—whom Cacho alleged was indirectly involved in a child prostitution ring in her book *Los Demonios del Eden*—and Puebla governor Mario Marin plotting the journalist's arrest, the Supreme Court ordered an investigation into the matter. Ironically, in 2006 a political ally of Governor Marin was named the new special prosecutor for crimes against journalists.

In 2006, a new Radio and Television Law was also passed, although a minority coalition of senators appealed the decision to the Supreme Court. Advocates of the two major TV networks, Televisa and TV Azteca, claimed that the law reduced political discretion for awarding broadcast concessions. Critics pointed out that it could solidify the two networks' duopoly status, give away lucrative digital rights, and offer no financial or legal assistance for noncommercial broadcasters.

According to the Organization of American States, during 2006 a record nine journalists were killed, and in the majority of cases their deaths were likely connected to their profession. The journalists were targeted for their coverage of drug trafficking, organized crime, public corruption, and police brutality. The Popular Assembly of the District of Oaxaca attacked several journalists and took over media outlets throughout the year. Political violence in Oaxaca led to the deaths of two journalists. Raul Marcial Perez from the regional newspaper *El Grafico* was murdered on December 8 in Juxtlahuaca by gunmen who opened fire in the newsroom. Perez's columns often criticized the local government. On October 27, an American cameraman for Indymedia, Bradley Will, was gunned down while covering protests in Oaxaca City. The shots came from an area where the municipal police were located. Two suspects were detained but released a month later, despite witness accounts of them firing in Will's direction. The Office of the Special Prosecutor failed to solve any major crimes against the press but documented 108 complaints between February and November 2006. Threats against journalists were a major issue in 2006, as were arrests, and during the Oaxaca demonstrations, several news outlets were seized by protesters. Self-censorship along the drug-plagued northern border was well documented in testimonials. Attempts by media to investigate drug-related attacks were stalled by fear.

There is a diversity of perspectives represented in media in the largest cities, less so in smaller states and the countryside. Television remains limited because of concentration of wealth inherited from the authoritarian era. President Felipe Calderon's six-year administration announced plans to create a third national commercial television network as well as several regional networks. Coupled with measures to strengthen noncommercial radio, this could increase media diversity. There are about 300 independently owned newspapers. The government does not restrict the internet, which was used by 19 percent of the population.

| | | | LEGAL ENVIRONMENT: 1 |
| | | | POLITICAL ENVIRONMENT: 8 |

Micronesia

ECONOMIC ENVIRONMENT: 11

Status: Free   TOTAL SCORE: 20

Survey Edition	2002	2003	2004	2005	2006
Total Score, Status	20,F	17,F	19,F	18,F	20,F

Article 4, Section 1, of the constitution states that no law may deny or impair freedom of expression, peaceable assembly, association, or petition; there are no specific safeguards for speech or the press. Free speech was generally respected by the government, and there were no documented attacks on the press. A lack of economic resources is the biggest constraint on Micronesian media. Micronesia has five newspapers; the broadest reaching is the state-owned *Kaselehlie Press*, which is published biweekly. In 2005, two new independent weeklies emerged, the *Sinlaku Sun Times* and *Da Rohng*, which have quickly earned a reputation as being critical of the government. There is also an online daily, the *Mariana Variety*. Each of the four state governments has a radio station that broadcasts in the local language; however, broadcasting was down for much of the year because of weather-related damages to equipment. The states of Pohnpei and Chuuk have commercial television, and Yap has a government-run television station. Foreign television is available via satellite. The internet is unrestricted by the government but was accessed by only 13 percent of the population in 2006.

Moldova

Status: Not Free

LEGAL ENVIRONMENT: 20
POLITICAL ENVIRONMENT: 25
ECONOMIC ENVIRONMENT: 20
TOTAL SCORE: 65

Survey Edition	2002	2003	2004	2005	2006
Total Score, Status	59,PF	59,PF	63,NF	65,NF	65,NF

The government often infringes on legally guaranteed press freedoms. Libel is no longer punishable by imprisonment, and legislation was passed in July aimed at capping previously unlimited fines in libel cases. An existing Access to Information Law permits legal residents of Moldova to request information or documents from state entities without an explanation, but draft legislation affecting transparency in the decision making of public authorities was still under consideration in 2006. In March, after neglecting to involve civil society in the development of a draft audiovisual code, Moldova's Parliament made the draft available for public comment and passed it in July. Media watchdogs commended the government for trying to bring Moldovan law in line with international standards. However, they also expressed various concerns, warning in part that the draft code's proposed broadcast regulatory body should not, as suggested, also act as a supervisory body for the public service broadcaster. In Moldova, any person has the freedom to become a journalist, and journalists do not require accreditation for exercising their profession, but the Press Law gives authorities the right to introduce required accreditation if they believe it to be necessary. A new Chisinau School of Advanced Journalism opened in September, offering a one-year program in print and broadcast journalism leading to certificates signed by the Independent Journalism Center and the U.S.-based Missouri School of Journalism.

President Vladimir Voronin's government controls the public company Teleradio Moldova, which is the only national public company and includes one radio station and one television channel, and censorship is reportedly imposed on the stations. Owners of both state-run and private media continue to promote self-censorship, and many journalists avoid controversial issues that might cost them their jobs or draw libel suits, particularly when investigating issues of corruption. Journalists tend to be divided along political lines, reflecting the viewpoint of either the authorities or the opposition. In September, after the Romanian television station Pro-TV broadcast reports that were highly critical of the Moldovan interior minister, ministry officials arrested Ghenadie Braghis, a sales director of the Chisinau branch of Pro-TV. They denied him access to legal counsel and accused him of seeking a US$1,000 bribe from a client to seal an advertising deal. After publishing articles related to crime and corruption in Moldova's legal system, journalists from the Chisinau-based weekly newspaper *Ziarul de Garda* reported pressure from various state entities in October.

In the separatist Transnistria region, media are sharply restricted and politicized. Most news outlets are controlled, owned, or funded by the Transnistrian authorities. Print media in Transnistria are required to register with the local Ministry of Information rather than the Moldovan government.

Moldova's print media were able to express diverse political and public views throughout the year. Broadcast media were weaker, as there is little private local broadcasting and most programs are rebroadcast from either Romania or Russia. However, in a particularly serious transgression of the need for open public broadcasting following the passage of the new audiovisual code, Radio Antena C and Euro TV, the public municipal stations, were privatized in a process that was not open to public scrutiny. Most private media are dependent on funds they receive through foundations created by foreign governments. The government frequently uses financial measures to harass the media, such as dissuading business owners from advertising in independent outlets. Foreign publications were available in limited quantities. Authorities do not control internet access, although internet services are limited to roughly 15 percent of the population owing to an underdeveloped telecommunications infrastructure.

Monaco

LEGAL ENVIRONMENT: 3
POLITICAL ENVIRONMENT: 7
ECONOMIC ENVIRONMENT: 6

Status: Free

TOTAL SCORE: 16

Survey Edition	2002	2003	2004	2005	2006
Total Score, Status	NA	9,F	13,F	14,F	16,F

Freedom of expression is guaranteed under Article 23 of the 1962 Monegasque constitution. However, it is prohibited by law to publicly denounce the ruling family. This exception is generally observed by the media, leading to occasional self-censorship. No violations of press freedom were reported in 2006. Monaco has no daily newspapers, but French dailies that cover news in Monaco are available, as are French television and radio broadcasts. Two domestic weekly newspapers, the government-produced *Journal de Monaco* and *Monaco Hebdo*, are also available. Monaco has one government-run television station, one privately owned English-language radio station, Riviera Radio, and the government-run Radio Monte-Carlo, which broadcasts in several languages both in and outside of Monaco. The internet is available and unrestricted and used by more than 50 percent of the population.

Mongolia
Status: Partly Free

LEGAL ENVIRONMENT: 12
POLITICAL ENVIRONMENT: 13
ECONOMIC ENVIRONMENT: 11
TOTAL SCORE: 36

Survey Edition	2002	2003	2004	2005	2006
Total Score, Status	31,PF	36,PF	36,PF	35,PF	34,PF

Freedom of speech and of the press are protected by law, and the government generally respects these rights in practice. However, media freedom deteriorated somewhat in 2006 owing to an increase in attacks and harassment of journalists. Censorship of public information is banned under the 1998 Media Freedom Law, which also prohibits the government from owning media outlets. The State Secrets Law limits access to government information to a degree, as many archived historical records have been given classified status. The government monitors media content for compliance with antiviolence, antipornography, and antialcohol content restrictions. The use of criminal and civil defamation suits also remains problematic. Officials have at times filed libel suits against media practitioners and publications in the wake of critical articles. In June, two journalists lost court cases brought by a plaintiff named in their articles, but were spared fines owing to an amnesty. Another journalist, Uyanga Gantumur, lost a suit brought by a bank after she wrote that the president might own shares in the bank. Libel charges are hard to defend against because Mongolian civil law places the burden on the defendant to prove the truth of the statement at issue. To avoid being sued for libel, many independent publications practice a degree of self-censorship.

While no direct government censorship exists, journalists complain of indirect forms of censorship such as harassment and intimidation, as well as pressure to reveal confidential sources. In early 2006, reporter Sh. Otgonjargal of the Mongolian People's Revolutionary Party daily *Unen* was harassed and threatened with arrest by a security official demanding to know the sources behind an article concerning official corruption. In July, B. Tsevegmid, editor in chief of the Nomin television station, was assaulted outside the station. She was hospitalized for treatment. The beating followed the airing of a controversial investigative program on the mining industry. In October, two journalists and two photographers from newspapers were beaten and detained while covering a protest demonstration in the capital city of Ulaanbaatar.

Although independent print media outlets are common and popular in cities, the main source of news in the vast countryside is the formerly state-owned Radio Mongolia. Under the new Law on the Public Radio and TV passed in January 2005, state-owned radio and television broadcasting outlets, like Radio Mongolia, are currently transitioning into public service broadcasting operations. Nonetheless, both the state-owned and public media still frequently experience political pressures, and most provincial media outlets continue to be controlled by local authorities. Mongolians have access to local, privately owned television stations, English-language broadcasts of the British Broadcasting Corporation and Voice of America on private FM stations, and, in Ulaanbaatar, foreign television programming via cable and commercial satellite systems. In this country of 2.5 million, only 220,000 people are internet users, or slightly more than 10 percent of the population. Owing to widespread poverty in Mongolia, the internet has yet to serve as a significant source of information.

Montenegro

LEGAL ENVIRONMENT: 11
POLITICAL ENVIRONMENT: 16
ECONOMIC ENVIRONMENT: 10

Status: Partly Free

TOTAL SCORE: 37

Survey Edition	2002	2003	2004	2005	2006
Total Score, Status	NA	NA	NA	NA	NA

The constitution of the newly independent state of Montenegro guarantees freedom of the press, but in practice the government has been known to restrict this right and interfere in the work of media outlets. Libel is punishable by fines of up to US$18,400, and frequent lawsuits against journalists threaten to encourage self-censorship. A Podgorica court in February and April dismissed a libel case brought by the minister of education against the opposition daily *Dan*. The administration accused several media outlets of unprofessional reporting and inciting nationalist sentiment ahead of the May referendum on independence from the State Union of Serbia and Montenegro and the September parliamentary elections. In September, a Podgorica court fined a *Dan* columnist for ridiculing those who voted for independence. The television broadcaster Elmag was fined for airing viewer text messages mocking different ethnic groups. The members of the Radio and Television Council (RTVCG), the body that oversees the national broadcast media, are appointed by nongovernmental organizations (NGOs) and professional groups. The Parliament twice rejected NGO nominations for RTVCG members in 2006, leading observers to speculate that the Parliament was seeking to influence the council. The regulatory body in charge of issuing broadcast licenses is independent from the government.

The media are active and express diverse views. There is no direct censorship, although certain government actions in 2006 suggested that officials were seeking to maintain a moderate level of control over major national media outlets. In January, a new television director was appointed by the director general of the public Radio and Television of Montenegro; the previous television director had been dismissed in 2005, and critics pointed out that the new appointee was a close government ally. Media are at times highly politicized and reflect the divisive nature of the Montenegrin Parliament, which remains split between pro-union and pro-independence factions. Although the ruling party received more airtime than the opposition, most media acted professionally during the politically sensitive referendum and elections. There were a few reports of harassment and violence directed at journalists. In October, a political novelist was beaten and his bodyguard was shot dead. The 2005 murder of *Dan* director and editor, Dusko Jovanovic, remained unresolved, and in December, a man accused of participating in the killing was acquitted.

The print media are privately owned, with the exception of one major national newspaper that is still state owned. The privatization process for that paper stalled in 2006. There are no restrictions on advertising or distribution, although smaller media outlets struggle to attract advertising and reach rural areas. There are a number of privately owned radio and television stations in addition to the public broadcasters, and Montenegrin stations routinely rebroadcast foreign content. There are no restrictions on the internet, with 17 percent of the population able to access this new medium in 2006.

LEGAL ENVIRONMENT: 23
POLITICAL ENVIRONMENT: 22

Morocco
ECONOMIC ENVIRONMENT: 17

Status: Not Free

TOTAL SCORE: 62

Survey Edition	2002	2003	2004	2005	2006
Total Score, Status	58,PF	57,PF	61,NF	63,NF	61,NF

The Moroccan constitution offers freedom of expression, but the Press Law prohibits criticism of the monarchy and Islam and effectively bars material challenging the government's position on the status of Western Sahara. Those who violate the law are subject to heavy fines and lengthy prison sentences. Government promises to reform the Press Law have largely gone unfulfilled. While some international human rights activists have pointed to evidence that Morocco is turning the page on its troubled past and moving toward more openness and democratization, the story of the country's press paints a somewhat different picture. Over the past decade, as the pioneering independent press continued to tackle taboo subjects despite the harsh press laws, the government began to adopt a subtler approach in its responses to critics who crossed the "red lines." Rather than imprisoning journalists, which would draw unwanted attention, the government now employs a series of tactics that make it nearly impossible for them to practice their profession.

The state largely refrained from direct censorship and manipulation of the licensing process in 2006, but the imposition of punitive fines and suspended prison sentences, and the use of third parties to apply indirect pressure, served to encourage self-censorship in the media. *Le Journal Hebdomadaire*, published and edited by journalists Aboubakr Jamai and Ali Amar respectively, suffered such government harassment throughout the year. In February, the weekly ran a small photograph of someone holding a newspaper that had published controversial cartoons of the prophet Muhammad. Within days, the magazine's office was besieged by protesters who were apparently bused in by the government. Meanwhile, pro-government media outlets attacked *Le Journal* in print and on the airwaves. Later in February, a Rabat court awarded security analyst Claude Moniquet a record 3 million Moroccan dirhams (US$340,000) in a defamation suit he brought against *Le Journal*. Moniquet's Brussels-based think tank, the European Strategic Intelligence and Security Center, had published a report on Western Sahara, and *Le Journal*'s editors questioned the study's independence. An appeals court subsequently confirmed the damages sum.

The case appeared to have been a politically motivated effort to bankrupt the magazine. In order to save it, Jamai relinquished his position, which was taken up by Amar, and left the country. In addition to *Le Journal*, several other publications suffered legal harassment during the year. The weekly *Nichane* was banned in December after it ran jokes about religion. The paper's editor and a reporter were charged with defamation of Islam and faced possible prison time; the publication would remain shuttered until their trial's completion. Foreign journalists can work with relative ease in Morocco but face government pressure and even expulsion from the country if they report on Western Sahara in a manner that offends authorities.

Morocco is home to a large number of private print publications, many of them critical of the government. However, circulation is limited, and most papers receive some government subsidies. Broadcast media that report news are still dominated by the state, but as in most Arab countries, residents can access critical reports through Pan-Arab satellite channels. Francophone Moroccans can also access French-language broadcasts that provide alternative viewpoints. Foreign journalists can work with relative freedom in Morocco, but authorities are as sensitive with the foreign press as they are with local journalists when it comes to covering the Western Sahara issue. The minority of Moroccans with internet access (roughly 15 percent of the population) also receive alternative viewpoints from online sources, though the government sometimes blocks certain websites.

Mozambique

Status: Partly Free

LEGAL ENVIRONMENT: 11
POLITICAL ENVIRONMENT: 15
ECONOMIC ENVIRONMENT: 14
TOTAL SCORE: 40

Survey Edition	2002	2003	2004	2005	2006
Total Score, Status	48,PF	47,PF	45,PF	45,PF	43,PF

Press freedom conditions continued to improve in 2006 owing to fewer instances of physical harassment of journalists and limited progress in the key Cardoso murder case. The 1990 constitution provides for press freedom but restricts this right according to respect for the constitution, human dignity, the imperatives of foreign policy, and national defense. Reporters continue to face problems accessing official information. In August 2005, the government introduced a draft freedom of information bill, the product of five years of consultations with journalists and press freedom advocates, but a final version had not been passed by the end of 2006. The 1991 Press Law, considered one of the more progressive in Africa, was reviewed in 2006 by Gabinfo, the government press office, which suggested possible "improvements" such as provisions for mandatory licenses for working journalists and pointed to the omission of much needed freedom of information legislation. Defamation of the president is illegal, and criminal libel laws are sometimes used to prosecute media outlets. In May, three journalists with *Mabarwe*, a community paper in Manica province, were arrested as a "preventive measure" after being sued for libel and were detained for a week.

Journalists continue to be at risk of being threatened or harassed by officials or nonstate actors, although no such cases were reported during 2006. Developments concerning the 2000 murder of prominent investigative journalist Carlos Cardoso continued to unfold during the year. The retrial of Anibal dos Santos Jr. began in December 2005, and in January 2006 he was convicted for a second time of recruiting the men who killed Cardoso and was sentenced to almost 30 years in prison. After several years of refusing to investigate the role in Cardoso's murder of former president Joaquim Alberto Chissano's son, Nyimpine Chissano, who had been implicated in the testimony of several of the accused killers, authorities charged Nyimpine Chissano with "joint moral authorship" of the crime in May 2006, but he had not been arrested by year's end. Despite these positive steps, the chilling effect cast by Cardoso's murder remains; many investigative reporters are hesitant to examine sensitive topics, and self-censorship is an issue.

The private media have enjoyed moderate growth in recent years, and independent daily and weekly newspapers routinely provide scrutiny of the government. However, publications based in the capital, Maputo, have little influence on the largely illiterate rural population. The state owns a majority stake in the main national daily, *Noticias,* and the largest broadcast networks, Radio Mozambique (RM) and Televisao de Mozambique, although dozens of private radio and television stations also operate. While state-owned media have displayed greater editorial independence, the opposition still receives inadequate coverage and establishment views are favored. According to the Media Institute of Southern Africa's African Media Barometer, the development of private commercial radio continues to be hampered by the fact that state advertisements are broadcast exclusively on RM. Instances have also occurred where newspapers have had advertising from state-owned companies withdrawn after publishing unfavorable stories. The financial viability of many outlets is affected as well by a law limiting foreign investment in any media enterprise to a 20 percent stake.

Internet access is unrestricted, though less than 1 percent of the population has access because of a scarcity of electricity and computers.

		LEGAL ENVIRONMENT: 8			
		POLITICAL ENVIRONMENT: 10			
Namibia		ECONOMIC ENVIRONMENT: 12			
Status: Free		TOTAL SCORE: 30			

Survey Edition	2002	2003	2004	2005	2006
Total Score, Status	34,PF	37,PF	34,PF	29,F	30,F

Namibia's press is generally considered to be one of the freest on the continent. The constitution guarantees freedom of speech and of the press, and the government generally respects these rights in practice. Independent media routinely criticize the government, though government pressure and sensitivity to negative coverage have led to some self-censorship. The Freedom of Information Act, introduced in 1999 as a fundamental component of the government's anticorruption initiative, was put into effect only in 2005.

In recent years, the most serious media restrictions in Namibia have been isolated incidents in which the government has canceled advertisements in a few newspapers for their supposedly critical coverage. In February, the Media Institute of Southern Africa reported that a government ban on the English-language independent daily *The Namibian*—in place since March 2001—persists to date. In September, Sam Nujoma former president and head of the ruling South-West Africa People's Organization (SWAPO) initiated a N$5 million (approximately US$650,000) defamation suit against *The Namibian* because of an August 2005 story implicating Nujoma in a corruption scandal. In addition, some restrictions have been sought in media coverage of the mass trials of accused secessionists from the Caprivi region. In May, John Liebenberg, a South African photographer, was arrested for attempting to photograph actors Brad Pitt and Angelina Jolie, who were in the country for the birth of their child. In December, the youth league of the ruling SWAPO party called for restrictions on "cancerous, racist, and parasitic media operators" after some newspapers reported critically on former president Sam Nujoma's role in a 1989 battle with South African forces.

Eight newspapers are in circulation, 6 of which are privately owned. There are at least 11 private radio stations and 2 private television stations that broadcast in English and German. A subscription satellite television service broadcasts CNN, the British Broadcasting Corporation, and a range of South African and international news and entertainment programs. Private radio stations and newspapers usually operate without official interference, but reporters for state-run media have been subjected to indirect and direct pressure to avoid reporting on controversial topics. While many journalists insist that the state-run Namibia Broadcasting Corporation (NBC) enjoys complete freedom to criticize the government, others believe that it is biased toward the ruling party. In February, the government attempted to allow only photographers from the NBC to cover the opening of parliament; after vocal protests from nonstate media and press freedom organizations, the government granted access to a wide range of media organizations. There are no government restrictions on the internet, and several print publications have popular websites, but access to this new medium is limited to less than 4 percent of the population owing to financial and infrastructure constraints.

Nauru

Status: Free

LEGAL ENVIRONMENT: 4
POLITICAL ENVIRONMENT: 11
ECONOMIC ENVIRONMENT: 13
TOTAL SCORE: 28

Survey Edition	2002	2003	2004	2005	2006
Total Score, Status	27,F	26,F	25,F	29,F	30,F

Freedom of expression is safeguarded in Article 12 of the constitution, though there are limitations for libel and national security. There are no protections for freedom of information under the law, and in the past the government has proven uncooperative in granting access to documents. The 2004 freedom of information bill was rejected, and no comparable bills have been presented since. There were no attacks on the press in 2006. Environmental challenges, a poor communications infrastructure, and a failing economy have limited the country's media scene. Nauru publishes no daily papers, and there are no private newspaper companies, though the government releases the weekly *Nauru Bulletin*, the fortnightly *Central Star News*, and the *Nauru Chronicle*. A newsletter, the *People's Voice*, is published by the opposition party. The state runs one radio and one television station that both carry material from foreign media, though no private broadcasting exists. The internet is unrestricted by the government, although access remains limited—available to less than 3 percent of the population owing to a poor telecommunications infrastructure.

LEGAL ENVIRONMENT: 17
POLITICAL ENVIRONMENT: 27

Nepal

ECONOMIC ENVIRONMENT: 14

Status: Partly Free

TOTAL SCORE: 58

Survey Edition	2002	2003	2004	2005	2006
Total Score, Status	60,PF	65,NF	65,NF	69,NF	77,NF

Status change explanation: Nepal's status improved from Not Free to Partly Free as a result of a dramatic shift in the media environment that accompanied equally dramatic political change, including the overthrow of direct rule by the monarchy, the reintroduction of a parliamentary form of government, and the peace accords reached with the Maoist rebels.

Media freedom improved dramatically in Nepal during 2006 as a result of equally dramatic political change in which massive street protests forced an end to King Gyanendra Bir Bikram Shah Dev's direct rule in April. While the king agreed to step out of political life and restore the 1990 Parliament, the Maoist insurgents agreed to a cease-fire and a restarting of peace talks designed to end the violence and bring them into the political process. Journalists, local press freedom organizations, and other civil society activists played a key role in restoring greater democratic rights through organizing a number of demonstrations in addition to pressing the Supreme Court to uphold media freedom.

Nepali media started the year under heavy legal restrictions, including a state of emergency, overt censorship of news, and frequent arrests and detention of editors. In addition, an October 2005 ordinance gave the government the power to revoke journalists' press accreditation and to impose high fines for publishing banned items; permanently barred private radio stations from broadcasting news; criminalized criticism of the royal family; and restricted media cross-ownership. However, beginning in May, the interim government rescinded this and several other pieces of "antimedia" legislation. Parts of the Press and Publications Act, which allowed for restrictions on speech and writing that could undermine the monarchy, national security, public order, or interethnic or intercaste relations, were repealed by the Parliament in May. Similarly, provisions of the 1992 National Broadcasting Act, which gave the government the right to cancel the licenses of radio and television stations, were deemed incompatible with constitutional guarantees for press freedom. A high-level media commission was formed in June to further review media laws and practices. Antiterrorism legislation permitting authorities to detain for renewable six-month periods individuals suspected of supporting the Maoists had been used regularly to arrest and detain journalists suspected of pro-Maoist leanings for long periods. In July, the government announced that all prisoners held under the law would be freed and that no new cases would be filed, according to the Committee to Protect Journalists. Finally, the interim constitution signed in December provides for press freedom and specifically prohibits censorship or the closure of, or cancellation of registration to, print and broadcast media outlets.

The media now function in a less threatening environment than under Gyanendra's rule, when harassment, intimidation, and violence toward journalists were commonplace. Following the king's overthrow, the interim government as well as the Maoist leadership promised to respect press freedom, and an improvement in conditions was clear. However, journalists still face harassment from Maoist cadres, local-level officials and politicians, police and military forces, and criminal groups, especially when reporting on sensitive topics. Although instances in which the government was directly responsible for attacks or threats toward the press were less frequent, there have been cases in which police or soldiers have mistreated journalists. Maoists continue to regularly intimidate, detain, kidnap, and assault reporters owing to their coverage of the rebels or the peace process. Journalists have also come under attack by activists or mobs when covering the news or reporting on sensitive topics; reporters covering the treatment of minority groups in rural areas have been threatened or attacked. With dozens of cases of threats and attacks documented in the latter half of the year by groups such as the Kathmandu-based Federation of Nepalese Journalists and the Center for Human Rights and Democratic Studies, journalists' ability to operate freely, particularly in the rural areas, remains constrained.

The government owns several of the major English-language and vernacular dailies; these news outlets generally provide pro-government coverage. Hundreds of private publications, some with particular political viewpoints, provide a range of diverse views, and many have resumed their critical coverage of sensitive issues such as human rights violations, the insurgency, and corruption. The government owns both the influential Radio Nepal, whose political coverage is supportive of official policies, and NTV, Nepal's main television station. Private FM and community radio stations, which together with the national radio network reach some 90 percent of the population, flourished prior to the 2005 coup and are a primary source of information, particularly in the rural areas. Under Gyanendra's direct rule, censorship and news bans caused the closure of many stations, forcing several thousand reporters out of work. However, this situation was reversed in 2006, with many radio journalists returning to their jobs. Requirements for registering broadcast stations were eased, and by October the government had awarded licenses for 6 new television channels and 50 FM radio stations across the country. A 2005 decision to ban official advertising in private news outlets was also reversed. The internet is generally unrestricted but was accessed by less than 1 percent of the population. During 2005 and early 2006, some pro-Maoist or antimonarchy websites were reportedly blocked or monitored, but this surveillance ceased after the April transition. Restrictions on foreign broadcasts were similarly lifted.

Netherlands

Status: Free

LEGAL ENVIRONMENT: 2
POLITICAL ENVIRONMENT: 7
ECONOMIC ENVIRONMENT: 4
TOTAL SCORE: 13

Survey Edition	2002	2003	2004	2005	2006
Total Score, Status	15,F	15,F	12,F	11,F	11,F

The media in the Netherlands are free and independent. Restrictions against insulting the monarch and royal family exist but are rarely enforced. The Netherlands does not have legislation ensuring the right of journalists to protect their sources, although this right can be invoked under Article 10 of the European Convention on Human Rights. In November, two respected journalists, Bart Mos and Joost de Haas, of the Netherlands' largest newspaper, *De Telegraaf*, were imprisoned for refusing to reveal their sources in the case of an intelligence service agent who was suspected of leaking classified information to crime syndicates. After fierce protests from the media sector, Mos and de Haas were released a few days later and the court order to reveal their sources was dropped. Nonetheless, this is a worrying sign for journalists in the Netherlands, many of whom now fear that potential sources will be deterred from confiding in them as a result of this case. *De Telegraaf* was also at the center of a separate debate over the legality of wiretapping when it was revealed that the Dutch intelligence service had been taping the phone conversations of two of *De Telegraaf*'s leading reporters. In defense of the wiretapping, Interior Minister Johan Remkes told the Dutch Parliament that journalists should not be given special protections and, like the rest of the population, ought to be subject to investigation and telephone tapping if necessary.

In 2005, Mohammed Bouyeri, the radical Islamist who killed the controversial filmmaker Theo van Gogh, was sentenced to life imprisonment for murder. Although this particular case resulted in the trial and conviction of the perpetrator, the legacy left by van Gogh's murder is a climate of fear among journalists and filmmakers interested in pursuing controversial topics, particularly those related to immigration and the increasing influence of Islam in the Netherlands. Ayaan Hirsi Ali, the Somali-born parliamentarian known for her outspoken criticisms of Islam and for the film *Submission*, on which she collaborated with Theo van Gogh, also received death threats during the year. In January, two satellite television stations that transmit from Iran were blocked in an attempt to censor extremist views. In November, according to the International Press Institute, a rocket-propelled grenade was fired at newspaper printer PCM. Minor damage was caused, though the perpetrators were not caught and the motives were unclear.

Despite a high concentration of newspaper ownership, a wide variety of opinions are expressed in the print media. In a remnant of the traditional "pillar" system, the state allocates public radio and television programming to political, religious, and social groups according to their membership size. While every province has at least one public television channel, public broadcasting has faced stiff competition from commercial stations since their legalization in 1988. International news sources are widely accessible, and the internet is unrestricted by the government and used regularly by roughly 75 percent of the population.

New Zealand

Status: Free

LEGAL ENVIRONMENT: 3
POLITICAL ENVIRONMENT: 5
ECONOMIC ENVIRONMENT: 5
TOTAL SCORE: 13

Survey Edition	2002	2003	2004	2005	2006
Total Score, Status	8,F	8,F	10,F	12,F	13,F

While the news media are generally free and vigorous, the country's first sedition case in more than 80 years prompted debate on the implications for the press. Pamphleteer Tim Selwyn was jailed for two months in July 2006 under Section 81 of the Crimes Law. He had admitted to conspiring to commit willful damage when an ax was embedded in Prime Minister Helen Clark's electoral office window in November 2004. Selwyn had admitted in court to "having a hand" in media releases and pamphlets claiming responsibility for the attack and calling on other New Zealanders to take "similar action."

The controversy over the publication of Danish cartoons depicting the prophet Muhammad early in 2006 had an impact in New Zealand with differences among leading news media on how the issue should be covered. The country's largest daily newspaper, the *New Zealand Herald*, opted not to publish such a "gratuitous offence." Two other daily newspapers, the *Dominion Post* and *Nelson Mail*, published all 12 cartoons and defended their free speech action in the face of criticism by the country's tiny Muslim minority and fears of damage to New Zealand's growing trade with the Middle East. Race Relations Commissioner Joris de Bres initiated a dialogue with newspaper editors in February, "cultural diversity" guidelines were drawn up, and the editors of the two dailies apologized for any offense caused to the Muslim population.

Four companies, all foreign owned, continue to control a significant portion of the country's print media sector. Australia's John Fairfax Holdings owns almost 48 percent of New Zealand's daily newspaper circulation. The *New Zealand Herald* and a significant slice of smaller provincial and suburban newspapers are owned by the rival Australian Provincial Newspapers group, while the Australian Consolidated Press dominates New Zealand magazines. The state-owned corporation Television New Zealand dominates television with two free-to-air channels and was increasingly at the center of controversy over management issues. Maori Television Service, a bilingual second public broadcaster, had a successful debut broadcasting in English and Maori. There were a reported 3.2 million internet users, or roughly 75 percent of the population, and the internet is open and unrestricted.

Nicaragua

Status: Partly Free

LEGAL ENVIRONMENT: 14
POLITICAL ENVIRONMENT: 16
ECONOMIC ENVIRONMENT: 12
TOTAL SCORE: 42

Survey Edition	2002	2003	2004	2005	2006
Total Score, Status	32,PF	40,PF	37,PF	42,PF	44,PF

The Nicaraguan constitution provides for freedom of the press but also allows for some forms of restriction, including criminal defamation legislation. Although physical attacks on journalists have been reduced, the possibility of harassment and death threats remains high. Legal actions to improve the situation for the media remain stagnant. The administration of President Enrique Bolanos, ruling Nicaragua since 2002, tolerated criticism and diverse views expressed by the media. In November 2006, Daniel Ortega, leader of the left-wing Sandinista party, won the presidential election. Ortega has promised to fight corruption and to resolve the country's widespread poverty issue, but his desire to follow in his predecessor's footsteps and respect freedom of the press is currently unclear.

Judges are often aligned with political parties, and some have restricted reporters from covering certain stories; cases of judicial intimidation have also been reported. New initiatives to promote access to information were discussed during the year, but no laws were actually passed owing to a lack of political will. A court appeal on constitutional grounds against Law 372, which requires all journalists to register with the Colegio de Periodistas, was still pending in the Supreme Court at year's end. However, a number of recent court cases have recognized the importance of freedom of the press. In November 2006, the 2005 conviction of Eugenio Hernandez for killing *La Prensa* journalist Maria Jose Bravo Sanchez was upheld. In addition, in June a criminal court judge upheld the acquittal of journalists Heberto Rodriguez, Oliver Bodan, and Darling Moises Lopez, who had been sued for libel.

Physical attacks on journalists have diminished, but a number of reporters received death threats or were harassed at gunpoint throughout the year. Although two of the recent killings were linked directly to the polarized political scene, threats against journalists from narcotics traffickers and corrupt police hindered press freedom in some of the more isolated regions of the country. Politicians have also often criticized the media for trying to undermine their credibility and limit public debate. On February 23, approximately 250 supporters of Alvaro Chamorro Mora, the mayor of Granada, traveled to Managua, where they blocked the entrance to the privately owned daily *La Prensa*. They demanded a meeting with the editors and insisted that the paper refrain from publishing news on alleged irregularities in city hall. That same month, while attempting to cover a meeting of the Granada City Council, *La Prensa* correspondent Arlen Cerda and photographer Guillermo Flores were surrounded, verbally insulted, and assaulted. At another political meeting in November, Canal 2 reporter Martha Irene Sanchez was beaten and forcibly removed when she attempted to move closer to speaker Daniel Ortega. President Bolanos also publicly asked the private daily *El Nuevo Diario* to fire reporter Oliver Bodan, who had investigated a corruption scandal at the Ministry of Transportation and Infrastructure.

There are 10 Managua-based television stations, some of which carry obviously partisan content, as well as more than 100 radio stations, which serve as the main source of news for most citizens. Nicaragua is one of the poorest countries in the hemisphere, and its media rely on government advertising. There are still complaints about the political manipulation of government propaganda. Newspaper ownership is concentrated in the hands of various factions of the Chamorro family. The prominent Sacasa family similarly dominates the television industry. Angel Gonzalez, noted for his holdings in Guatemala and Costa Rica, also owns significant electronic media interests. The poor economic climate leaves journalists vulnerable to bribery. A new generation of journalists in Nicaragua is rejecting the old ways of self-censorship and bribery, but this process has been slow. There are no government restrictions on the internet, which is used by less than 3 percent of the population.

Niger

LEGAL ENVIRONMENT: 21
POLITICAL ENVIRONMENT: 20
ECONOMIC ENVIRONMENT: 17

Status: Partly Free

TOTAL SCORE: 58

Survey Edition	2002	2003	2004	2005	2006
Total Score, Status	49,PF	53,PF	56,PF	53,PF	56,PF

The rights to freedom of speech and of the press are protected by the constitution, but in practice they are often ignored. The life of a journalist is made particularly difficult by a government that frequently implements a law criminalizing defamation and a judiciary ready to enforce it. In 2006, all on charges of libel or defamation, five different journalists spent time in prison. One newspaper, *L'Opinion*, was banned, and a talk show on the private radio station Tenere FM received a three-month suspension. Journalists who wrote or spoke about problems of corruption within business or government were particularly targeted. The most high-profile case began on August 4, when Mamane Abou and Oumarou Keita, the director and editor, respectively, of the private weekly *Le Republicain*, were detained and interrogated over an article accusing the prime minister of "courting the Iranians" and thereby risking a rupture with Western donors. A month later, after being held in preventive detention, Abou and Keita were found guilty and each sentenced to 18 months in prison and a US$9,800 fine. However, the appeal of the case went all the way to the Supreme Court of Appeals in the capital, Niamey, where the Court decided the previous sentence had been too harsh and reduced the journalists' prison time to nine months, six of them suspended. As Abou and Keita had already spent nearly four months in detention awaiting the appeal, they were immediately released. Notably, this ruling came soon after hundreds of people protested in the streets of the central town of Agadez, calling for the release of the journalists.

Although in 2006 there were no direct physical attacks on journalists, the government did continue its efforts to conceal the existence and impact of the famine that hit Niger in 2005. In April, the government withdrew the accreditation of a British Broadcasting Corporation television crew following its investigation into the hunger problem in central Niger. In addition, government officials have been formally prohibited from talking to the media about the hunger crisis.

The state-owned media consistently reflect the government line, while private publications have been very critical of government action. The broadcast media have a greater influence than the newspaper industry owing to the nation's low literacy level. The state continues to dominate the broadcasting landscape. Nonetheless, at least eight private radio stations broadcast reports critical of the government in French and local languages. Restrictive press licensing legislation and a heavy tax on private media outlets continue to prohibit the growth of a vibrant and dynamic press. Internet access is hard to acquire for most (less than 0.2 percent of the population access it regularly), but this is a result more of the country's high level of poverty and lack of infrastructure than direct government interference.

	LEGAL ENVIRONMENT: 14
	POLITICAL ENVIRONMENT: 24
Nigeria	ECONOMIC ENVIRONMENT: 17
Status: Partly Free	TOTAL SCORE: 55

Survey Edition	2002	2003	2004	2005	2006
Total Score, Status	57,PF	53,PF	53,PF	52,PF	54,PF

Even though the 1999 constitution guarantees freedom of expression, of the press, and of assembly, the state often uses arbitrary actions and extralegal measures to suppress political criticism and expression in the media. Libel still remains a criminal offense, and the burden of proof rests with the defendant. In 2006, two journalists were jailed for two months for allegedly libeling a state governor and were released only because of strong international and local pressure. In July, the government issued new accreditation requirements for journalists covering the House of Representatives, causing even journalists with proper accreditation to reapply. On November 15, the Senate finally approved the much awaited freedom of information bill to facilitate access to information, particularly important for media practitioners. Among other things, the bill makes it a criminal offense, punishable by three years' imprisonment, for any officer, government administrator (including the head of state), or public institution to destroy or falsify any official record before its release. But President Olusegun Obasanjo has so far refused to sign the bill into law, saying it would undermine Nigeria's security. Despite the passage of this bill by the National Assembly, the situation for access to information is not yet ideal in Nigeria, as there are still laws that restrict public access to government-held information, speech, and assembly, including the 1962 Official Secrets Act and the Sedition Law, among others. On August 28, the Senate rejected guidelines that would have limited the number of reporters covering the federal legislature from four to two.

Despite these encouraging legislative actions, various security agencies, particularly the State Security Service (SSS), continued to use arbitrary detention and extrajudicial measures in attempts to suppress expression in the press and to muffle political activism and criticism. This was a particularly acute problem for journalists who chose to critically cover President Obasanjo's attempts to change the constitution in order to legally run for a third term. For example, in March Mahmud Jega, editor of the *New Nigerian,* was sacked after running a story that criticized Obasanjo's ambitions to continue in the presidency. Also, on May 14

SSS officers raided the Abuja station of Africa Independent Television (AIT), the leading independent television station, during its broadcast of a documentary program comparing Obasanjo's ambitions to the failed efforts made by previous presidents to extend their respective term limits. The security officers confiscated a master tape of the documentary after stopping its further transmission. AIT was targeted a number of other times by the SSS throughout 2006. The editorial staff was threatened as a result of their plans to broadcast live the parliamentary debates on the term limit extension amendment; and in June, the SSS detained AIT presenter Mike Gbenga Aruleba for a program he hosted investigating the cost of Obasanjo's presidential jet. Later, Aruleba and another journalist, Rotimi Durojaiye—who worked for the *Daily Independent* but contributed to the controversial report on the presidential jet—were both arrested, detained, and charged with sedition. By October, the courts had dropped the charges against Aruleba but refused to do so for Durojaiye even by year's end.

In 2006, the National Broadcasting Commission (NBC) clamped down and imposed sanctions or bans on a number of media outlets. In March, the privately owned Kano-based Freedom Radio was shut down for five hours and fined approximately US$1,700 for an alleged infraction of the broadcasting code. The NBC threatened to revoke the station's license if it failed to pay the fine. In January, the NBC also suspended the operations of five private television stations and five private radio stations owing to their failure to pay their licensing fees. There was no apparent political motive behind the suspension of these stations. Violence against journalists is also a common occurrence, but often this is more a factor of the environment in which they report than the particular content of their work. In one especially violent incident in December, Godwin Agbroko—the editorial board chairman of the privately owned *ThisDay* newspaper—was assassinated while returning home from work. He was found dead in his car. However, at year's end no evidence had been put forward to suspect that the murder had been tied to his work.

There are about 100 national and local publications, the most influential of which are privately owned. The press is vibrant and vocal against unpopular state policies and was particularly critical when covering Obasanjo's third-term ambitions. The broadcast industry has been liberalized since 1992, and by 2006 about 300 licenses had been granted by the NBC, although most of the licensees have yet to take off or remain on the air owing to financial difficulties. Radio tends to be the main source of information for Nigerians, while television is used mostly in urban areas and by the affluent. Foreign broadcasters, particularly the Voice of America and the

British Broadcasting Corporation, are important sources of news in the country. Over five million Nigerians reportedly had access to the internet in 2006—more than three times the figure from last year. While this is only 3 percent of Nigeria's 140 million people, the percentage of Nigerians making use of this new medium is rising significantly every year, even if access is limited primarily to urban areas and the wealthy.

North Korea

Legal Environment: 30
Political Environment: 38
Economic Environment: 29

Status: Not Free

Total Score: 97

Survey Edition	2002	2003	2004	2005	2006
Total Score, Status	96,NF	96,NF	98,NF	97,NF	97,NF

Second-generation dictator Kim Jong-il rules this one-party state with military force and places severe restrictions on media freedom and the ability of North Koreans to access information. Although the constitution guarantees freedom of speech, in practice constitutional provisions for obeying a "collective spirit" restrict all reporting not sanctioned by the government. All journalists are members of the ruling party, and all media are mouthpieces for the regime. Journalists are punished harshly for even the smallest errors. The North Korean media portray all dissidents and the foreign media as liars attempting to "destabilize the government," and the government severely restricts the ability of foreign journalists to access information by claiming their cell phone upon arrival and preventing them from talking to people in the street, all the while monitoring their movements. North Koreans face harsh punishments, including prison sentences and hard labor, for accessing foreign media.

Newspaper, television, and radio reports typically consist of praise of Kim Jong-il, often focusing on his daily activities. Radios must be registered with the police and are preset to government frequencies. Some North Koreans purchase a second radio set that is not registered with the police, enabling them to listen to broadcasts by Radio Free Asia and the South Korean public radio station KBS. Free North Korea (FNK), the first radio station run by North Korean refugees living in South Korea, began broadcasting in February 2004. On October 12, 2006, the North Korean TV station Joon Gang Bang Song condemned the activities of FNK, which broadcasts criticism of the Kim Jong-Il regime. Simultaneously, the North Korean official news agency KCNA criticized Radio Free Chosun and

Open Radio for North Korea, both based in South Korea and supported by U.S. organizations, and asked the South Korean government to stop the broadcasts of both stations. Internet access is restricted to a handful of high-level officials who have received state approval and to 200 or so foreigners living in the capital, Pyongyang; all foreign websites are blocked by the state. For most North Koreans with computer access, web surfing takes place only on the state-run intranet.

Norway

LEGAL ENVIRONMENT: 3
POLITICAL ENVIRONMENT: 4
ECONOMIC ENVIRONMENT: 4

Status: Free

TOTAL SCORE: 11

Survey Edition	2002	2003	2004	2005	2006
Total Score, Status	9,F	9,F	9,F	10,F	10,F

Freedom of the press and of information are guaranteed under Article 100 of the constitution. A government ban on political commercials, designed to ensure equal opportunity to the media for all candidates regardless of varying resources, violates the European Convention on Human Rights, which Norway has signed.

In January 2006, "in the name of freedom of expression," *Magazinet*, a Christian magazine, published cartoons of the prophet Muhammad that were originally published in Denmark at the end of 2005 and sparked an international furor across the Muslim world. The cartoons were removed from the magazine's website after a series of death threats were received. In June, 1,500 workers went on strike against public broadcaster NRK over pay as well as conditions for freelance journalists. In July, the home of Nina Johnsrud came under attack after she published a story in the *Dagsavisen* exposing election fraud by Yogaraja Balasingham, a supporter of the Liberation Tigers of Tamil Eelam, a Sri-Lanka based rebel group.

Norway has one of the highest newspaper readerships in the world and distributes over 200 newspapers that express a diversity of opinions. Concerns were raised over the editorial independence of several papers upon the sale of media giant Orkla Media to the British company Mecom in September 2006. Media concentration is a concern in Norway, with three main companies dominating print media. Amendments to the Media Ownership Act were proposed in March to reduce the limit for ownership of media outlets to one-third of the market, down from the current 40 percent. The bill was still pending at year's end. The internet is widely used in Norway, accessed by 67 percent of the population.

Oman

Status: Not Free

LEGAL ENVIRONMENT: 24
POLITICAL ENVIRONMENT: 28
ECONOMIC ENVIRONMENT: 19

TOTAL SCORE: 71

Survey Edition	2002	2003	2004	2005	2006
Total Score, Status	68,NF	73,NF	74,NF	72,NF	70,NF

Although Oman's basic charter provides for freedom of the press, government laws and actions tightly restrict this freedom in practice. Article 29 of the Basic Law provides for freedom of the press "within the limits of the law," but this right is restricted in practice by the government and the repressive 1984 Press and Publication Law. Libel is treated as a criminal offense, and journalists can be imprisoned or given high fines for such transgressions, particularly if they voice criticisms of longtime ruler Sultan Qaboos. The Ministry of Information may legally censor any material regarded as politically, culturally, or sexually offensive in both domestic and foreign media. Articles 61 and 62 of the 2002 Telecommunications Act prohibit individuals from knowingly sending a message over any form of telecommunications that violates laws for public order and morals or is harmful to an individual's safety. On January 30, Taybah al-Ma'wali, a former parliamentarian, was released from prison after serving a six-month term for insulting public officials via telephone and the internet. Journalists practice a high degree of self-censorship out of fear of violating vaguely written laws such as those prohibiting the publication of material that may lead to public discord, the abuse of a person's dignity, or the violation of state security. The penal code allows for defendants considered to have endangered national security to be prosecuted before the State Security Court, where fewer due process rights exist.

Despite such restrictive press laws, information is widely available and "constructive" criticism of the government is allowed, particularly in online publications. Journalists do not have open or equal access to sources and are not able to cover the news freely. There were no reported cases of physical intimidation of journalists, but self-censorship is widespread. Public information is often made available through the official Oman News Agency before being distributed to media outlets. While journalists do not often face obstacles in acquiring the required licenses to practice journalism, increased requirements regarding journalistic identification cards were introduced in 2005. Every journalist had to reapply for a new ID card in 2005 and must now reapply every year as a employee of a specific media outlet, thus forbidding the practice of freelance journalism. The first Oman Journalists Association was officially launched in early 2006, although it is widely believed to be too closely connected to government agencies to function independently.

Print media serve as the main source for local news. There are four privately owned daily newspapers and two state-run dailies. Each daily has its own printing press; however, the government places regulations on the use of printing materials and distribution. Privately owned publications reportedly receive government subsidies, although the increasing amount of foreign advertising revenue is slowly allowing some private publications to rely less on state funding. The government's monopoly on radio and television broadcasts continued in 2006, and the licensing conditions for establishing private broadcast media, under the 2004 Private Radio and Television Companies Law, are difficult to meet. Applicants are limited to Omani nationals with high capital owing to the US$1.25 million required to establish an outlet. Nonetheless, in October 2005 the state issued licenses to two different companies to establish a private television station and three private radio stations, which are expected to launch in 2007. Satellite access in mostly urban areas provided foreign news and information. Although the internet was widely available (approximately 12 percent of the population accessed it), it was also heavily filtered by the government-owned internet service provider, Omantel. Because of such restrictions, fewer local blogs and websites exist, and those that do are monitored. Authorities created an Internet Service Manual, which contains a lengthy list of prohibited online topics, including defamation of the royal family and false data or rumors.

Pakistan

LEGAL ENVIRONMENT: 17
POLITICAL ENVIRONMENT: 28
ECONOMIC ENVIRONMENT: 18

Status: Not Free

TOTAL SCORE: 63

Survey Edition	2002	2003	2004	2005	2006
Total Score, Status	57,PF	58,PF	59,PF	61,NF	61,NF

Although the already outspoken Pakistani media have grown more diverse, they continue to face a range of pressures, harassment, and attacks from both the government and other sources, all of which intensified during 2006. The constitution and other laws such as the Official Secrets Act authorize the government to curb freedom of speech on subjects including the constitution, the armed forces, the judiciary, and religion. Harsh blasphemy laws have also been used in past years to suppress the media. In April, the Supreme Court reaffirmed a sentence of life imprisonment imposed on Rehmat Shah Afridi, former editor of the *Frontier Post* and *Maidan* dailies, who had been arrested on alleged drug-trafficking charges in 1999; Afridi continues to declare his innocence. The controversial Defamation (Amendment) Act, passed in 2004, expanded the definition of defamation and increased the punishment for offenders to minimum fines of 100,000 rupees (approximately US$1,700) and/or prison sentences of up to five years; however, this legislation has not yet been used to convict members of the press. A bill that would allow the Pakistan Electronic Media Regulatory Authority (PEMRA) to ban broadcast outlets in the name of "vulgarity" or "national security" and provides for large fines or prison terms for violators was passed by the lower house of Parliament in 2005 but lapsed before being brought before the Senate and was enacted. The PEMRA did temporarily shut down or ban access to several television and radio stations during the year, including two Afghanistan–based broadcasters in March. On a number of occasions, General Pervez Musharraf and other members of his administration contributed to an atmosphere inimical to free speech by making public threats against or derogatory comments about specific members of the press. Government plans to establish a new body called the Press and Publication Regulatory Authority, which would supersede existing self-regulatory mechanisms, were criticized by local and international watchdog groups.

Over the past several years, military authorities have used increasingly aggressive tactics to silence critical or investigative voices in the media. A number of journalists have been pressured to resign from prominent publications or charged with sedition, while media outlets have been shut down. On numerous occasions, police, security forces, and military intelligence officials subjected journalists to physical assaults, intimidation, torture, and arbitrary arrest and detention, with some reporters being held for several months at a time. Islamic fundamentalists and thugs hired by feudal landlords or local politicians continue to harass journalists and attack newspaper offices. Several press clubs were also attacked. Reporters in Sindh province faced threats and attacks from local-level authorities and political or tribal figures during the year. In total, more than 100 such instances were reported throughout 2006.

As in 2005, conditions for reporters covering the ongoing unrest in the tribal areas bordering Afghanistan were particularly difficult during the year, with a number of local and foreign correspondents detained, threatened, or otherwise prevented from covering events there, both by the Taliban and local tribal groups or by the army and intelligence services. Reporter Hayatullah Khan, who had been abducted near his home in the semiautonomous North Waziristan tribal region in December 2005, was found dead in June 2006; intelligence agencies were suspected of being involved in the murder. Unknown assailants seized Dilawar Khan, a reporter for the British Broadcasting Corporation's Urdu service based in South Waziristan, in November, in order to interrogate him regarding his news sources. In a chilling trend, the child siblings of both men were also killed, apparently to threaten the journalists and their families. In general, foreign journalists experience visa and travel restrictions that can inhibit their scope of reporting and are subject to arrest and deportation if found in areas not specifically covered by the terms of their visas; a number of such cases have been reported in the past several years. In December, *New York Times* reporter Carlotta Gall was assaulted by military intelligence officers in Quetta; the assailants beat her, searched her hotel room and confiscated equipment, and for several hours detained the Pakistani photographer who was accompanying her. Conditions for media remain much more tightly restricted in Pakistani-administered Kashmir, where pro-independence publications are refused permission to operate.

While some journalists practice self-censorship, many privately owned daily and weekly newspapers and magazines provide diverse and critical coverage of national affairs. Authorities attempt to wield some control over content by reportedly providing unofficial "guidance" to newspaper editors on suggested placement of front-page stories or permissible topics of coverage. Restrictions on the ownership of broadcast media were eased in late 2002, and media cross-ownership was allowed in July 2003. The government continues to control Pakistan Television and Radio Pakistan, the only free broadcast outlets with a national reach, where coverage supports official viewpoints. Private radio stations operate in some major cities but are prohibited from broadcasting news programming. In a positive change for the media landscape in recent years, a growing number of private cable and satellite television channels such as GEO and ARY, all of which broadcast from outside the country but are widely available, provide live news coverage and a much wider variety of viewpoints than was previously available.

Authorities wield some economic influence over the media through the selective allocation of advertising, and both official and private interests reportedly pay for favorable press coverage. State-level and national officials regularly use advertising boycotts to put economic pressure on publications that do not heed unofficial directives on coverage. Internews reported that at least 11 newspapers or magazines were denied state-sponsored advertising from public funds in 2006 for being critical of government policies.

The internet is not widely used, with less than 5 percent of the population able to gain access. Despite this, the government did invade online privacy by monitoring the e-mail accounts of some journalists. During 2006, authorities blocked access to certain websites, particularly those that concern Baluch nationalist issues, with several dozen blocked at various points during the year. In February, the decision of the Pakistan Telecommunication Authority to block access to the hosting site blogspot. com was met with protests from the expanding community of Pakistani bloggers as well as freedom of expression groups.

Palau

Status: Free

LEGAL ENVIRONMENT: 1
POLITICAL ENVIRONMENT: 6
ECONOMIC ENVIRONMENT: 7
TOTAL SCORE: 14

Survey Edition	2002	2003	2004	2005	2006
Total Score, Status	NA	9,F	11,F	13,F	14,F

The Pacific island republic of Palau has a small but vibrant media environment, and Article 4, Section 2, of the constitution protects freedom of expression and of the press. Censorship is rare, and the press is free to report on a diversity of issues, including official corruption. In November, the Consolidated Boards Act of 2006 was passed, combining four government entities—including the Palau National Communications Corporation, which controls internet and satellite television transmissions—into one commission. The officials of the new commission will be publicly elected rather than appointed by the government, as was previously the case. There were no attacks on the press in 2006.

Palau has a relatively diverse media considering its small population. There are two weeklies and one regular biweekly. President Tommy Esang Remengesau Jr. meets every Wednesday with the press on the government radio station Eco-Paradise. There are also two private and two church radio stations. Diaz Radio, owned by outspoken journalist and senator Alfonso Diaz, started airing a weekly program in April for Filipinos in Palau. In April, members of the political group Voices of Palau demanded equal airtime on Diaz Radio to rebut statements Senator Diaz made on the air attacking their character. Senator Diaz and members of Voices of Palau filed harassment suits against each other after encounters heated up concerning the disputed airtime. The internet is unregulated by the government but is not a significant news source, as it is accessed by only 1 percent of the population.

Panama

LEGAL ENVIRONMENT: 18
POLITICAL ENVIRONMENT: 16
ECONOMIC ENVIRONMENT: 9

Status: Partly Free

TOTAL SCORE: 43

Survey Edition	2002	2003	2004	2005	2006
Total Score, Status	30,F	34,PF	45,PF	44,PF	43,PF

Panama is notable for its harsh legal environment for journalists, and events in 2006 did very little to improve the situation. President Martin Torrijos had ratified the repeal of the country's "gag laws," enacted under military rule more than 30 years ago; however, a commission of lawyers and academics, which was set up by Torrijos to examine penal code reform, in July submitted a proposal that included harsh penalties for criminal defamation. Among the amendments, Article 214 would drastically increase penalties and raise the maximum prison term for defamation to three years. More than 100 journalists took to the streets demanding the withdrawal of the draft bill, which was designed to protect the reputation of government officials.

A new bill, which still considered defamation and libel to be criminal offenses, was also being considered at the end of the year. The draft bill would make it a crime punishable by up to four years' imprisonment to publish "confidential information involving state security." There are also concerns about other existing provisions, including Articles 307 and 308 of the criminal code, which contain two insult laws with similar language to the *desacato* (disrespect) laws. Several cases against journalists under this law are pending in the courts, including that of Jean Marcel Chery, a former reporter with the daily *El Panama America*, who was accused of libel by the Supreme Court judge Winston Spadafora. Chery had written about a Supreme Court decision that canceled Spadafora's US$2 million debt to a government canal agency known as the Interoceanic Regional Authority. In another case, Spadafora filed a civil lawsuit that sought US$2 million in damages from the publisher of *El Panama America,* for a 2001 story that allegedly "insulted" him when he was minister of government and justice. Such legal tensions cause many journalists to practice self-censorship.

Access to public information still remains limited because government officials are not held accountable for refusing to release information and public institutions still lack an effective mechanism for expediting information requests. There were no attacks on the media in Panama in 2006.

Independent media are very active and express diverse views. The media often reflect the polarized political scene, with different outlets openly supporting various factions. All Panamanian media outlets are privately owned with the exception of one state-owned television network. The law prohibits cross-ownership, but there is considerable concentration of media ownership by relatives and associates of former president Ernesto Perez Balladares, whose party President Torrijos now leads. Poor salaries encourage corruption among some journalists. A number of domestic journalists and press freedom advocacy groups allege that the government manipulates the "free flow of information" by buying advertising space from organizations that report positively on the government while withdrawing funding from organizations that do not. A bill to standardize government advertising and reduce this was under consideration but not acted upon before the end of the year. There are no government restrictions on the internet, which was accessed by nearly 7 percent of the population during 2006.

Papua New Guinea

Legal Environment: 4
Political Environment: 14
Economic Environment: 12

Status: Free

Total Score: 30

Survey Edition	2002	2003	2004	2005	2006
Total Score, Status	26,F	25,F	25,F	29,F	29,F

The relatively vibrant media environment worsened this year owing primarily to new government restrictions on reporters. Media freedom is guaranteed under the constitution adopted at independence in 1975 and the Papua New Guinea Media Council (PNGMC) is a strong lobby group in support of news organizations and professional standards. However, at times the news media clash with the government when defending freedom of the press. In August 2006, the government imposed restrictions on journalists covering a state of emergency in the Southern Highlands province. Among these restrictions was the introduction of a permit system for journalists wishing to travel to the mountainous province, which has been troubled by prolonged tribal warfare. Acting Information and Communications Minister Patrick Pruaitch justified the new requirements as a way to ensure "positive reporting" by local and international media. The media saw the requirements as an attempt to control negative reporting that may reflect poorly on the government, and PNGMC president Peter Aitsi called for the restrictions to be lifted. Despite these restrictions, no journalists were attacked for their reporting in 2006.

Both daily newspapers are foreign owned but provide contrasting viewpoints. The *PNG Post-Courier*, founded in 1969, is owned by a subsidiary of Rupert Murdoch's News Corporation, and the rival *National* is owned by a prominent Malaysian logging company with a major timber and investment stake in the country. Papua New Guinea's only television station, EM TV, is owned by Fiji Television Ltd. The state-run National Broadcasting Corporation is also a significant media company, and the major commercial radio network is run by partly Fiji-owned PNG FM Pty. Ltd., operating Nau FM and Yumi FM. The internet is unrestricted by the government but is accessible to less than 5 percent of the population.

Paraguay

Status: Partly Free

LEGAL ENVIRONMENT: 19
POLITICAL ENVIRONMENT: 23
ECONOMIC ENVIRONMENT: 18
TOTAL SCORE: 60

Survey Edition	2002	2003	2004	2005	2006
Total Score, Status	51,PF	55,PF	54,PF	56,PF	57,PF

Paraguay remains one of the most troubled democracies in Latin America, with widespread corruption and a political system that has been dominated by the Colorado Party for the last seven decades. Criminal organizations frequently attack the press, often with the complicity of state authorities. This unfavorable context has contributed to further deterioration in the environment for press freedom in 2006. Article 26, Section 1 of the constitution provides a general guarantee for freedom of expression and of the media, but other articles are contradictory or vague and allow for loopholes in the interpretation of freedom of expression. Repressive libel and defamation laws severely restrict criticism of public authorities. The application of such laws was irregular throughout the year, with judges often demonstrating a bias toward the plaintiffs regardless of the case.

The Union of Paraguayan Journalists (SPP) concluded in a recent report that attacks on freedom of expression in 2006 frequently originated from inside the state and from the government's inaction toward criminal groups. The disappearance of journalist Enrique Galeano in February illustrates the difficult situation for the country's news organizations. Galeano disappeared after receiving several death threats for his denunciations of drug traffickers and their links to local Colorado Party politicians. Although President Nicanor Duarte Frutos promised a thorough investigation of Galeano's disappearance, the Ministry of the Interior did not question the police's decision to close the case after arguing that Galeano had disappeared on his own, most probably running away from the country. Several other journalists were victims of violent acts throughout the year, including Alberto Nunez, correspondent for the private dailies *La Nacion* and *Cronica*, who was kidnapped and beaten in the city of Capiibary by a group of lumber traffickers. In December, Colorado mayoral candidate and journalist Julio Benitez Ruiz Diaz was killed in his home; the investigation remained unresolved at the end of 2006. Community radio stations Manantial FM and Temonde FM were shut down while awaiting a ruling on their broadcasting frequency, and a local newspaper, *El Espectador Luqueno*, had its equipment destroyed by order of the mayor on the pretext of a land dispute.

Paraguay has a diverse media system, with a number of private broadcasting stations and independent newspapers. But the dominance of the Colorado Party elite and a hostile political environment for assertive journalism have prevented the media from offering a diversity of viewpoints. The manipulation of government advertising to ensure political quiescence continues, especially in the country's interior. The SPP estimates that about 80 percent of radio stations are controlled by members of the Colorado Party. The union also reports that the growing trend of hiring journalists on the basis of informal labor contracts has eliminated basic social rights—including social security, minimum wages, and paid vacations—and has affected the quality of information. There were no reported restrictions on the internet imposed by the government, though less than 4 percent of the population had regular access to this medium during the year.

Peru

LEGAL ENVIRONMENT: 13
POLITICAL ENVIRONMENT: 18
ECONOMIC ENVIRONMENT: 11

Status: Partly Free

TOTAL SCORE: 42

Survey Edition	2002	2003	2004	2005	2006
Total Score, Status	30,F	35,PF	34,PF	40,PF	39,PF

Peru's media freedom declined in 2006 amid a series of threats and physical attacks against media workers. Freedom of the press is guaranteed in the 1993 constitution, but local and international media organizations continued to express concern about the state of press freedom. In 2002 and 2003, the government of President Alejandro Toledo passed laws expanding access to public information. The willingness of many agencies to provide information has grown, despite a July 2005 measure that tightened restrictions on access to information in certain categories and extended the timelines for release of classified information. In 2006, the government attempted unsuccessfully to prosecute one reporter for revealing state secrets, even though the supposedly damaging footage had been used in campaign ads by former president Alberto Fujimori. *Desacato* (disrespect) laws continue to be a problem. A number of journalists were entangled in court cases in 2006, charged with defamation by public officials and private citizens, and two reporters were given suspended prison sentences. Press watchdog groups also decried a new law that could limit free expression by subjecting nongovernmental organizations to onerous registration requirements.

In addition to judicial harassment, the hostile climate for the press is evidenced by numerous instances of physical attacks and verbal threats. Local press watchdog Instituto de Prensa y Sociedad dramatically increased the number of alerts it issued, from 73 in 2005 to 96 in 2006. Journalists working in the country's interior provinces are especially vulnerable. Reporters covering crime stories and scandals were targeted largely after reporting on corruption. In April, Chimbote journalist Marilu Gambini was forced to flee the country after her reporting on drug trafficking resulted in a series of death threats, which continued even after she went into hiding. Elias Navarro, a reporter from the Ayacucho region, was threatened and an attempt was made to bomb his home in September following his reports on a local corruption scandal. Political campaigns and protests also resulted in violence against journalists; in fact, the largest number of reported press violations occurred in the periods prior to the April national elections and the November local elections. In December, two journalists were injured—one shot and severely wounded—during a large protest in the city of Abancay.

Most abuses of journalists by public officials and private citizens continue to go unpunished. The progress made in 2005 when the former mayor of Yungay, Amaro Leon, was found guilty of ordering the 2004 assassination of Antonio de la Torre, a radio journalist and harsh critic of the mayor, was tarnished when the Supreme Court released Leon owing to what it said was a lack of evidence. In the case of the 2004 murder of radio journalist Alberto Rivera in the city of Pucallpa, several individuals were sentenced, but the arrest order against the Pucallpa mayor, under suspicion as an intellectual author of the crime, was revoked after a dubious court ruling.

Private investors dominate the media industry, and in comparison the audience for state-run media is relatively small. The government owns two television networks and one radio station and operates the print news agency Andina. Radio is an important medium, especially in the countryside. Peru's media are diverse and express a broad range of viewpoints. The media corruption that was endemic in the Fujimori era continues to an extent today, with both owners and individual journalists sometimes accepting bribes in exchange for slanted coverage. Several newspapers were accused in 2006 of coordinating smear campaigns with high-level government officials. These activities contribute to a long-standing lack of confidence in the press as a credible institution. National newspapers are also dependent on advertising revenue from a small number of large companies. The internet is open and unrestricted by the government, with just under 16 percent of the population accessing the web in 2006.

Philippines

Status: Partly Free

LEGAL ENVIRONMENT: 11
POLITICAL ENVIRONMENT: 24
ECONOMIC ENVIRONMENT: 11
TOTAL SCORE: 46

Survey Edition	2002	2003	2004	2005	2006
Total Score, Status	30,F	30,F	34,PF	35,PF	40,PF

Media in the Philippines have historically ranked among the freest, most vibrant, and outspoken in Southeast Asia, although reports are often rooted in sensationalism and innuendo. However, the year saw an overall decline in press freedom as a result of the excessive use of defamation suits to silence criticism of public officials, the government's clampdown on opposition media during the state of emergency in February, and the continued threat posed by journalist-targeted violence.

The constitution guarantees freedom of speech, of expression, and of peaceful assembly. There are no restrictive licensing requirements for newspapers or journalists and few legal limitations such as national security, privacy, or obscenity laws. However, the country's penal code makes libel a criminal offense punishable by fines and imprisonment. In July 2006, columnist and television broadcaster Raffy Tulfo was sentenced to 32 years in prison and fined 14.7 million pesos (US$285,000) for showing "reckless disregard" for the truth in several articles written nearly a decade ago. In response to the extreme Tulfo verdict and the subsequent revelation that Jose Miguel Arroyo, the president's husband, had filed libel charges against at least 43 reporters, columnists, editors, and publishers since 2003, a number of press freedom watchdog groups along with more than 600 Filipino journalists signed a petition calling for the decriminalization of defamation, submitting it to the Senate in November. In what proved a limited effort to mitigate the use of libel laws to prevent scrutiny of public officials, in August the House of Representatives approved a bill which would require that libel suits against members of the press be filed at the court in the province or city where the journalist or media outlet maintains its principal office and that civil actions connected with such libel suits be filed in the same court as the criminal complaint. Nevertheless, a number of journalists were held for a few nights in jail on arrest warrants for defamation, even though the bill had yet to receive bicameral approval.

Although a censorship board broadly has the power to edit or ban content for both television media and film, government censorship does not generally enforce political orientation. Both the private press (most print and electronic media) and the country's many state-owned television and radio stations cover controversial topics—including, in 2006, developments in the constitutional reform debate and the second unsuccessful impeachment bid against President Macapagal-Arroyo in June. The February 2006 state of emergency brought a significant blow to critical voices when police officers raided the leading pro-opposition newspaper, the *Daily Tribune*, and placed the office under guard. Troops were also positioned around the Manila headquarters of the country's two largest television broadcasters, ABS-CBN and GMA-7. In the same week, as part of the official effort to silence media outlets "recklessly" promoting the cause of those working to overthrow the government, critical media figures were charged with incitement to rebellion and several journalists with the *Daily Tribune* were arrested and served time in jail until they were freed on bail. After emergency rule was lifted, the National Telecommunications Commission warned the media not to air materials that could "incite treason, rebellion, sedition, or pose a clear and present danger to the state" and threatened broadcast networks with closure or takeover for failing to comply with such regulations. According to the International Federation of Journalists, radio stations subsequently stopped airing interviews with union and other popular leaders critical of the state of emergency. In a May ruling, the Supreme Court confirmed that the administration's clampdown on the press during the state of emergency was unjustified.

Journalists continued to face extreme danger in the course of their work throughout the year. With the Committee to Protect Journalists counting 32 total journalists killed in the last 15 years and at least 3 murdered in 2006 alone, the Philippines continues to rank as one of the most dangerous places in the world for journalists. Several cases over the last few years have involved journalists who were well-known for exposing corruption scandals or being critical of the government, army, or police. Watchdog groups allege that unknown gunmen are hired by local government officials who are never held accountable and continued in 2006 to call on the president to end the prevailing culture of impunity. For example, while three people were found guilty in October 2006 of the 2005 murder of investigative reporter Marlene Garcia-Esperat, there have been no convictions against those who allegedly ordered the killings. In May, the president established Task Force Usig, a police task force intended as a first step toward investigating the murders, yet the effort was complicated by the fact that police are believed to be complicit in many of the killings. The Melo Commission to Investigate Media and Activist Killings, established by the president in response to international pressure in August, marked a second, if largely cosmetic, government effort to investigate journalist-targeted violence. Yet additional death threats and murders followed, including the stabbing of radio broadcaster Andres Acosta in Batac, Ilocos Norte, in December.

Most print and electronic media are privately owned, and while some television and radio stations are government owned, they too present a wide variety of views. Since 1986, however, there has been a general trend toward concentration of ownership, with two broadcast networks owned by companies of wealthy families, dominant among audiences and advertising. Often criticized for lacking journalistic ethics, the press is likely to reflect the political or economic orientations of owners and patrons, and special interests reportedly use inducements to solicit favorable coverage. Approximately 9 percent of the population made use of the internet in 2006, and the government did not restrict their access.

Poland

LEGAL ENVIRONMENT: 7
POLITICAL ENVIRONMENT: 8
ECONOMIC ENVIRONMENT: 7

Status: Free

TOTAL SCORE: 22

Survey Edition	2002	2003	2004	2005	2006
Total Score, Status	18,F	18,F	19,F	20,F	21,F

The Polish media remained vibrant, highly independent, and resistant to pressures from political and economic interests in 2006. The constitution forbids censorship and guarantees freedom of the press, and those principles were successfully upheld by the Constitutional Tribunal. For example, when a new Media Law went into effect in March 2006, the Tribunal struck down several articles, including provisions that would have given greater powers to the State Committee on Radio and Television (SCRT) and rules providing preferential treatment for Catholic-oriented media outlets. Libel and some forms of insult—including defamation of public officials, the state, and constitutional institutions—are criminal offenses punishable by fines and up to two years in prison. In January, when the editor in chief of *Wiesci Polickie* was sentenced to three months in jail for libeling a local government spokesman, the Tribunal suspended the sentence.

In 2006, the media's tendency towards politicization was reinforced by the government's open criticism of the media. For example, after several scandals involving the ruling coalition were revealed by investigative journalists, the government announced plans for a state-sponsored media monitoring institute and more restrictive media regulations. Officials continue to exert influence over public media, as seats on regulatory agencies and directorships of state-owned media outlets are typically political appointments. During 2006, the SCRT dealt with the media more aggressively than in previous years, imposing punitive fines on a number of occasions. In one case, a US$170,000 fine was imposed on a television station after a commentator on a satirical talk show mocked a disabled religious figure from the populist Catholic radio station Radio Maryja. The radio station Tok FM was also censured for allowing the broadcast of a satirical poem about the president. A media watchdog also showed that public television favored candidates of the ruling coalition in local elections in several major cities. Separately, in a step media freedom advocates saw as analogous to censorship, the Warsaw Regional Court in May imposed a gag order on a newspaper that was printing an investigative report into alleged financial improprieties by the previous president. In contrast, Radio

Maryja was granted the status of a public broadcaster, which included an exemption from paying nearly US$500,000 in licensing fees.

Print media, including two newly launched national dailies and over 300 other newspapers, are for the most part privately owned, highly diversified, and regional papers in scope. The biggest-selling daily, the *Fakt* tabloid, was launched in 2003. Government-owned Polish Television and its four channels remain a major source of information for most citizens, but the private television stations TVN and PolSat continue to gain market share. The portion of the population with internet access is around 30 percent and growing, and there have been no reports of the government restricting its use.

Portugal

Status: Free

LEGAL ENVIRONMENT: 2
POLITICAL ENVIRONMENT: 6
ECONOMIC ENVIRONMENT: 6
TOTAL SCORE: 14

Survey Edition	2002	2003	2004	2005	2006
Total Score, Status	15,F	15,F	14,F	14,F	14,F

Portuguese media remained free in 2006, despite the proposal of a new law that would restrict journalists' ability to protect their sources. Freedom of the press is guaranteed by the constitution, and laws against insulting the government or the armed forces are rarely enforced. Changes to the country's Journalism Law were proposed in 2006 that would make it easier for courts to order journalists to disclose confidential sources if the courts decided that it would be "difficult to obtain [the] information in any other way." If passed, the revised law would most likely be challenged in the European Court of Human Rights. An appeal by two journalists in April 2006 to block a court order to examine their computers was rejected. The reporters claimed that the search violated their right to source protection, while the court held that the reporters were guilty of "illegal access to personal data." This came after the journalists had published a piece claiming that Telecom Portugal was in possession of a list of 80,000 phone numbers of public officials, including the president's, in connection with the Casa Pia pedophile case.

The proposed changes to the Journalism Law would also give journalists' employers and clients the right to reuse work in any way for 30 days following their first publication. Journalists would have the right to reject any modifications to their work if such changes might affect their reputation; they could also remove their names from badly edited pieces. However, the European Federation of Journalists has argued that such protections are "impracticable," especially because such "modifications are made without the journalist's knowledge" and will be discovered only after their publication.

Six main national newspapers, four daily and two weekly, make up the bulk of the printed press in Portugal. There are some 300 local and regional private radio stations. The Catholic station Radio Renascenca commands a wide listening audience. Commercial television has been making gains in recent years, providing serious competition for the public broadcasting channels that lack funds. The internet is unrestricted, with more than 70 percent of the population able to access it regularly.

Qatar

Status: Not Free

LEGAL ENVIRONMENT: 18
POLITICAL ENVIRONMENT: 24
ECONOMIC ENVIRONMENT: 21
TOTAL SCORE: 63

Survey Edition	2002	2003	2004	2005	2006
Total Score, Status	62,NF	61,NF	61,NF	62,NF	61,NF

The government professes to respect freedom of the press, but aside from selected constitutional provisions, including Section 47, there are no laws that protect media freedom. Journalists are forbidden from criticizing the government, the ruling family, or Islam and are subject to prosecution under the penal code for such violations. Press laws are administered by the criminal courts, under which journalists can face jail sentences if convicted of libel or slander. By law, all publications are subject to licensing by the government. The law also authorizes the government, the Qatar Radio and Television Corporation, and even customs officers to censor both domestic and foreign publications and broadcast media for religious, political, and sexual content prior to distribution.

Journalists suffer several forms of intimidation, although there were no reports of physical violence directed at members of the press during the year. While local journalists usually face warnings and threats whenever the government feels they have crossed a line, noncitizens employed by Qatari media outlets can face harsher measures, including termination, deportation, and imprisonment. Such disparity in the application of these laws for Qatari and non-Qatari journalists, who represent the majority of journalists in Qatar, is widely known. Even a noncitizen journalist has been convicted and sentenced to one year in prison for slander of a Qatari citizen. As a result, most journalists censor themselves heavily.

Qatar has six newspapers, four of them Arabic language, and two in English. These six newspapers are not owned by the government, but by members of the ruling family or businessmen with close business ties to the ruling family. The state owns and operates all broadcast media, and there are only two television networks in the country, Qatar TV and the Al-Jazeera satellite channel. While Qatar TV broadcasts mostly official news and views, Al-Jazeera focuses its coverage solely on international topics. As a government-subsidized channel, Al-Jazeera is commissioned to focus on all news except local. The channel refrains from any criticism of its subsidizer and covers local news only if it has an international angle to it, with no critical commentary. Shows on the local radio station are more accommodating to voices criticizing government services and operations. The concentration of media ownership within the ruling family and the high financial and citizenship requirements for granting media ownership licenses continue to hinder the expansion and freedom of the press.

The internet is used by almost 27 percent of Qataris. The government restricts freedom of expression and censors the internet for political, religious, and pornographic content by controlling the local internet service provider. Both high-speed and dial-up internet users find themselves directed to a proxy server that blocks materials deemed inconsistent with the "religious, cultural, political, and moral values of the country." This proxy server maintains a list of banned websites and blocks users from accessing them.

Romania

Status: Partly Free

LEGAL ENVIRONMENT: 12
POLITICAL ENVIRONMENT: 15
ECONOMIC ENVIRONMENT: 15
TOTAL SCORE: 42

Survey Edition	2002	2003	2004	2005	2006
Total Score, Status	35,PF	38,PF	47,PF	47,PF	44,PF

The constitution protects freedom of the press, and the government has become increasingly respectful of these rights. In June, the Parliament passed a measure that decriminalized defamation and similar offenses, meaning journalists would no longer face jail time if convicted. Lawmakers had initially removed the infractions from the criminal code in 2005, but the changes were subsequently suspended. In February 2006, several journalists were drawn into the case of a former soldier, Ionel Popa, who had allegedly leaked classified information about Romanian forces in Iraq and Afghanistan to a number of news organizations. While the information was reportedly not sensitive enough to endanger the troops, many media outlets declined to publish it and in some cases voluntarily handed it over to the authorities. Nevertheless, one reporter, Marian Garleanu of the *Romania Libera* daily, was arrested for possessing state secrets and jailed for two days. Sebastian Oancea of the privately owned *Ziua* daily was also charged; both men face up to seven years in prison if convicted. Recent progress toward implementing freedom of information legislation has been difficult, and the government still appoints the boards of the public television and radio operators.

The 2004 election of President Traian Basescu brought substantial improvements in the political environment for the press as he has proven to be less controlling and manipulative of the media than his predecessors. Self-censorship also appears to have decreased. However, the government and state institutions remain sensitive to media criticism. Media tycoon and Conservative Party leader Dan Voiculescu withdrew his candidacy for deputy prime minister after an official body tasked with studying the Communist-era secret police archives revealed that he had been a collaborator. The media had often aired unproven claims that various public figures had worked with the security services, but none had previously been confirmed officially. Voiculescu maintained that he had merely provided security officials with obligatory reports on his trade-related activities abroad. There were a few attacks on journalists in Romania in 2006, although they were all minor and not directly politically motivated. Two such incidents occurred when a businessman spat on a reporter and when a member of a rock group tried to take a camera from a photographer after having his picture taken.

The number of media outlets and news sources has increased in recent years, and they are becoming more active and self-sufficient. There are five private television stations and one public station. Four main private radio stations also compete with a single state-owned station, which operates both national and regional networks. Many media outlets still face significant economic pressure owing to ownership concentration, lack of revenue, and a limited advertising market. Most media rely on government-funded advertising. The situation is worse for smaller newspapers outside of Bucharest, where the advertising market is less developed and local officials own many media outlets. Western European media groups Ringier and

WAZ own the three highest-circulating dailies, and journalists report that the owners are increasingly toning down critical coverage. According to a 2005 European Union study, media outlets are frequently registering abroad to avoid disclosing ownership structures.

Usage of the internet is increasing, but rural areas suffer from inadequate infrastructure; about 25 percent of the population is able to gain access, with few reports of government interference. However, interference did take place in June, when the Foreign Ministry convinced a private internet service provider (ISP) to shut down a website created by two *Ziua* reporters intended to parody the ministry's own site. The ISP agreed to hand over the journalists' personal information in an apparent violation of Romanian privacy law.

Russia

LEGAL ENVIRONMENT: 18
POLITICAL ENVIRONMENT: 33
ECONOMIC ENVIRONMENT: 24

Status: Not Free

TOTAL SCORE: 75

Survey Edition	2002	2003	2004	2005	2006
Total Score, Status	60,PF	66,NF	67,NF	68,NF	72,NF

Media freedom in Russia continued to be curtailed in 2006 as President Vladimir Putin's government passed legislation restricting news reporting and journalists were subjected to physical violence and intimidation. Although the constitution provides for freedom of speech and of the press, authorities are able to use the legislative and judicial systems to harass and prosecute independent journalists. In January, Putin signed into law new regulations that required stricter registration and reporting for nongovernmental organizations (NGOs), thus asserting greater government control over civil society and potentially hindering journalists from obtaining news from NGOs. Despite public objections, Russia's Parliament also passed amendments to the Law on Fighting Extremist Activity, which Putin signed in July. The measure expanded the definition of extremism to include media criticism of public officials and authorized up to three years' imprisonment for journalists as well as the suspension or closure of their publications if they were convicted.

Throughout 2006, journalists continued to face criminal libel charges for printing and broadcasting statements that were unfavorable to public officials. Criminal courts also sentenced several journalists on charges of "inciting racial hatred" for publicizing controversial events in Chechnya. Stanislav Dmitriyevsky, head of the Russian-Chechen Friendship Society, was convicted of such an offense in February after publishing statements by leading Chechen separatists. He received a suspended prison sentence and probation, but his conviction allowed the government to shutter his organization in October under a provision of the new NGO law. However, the office remained open, with appeals pending, at year's end. Separately, Boris Stomakhin of the monthly *Radikalnaya Politika*, who has written various critical articles on Russia's actions in Chechnya, was sentenced in November to five years in prison.

The international community expressed its shock at the October murder of *Novaya Gazeta* journalist Anna Politkovskaya, who was renowned for her independent reporting of abuses committed in Chechnya. Other journalists who were killed in 2006—likely for reasons tied to their work—included Ilya Zimin, a correspondent for the national television station NTV; Vagif Kochetkov, a correspondent for the Moscow daily *Trud* and columnist for the Tula paper *Tulskii Molodoi Kommunar*; Yevgeny Gerasimenko, a correspondent for the Saratov independent weekly *Saratovksy Rasklad*; and Anatoly Voronin, deputy director of the Russian news agency ITAR-TASS. The freelance journalist Elina Ersenoyeva and her mother, Margarita, were both abducted in Chechnya amid rumors that Elina had been married to the infamous Chechen separatist fighter Shamil Basayev. She had recently reported on prison conditions in the republic. In the case of the 2004 murder of *Forbes* editor Paul Klebnikov, two ethnic Chechen suspects, Kazbek Dukuzov and Musa Vakhayev, were acquitted in May after a trial that was closed to the public to protect classified evidence. However, the Klebnikov family appealed and Russia's Supreme Court overturned the acquittal in November, ordering a retrial. Journalists remained unable to cover the news freely, particularly with regard to contentious topics like Chechnya or the environment, and were subject to physical attacks, arrests, detentions, random searches, threats, and self-censorship. While Russia assumed the presidency of the Group of 8 in 2006 and hosted the international club's summit in St. Petersburg in July, the authorities used police violence and detentions to bar foreign journalists from covering civic protests that took place.

Authorities continued to exert influence on media outlets and determine news content. The state owns or controls significant stakes in the country's three main national television networks: Channel One, Rossiya, and NTV. Some diversity of perspective exists with national-level print media, which are privately owned. Ownership of regional print media is less diverse and often concentrated in the hands of local authorities. Private owners of media outlets are generally billionaire business magnates or large companies like the state-controlled energy conglomerate Gazprom, which holds majority stakes in the newspaper *Izvestia* and radio station Ekho Moskvy. However, the law requires little transparency in media ownership, and media watchdogs expressed concern in 2006 that companies like Gazprom would purchase additional newspapers, such as *Komsomolskaya Pravda*, and tighten the establishment's grip on the media ahead of the 2008 presidential election. The government continued to disadvantage private media by allocating subsidies to state-controlled outlets and controlling the means of production and distribution. With online media developing and 16 percent of the population now online, the government also harassed some of Russia's leading news websites. For example, officials accused Pravda.ru, Bankfax.ru, and Gazeta.ru of spreading extremist ideas and fined the editor of the internet publication *Kursiv* for publishing an "offensive" article about Putin.

Rwanda

Status: Not Free

LEGAL ENVIRONMENT: 24
POLITICAL ENVIRONMENT: 34
ECONOMIC ENVIRONMENT: 26
TOTAL SCORE: 84

Survey Edition	2002	2003	2004	2005	2006
Total Score, Status	87,NF	80,NF	82,NF	84,NF	85,NF

Rwanda's media remain restricted by persistent government censorship. The constitution provides for freedom of the press "in conditions prescribed by the law." However, in 2006 the government continued to sharply restrict the ability of media to operate, citing the role that certain media outlets played in provoking violence during the 1994 genocide. A law passed in 2002 guarantees media independence by formally forbidding censorship, but in practice the media are still tightly controlled by the government. Articles of the same law impose criminal sanctions on the media for a wide range of offenses such as "divisionism" and "genocide ideology," punishable by up to five years in prison. Libel is still a criminal offense; however, in August 2006 the High Court overturned a criminal libel conviction made by the lower courts against Charles Kabonero, editor of *Umuseso*. Nonetheless, the court upheld his conviction of "insulting a public figure" and the one-year suspended prison sentence and US$1,900 fine that went with that conviction. In 2006, the government debated a new press law that could provide marginal improvements to the 2002 law by protecting newspaper printers and vendors from criminal libel prosecutions and removing a judge's obligation to impose the maximum sentence on journalists convicted of certain criminal offenses.

The government's attitude toward the press continued to be one of suspicion and control. Although there were no formal arrests of journalists in 2006, attacks on those critical of the government remained a consistent problem throughout the year. In particular, the biweekly independent *Umuco* and its personnel have been repeatedly harassed and threatened for their criticism of the government. In January and again in August, *Umuco*'s editor was forced into hiding after the publication of articles critical of the ruling party led to threats and a police summons. In a positive turn, an *Umuco* journalist was finally released from prison in July after spending nearly 11 months in jail on a murder charge related to the 1994 genocide, a charge of which he had been acquitted several years earlier. In June 2006, Sonia Rolley, a correspondent with Radio France Internationale (RFI), was expelled from the country even after she received press accreditation from the Ministry of Information. Then in November, when a French court accused Rwandan president Paul Kagame of involvement in the 1994 assassination of former president Juvenal Habyarimana that triggered the genocide, the Rwandan government formally severed diplomatic relations with France and ordered the entire RFI office to leave the country.

Although the government continued its confrontational approach to relations with the media in 2006, many independent print publications refused to censor themselves and published articles critical of government behavior. Nonetheless, all newspapers operating in Rwanda, including the state-owned papers, face financial constraints that make it impossible for them to publish on a daily basis, and most private publications do so only twice a month. In addition, the government has the potential to influence print publication content through its purchase of advertising space, upon which many newspapers are financially dependent, as well as its operation of the sole domestic printing press available to nonreligious media. In 2006, the government issued a number of new radio licenses; however, the authorities maintain tight control over the broadcast media, and most of the independent stations avoid political content and focus instead on music. Independent television is legally permitted, but the government continues to maintain a monopoly on the industry. Despite the expulsion of RFI this year, other foreign media like the British Broadcasting Corporation and Voice of America are able to broadcast from Rwanda. Internet access appears to be unrestricted but is available to less than 1 percent of the population.

St. Kitts and Nevis

Status: Free

LEGAL ENVIRONMENT: 4
POLITICAL ENVIRONMENT: 8
ECONOMIC ENVIRONMENT: 8
TOTAL SCORE: 20

Survey Edition	2002	2003	2004	2005	2006
Total Score, Status	18,F	18,F	21,F	23,F	21,F

Freedom of the press is enshrined in the constitution. The independent media were active in 2006 and expressed a wide variety of views without restriction. One of the only notes of discord during the year came in August, when some opposition politicians expressed concerns about the appointment of Clive Bacchus, a Guyanese national and manager of the private WINN FM radio station, to the government's seven-member electoral reform consultative committee. The *Democrat*, the paper of the opposition People's Action Movement, suggested that Bacchus's appointment was an attempt by the ruling St. Kitts and Nevis Labour Party to curb WINN FM's participation in the electoral reform debate. Bacchus was instrumental in solidifying the newly reconstituted Media Association of St. Kitts and Nevis. Both the main parties publish weekly newspapers, and there are three other nonaligned weekly newspapers. ZIZ Broadcasting Corporation, a company in which the government is a majority shareholder, operates both radio and television services, while seven private radio stations and a multichannel cable television service also operate regularly. There are no government restrictions on the internet, and approximately 25 percent of the population used the medium in 2006.

St. Lucia

Status: Free

LEGAL ENVIRONMENT: 4
POLITICAL ENVIRONMENT: 7
ECONOMIC ENVIRONMENT: 5
TOTAL SCORE: 16

Survey Edition	2002	2003	2004	2005	2006
Total Score, Status	11,F	8,F	11,F	16,F	18,F

Freedom of speech and of the press are legally guaranteed and generally upheld by the authorities. In November 2006, the Parliament repealed Section 361 of the criminal code, which had prescribed imprisonment for those convicted of publishing news that endangered the "public good."

Prime Minister Kenny Anthony admitted that it had been difficult to successfully prosecute cases under the provision since it took effect in early 2005. The Association of Caribbean Media Workers, which had led a campaign against Section 361, hailed the repeal of what it called a dangerous measure. No attacks on the media were reported during the year. St. Lucia has three television stations and seven radio stations, all of them private apart from the state-owned Radio St. Lucia. There are three weekly newspapers and two that are published three times a week. There are no government restrictions on the internet, which was accessed by over 32 percent of the population in 2006.

St. Vincent and the Grenadines

LEGAL ENVIRONMENT: 4
POLITICAL ENVIRONMENT: 7
ECONOMIC ENVIRONMENT: 6

Status: Free

TOTAL SCORE: 17

Survey Edition	2002	2003	2004	2005	2006
Total Score, Status	16,F	17,F	14,F	16,F	16,F

The constitution guarantees a free press, and publications openly criticize government policies. In January 2006, Minister of Information Selmon Walter announced that the government had started examining broadcast policies from across the region and would be consulting with "knowledgeable" persons to formulate a new local broadcasting policy in an effort to raise the quality of programming. Walter told members of the Parliament that the content of talk radio programs had made St. Vincent and the Grenadines the "laughingstock of the Caribbean." In a particularly serious incident, Glenn Jackson, press secretary of Prime Minister Ralph Gonsalves and a former head of the local media association, was found shot dead on March 8. A man was later arrested and charged with Jackson's murder, but no motive was revealed. Jackson had ended his career as a journalist in 2001 when he was appointed the prime minister's press secretary; however, he continued to make regular appearances as host of the pro-government *Shake-Up* interactive radio program on the WE FM 99.9 station. The main newspapers—the daily *Herald* and weeklies *Searchlight* and the *Vincentian*—are all privately owned. The state-run St. Vincent and the Grenadines Broadcasting Corporation operates SVG Television and the Hitz FM music radio station. NBC is a partly government-funded national FM radio service, while there are numerous other private outlets. There are no government restrictions on the internet, but it is not a significant source of information, with only about 8 percent of the population using the medium in 2006.

Samoa

LEGAL ENVIRONMENT: 7
POLITICAL ENVIRONMENT: 12
ECONOMIC ENVIRONMENT: 11

Status: Free

TOTAL SCORE: 30

Survey Edition	2002	2003	2004	2005	2006
Total Score, Status	23,F	24,F	24,F	25,F	29,F

While the constitution protects press freedom in Samoa, publishers remain vigilant against political attempts to intimidate the media. Samoan law mandates imprisonment for refusal to reveal a confidential source, but the rule has never been enforced in court. The most significant media freedom issue in 2006 involved an alleged attack by a media executive on a local reporter. The Samoa Broadcasting Corporation's (SBC) chief executive, Galumalemana Faiesea Matafeo, was charged with assaulting journalist Atofu Moana from the private *Le Samoa* newspaper. Police also investigated a case of possible sabotage against the traditionally independent and outspoken newspaper, the *Samoa Observer*. In May, following complaints made by the Samoa Council of Churches, Samoa's principal censor banned the screening of the film *The Da Vinci Code* in cinemas and on local television stations. Samoa has three English-language and several Samoan-language newspapers. It also has five private radio stations, the state-run SBC, and some access to local and foreign satellite television. Internet access is unrestricted but is used by only 3.2 percent of the population.

San Marino

LEGAL ENVIRONMENT: 4
POLITICAL ENVIRONMENT: 6
ECONOMIC ENVIRONMENT: 7

Status: Free

TOTAL SCORE: 17

Survey Edition	2002	2003	2004	2005	2006
Total Score, Status	NA	9,F	14,F	16,F	17,F

The 1974 San Marino Constitutional Order guarantees freedom of expression, and Article 183 of the criminal code protects against libel and slander. However, there are restrictions when freedom of expression comes into conflict with the right to confidentiality and to secrecy. No direct violations of freedom of the press by either state or nonstate actors were reported in 2006. By law, radio and television broadcasting is monopolized by the San Marino Broadcasting Company, whose responsibility it is to grant concessions to private broadcasters. State-owned San Marino RTV runs both a radio and a television station. Three daily private papers are published in the republic, one of which is electronic, and a local weekly paper reports on economics, finance, and politics. There is a plethora of Italian news in San Marino including two private newspapers as well as radio and television stations. The internet is available, unrestricted, and used by about 45 percent of the population.

Sao Tome and Principe

LEGAL ENVIRONMENT: 4
POLITICAL ENVIRONMENT: 11
ECONOMIC ENVIRONMENT: 14
TOTAL SCORE: 29

Status: Free

Survey Edition	2002	2003	2004	2005	2006
Total Score, Status	19,F	19,F	28,F	28,F	29,F

The constitution provides for freedom of the press, and this right is respected in practice and upheld by the state. There were no known cases of government restrictions on local or foreign media during the year, and publications that regularly criticize the administration are freely circulated without government interference. Nonetheless, self-censorship is widely practiced, and newspapers often depend on official news releases as primary sources of information, which inhibits the growth of investigative journalism. Some writers accept financial favors from news sources for doing their jobs. Severe problems with infrastructure, including inadequate telecommunications and media distribution networks, constitute a major obstacle for the media. There are seven privately owned and two state-run newspapers in addition to a number of state-operated radio and television stations. In 2005, the government authorized two new private radio stations to operate within the country, both of which began broadcasting by the end of 2006. Access to the internet is not restricted by the government but is limited by a lack of infrastructure; nonetheless, over 11 percent of the population accessed this new medium during the year.

Saudi Arabia

LEGAL ENVIRONMENT: 28
POLITICAL ENVIRONMENT: 30
ECONOMIC ENVIRONMENT: 24

Status: Not Free

TOTAL SCORE: 82

Survey Edition	2002	2003	2004	2005	2006
Total Score, Status	80,NF	80,NF	80,NF	80,NF	79,NF

Saudi Arabia has few safeguards to protect press freedom. Since there is no constitutional guarantee of freedom of speech or of the press, the media are regulated under a 1963 Publishing and Printing Law. The 49 provisions of this law cover the establishment of media outlets, address the rights and responsibilities of journalists, and explain the penalties that can be imposed on them. The lack of a theoretical framework for freedom of the press in Saudi Arabia is due largely to the government's position on the role of the press in society. The press, according to the government and the conservative religious establishment, is a tool to educate the masses, propagate government views, and promote national unity. Through harsh measures, and with the help of heavy self-censorship, the government and allied clerics are able to overcome all attempts by journalists to exercise limited freedom of action. Criticism of the royal family and the religious authorities is forbidden, and press offenses are punishable by fines and imprisonment. All journalists must register with the Ministry of Information, and foreign journalists face visa obstacles and restrictions on freedom of movement. However, recently there have been marginal improvements for both domestic and foreign journalists, allowing freedom to report on social issues and gesture toward government accountability, but those efforts are, at this point, relatively isolated.

Even when the government has been inclined to permit some freedom of expression, it finds itself at odds with the strong ultraconservative Islamic forces in the kingdom. In many instances, it has been forced to back down. In 2006, several episodes of the very popular television sitcom *Tash Ma Tash* were canceled after a fatwa was issued against the show amid protests and threats from the ultrareligious Right. An episode criticizing the powerful religious agency tasked with "Promoting the Good and Forbidding the Evil" was canceled as soon as the agency learned of its content.

Journalists in the kingdom face threats, harassment, and detention if they publish material that the authorities deem objectionable. In February 2006, journalist Batal al-Qaws, editor of the privately owned daily *Shams*, was dismissed from his job after his newspaper published controversial Danish cartoons of the prophet Muhammad. Among a number of other such incidents, in March journalist Mohsen al-Awajy was detained for 10 days for criticizing the king and Fawaz Turki, a journalist with the daily *Arab News* newspaper, was dismissed from his job for writing about atrocities committed in East Timor. Separately, writer and women's rights activist Wajiha al-Howaider was arrested in August, threatened with the loss of her job, and forced to sign a pledge to cease all human rights activities, including writing and talking to the media. These tactics of arrest, interrogation, dismissal, and harassment have forced journalists and editors to practice and enforce extreme levels of self-censorship.

There are 10 daily newspapers in Saudi Arabia, all owned by either the government, members of the royal family, or close associates of the royal family. Broadcast media are also in the grip of the government, which owns and operates all television and radio stations. Satellite television has become widespread despite its illegal status and is an important source of foreign news; nonetheless, much of the satellite industry is controlled by Saudi investors and is respectful of local sensibilities. About 11 percent of Saudi residents used the internet in 2006. King Abdul-Aziz City for Science and Technology (KACST)—a government institution charged with developing and coordinating internet-related policies—is the sole gateway for Saudi internet users and manages the connections between the national and international internet. Although the authorities approved applications for over 40 privately owned internet service providers in 1998, all of them are linked to the main server at KACST. Through this agency, the government continues to block and filter websites deemed offensive, critical, or immoral. Updated lists of undesirable websites are continuously fed to the filters, and users attempting to access banned sites receive warnings and are told that their attempts are being logged. In 2006, the Saudi government approved the first law to combat "electronic crimes," defined as defamation on the internet and computer hacking. Online journalists are generally subject to the same restrictions as their print colleagues.

Senegal

Status: Partly Free

LEGAL ENVIRONMENT: 13
POLITICAL ENVIRONMENT: 21
ECONOMIC ENVIRONMENT: 12
TOTAL SCORE: 46

Survey Edition	2002	2003	2004	2005	2006
Total Score, Status	39,PF	38,PF	37,PF	37,PF	44,PF

Criminal prosecutions of journalists for libel during the year and the passage of a controversial broadcasting reform bill intended to muzzle the media together confirmed earlier indications that President Abdoulaye Wade does not intend to live up to his promises to protect press freedom. Although the constitution formally guarantees freedom of expression and of the press, the government often restricts these rights in practice. Article 80 of the penal code is particularly harsh, imposing severe penalties for libel and the publication of materials that compromise national security. In July, Mustapha Sow, managing editor of the private newspaper *L'Office*, was imprisoned on charges that he defamed a local businessman. Sow was released on bail after two weeks when his lawyer filed an appeal. He had been convicted of criminal defamation charges and sentenced to six months in prison in February, but the arrest warrant was not carried out until June. In September, two more journalists were given suspended sentences and fined the equivalent of US$100 each for a story involving a construction company accused of bribing government officials for contracts. According to Diatou Cisse Coulibaly, secretary general of the Senegalese press union, criminal libel accusations have been a particular problem under the Wade administration, resulting in broad intimidation of critical journalists and increased self-censorship.

A controversial broadcasting bill that was passed by a vote of 11 to 2 in the 120-seat National Assembly in December 2005 still awaited the signature of President Wade at the end of 2006; if approved, it would create the National Council for the Regulation of Broadcasting (CNRA). The new nine-member panel would be made up of the president's appointees, only one of whom would be a professional with broadcasting credentials. The CNRA would function as a supreme tribunal with the power to monitor media behavior and impose punishments ranging from temporary closures to fines of up to US$18,000. The new bill would also strip the media profession's self-regulatory body—the Council for the Respect of Professional Ethics and Conduct—of its authority to monitor and sanction members of the media who act unprofessionally.

Despite intimidation caused by the wave of criminal defamation prosecutions, much of the private media still frequently criticize the government in their reporting. Near the end of 2006, during the campaign for the February 2007 presidential election, journalists working for the private newspaper *Sud Quotidien* and the private radio station Sud FM reported receiving intimidating and threatening telephone calls from unknown persons. And in the central city of Mbacke, a correspondent for a local private radio station was beaten with metal cables and suffered head and back injuries after he broadcast a report critical of a local religious leader who was mobilizing his supporters for President Wade in the election. On a promising note, a court dismissed charges of breaching national security that had been leveled against several journalists whose private media company—Sud Communications Group, which operates *Sud Quotidien* and Sud FM—broadcast an interview in October 2005 with the rebel leader of the southern Casamance region. The court's dismissal of the case was seen as a rebuke to the Wade administration.

Senegal has many private, independent print publications. A number of community, private, and public radio stations operate all over the country, and 70 separate radio frequencies have been granted so far by the state. Nevertheless, the Wade administration refuses to accept private participation in the television sector except for entertainment channels. The only national television station, Radiodiffusion Television Senegalaise, is required by law to be majority controlled by the state, and it broadcasts generally favorable coverage of the government. In the past, Senegal's media watchdog, the High Audiovisual Council, has criticized the government-run television station for not reflecting diverse viewpoints and not allowing equal coverage of opposition members and religious groups. Foreign satellite television and radio stations, including Radio France Internationale and the British Broadcasting Corporation, are available. Internet access is unrestricted, but usage was estimated at just 5 percent of the population in 2006.

Serbia

Status: Partly Free

LEGAL ENVIRONMENT: 13
POLITICAL ENVIRONMENT: 17
ECONOMIC ENVIRONMENT: 9
TOTAL SCORE: 39

Survey Edition	2002	2003	2004	2005	2006
Total Score, Status	45,PF	40,PF	40,PF	40,PF	40,PF

The constitution of the newly independent Serbia, adopted in October 2006, provides for freedom of the press. However, the government, media owners, local officials, and businessmen continue to place undue pressure on journalists. Libel remains a criminal offense, punishable by imprisonment or fines of up to US$13,800. In August, a senior editor at local television channel RTV Kursumlija received a suspended four-month prison sentence after the station aired viewers' text messages that were critical of a local official. In October, despite international criticism and objections from local nongovernmental organizations, the Parliament adopted controversial amendments to the Broadcasting Law. The legislation made Serbia's Republic Broadcasting Agency (RBA) financially and politically dependent on the government, since it required the government to approve the budget of the agency's nominally independent council. The changes also limited broadcasters' ability to appeal council decisions and required them to carry out the council's directives. Furthermore, the amendments gave the council greater latitude to deny commercial broadcasting licenses. The licenses themselves would entail the payment of substantial fees, and the RBA had already been criticized for carrying out its licensing procedures in a discriminatory way. In April, the council had temporarily suspended the license of the private BK television station. Local media watchdog organizations reported that the suspension was a direct attack on opposition politician and BK owner Bogoljub Karic. However, the decision was overturned by the Supreme Court in May.

Both broadcast and print media in Serbia are highly active and promote diverse views. However, news outlets operate with a significant level of politicization, which increased toward the end of the year as the fall constitutional referendum and the January 2007 parliamentary elections approached. Journalists at times practice self-censorship, and many avoid politically charged topics, such as Serbia's failure to comply with the UN war crimes tribunal in The Hague, negotiations on the future status of the UN-administered province of Kosovo, and the May 2006 referendum on Montenegrin independence. Media organizations and journalists were again the victims of harassment, intimidation, and physical violence in 2006. Employees of the private broadcaster B92 were threatened throughout the year. Most incidents involving extralegal intimidation and physical violence against journalists occurred in smaller towns. Local police often failed to properly investigate attacks on journalists, and on several occasions, local officials and police blocked journalists' access to public documents or events. The 2001 murder of journalist Milan Pantic and the 1999 murder of Slavko Curuvija remain unresolved, and investigations into both crimes have stalled.

Serbia's broadcast and print media are for the most part privately owned. The government owns a stake in the oldest and best-selling daily, *Politika*, but has little direct editorial influence. The state still controls Radio Television Serbia, and reports indicate that the broadcaster, which operates three nationwide television stations and a radio station, has a slight pro-government bias. Media ownership concentration has increased slightly with the growing presence of foreign firms. Internet access is unrestricted, but authorities selectively monitor e-mail and other online communications for the 14 percent of the population that use the medium.

The media environment in Kosovo is regulated by the UN Mission in Kosovo (UNMIK) and the constitutional framework. While UNMIK, the NATO-led Kosovo Force, and Kosovo's Provisional Institutions of Self-Government largely uphold press freedom, the media face a difficult operating environment owing to political pressure and financial difficulties. In January 2006, the Parliament passed legislation transferring authority over the public broadcaster, Radio Television Kosovo, from UNMIK to local government control and placed its budget under the direct control of the Ministry of Finance. Journalists faced indirect pressure and were offered bribes in exchange for positive coverage. Throughout the year, journalists were the victims of violence and harassment. In September, a reporter with the daily *Lajm Ekskluzive* was assaulted by a security officer in the Kosovo assembly building. Lack of advertising funds leaves media outlets vulnerable to editorial pressure from government and business interests. The Pristina branch of the Albanian newspaper *Bota Sot* was closed down in November for failing to pay taxes, reducing the number of daily newspapers in Kosovo to nine. Media operating with foreign financial aid were more editorially independent and expressed a wider range of views, but they remained vulnerable to future fluctuations in foreign assistance.

Seychelles

LEGAL ENVIRONMENT: 20
POLITICAL ENVIRONMENT: 21
ECONOMIC ENVIRONMENT: 19

Status: Partly Free

TOTAL SCORE: 60

Survey Edition	2002	2003	2004	2005	2006
Total Score, Status	51,PF	50,PF	52,PF	58,PF	60,PF

The constitution provides for freedom of speech but also restricts this right by protecting the reputation, rights, and privacy of citizens as well as the "interest of defense, public safety, public order, public morality, or public health." These restrictions have limited freedom of the press, particularly because libel charges can easily be filed to penalize journalists. The law also allows the minister of information to prohibit the broadcast of any material that is against the "national interest." The Seychelles Broadcasting Corporation, the state-controlled media regulation body, continued to ban a local singer's music on the grounds that it was seditious.

In the past, the *Regar*, one of the county's two independent weekly newspapers, has been sued regularly for libel by the government. In October 2006, the *Regar* stopped publication to protest a lawsuit in which the paper was ordered to pay excessive damages (US$58,500) to Seychelles Tourism Board President Maurice Lousteau-Lalanne for publishing a photograph of him that had already appeared in the pro-government paper the *Nation*—the country's only daily newspaper. Also in October, violent protests erupted after the Parliament rejected a motion to amend the law banning political parties from setting up their own radio stations. Several people were injured during the protests, and *Regar* editor Roger Mancienne was arrested and then released on bail after being charged with "unlawful assembly."

The state has a de facto monopoly over the widely consumed broadcast media, and private broadcasters have been slow to develop because of restrictive licensing fees of more than US$185,000 per year. Telecommunications companies must submit subscriber information to the government. The internet was available and unrestricted in Seychelles for the nearly 25 percent of the population that accessed it in 2006.

Sierra Leone
Status: Partly Free

LEGAL ENVIRONMENT: 17
POLITICAL ENVIRONMENT: 21
ECONOMIC ENVIRONMENT: 18
TOTAL SCORE: 56

Survey Edition	2002	2003	2004	2005	2006
Total Score, Status	62,NF	61,NF	58,PF	59,PF	59,PF

The constitution guarantees freedom of expression, but this right is not upheld in practice. The Public Order Act of 1965 criminalizes libel and holds accountable not only journalists, but also vendors, printers, and publishers, rendering any guarantee of press freedom illusory. The law was applied as recently as 2005, when the managing editor and a reporter with the weekly *Trumpet* were jailed and charged with seditious libel; they were acquitted the following month. No new criminal libel cases were filed in 2006. In fact, during the year President Ahmad Tejan Kabbah pledged to decriminalize libel, though this promise remained unfulfilled at year's end.

In February, the attorney general of Sierra Leone declined to press manslaughter charges against lawmaker Fatmata Hassan Komeh and two others accused of assaulting journalist Harry Yansaneh, acting editor of the independent newspaper *For Di People*. The suspects had attacked Yansaneh in May 2005; two months later he died of complications from his injuries. Komeh and her accomplices had been arrested in August 2005 but were subsequently released on bail. Explaining his decision not to pursue manslaughter charges, the attorney general said he relied on the report of the inquest into Yansaneh's death where a physician testified that Yansaneh died from chronic kidney failure unrelated to the assault. The attorney general said he was considering lesser charges against the three suspects. In August, the High Court requested the extradition of Komeh's three children, residents of the United Kingdom who were also implicated in the assault, but this was still pending at year's end.

Despite frequent harassment, newspapers openly and routinely criticize the government, its officials, opposition political parties, and former rebel forces. The diverse and lively media, particularly the growing print media (more than 25 newspapers published in 2006, many of varying political persuasions) have been a strong voice against government corruption. Nonetheless, poor journalistic skills, insufficient resources, a high degree of politicization, and a lack of professional ethics all pose enduring problems for the quality of the press. Several government and private radio stations, as well as international stations like United Nations Radio, all provide coverage of domestic news and political commentary. The radio remains the medium of choice for most Sierra Leoneans, who for economic reasons have limited access to television, newspapers, and the internet. Less than 0.5 percent of the population accessed the internet in 2006, though the government did not place any explicit restrictions on internet use.

LEGAL ENVIRONMENT: 24
POLITICAL ENVIRONMENT: 24
ECONOMIC ENVIRONMENT: 21

Singapore

Status: Not Free

TOTAL SCORE: 69

Survey Edition	2002	2003	2004	2005	2006
Total Score, Status	68,NF	66,NF	64,NF	66,NF	66,NF

Media freedom in Singapore is constrained to such a degree that the vast majority of journalists practice self-censorship rather than risk being charged with defamation or breaking the country's criminal laws on permissible speech. The constitution guarantees freedom of speech and of expression in Article 14, but it also permits restrictions on these rights. Legal constraints include the Newspapers and Printing Presses Act, the Defamation Act, and the Internal Security Act, all of which allow authorities to restrict the circulation of news deemed to incite violence, arouse racial or religious tensions, interfere in domestic politics, or threaten public order, national interest, or national security. The government proposed a series of amendments to the penal code in 2006 that would cover offenses committed via digital media. The draft amendments would not only provide jail terms or fines for defamation, "statements that would cause public mischief," and the "wounding" of racial or religious feeling, they would also make it a crime for anyone outside the country to abet an offense committed inside the country, thereby allowing the authorities to prosecute internet users living abroad. Singaporean students studying overseas are the presumed targets of this amendment.

The government is quick to sue critics under harsh criminal defamation laws. In May 2006, for example, Prime Minister Lee Hsien Loong and his father filed criminal charges against the publishers of opposition newspaper the *New Democrat*, which is put out several times a year by a committee of the Singapore Democratic Party. The lawsuit stemmed from an unsigned story that described the ruling party's handling of a corruption scandal at the National Kidney Foundation as "secretive and non-accountable." Foreign media in Singapore are also subject to restrictive laws. In August, after the *Far Eastern Economic Review* published an interview with opposition party leader Chee Soon Juan, it and four other foreign publications were advised that they needed to post bonds and appoint legal representatives in order to continue to operate in Singapore. When the *Far Eastern Economic Review* did not comply, its circulation permit was revoked, effectively banning the publication. Meanwhile, in September the prime minister and his father filed defamation suits against it over the article.

Nearly all print and broadcast media outlets, internet service providers, and cable television services are either owned or controlled by the state or by companies with close ties to the ruling party. Annual licensing requirements for all media outlets, including political and religious websites, have been used to inhibit criticism of the government. Approximately 66 percent of the population accessed the internet in 2006. Nonetheless, the government restricts internet access, and Singapore has no tolerance for bloggers who challenge the government in any way. Prior to the May 6 parliamentary elections, the communications and arts minister warned bloggers and website managers that they did not have the right to back a particular candidate's program or to express opinions on political issues. The same rules were applied to other new media, including podcasting and videocasting. On April 26, the opposition Singapore Democratic Party was ordered to withdraw a podcast from its website. In June, popular blogger Lee Kin Mun, known online as Mr. Brown, was informed by the state-owned newspaper *Today* that his weekly column, which had satirized the high cost of living, would be suspended. On November 6, a judge ordered Yap Keng Ho, a member of the opposition, to remove from his blog a video of himself speaking in public during the general elections.

Slovakia

LEGAL ENVIRONMENT: 5
POLITICAL ENVIRONMENT: 8
ECONOMIC ENVIRONMENT: 7

Status: Free

TOTAL SCORE: 20

Survey Edition	2002	2003	2004	2005	2006
Total Score, Status	22,F	21,F	21,F	21,F	20,F

Press freedom in Slovakia is constitutionally guaranteed and generally respected, and independent media outlets freely disseminate diverse views. Defamation is not a criminal offense, and in a break from the pattern of recent years, no new civil defamation cases were brought before the courts in 2006. In one case that was pending, a court in February ordered a daily newspaper to apologize and pay damages of US$100,000 to a former Supreme Court judge for reporting on bonuses paid to court members and alleged improprieties in assigning cases to judges. A new media bill that has lingered in draft form since 2005 was not passed in 2006, though the Parliament approved several amendments to current legislation that improved the oversight of public service media. The existing Press Act, which has been in force for 40 years, is widely considered to be inadequate to the needs of a modern media market, particularly with respect to the regulation of digital media.

Political pressures on the media in 2006 were low for an election year. The only notable incident was an alleged attempt in October by the Office of the Prime Minister to interfere with the public broadcaster's reporting about the prime minister's trips abroad. Most Slovak media outlets, including all major print outlets, are privately owned. Following legislative changes in 2004, the heads of state-owned media enterprises are no longer political appointees, and generally journalists in both print and electronic media exercise broad editorial independence. A lack of transparency in media ownership remains a concern, as does inadequate enforcement of regulations on cross-ownership of media outlets. Electronic media are diverse and pluralistic, and many Slovak citizens also regularly watch television from the neighboring Czech Republic and Hungary. Slovaks enjoy growing access to the internet, though the proportion of users (nearly 47 percent of the population) is among the lowest in the European Union. Public authorities in 2006 redoubled their efforts to increase internet access in the schools and subsidize access in homes.

Slovenia

LEGAL ENVIRONMENT: 5
POLITICAL ENVIRONMENT: 9
ECONOMIC ENVIRONMENT: 7

Status: Free

TOTAL SCORE: 21

Survey Edition	2002	2003	2004	2005	2006
Total Score, Status	20,F	19,F	19,F	19,F	20,F

The Slovenian constitution and legal system guarantee freedom of the press, and the government typically respects this right in practice. However, reports of government pressure and interference in the media are a growing cause for concern. Although libel is not punishable with prison terms, it remains a criminal offense. A controversial law that took effect in late 2005 served to increase government influence on public media outlets, establishing a programming council and a supervisory board to oversee the public television and radio network. The Parliament appoints 21 of the 29 Programming Council members, as well as 5 members of the 11-member

Supervisory Board. The government names 4 of the board's members, leaving only 2 seats controlled by employees.

Media are able to report freely on government activities and express a diversity of viewpoints. However, there were several reports of police using unnecessary force against journalists in 2006, and news outlets faced indirect political and economic pressure from the government and business interests. On occasion, government officials have openly criticized members of the media, treating them as political opposition. Major print outlets are adequately financed through advertising sales and private investment, but the government owns stakes in companies that hold shares in major media firms. The public broadcaster's television and radio channels compete with a handful of commercial stations. Freelance journalists do not fall under the current labor legislation, leaving them vulnerable to pressure from media owners, who are themselves strongly influenced by investors and public officials. Internet access is unrestricted and widely available, with about 56 percent of the population reportedly using the internet in 2006.

Solomon Islands

LEGAL ENVIRONMENT: 5
POLITICAL ENVIRONMENT: 14
ECONOMIC ENVIRONMENT: 11

Status: Free

TOTAL SCORE: 30

Survey Edition	2002	2003	2004	2005	2006
Total Score, Status	24,F	25,F	30,F	30,F	30,F

The law in the Solomon Islands provides for freedom of speech and of the press, but the news media were challenged by renewed ethnic violence in 2006. On April 18, protests against the election of Prime Minister Snyder Rini led to rioting that devastated the Chinatown district of Honiara, the capital, amid suspicions that local Chinese businessmen had used bribery to influence the election result. The widespread violence led to a more dangerous atmosphere for journalists and had a chilling effect on free speech. Australia and New Zealand deployed troops and police to assist the local security forces and the existing Regional Assistance Mission to the Solomon Islands (RAMSI), and Rini resigned shortly thereafter. RAMSI officials later praised the conduct of local journalists during the crisis and offered a series of training and support programs to bolster the country's press.

One daily newspaper, the independent *Solomon Star*, dominates the media scene. Three private weekly papers—*Solomons Voice, Solomon Times*, and the new *Island Sun*, established in November—are also published, along with the monthly newsletters *Agrikalsa Nius* and the *Citizen's Press*. Low literacy rates mean that the broadcast media are major news sources. The Solomon Islands Broadcasting Corporation operates the national public station Radio Hapi Isles, Wantok FM, and the provincial stations Radio Hapi Lagun and Radio Temotu. One private commercial station, Paoa FM, also operates. There are no domestic television stations, although the Australian Broadcasting Corporation, the British Broadcasting Corporation, and other satellite channels can be received. The internet is not restricted by the government, but it is accessed by less than 2 percent of the population.

Somalia

Status: Not Free

LEGAL ENVIRONMENT: 27
POLITICAL ENVIRONMENT: 34
ECONOMIC ENVIRONMENT: 24

TOTAL SCORE: 85

Survey Edition	2002	2003	2004	2005	2006
Total Score, Status	88,NF	80,NF	80,NF	83,NF	83,NF

The media environment experienced a noticeable deterioration in 2006 with the escalation of armed conflict between the internationally recognized Transitional Federal Government (TFG), which was based in Baidoa, and the Islamic Courts Union (ICU), an Islamist group that took control of much of Somalia, including the capital, Mogadishu, beginning in June. By the end of the year, however, the ICU had been largely routed by Ethiopian troops intervening on behalf of the TFG, which was able to relocate to Mogadishu following the defeat of the ICU in December. According to the National Union of Somali Journalists (NUSOJ), 2006 was the most dangerous year for press freedom in more than a decade.

In principle, Somalia's charter provides for freedom of the press, but given the lawless conditions in much of the country, many of the local clan leaders have disregarded this in favor of a more aggressive approach to critical reporting. In October, the ICU proposed the establishment of a 13-point program with which it would regulate the conduct of the media that would have effectively eliminated press freedom in the areas under its control. It would have prohibited the publication of articles that could create division between the ICU and the public, required journalists to reveal their sources, and forbidden media outlets from receiving foreign funding. However, the ICU eventually agreed to discuss the proposal with the media before it could be passed; at year's end, no aspect of the proposed media regulations had been formally approved or implemented. In general, the ICU was able to severely curtail the freedoms of the independent press and its efforts to impose further legal restrictions helped to cultivate an atmosphere of fear and pervasive self-censorship across the country.

In 2006, the number of violent attacks, arbitrary arrests, and instances of censorship noticeably increased. The NUSOJ logged 30 such cases—10 more than it had recorded in 2005. The most egregious incident occurred in June, less than three weeks after the ICU seized control of Mogadishu, when Martin Adler, the award-winning Swedish freelance journalist and photographer, was shot in the back and killed while filming a pro-ICU demonstration in the capital. Despite ICU promises that his killer would be brought to justice, at year's end no one had been identified or arrested. Among numerous other press freedom violations that occurred in territories held by the Islamists, in September the ICU began closing critical radio stations and detaining journalists. Private Radio HornAfrik, Radio Jowhar, and Radio Simba were all temporarily shuttered for their critical reporting. Radio Jowhar in the Middle Shabelle region was told it could resume broadcasting if it agreed to stop playing romantic music and refrained from critical reporting about the ICU.

Intimidation and harassment of the media was not unique to Mogadishu or the ICU. In fact, self-censorship was a particular problem in Baidoa, where journalists were expressly targeted by the TFG for reporting on the presence of Ethiopian troops in Somalia prior to their announced entry on December 20. TFG actions included the June closure of Radio Shabelle, a local radio station, and the October arrest and temporary detention of Abdullahi Yassin Jama, a journalist with private outlets Radio Warsan and the Somali Broadcasting Corporation.

Despite the high number of press freedom violations reported in 2006, many more are believed to have gone completely unreported, often out of fear of reprisal or an acceptance of the futility of attempts to bring perpetrators to justice. In fact, near total impunity currently exists in Somalia for perpetrators of crimes against the press; in the last two years, no suspects have been arrested for any of the multiple instances of harassment, intimidation, murder, abuse, or torture of journalists. Such is the case with two journalists murdered in 2005; British Broadcasting Corporation correspondent Kate Peyton and Duniya Muhyadin Nur, a reporter for the

Somali-based radio station Capital Voice, were both shot and killed while working in and around Mogadishu.

Photocopied dailies and low-grade radio stations have proliferated in Mogadishu and elsewhere since 1991; some 50 private newspapers and a dozen radio and television stations exist in the country. Nonetheless, a number of outlets ceased operations in 2006 or censored the subject matter of their reporting. Of those that continue to operate, many have been accused of bias, particularly in their coverage of the war or ethnic and clan rivalries. The infrastructure for journalism in Somalia is relatively undeveloped, as many journalists work with little to no pay and most are employed without a written contract. Unlike many other African nations, Somalia has a rich internet presence, fueled predominantly by the Somali diaspora in Europe, North America, and the Gulf states. Nevertheless, owing to pervasive poverty, less than 1 percent of the domestic Somali population has been able to access this resource. While the online community has traditionally operated unhindered, there were reports in 2006 that the ICU monitored internet activity closely.

In 2006, the status of press freedom was visibly better in Puntland (a self-declared autonomous region) and Somaliland (which claimed, but has not been granted, full independence from Somalia) than in the rest of the country, although restrictions are still harsh and coverage of political and security issues is particularly perilous. The Puntland charter provides for freedom of the press "as long as [media practitioners] respect the law." In January, Radio Las Anod—the only radio station in the city of Las Anod, in the Sool region between Somaliland and Puntland—was temporarily closed and all employees were briefly detained, reportedly for airing criticism of the Puntland government's decision to move a planned vaccination program out of the city. In Somaliland, liberal decrees nominally guaranteeing press freedom do not prevent the local administration from continuing to harass and detain journalists. In June, soldiers from the Somaliland Criminal Investigation Department arrested the editor of a popular newspaper on charges that he had published an article written by a U.S. reader; the editor was released the next day, but only following persistent demands by human rights groups. In March, the government in Somaliland gave its permission for Hargeisa Cable Television to begin operating an independent broadcast in the region; until 2006, the Somaliland government had maintained a monopoly on broadcast television.

LEGAL ENVIRONMENT: 7
POLITICAL ENVIRONMENT: 12

South Africa

ECONOMIC ENVIRONMENT: 9

Status: Free

TOTAL SCORE: 28

Survey Edition	2002	2003	2004	2005	2006
Total Score, Status	23,F	25,F	24,F	26,F	27,F

Freedom of expression and of the press, protected in principle by the constitution, are generally respected in practice in South Africa. Nevertheless, several apartheid-era laws that remain in effect permit authorities to restrict the publication of information about the police, national defense forces, prisons, and mental institutions and to compel journalists to reveal sources. A proposed film and publication amendment bill was sent to Parliament in August 2006; it would subject print and broadcast media to the same prepublication screening for "indecent content" that is currently required for films, computer games, and magazines. After vociferous protest from media outlets and press freedom advocates, President Thabo Mbeki postponed a decision on the bill until 2007. Recent years have seen an increase in the use of interdictions and gag orders by both governmental and nonstate actors, a trend the Johannesburg-based Freedom of Expression Institute likens to prepublication censorship. In February, the Johannesburg High Court approved an interdiction request from a Muslim religious organization to prevent the country's largest newspaper, the *Sunday Times*, from reprinting allegedly offensive cartoons of the prophet Muhammad. In September, the Johannesburg High Court granted an interdiction request brought by the former head of the national postal service against the *Mail & Guardian* newspaper; the Court overturned the gag order 10 days later. The *Mail & Guardian* had been the subject of a May 2005 gag order that delayed for over a month the publication of an article on the "Oilgate" corruption scandal.

South Africa features vibrant press freedom advocacy and journalists' organizations, and a number of private newspapers and magazines—including the *Mail & Guardian*, the *Cape Times*, and the *Sunday Times*—are sharply critical of the government, political parties, and other societal actors. The state-owned South African Broadcasting Corporation (SABC) dominates broadcast media. Although editorially independent, the SABC has come under fire for displaying pro-government bias and for encouraging self-censorship. In June, the SABC—apparently under pressure from the government—opted not to air a commissioned documentary about President Mbeki because it contained allegedly defamatory statements about him. In the year's most worrying development for press freedom, in October the *Mail & Guardian* website leaked excerpts from an internal SABC report that found several outspoken government critics had been barred from SABC airwaves. The leaked report accused head of news Snuki Zikalala of repeated and inappropriate interventions in the SABC's news programs. The SABC then attempted to interdict the *Mail & Guardian*'s online publication of the "blacklist" report, but the interdiction request was struck down by the Johannesburg High Court. In October, the SABC decided not to release the full report, making available only selected excerpts and summaries. In addition, members of government and other political figures continued to reveal a heightened sensitivity to media criticism, in some cases accusing critical journalists of racism and betraying the state.

Most South Africans receive the news via radio outlets associated with the SABC. However, efforts are being made to expand the number and broadcasting range of community radio stations via the Independent Communications Authority of South Africa (ICASA). In April, press freedom organizations praised Mbeki's decision not to sign controversial legislation that would have enabled the minister of communications to select the ICASA council. While the SABC's three stations claim most of the television market, the country's two commercial television stations, e.tv and M-Net, are reaching ever greater proportions of the population—78 percent of the population accessed e.tv in 2006. Internet access is unrestricted and growing rapidly, although many South Africans cannot afford the service fee and only 10 percent of the population accessed it in 2006.

South Korea

LEGAL ENVIRONMENT: 9
POLITICAL ENVIRONMENT: 11
ECONOMIC ENVIRONMENT: 10

Status: Free   TOTAL SCORE: 30

Survey Edition	2002	2003	2004	2005	2006
Total Score, Status	30,F	29,F	29,F	29,F	30,F

Freedom of the press is guaranteed under South Korean law and is generally respected in practice. Censorship of the media is against the law, though some websites have been blocked for posting pro–North Korean content, and the government requires all website operators to indicate whether their sites might be harmful to youths. Article 7 of the 1948 National Security

Law allows imprisonment for praising or expressing sympathy for North Korea. However, the government also blocks the sale of video games that vilify North Korea. President Roh Moo-hyun's tenure has been marked by disputes with conservative media outlets, and critics alleged that the liberal Uri Party government was seeking to reduce the media's influence through two media reform laws that were passed in January 2005. But in June 2006, the Supreme Court struck down several measures in one of the January 2005 laws, the Law Governing the Guarantee of Freedom and Functions of Newspapers Etc. (also known as the Newspaper Law), which had required all newspapers, including those with internet sites, to register with the government and designated newspapers with a market share of more than 30 percent, or a combined total of 60 percent for three dailies, as "dominant market players." Such a designation would allow antimonopoly restrictions to be imposed. The legislation was believed to be aimed at the three major daily newspapers in South Korea, which are politically conservative and have voiced disapproval of many policies of the Roh administration. The three dailies, *Chosun Ilbo*, *Dong-a Ilbo*, and *JoonAng Ilbo*, had challenged the Newspaper Law, and the court determined by a vote of seven to two that the law was contrary to press freedom "because readers can freely decide which paper they want to read."

South Korea has vibrant and diverse media, with numerous cable, terrestrial, and satellite television stations and over 100 daily newspapers in Korean and English. Many newspapers depend on large corporations for their advertising revenue. There are both public and private radio and television stations, including an American Forces Network for the U.S. military. The internet is unrestricted by government regulation, and nearly 67 percent of the population was recorded as being online in 2006; a significant number of young people get their news exclusively from online sources. The South Korean online media are especially vigorous and innovative. For example, in 2000 an interactive internet news site called OhmyNews was launched, allowing citizens to submit their own news articles for immediate publication on the site.

Spain

Status: Free

Legal Environment: 4
Political Environment: 13
Economic Environment: 5
Total Score: 22

Survey Edition	2002	2003	2004	2005	2006
Total Score, Status	17,F	16,F	19,F	22,F	21,F

Freedom of speech is protected by Spanish law and is generally respected in practice. However, threats to press freedom include antiterrorism legislation and high awards in defamation suits against journalists. In November 2005, the national court began hearing appeals by journalists of the Basque-language daily *Euskaldunon Egunkaria* who had been charged in December 2004 by lower court judge Juan del Olmo with creating an "illegal association" and in some cases with "membership of a terrorist group" as well. In 2003, the newspaper had been shut down under suspicion of collaborating with the Basque separatist group Euskadi Ta Askatasuna (ETA, or Basque Fatherland and Freedom). The journalists, who are all free on bail, face prison terms ranging from 1 to 14 years. *Euskaldunon Egunkaria* remains closed.

According to observers, ETA still poses a threat to journalists, many of whom employ bodyguards. Journalists who oppose the political views of ETA are often targeted by the group. The publicly owned Vitoria radio station EITB in particular was threatened with reprisals by ETA in February 2006. In October 2006, a Spanish court ruled that Tayssir Allouni, the presenter for Qatar-based satellite television station Al-Jazeera who became famous for interviewing terrorist leader Osama bin Laden, could serve the remainder of his seven-year sentence under house arrest. Allouni had been sentenced in September 2005 along with 23 other people after being implicated in terrorist activities.

Spain has a free and lively press, with more than 100 newspapers that cover a wide range of perspectives and are active in investigating high-level corruption. However, daily newspaper ownership is concentrated within large media groups like Prisa and Zeta. During the year, the Spanish public broadcaster RTVE threatened to cut up to 3,000 jobs, around 40 percent of its workforce, sparking protests and strikes. The internet is unrestricted by the government. The growth in internet usage was among the highest in Western Europe in 2006, with 44 percent of the population accessing the internet that year—nearly triple the number of users from the previous year.

Sri Lanka

LEGAL ENVIRONMENT: 17
POLITICAL ENVIRONMENT: 29
ECONOMIC ENVIRONMENT: 17

Status: Not Free

TOTAL SCORE: 63

Survey Edition	2002	2003	2004	2005	2006
Total Score, Status	63,NF	52,PF	53,PF	56,PF	58,PF

Status change explanation: Sri Lanka's status changed from Partly Free to Not Free to reflect new restrictions on media coverage as well as a rise in attacks against journalists, particularly ethnic Tamils.

Media freedom was one of the main casualties of Sri Lanka's slide into war in 2006, as increasing numbers of journalists, particularly ethnic Tamils, were targeted and media outlets faced censorship and other restrictions. Although freedom of expression is provided for in the constitution, a growing number of laws and regulations restrict this right. Contempt-of-court laws are occasionally used to punish reporters who investigate judicial misconduct. However, in June the Supreme Court refused to pursue a case against three journalists, including the editor in chief of the *Sunday Leader*, Lasantha Wickrematunga, who had been charged with five counts of contempt. The Official Secrets Act bans reporting on information designated "secret." Although those convicted of gathering secret information can be sentenced to up to 14 years in prison, no journalist has ever been charged under the act. Emergency regulations reintroduced in August 2005 allow the government to bar the publication, distribution, performance, or airing of any print or broadcast material deemed likely to cause public disorder; however, it did not use this authority during 2006. In September, unofficial prepublication censorship concerning issues of "national security and defense" was imposed by the government's Media Centre for National Security. The Emergency (Prevention and Prohibition of Terrorism and Specified Terrorist Activities) Regulations, introduced in December, contain excessively broad language that local rights activists noted could restrict media freedom. Within a month of the new regulations' enactment, several journalists were summoned for questioning and asked to reveal their sources, one was detained, and a senior correspondent openly admitted to self-censoring his column. Official rhetoric has become more unfriendly toward journalists and media outlets perceived to be "unpatriotic" or critical. In June, the government announced that it planned to reconstitute the state-controlled Press Council in order to regulate the media.

The Liberation Tigers of Tamil Eelam (LTTE) separatist rebel group, which controls parts of the north and east of the country, does not permit free expression in the areas under its control and continues to terrorize a number of Tamil journalists and other critics. The government and a breakaway rebel faction in the east led by "Colonel Karuna" have also been responsible for abuses. A sharp increase in tension and violence during the year—both between the government and the LTTE, and between the LTTE and the Karuna faction—severely curtailed journalists' ability to cover the news freely, particularly in the troubled north and east. A number of Tamil newspapers have been banned or seized by various factions, and distributors have been attacked or warned not to sell certain papers. According to a report by the Colombo-based Centre for Policy Alternatives, over two dozen Tamil journalists were abducted, severely assaulted, or killed during the year. Despite its calls for protection, the largest-circulation daily in Jaffna, *Uthayan*, faced repeated attacks and harassment in 2006, including killings of staff by unidentified gunmen in May and an arson attack on its printing facilities in August.

Journalists throughout Sri Lanka, particularly those who covered human rights issues or official misconduct, continued to face intimidation and threats from the security forces and government officials. In several other instances, police or security forces manhandled reporters as they attempted to cover the news. In a growing trend, journalists and civil society groups perceived as being supportive of Tamil interests have also drawn ire from Sinhalese nationalist groups. Increased threats coupled with expanded legal restrictions have led a growing number of journalists to practice self-censorship. Previous cases of attacks and killings of journalists have not been adequately investigated or prosecuted.

While numerous privately owned newspapers and broadcasters scrutinize government policies and provide diverse views, private outlets have become more polarized, shrinking the space for balanced coverage. The Colombo-based Free Media Movement has noted that state-run media—including Sri Lanka's largest newspaper chain, two major television stations, and a radio station—remain heavily influenced by the government, citing cases of pressure on editors, several unwarranted dismissals of high-level staff, and biased coverage of the November 2005 elections. Business and political interests exercise some control over content through selective advertising and bribery. Owing to the closure of a major road, newspapers on the Jaffna peninsula faced shortages of newsprint and other key supplies, hindering their production abilities. Access to the internet and to foreign broadcasts is not restricted, but only 1.4 percent of the population used the internet in 2006 because of the high costs involved.

Sudan

Status: Not Free

LEGAL ENVIRONMENT: 27
POLITICAL ENVIRONMENT: 30
ECONOMIC ENVIRONMENT: 24
TOTAL SCORE: 81

Survey Edition	2002	2003	2004	2005	2006
Total Score, Status	87,NF	84,NF	85,NF	86,NF	85,NF

While the situation for the press in the north of Sudan and the Darfur region remained largely as restrictive in 2006 as in previous years, improvements in media freedom were noticeable in the southern region, particularly as a result of the autonomous southern government's increased tolerance of critical reportage. President Omar al-Bashir's concentration of power has been reduced somewhat by the January 2005 Comprehensive Peace Agreement between north and south and its attendant power-sharing arrangements. The interim constitution provides for freedom of thought and expression, but this is respected only on a rhetorical level by those in power. The Sudanese government's main preoccupation in 2006 was how best to manage international reaction to the Darfur situation. While prepublication censorship has been officially lifted, security personnel regularly harass and censor journalists. In addition to the security forces, the National Press Council (NPC) has the right to sanction journalists and suspend publications, and it regularly abuses these rights in order to censor outlets that produce critical material.

Throughout 2006, journalists faced harassment, violent attacks, intimidation, and direct censorship at the hands of both government and nongovernmental forces. In a September case that shocked the Sudanese public and press corps, gunmen kidnapped and beheaded Mohammed Taha Mohammed Ahmed, editor of the pro-government, Khartoum-based daily *Al-Wifaq*. Taha Mohammed Ahmed in 2005 had published an article about the prophet Muhammad's lineage, for which he was detained and questioned. The article's publication raised the ire of Sudan's religious establishment. A group linked to al-Qaeda later claimed responsibility for the killing, but no arrests had been made by year's end. Several major private Khartoum–based dailies were censored or confiscated after reporting on the case. According to the Committee to Protect Journalists, Sudanese journalists said that the censored publications also carried articles about local demonstrations against rising fuel and sugar prices and the slow pace of democratic reform. Several television and print journalists were also detained, beaten, and harassed during coverage of demonstrations in the summer over the rising prices as well as antigovernment protests. Another major issue for Sudan in 2006 was control of journalists—especially foreign journalists—covering Darfur. Government spokesmen have regularly attacked the foreign media's coverage of Darfur as anti-Sudanese. In August, government forces in Darfur detained U.S. reporter Paul Salopek, on assignment for *National Geographic* magazine, as well as his translator and driver and eventually charged the three with espionage. They spent a month in detention before al-Bashir ordered their release in September.

Press freedom conditions in autonomous southern Sudan continued to improve in 2006, in contrast with areas controlled directly by Khartoum. Journalists in the south are not as restricted as those in the north and have more leeway to criticize government policies. While there were no reports of direct censorship by authorities in the south during the year, local provincial governments did interfere with the independence of the press. One such case occurred in July, when the local radio station Liberty FM was forced to shut down after a caller on a talk show voiced criticisms of the provincial government.

Many daily newspapers operate in Sudan—though none are currently able to function regularly in Darfur—and most experienced intense scrutiny from the government during the year. Still, some private newspapers are critical, and many employ columnists that regularly question and attack al-Bashir's policies. In 2006, newspapers published articles about cases of torture and abuse at the hands of government forces and identified officials alleged to be responsible. The al-Bashir administration in Khartoum runs one Arabic- and one English-language newspaper and also dominates the broadcast media, the main source of information for much of Sudan's population. Formal censorship is mandatory for television broadcasts, ensuring that the news reflects the government's viewpoint. But Arabic satellite channels like Al-Jazeera and Al-Arabiya are popular in Sudan and are increasingly relied upon as an alternative to the pro-government domestic television and radio stations. The government exerts pressure on international correspondents for such foreign broadcasters; in 2006, Al-Arabiya's Khartoum reporter quit after the NPC harassed him and he was repeatedly called in by security agents for questioning. The government is also trying to limit the broadcast reach of the UN radio station in Sudan, which operates as part of the Comprehensive Peace Agreement.

Internet penetration in Sudan is among the highest in sub-Saharan Africa—though still low by global standards—with 7.6 percent of the population accessing the internet in 2006, almost exclusively in urban areas. The government has not traditionally displayed much interest in censoring this new medium, but with the high rate of expansion in internet consumption in Khartoum and other major cities, the government was reported to have monitored e-mail communications and internet activity in 2006. The National Telecommunication Corporation also censored websites during the year, though it claimed that most were of a pornographic nature and that none were shut down for political reasons.

Suriname

LEGAL ENVIRONMENT: 5
POLITICAL ENVIRONMENT: 11
ECONOMIC ENVIRONMENT: 6

Status: Free

TOTAL SCORE: 22

Survey Edition	2002	2003	2004	2005	2006
Total Score, Status	25,F	26,F	18,F	20,F	23,F

The government generally respects freedom of expression and of the press, as provided for in the country's constitution. However, little investigative reporting takes place, and some journalists practice self-censorship on certain issues, particularly drug trafficking and the human rights abuses that took place under the Desi Bouterse dictatorship in the 1980s. A December 2005 libel ruling against *De West*, one of the country's two national independent newspapers, continues to cause concern. George Findlay, publisher of *De West*, faces imprisonment on a charge of insulting members of the country's Foreign Exchange Commission and heavy fines for not submitting a retraction of the original story for publication in the competing newspaper, *De Ware Tijd*. In May, a minister's bodyguard harassed a journalist and confiscated his equipment for photographing the minister's vehicle.

According to the Association of Surinamese Journalists, poor salaries and lack of training are leading to unprofessional conduct and undermining the profession. In August, the government announced that, after a three-year selection process, Caribbean telecommunications giants Digicel and Intelsur would be granted licenses to offer telecommunications services in Suriname.

The actual liberalization will take place when the new Telecommunications Act goes into effect. *De West* and *De Ware Tijd*, both privately owned, are the country's main newspapers. There are seven radio stations and a number of community radio stations. Both television stations—Algemene Televisie Verzorging and Surinaamse Televisie Stichting—and the national radio station are state owned. There are no government restrictions on the internet, though only 6 percent of the population accessed it in 2006.

Swaziland

Status: Not Free

LEGAL ENVIRONMENT: 25
POLITICAL ENVIRONMENT: 26
ECONOMIC ENVIRONMENT: 25
TOTAL SCORE: 76

Survey Edition	2002	2003	2004	2005	2006
Total Score, Status	77,NF	74,NF	77,NF	79,NF	77,NF

Freedom of expression is severely restricted in Swaziland, especially regarding political issues or matters concerning the royal family. There are very few legal protections for journalists and media workers. While a new constitution—which went into effect in February 2006—provides for freedom of speech, the king may waive these rights at his discretion. The 1938 Sedition and Subversive Activities Act bans publication of any criticism of the monarchy, and self-censorship is widespread, particularly regarding the king's lavish lifestyle. The 1968 Proscribed Publications Act also empowers the government to ban publications if they are deemed "prejudicial or potentially prejudicial to the interests of defense, public safety, public order, public morality, or public health." The law has been used several times in recent years to punish newspapers that criticized or embarrassed the monarchy. In a potentially positive development, in April the government announced that it had hired consultants to assist in the drafting of the kingdom's first freedom of information legislation.

Harsh defamation laws are also used to stifle the press. In 2006, the *Times of Swaziland* lost three separate defamation cases and was ordered to pay damages to the government's United Nations envoy, a member of Parliament, and a Mbabane businessman. However, in May the Supreme Court overturned massive fines (approximately US$116,000) levied against the newspaper in a 2005 defamation case brought by the late deputy prime minister Albert Shabangu. In October, a parliamentary committee charged the newspaper with damaging "the dignity and reputation of

Parliament" and mandated an unconditional apology for an article that accused lawmakers of interfering in the management of the state radio station, run by the Swaziland Broadcasting and Information Services (SBIS). The government routinely warns against negative news coverage. In August, Minister for Public Service and Information Themba Msibi warned the media against criticizing the king after Thulani Maseko, a human rights lawyer, voiced concerns about the king's wide-ranging constitutional powers on an SBIS program. In addition, journalists are subject to harassment and assault by both state and nonstate actors. In May, Musa Ndlangamandla, editor of the state-owned *Swazi Observer*, claimed to have received death threats related to the newspaper's campaign against unscrupulous moneylenders.

The two major newspapers in circulation are the *Times of Swaziland* and the *Swazi Observer*. The *Times*, founded in 1897, is the oldest newspaper in the kingdom and the only major news source that is free of government control. Generally, the government withheld its advertising from the *Times*. Despite being owned by a royal conglomerate, the *Swazi Observer* was shut down temporarily in 2002 because its editorial direction was viewed as too liberal. Both newspapers continued to criticize government corruption and inefficiency in 2006 but steered clear of the royal family. The Swaziland Television Authority, which is both the state broadcaster and the industry regulatory agency, dominates the airwaves. There is one independent radio station, Voice of the Church, which focuses on religious programming. A member of the royal family owns the country's lone private television station. However, broadcast and print media from South Africa are received in the country, and state broadcasters retransmitted Voice of America and British Broadcasting Corporation programs without censorship. The government does not restrict internet-based media, though only 3 percent of the population used the internet in 2006.

Sweden

Status: Free

LEGAL ENVIRONMENT: 2
POLITICAL ENVIRONMENT: 5
ECONOMIC ENVIRONMENT: 4

TOTAL SCORE: 11

Survey Edition	2002	2003	2004	2005	2006
Total Score, Status	8,F	8,F	8,F	9,F	10,F

Sweden has strong legal protections for press freedom under the Freedom of the Press Act and the Fundamental Law of Freedom of Expression. In 2006, the government considered the possibility of reviewing current press legislation to address new technologies. Journalists' sources are protected by law, as is access to information for all citizens. In March, Swedish foreign minister Laila Freivalds resigned after receiving strong criticism for her involvement in the forced closure of a far-right website in February. The website had planned to post controversial Danish cartoons depicting the prophet Muhammad. In a study by the Mid Sweden University in Sundsvall, it was reported that journalists at half of Sweden's newspapers and two-thirds of all newspaper editors received threats in 2006. In some instances, the threats led to stories being dropped.

In late 2006, the European Commission referred Sweden to the European Court of Justice owing to its failure to break down the monopoly of state-owned Boxer TV–Access AB on digital terrestrial broadcasting. Public broadcasting has a strong presence in Sweden, consisting of Sveriges Television and Sveriges Radio. Public television and radio is funded through a license fee. Private broadcasting ownership is highly concentrated under the media companies Bonnier and the Modern Times Group. The government offers subsidies to newspapers in order to encourage competition, and media content in immigrant languages is also supported by the state. According to the British Broadcasting Corporation, Sweden is among the top consumers of newspapers in the world. Access to the internet is unrestricted by the government, and 76 percent of the population used the medium in 2006, one of the highest proportions of internet users in the world.

Switzerland

LEGAL ENVIRONMENT: 4
POLITICAL ENVIRONMENT: 3
ECONOMIC ENVIRONMENT: 5

Status: Free

TOTAL SCORE: 12

Survey Edition	2002	2003	2004	2005	2006
Total Score, Status	8,F	10,F	9,F	11,F	11,F

Media freedom is guaranteed in the constitution and generally respected by the government. The penal code prohibits racial hatred or discrimination. Even though the law does not explicitly prohibit anti-Semitic speech or Holocaust denial, there have been convictions for such forms of expression.

In 2006, the Swiss courts decided to investigate Dogu Perincek, a Turkish politician, after he publicly denied the Armenian genocide while in Switzerland. Formal court proceedings had yet to commence in this case at year's end. Transparency legislation adopted in December 2004 went into effect in July 2006. The law applies only to documents produced after July 1, 2006, and contains numerous exceptions.

In 1997, a Swiss federal court found two journalists guilty of inciting an official to disclose a secret, an act considered to be a criminal offense under Article 293 of the Swiss criminal code. However, in April 2006 the European Court of Human Rights overturned the ruling, arguing that a reporter's right to protect his or her sources superseded the domestic Swiss judgment. In 2006, a debate concerning the possibility of amending the Swiss punitive provisions for a breach of confidentiality became particularly relevant when the Swiss Defense Ministry took legal action against two journalists working for *SonntagsBlick*—one of the most popular newspapers in the country—for reproducing a fax that had been intercepted by the Swiss Intelligence Service and that referred to confidential allegations of CIA prisons in Eastern Europe. The two journalists face up to five years in prison if convicted under the Swiss military penal code.

Broadcast media are dominated by the Swiss Broadcasting Corporation, a public service association subject to private law that operates 7 television networks and 18 radio stations. The corporation is dependent on the government for financing, although its news reporting is politically neutral. Owing to market forces and the multilingual nature of the country, most private stations are limited to local and regional broadcasts. Nearly all homes are connected to cable networks, which provide access to international commercial stations. Daily newspapers are owned by large media conglomerates, which have steadily pushed smaller publications out of the market. The internet is unrestricted by the government and accessed by nearly 68 percent of the population.

Syria

LEGAL ENVIRONMENT: 29
POLITICAL ENVIRONMENT: 33
ECONOMIC ENVIRONMENT: 21

Status: Not Free

TOTAL SCORE: 83

Survey Edition	2002	2003	2004	2005	2006
Total Score, Status	78,NF	80,NF	80,NF	83,NF	84,NF

The Syrian government continued to place severe restrictions on press freedom in 2006. Although the constitution provides for freedom of speech and of the press, a constellation of repressive laws restricts such rights in practice. First among them is the Emergency Law, in place since December 1962, which broadly mandates the censorship of letters, publications, broadcasts, and other forms of communication. The 2001 Press Law sets out sweeping controls over newspapers, magazines, and other periodicals, as well as virtually anything else printed in Syria. The decree forbids writing on a wide variety of topics, including reports that touch on what authorities consider to be "national security" or "national unity." Articles 286 and 287 of the penal code criminalize spreading news abroad. Decree No. 6 of 1965 criminalizes "publishing news aimed at shaking the people's confidence in the revolution." Other laws criminalize "opposition to the revolution, its goals, or socialism." At the June 2005 conference of the ruling Baath Party, the Ministry of Information announced that it would issue new press legislation. However, no such legislation had been introduced by the end of 2006. Syria's first independent media union was created in May 2005 by journalists and human rights activists hoping to liberalize the media. The union, called Hurriyat (Freedom), was still in existence at the end of 2006.

Journalists continue to be subject to legal prosecution as well as other forms of extralegal harassment and threats. Eight journalists and cyberdissidents were imprisoned during the year, and dozens of people who had spoken out or were suspected of opposition to the government were detained. On February 7, authorities arrested Adel Mahfouz, who had published an article arguing that violent protests in reaction to cartoons caricaturing the prophet Muhammad could reinforce inaccurate perceptions of Islam as a violent religion. Mahfouz was charged with insulting public religious sentiment and could face up to three years in prison. Freelance journalist Ali Abdallah, who wrote for the Emirati daily *Al-Khaleej* and Lebanese dailies *Al-Nahar* and *Al-Safir*, was sentenced to six months in prison in March for criticizing the country's weak economy. His son was given the same sentence after contacting the Qatar–based satellite television station Al-Jazeera to report his father's arrest. In August, security forces arrested Ali Sayed al-Shihabi, a professor of English, for posting articles on left-wing websites. He was still in detention at the end of 2006.

Although most print media are state owned and operated and follow the official line, a handful of private and political party-affiliated newspapers sometimes publish mild criticism of the government. Except for a handful of radio stations that do not broadcast news or report on political issues, radio and television outlets are all state owned. Satellite dishes are common, and the government makes no attempt to interfere with satellite broadcasts. Recently, Syrian television has broached topics formerly considered taboo and conducted interviews with opposition figures. The internet has also been increasingly used by critical journalists to voice dissent, although the government has aggressively cracked down on internet freedom in recent years. The government censors the internet and monitors its use, but Syrians employ a range of technical tricks to circumvent censorship, and a handful of blocked domestic Syrian websites and e-mail lists openly criticize the government. However, only about 6 percent of the population used the internet in 2006.

Taiwan

LEGAL ENVIRONMENT: 7
POLITICAL ENVIRONMENT: 7
ECONOMIC ENVIRONMENT: 6

Status: Free

TOTAL SCORE: 20

Survey Edition	2002	2003	2004	2005	2006
Total Score, Status	21,F	24,F	23,F	21,F	20,F

Taiwan is known for having one of the freest media environments in East Asia because of its firm commitment to judicial independence and economic freedom. The constitution provides for freedom of speech and of the press, and the government generally respects these rights in practice. In April, a court in Taipei sentenced Kao Nien-yi, a journalist for the *United Daily News*, to a fine of NT $30,000 (US$1,000) per day for refusing to reveal his sources for an article that allegedly caused the stock of a company to lose two-thirds of its value. The sentence was applied for three days before it was suspended. In October, the Constitutional Court held that freedom of publication is not an absolute right, stipulating that certain sexually explicit materials are protected only as long as they are properly packaged and labeled.

The government announced in February that Taiwanese reporters, notorious for their aggressive behavior toward visiting officials and celebrities, will be denied access into restricted areas of Chiang Kai-Shek International Airport to help protect the island's image. In September, four journalists were attacked by supporters of President Chen Shui-bian during a pro-Chen demonstration in Taipei. At the same demonstration, a presenter for the satellite channel CTI was physically assaulted while interviewing two deputies in the ruling Democratic Progressive Party. In

December, leaders of the ruling party said they were refusing to reply to questions from the *China Times*, a pro-opposition daily.

Taiwan has over 360 privately owned newspapers, 169 radio stations, and widespread availability of cable and satellite television. Print media are completely independent, but broadcast media have been subject to government efforts to regulate programming and to impose licenses through the authority of the Government Information Office (GIO). In a positive move for media impartiality, the politically independent National Communications Commission replaced the GIO in 2006 and given that most Taiwanese can access about 100 cable television stations, the state's influence on the media is, on balance, minimal. Legislation approved in 2003 barred the government and political party officials from holding positions in broadcast media companies and government entities and political parties were required to divest themselves of all radio and broadcast companies by December 2005. In April 2006, the government donated its 70 percent share of the China Television System to the Public Television Service. The two companies merged into the Taiwan Broadcasting System, which was privatized in July. The government refrains from restricting internet access, which is currently accessed by approximately 63 percent of the population. Homosexual rights advocacy groups claim that government law enforcement agencies monitored internet chat-room and bulletin-board exchanges among adults. Several nongovernmental organizations reported that law enforcement officials prosecuted and punished adults for posting sexually suggestive messages.

Tajikistan

LEGAL ENVIRONMENT: 24
POLITICAL ENVIRONMENT: 28
ECONOMIC ENVIRONMENT: 24

Status: Not Free

TOTAL SCORE: 76

Survey Edition	2002	2003	2004	2005	2006
Total Score, Status	80,NF	76,NF	73,NF	74,NF	76,NF

Freedom of speech is guaranteed by the constitution, but government efforts to reduce the media to docility in 2004 and 2005 proved largely successful. Nonetheless, Tajikistan's media environment remained relatively stable in 2006, despite a court's decision to suspend the country's Union of Journalists from April through July—arguing that its charter violated Tajik law. Existing laws criminalize insults to individuals' dignity and set five-year prison terms for public criticism of the president; several dozen additional press restrictions were passed by the Parliament over the course of the year, including one that required all private media outlets to obtain licenses from the Ministry of Culture.

There were no reports of violence against journalists in 2006, although the murders of 29 journalists during the 1992–1997 civil war remain unsolved. The independent newspaper *Nerui Sukhan* remained closed, but the Supreme Court in January substituted a fine for the two-year corrective labor sentence that its editor in chief, Mukhtor Boqizoda, had received in 2005 for illegal use of electricity at his printing facility. *Adolat*, a weekly opposition newspaper published by the Democratic Party of Tajikistan, briefly resumed publication in September after a two-year hiatus but vanished in October when the Shafei publishing house refused to print it. *Adolat* editor in chief Rajab Mirzo managed to publish another edition of the paper on October 12, but faced a rival publication with the same name issued by a government-supported faction of the Democratic Party. Furthermore, two journalists investigating the use of forced labor in the cotton industry were detained briefly in September. In November, President Emomali Rakhmonov secured reelection in a presidential election. All major broadcast and print media, controlled either directly or indirectly by the state, provided favorable coverage of Rakhmonov, while virtually ignoring the four other opposition candidates, according to the Committee to Protect Journalists.

The dominant feature of Tajikistan's media environment remained state control over nationwide broadcast media from which most citizens get their news. The state maintains its control, even of the newspaper industry, through direct and indirect ownership, licensing requirements, control of printing and transmission facilities, and subsidies. The government maintained a near freeze on the registration of new media outlets, but two fledgling newspapers with political content were registered in 2006. International media had generally been allowed to operate freely, and rebroadcasts of Russian television and radio programs are reportedly available. However, many foreign broadcasts could be accessed only via satellite, and few Tajiks could afford such technology. In January, FM radio broadcasts by the British Broadcasting Corporation (BBC) were suspended in a dispute with the authorities over registration requirements. The government eventually denied the BBC a license for FM broadcasting in the capital city, Dushanbe, as well as in the northern city of Khujand, citing the lack of a broadcasting cooperation agreement between the British and Tajik governments. Internet services were limited to only one-tenth of one percent of the population. According to a letter obtained by Reuters, authorities asked Tajik internet providers to block websites that "aim to undermine the state's policies in the sphere of information," in the lead-up to the November election. Access to centrasia.ru, arianastorm.com, charogiruz.ru, ferghana.ru, and tajikistantimes.ru, which all feature material critical of Rakhmonov, was temporarily blocked in 2006 for a few days, but Tajik officials attributed the shutdown to maintenance issues.

Tanzania

LEGAL ENVIRONMENT: 16
POLITICAL ENVIRONMENT: 20
ECONOMIC ENVIRONMENT: 15

Status: Partly Free

TOTAL SCORE: 51

Survey Edition	2002	2003	2004	2005	2006
Total Score, Status	49,PF	47,PF	50,PF	51,PF	50,PF

Although the constitution provides for freedom of speech, several other laws limit the ability of the media to function effectively. Authorities are empowered to register and ban newspapers under the Newspaper Registration Act "in the interest of peace and good order," while the Broadcasting Services Act provides for state regulation of electronic media, and the National Security Act allows the government to control the dissemination of information to the public. Libel laws that impose criminal penalties intimidated journalists from reporting aggressively, particularly on issues of corruption. In August 2006, the minister of lands and settlement development, John Magufuli, initiated criminal proceedings against three journalists after publication of an article relating to funds for the construction of a road that had allegedly been diverted to the minister's constituency. There is no freedom of information legislation in place, but the government announced plans to table a draft bill in April 2007.

In 2006, journalists were subjected to extralegal intimidation, particularly threats of deportation. In August, the government threatened to strip the citizenship of and deport Richard Mgamba, a local investigative journalist with the daily newspaper *The Citizen*, after he appeared in a documentary film that the authorities allege damaged both the country's economy and its image. The resolution of the case was still pending at year's end. Earlier in the year, Ali Mohammed Nabwa, former editor of *Dira*, a defunct Zanzibar newspaper, was stripped of his Tanzanian nationality by the Zanzibar Immigration Department, just three and a half months after having it restored by the Tanzanian interior minister.

The situation in Zanzibar remains more restrictive than in the rest of the country. Journalists in Zanzibar must be licensed, and the state tightly controls the broadcast media. Locals can receive broadcasts and reports from the mainland. Zanzibar's first independent private newspaper, *Dira,* remains banned, and there are no private broadcasters on the island. In 2005, the government made direct attempts to bar journalists from reporting critically in the region; no such incidents were reported in 2006.

The number of media outlets continued to grow and now includes 47 FM radio stations, 537 registered newspapers, and a dozen television stations. Only 4 radio stations have a national reach—the state-run Radio Tanzania and three privately-run stations—and all are viewed as sympathetic to the ruling party. The government reportedly withholds advertising from critical newspapers and those that report favorably on the opposition. Private firms that are keen to remain on good terms with the government allegedly follow suit, thus making it difficult for critical media outlets to remain financially sustainable. Nonetheless, a number of independent media outlets regularly criticize official policies. There are no reports of government restriction of the internet, though less than 1 percent had the financial means to access it in 2006.

Thailand

Status: Not Free

LEGAL ENVIRONMENT: 20
POLITICAL ENVIRONMENT: 25
ECONOMIC ENVIRONMENT: 14
TOTAL SCORE: 59

Survey Edition	2002	2003	2004	2005	2006
Total Score, Status	30,F	36,PF	39,PF	42,PF	50,PF

Despite the extent of ousted prime minister Thaksin Shinawatra's intolerance for critical media, the September 2006 coup that installed a military-led government brought an even more dramatic decline for press freedom in Thailand. Rather than fostering a more open, diverse media as a key pillar of the stronger democracy it claims to be creating, the Council for Democratic Reform, later dubbed the Council for National Security (CNS), has largely treated the press as a potential threat to the new regime and restricted it as such.

The September 19 coup abrogated the 1997 constitution and its strong protections for freedom of expression. Despite heavy lobbying by a coalition of Thai media advocates and assurances by coup leader General Sondhi Boonyaratkalin, the interim constitution promulgated on October 1 does not explicitly protect freedom of expression and failed to rescind restrictions on the press imposed in the immediate aftermath of the coup. Several older laws that reserve the government's right to restrict the media to preserve national security or public order and prevent criticism of the king, royal family or Buddhism remain in force, including the 1941 Printing Act, which reserves the government's right to shut down media outlets. Access to information legislation, introduced in the 1997 constitution (although essentially reversed under Thaksin with a steady decline in disclosures), has also been erased.

Defamation legislation under the penal code is harsh and proved a favorite tool of the former Thaksin regime for silencing critical voices. Prior to being removed from office in September, Thaksin continued to file a series of criminal and civil defamation suits against critical journalists and editors, particularly for reporting on his family's controversial THB 73 billion (US$1.858 billion) sale of its shares in Shin Corporation, a Thaksin family conglomerate, to Temasek Holdings, the Singaporean government investment fund, in January 2006. As a political standoff emerged between Thaksin supporters and those calling for his resignation in mid-March, the prime minister increasingly filed libel and sedition charges against journalists and media outlets that covered the massive anti-Thaksin protests occurring around the country. By June 2006, Sondhi Limthongkul, a prominent journalist and fierce Thaksin critic who first came under fire from the prime minister in 2005, was facing 50 criminal lawsuits, largely for activities associated with his role as a leader of the People's Alliance for Democracy, a coalition of anti-Thaksin protesters. The status of many of these cases remained uncertain at year's end in light of Thaksin's retreat into exile. However, March 2006 brought the landmark acquittal of media activist Supinya Klangnarong and four journalists from the daily *Thai Post*, charged by the Shin Corporation in 2005 with suggesting a conflict of interest between Thaksin's public office and his family's private businesses. The court's ruling, which held that public companies, like public figures, should be open to criticism in the public interest, was widely lauded by local and international press freedom advocates. The pre-coup period also saw a number of closings in response to critical or investigative reporting, including that of the anti-graft website Corruption Watch after it covered the Shin Corporation–Temasek transaction in January.

Restrictions on media coverage during the coup itself were largely limited to disruptions of CNN and British Broadcasting Corporation broadcasts featuring background on Thaksin and a local broadcast airing a statement from Thaksin himself. Foreign and local journalists enjoyed relatively unfettered movement. However, a number of significant restrictions were imposed in the coup's immediate aftermath. On September 20, the military's Administrative Reform Council empowered the Ministry of Communications and Information Technology to "control, block, and destroy" information detrimental to the new administration and issued Military Order No. 10, urging media cooperation in promoting "peace and national unity."

The CNS took a proactive and direct approach to securing media compliance, calling a meeting with senior media representatives to convey a host of coverage directives on September 21. The broadcasting sector, with all radio and television frequencies owned by the government, incurred the greatest restrictions. Troops were positioned outside all broadcast stations, and station executives were ordered not to air materials that might challenge the new regime. All expressions of public opinion and discussions of the coup itself were essentially banned, with all media asked to stop broadcasting related text messages; radio stations ordered to cancel phone-in news programs; and more than 300 radio stations closed down in just a few days in three provinces known for being Thaksin strongholds. Thai editors expressed significant concern about the military's interference in the broadcasting sector in light of the fact that the National Telecommunications Commission and the National Broadcasting Commission, previously intended to serve as independent regulators of the airwaves, were made defunct by the new regime.

No specific guidelines were issued to print media, and the mainstream press and foreign media were generally allowed to operate as usual, although "negative" reporting was widely discouraged. Coverage directives were extended to webmasters responsible for online media, and a website designed to allow Thais to share opinions on the coup was shut down on orders from the Ministry of Information immediately after it was established, on the grounds that it was "in violation of rules imposed by the Council for Democratic Reform under Constitutional Monarchy." Another website, Midnight University, was shut down in early October for "insulting the monarchy" after its organizers launched a protest against the interim constitution. In November, the military government announced plans to push through a bill in question under Thaksin that would effectively allow the interim government to close down legitimate websites and take legal action against those who post content deemed to be a threat to national security.

Several press freedom watchdog groups expressed concerns about heightened self-censorship, particularly in television programming, and the Southeast Asia Press Alliance noted that websites typically supportive of Thaksin shifted to strictly covering the latest news. However, print and broadcast media continued to report news critical of the interim government and the CNS as well as Thaksin's statements and activities later in the year.

Radio and television remain under the control of the state—now the military—or formerly state-affiliated private businesses. iTV, Thailand's only independent nonstate-owned broadcast television station, is run by the Shin Corporation, owned by Thaksin until January 2006, when he sold his shares to Temasek in what has been considered the largest single deal in the Thai stock market. Stations are required to renew licenses annually and to feature government-produced newscasts daily. The National Broadcasting Commission, established in October 2005 to redistribute the country's frequencies from the state to the private sector, remained in limbo at year's end. The internet is accessed by approximately 12.5 percent of the Thai population. Government censorship of the internet has occurred since 2003, largely to prevent circulation of pornography or illegal products; after the coup, internet censorship shifted to prohibiting potentially disruptive political messages, while sites considered a threat to national security, including those of Muslim separatist groups, continue to be blocked in light of persistent violence in the south.

Togo

Status: Not Free

LEGAL ENVIRONMENT: 22
POLITICAL ENVIRONMENT: 31
ECONOMIC ENVIRONMENT: 21
TOTAL SCORE: 74

Survey Edition	2002	2003	2004	2005	2006
Total Score, Status	68,NF	74,NF	78,NF	73,NF	78,NF

After a period of heightened aggression toward journalists during the 2005 coup and an election intended to ensure Faure Gnassingbe's continuation as president, the media environment stabilized in 2006; nonetheless, the lack of any investigation into 2005's attacks on the press has led to widespread impunity. Freedom of speech and of the press are legally guaranteed in Togo, but these rights are not always respected in practice. In 2004, in a deal to end trade sanctions from the European Union, President Gnassingbe Eyadema initiated legal improvements to the status of press freedom, including abolishing prison sentences for libel and prohibiting the government from seizing and closing media outlets without judicial approval. However, following Eyadema's death in 2005, these legal improvements were disregarded as his son Faure Gnassingbe took over the presidency and began targeting and harassing independent media outlets in the wave of violence intended to secure his hold on power. In 2006, nominal respect for the 2004 press laws have returned, but very few, if any, prosecutions have taken place against those responsible for the 2005 crackdown and intimidation of the media.

The 1992 constitution established the High Authority for Audiovisual Communications (HAAC) as an independent body intended to protect freedom of the press and ensure ethical standards in media operations. Despite its nominal independence, the HAAC has traditionally resided in the breast pocket of Eyadema's regime and has served predominantly as a tool for government repression of opposition or dissenting media outlets. This is no less true today, even with last year's appointment of Philippe Evegno, a prominent opposition journalist, as chairman of the HAAC. In May 2006, the HAAC suspended for a month a daily political program on Radio Nostalgie, an independent station, charging that the program "attacked and systematically threatened national and international personalities" after a guest on the show criticized the support showed to the current regime by the Economic Community of West African States. The HAAC has also announced that community and faith-based radio stations will be heavily penalized for broadcasting political commentary.

In 2006, the political environment for the press appears to have returned to what it was under Eyadema, with journalists wary of criticizing the government but infrequently facing direct physical harassment. The most prominent threat to media freedom was the culture of impunity that pervaded the country. Although the number of attacks, harassments, and closures of media outlets has decreased dramatically since 2005, the memory of last year's campaign of intimidation has led to self-censorship among much of the press. A number of instances of physical attacks and intimidations did occur in 2006, originating primarily from the family of the current and former president. In September, a brother of the president—also the head of the football federation—threatened the host of a show on Radio Sport FM for criticizing a decision the football federation had made. A more direct assault occurred in November when two of Gnassingbe's brothers physically attacked a journalist with the private radio station Nana FM for having criticized their late father.

Despite government intimidation efforts that frequently result in self-censorship, Togo does house a lively and diverse independent media, even though many private print and broadcast outlets are heavily politicized. The government made consistent efforts to paint all independent media as puppets of the opposition and frequently denied press accreditation to local private media outlets for political events. Over 310 newspapers are registered in Togo, many of them able to publish only sporadically or having to close soon after they open. There are 15 regularly publishing private newspapers, though even these are habitually plagued by inconsistent readerships, as well as a number of private radio stations. The government owns and operates the only uninterrupted daily newspaper, *Togo Presse*, and the only national television station, and all government outlets maintain a heavy pro-government bias. Improving on 2005, access to the internet in 2006 was generally unrestricted with 5.4 percent of the population accessing the internet during the year, although proprietors of internet cafés were often required to provide records of clientele activity if asked to do so by a state official.

Tonga

Legal Environment: 11
Political Environment: 11
Economic Environment: 9

Status: Partly Free

Total Score: 31

Survey Edition	2002	2003	2004	2005	2006
Total Score, Status	36,PF	32,PF	44,PF	37,PF	32,PF

Freedom of the press is guaranteed under the constitution and is generally respected in practice. Tonga's media environment has been improving steadily since a 2004 Supreme Court ruling reinstated a press freedom clause in the constitution and invalidated the controversial 2003 Media Operators and Newspaper Acts, which had been used to harass newspapers such as *Taimi 'o Tonga*.

There were no physical attacks on the press in 2006, but the Overseas Broadcasting Network (OBN), which allocated significant airtime to pro-democracy leaders and functions as one of only two private television stations in the country, was prevented from broadcasting only days before riots broke out in November. Opposition campaigners believe this action was taken in response to OBN's frequent criticism of the government. 'Akilisi Pohiva, the leading pro-democracy parliamentarian and publisher of *Ko e Kele'a*—a popular investigative newsletter—was arrested and charged with sedition for displaying banners that the government claimed criticized King Taufa'ahau. However, charges were subsequently dropped.

Tonga has a remarkably diverse range of media considering the nation's small population and economy. Besides *Taimi 'o Tonga*, which has the largest circulation of the country's private newspapers (as well as editions in Australia, New Zealand, and the United States), other publications include the weekly government newspaper *Tonga Chronicle* and the independent monthly magazine and news website *Matangi Tonga*. The state-owned Tongan Broadcasting Commission owns one AM and one FM station and the free-to-air Television Tonga station. There are also two privately owned television stations and three private radio stations. The internet is open and unrestricted, but only 3 percent of the population had access to this medium in 2006.

Trinidad and Tobago

LEGAL ENVIRONMENT: 5
POLITICAL ENVIRONMENT: 11
ECONOMIC ENVIRONMENT: 8

Status: Free

TOTAL SCORE: 24

Survey Edition	2002	2003	2004	2005	2006
Total Score, Status	30,F	25,F	25,F	24,F	26,F

Freedom of the press is enshrined in the constitution of Trinidad and Tobago, but certain aspects of a draft constitution under consideration raise concerns. Although it maintains the right to press freedom, the draft includes a section stating that the rights of freedom of thought, belief, opinion, and expression do not preclude the state from regulating the broadcast or publication of information. Freedom of information legislation is in place, but the government has been criticized for gradually narrowing the categories of information accessible by the public under this law.

A major issue of contention in 2005 was the release of a draft national broadcasting code designed to deter talk radio stations from aggravating simmering ethnic tensions. By 2006, there had been such opposition to the draft code from media houses that it was withdrawn for possible redrafting. In November, there was also renewed concern about the use of libel legislation to restrict media operations when the Trinidad and Tobago News

Centre, publisher of the weekly *Mirror*, was ordered to pay a government minister the exorbitant sum of US$65,800 in libel damages. Separately, in July the Privy Council ordered the government to issue a commercial FM broadcasting license to Sanatan Dharma Maha Sabha (SDMS), the principal Hindu organization in the country, ending six years of rejected requests. In its decision, the Privy Council determined that the government had subjected the SDMS to unequal treatment under the law and, in the process, had denied it the right to freedom of expression. There were no physical attacks on the press in Trinidad and Tobago during the year.

There are 3 daily and 3 weekly newspapers operating in Trinidad and Tobago. In addition to the 3 television stations and over 30 radio stations that are privately owned, a new state-owned company, the Caribbean News Media Group, launched a new radio station in February and a new television station in September. Although the internet is not restricted by the government, broadband services are limited to a few upscale residential areas and only 12 percent of the population was able to access the internet in 2006.

Tunisia

Status: Not Free

LEGAL ENVIRONMENT: 28
POLITICAL ENVIRONMENT: 31
ECONOMIC ENVIRONMENT: 24
TOTAL SCORE: 83

Survey Edition	2002	2003	2004	2005	2006
Total Score, Status	73,NF	78,NF	80,NF	80,NF	83,NF

Tunisia continued to operate one of the world's most repressive media environments in 2006. The constitution guarantees freedom of the press except under "conditions laid down by law," but in reality assurances of press freedom are irrelevant to the government and have little bearing on the reality of Tunisian journalism. This untenable situation has been the state of affairs since President Zine el-Abidine Ben Ali seized office almost two decades ago. Tunisia's strong central authority controls most aspects of government and passes laws to ensure that media practitioners stay in line. The Press Law criminalizes defamation, and those who violate it can be imprisoned and fined. The print media are also required by law to obtain registration from the Ministry of the Interior. In January, the president signed a law abolishing the mandatory submission of all printed material for government approval prior to distribution. Nonetheless, authorities continue to vet and censor newspapers published locally as well as those coming from outside the country. While local publications are edited by persons close to the regime who know the restrictions, it is standard practice that foreign publications with reports critical of Tunisia are prevented from entering the country.

Journalists who cross the government's red lines have been harassed, beaten, imprisoned under harsh conditions, subjected to smear campaigns, prevented from leaving the country, and threatened. Tunisia released Hamadi Jebali in February after the journalist had served over 15 years of a 16-year sentence. According to the Committee to Protect Journalists, Jebali had served the longest prison term of any journalist in the Arab world. Jebali was tried by a military court in 1992 and accused of being a member of Ennahda, a banned Islamist movement, in a trial that did not satisfy international standards of fairness. Even after being freed from prison, some journalists faced further state interference.

Tunisia's print media comprise several private pro-government and government-owned newspapers. Editors of the private media are close associates of Ben Ali's government and typically heap praise on the leadership and its policies, while the government withholds advertising funds from publications that do not provide sufficiently favorable coverage. A few small independent newspapers, including *Al-Mawqif*, attempt to cover human rights issues and to publish mild criticisms of the government despite the difficult conditions, but their circulation is small owing to financial constraints. Many foreign satellite stations can be viewed in Tunisia, although the government blocks France 2 and has blocked Al-Jazeera for their negative coverage of Ben Ali. With the print and broadcast media firmly in the government's grip, the few independent voices in Tunisia publish on the internet or outside the country.

Compared with citizens of neighboring North African states, the more affluent Tunisians have wider access to the internet, with just over 9 percent of the population using it in 2006. The government blocks access to a number of sites, particularly those belonging to domestic human rights organizations, opposition groups, and Islamist associations, as well as websites that post material critical of the Tunisian government. In November, a collaborative university study found that the government blocked roughly 10 percent of the 2,000 websites it tested. Punishments for online dissidents are as severe as those for print and broadcast journalists who transgress. For example, in 2005 Mohamed Abbou, a human rights lawyer, was sentenced to three and a half years in prison after publishing an article on a banned website, Tunisnews, where he likened treatment of Tunisian prisoners to that of those in Iraq's Abu Ghraib prison under U.S. control.

	LEGAL ENVIRONMENT: 19
Turkey	POLITICAL ENVIRONMENT: 19
	ECONOMIC ENVIRONMENT: 11
Status: Partly Free	TOTAL SCORE: 49

Survey Edition	2002	2003	2004	2005	2006
Total Score, Status	58,PF	55,PF	52,PF	48,PF	48,PF

While efforts to meet European Union (EU) membership requirements have resulted in the passing of positive reforms, including a new Press Law in 2004, the greater national debate over Turkey's accession to the EU has fueled a nationalist movement that is driving a legalistic crackdown on free expression by journalists and writers. Constitutional provisions for freedom of the press and of expression exist but in practice are only partially upheld and have been increasingly undermined by the more restrictive measures of the new Turkish penal code, which came into force in June 2005.

According to Bianet, a Turkish press freedom organization, the number of prosecuted journalists, publishers, and activists rose to 293 in 2006 versus 157 in 2005. The same organization reports that 72 individuals were tried in 2006 under the new penal code's especially controversial Article 301 alone. This provision allows for prison terms of six months to three years for "the denigration of Turkishness" and has been used to charge journalists for crimes such as stating that genocide was committed against the Armenians in 1915, discussing the division of Cyprus, or writing critically on the security forces. Book publishers, translators, and authors have also faced prosecution for "insulting Turkish identity." Among the most prominent cases is that of Hrant Dink, editor of the Armenian weekly *Agos*, who was prosecuted for a second time under Article 301 in July 2006 following an interview with Reuters news agency where he confirmed his recognition of Armenian genocide allegations. In a more hopeful development, charges brought under the same article against Orhan Pamuk, the Nobel Prize–winning Turkish novelist, were dropped in January 2006. Article 277 of the penal code was invoked to charge several journalists covering controversial court cases with "attempting to influence court decisions," including Hrant Dink and four of his *Agos* colleagues for their coverage of a judge's decision to ban a conference on the Armenian genocide. Article 216 penalizes "inflaming hatred and hostility among peoples" and has been used against journalists who write about the Kurdish population. Human rights groups report that nationalist lawyers groups, such as the Turkish Union of Lawyers and Unity of Jurists, are leading the push for prosecutions.

Pressure from the EU and international press freedom watchdog groups prompted Prime Minister Recep Tayyip Erdogan to declare his commitment to revising Article 301 in September, but at year's end no progress had been made on this. Erdogan himself continued to launch defamation suits against members of the media, however, filing a total of 59 cases in 2006. Rights groups report that the total number of defamation cases increased from 2005, along with the fines issued as punishments. Convictions against journalists are made much less frequently than are prosecutions, but trials are time-consuming and expensive. A total of seven convictions were made for charges under Article 301 in 2006.

Causing further alarm, the Parliament approved amendments to the Antiterror Law in June that allow for imprisoning journalists for up to three years for the dissemination of statements and propaganda by terrorist organizations. The new legislation raises concerns that the broad definition of terrorism could allow for arbitrary prosecutions, particularly for members of the pro-Kurdish press who are sometimes charged with collaborating with the Kurdish Workers Party (PKK). For example, Rustu Demirkaya, a reporter with the pro-Kurdish news agency DIHA, was charged with collaborating with the PKK in June and then with disseminating terrorist propaganda for covering the return of an army private who had been kidnapped by the PKK in August. Journalist Ilyas Aktas, reportedly threatened by the police previously, was shot amid violent clashes between Kurdish demonstrators and security forces in southeastern Turkey in April and died a few weeks later.

The Supreme Council of Radio and Television, whose members are elected by the Parliament, has the authority to sanction broadcasters if they are not in compliance with the law or its expansive broadcasting principles. It is frequently subject to political pressure. Censorship is not explicit, but editors and journalists practice self-censorship out of fear of violating legal restrictions; Turkish press freedom advocates contend that self-censorship has become even more prevalent as a result of the onslaught of prosecutions under the new penal code. Further, media are highly concentrated in four major conglomerates, which subtly pressure their editors and journalists to refrain from reporting that will harm their business interests. This could include avoiding criticism of the government or potential advertisers, both of which could have contracts with other arms of the companies.

Turkey's broadcast media are well developed, with hundreds of private television channels, including cable and satellite as well as commercial radio stations. State television and radio provide limited broadcasting in minority languages, including Kurdish; this marked a major step forward for freedom of expression, although critics say that the broadcasts are too restricted and quality is poor. The quality of Turkish media is low, but independent domestic and foreign print media are able to provide diverse views, including criticism of the government and its policies. An estimated 21 percent of the Turkish population was able to access the internet in 2006, and the government refrains from restricting the internet, although on occasion it has accessed user records in the name of national security. Police must obtain permission from a judge or higher authority before obtaining such information.

Turkmenistan

LEGAL ENVIRONMENT: 30
POLITICAL ENVIRONMENT: 37
ECONOMIC ENVIRONMENT: 29

Status: Not Free

TOTAL SCORE: 96

Survey Edition	2002	2003	2004	2005	2006
Total Score, Status	91,NF	92,NF	95,NF	96,NF	96,NF

Turkmenistan's media environment remained one of the most repressive in the world in 2006, although the death of President Saparmurat Niyazov in December sparked hopes that limited improvements might be possible in 2007. In 2006, the state continued to control all domestic media, using them to advance Niyazov's personality cult and present an idealized picture of life under his rule. The government disregards any notion of press freedom, legal or otherwise, in its complete control of the country's media and information flow.

Journalists operate under the constant threat of physical attack in Turkmenistan and several journalists were victims of attacks. The death of Radio Free Europe/Radio Liberty (RFE/RL) correspondent Ogulsapar Muradova in police custody in September stood out as a potent reminder of the dangers that confronted independent media in Turkmenistan. Authorities arrested Muradova, along with two human rights activists, in June in the course of a convoluted espionage scandal. She was eventually sentenced after a closed trial in August to a six-year prison term for illegally possessing ammunition. When relatives were allowed to view Muradova's body, they said that it bore telltale signs of abuse, suggesting she may have died under torture. The government did not conduct any investigation into the circumstances of Muradova's suspicious death. Other instances of harassment of independent journalists by authorities included the detention of RFE/RL stringers Jumadurdy Ovezov and Meret Khommadov. The two were held briefly in March and released after they signed a statement pledging that they would no longer provide reports to RFE/RL's Turkmen service. Also in March, Anna Kurbanova, a stringer for the Russian news agency ITAR-TASS, was stripped of her accreditation in apparent retaliation for her reporting on "reforms" that deprived thousands of Turkmen citizens of their pensions.

As in past years, the government maintained an absolute monopoly over all media, directly controlling not only media outlets, but also the printing presses and other infrastructure on which they depended. State television rebroadcast some Russian entertainment programming, and satellite dishes remained available to citizens who could afford them. Turkmen opposition groups in exile operated a number of websites that were harshly critical of Turkmenistan's repressive political system, with original and translated materials in Turkmen and Russian. It is unclear whether these are accessible from within Turkmenistan, where the government controls and monitors the internet, but some reports indicate that individual access can be arranged for payment. Nonetheless, the cost is prohibitive for the vast bulk of the population, and less than 1 percent of citizens have regular access to the internet.

Tuvalu

LEGAL ENVIRONMENT: 3
POLITICAL ENVIRONMENT: 11
ECONOMIC ENVIRONMENT: 12

Status: Free

TOTAL SCORE: 26

Survey Edition	2002	2003	2004	2005	2006
Total Score, Status	NA	16,F	19,F	20,F	26,F

Article 24 of the constitution safeguards freedom of expression, though government regulations and a monopoly over the small media market sometimes limit this right in practice. The newly elected Prime Minister, Apisai Ielemia, vowed in August to make media freedom a top priority, but only minor improvements were reported by year's end. However, there were no recorded incidents of attacks on or harassment of journalists in 2006. The Tuvalu Media Corporation (TMC) controls the country's only newspaper, *Tuvalu Echoes*, and radio station, Radio Tuvalu; the TMC reportedly censors content considered to be in opposition to the government and restricted coverage of political and human rights issues in 2006. The TMC receives most of its funding from the state and is chaired by the secretary to the government. Tuvalu ISP is the sole internet provider for the 13.2 percent of the population with the means to access this new medium. However, only 16 percent of those connected can access the internet at any one time owing to a poor telecommunications infrastructure.

Uganda

Status: Partly Free

LEGAL ENVIRONMENT: 20
POLITICAL ENVIRONMENT: 21
ECONOMIC ENVIRONMENT: 13
TOTAL SCORE: 54

Survey Edition	2002	2003	2004	2005	2006
Total Score, Status	42,PF	45,PF	44,PF	44,PF	52,PF

The situation for the press worsened slightly during 2006 as a result of media harassment and criminal convictions against critical journalists surrounding the February presidential election. Although the constitution provides for freedom of expression, libel is still considered a criminal offense, and laws enacted in the name of national security have limited the constitutional provisions in practice. The government also set new restrictions on the accreditation of foreign journalists prior to the election; this included mandatory vetting of all foreign correspondents by a new Media Center established by the government in 2005. Even those who had previously received accreditation were told to reregister at the center. Information Minister James Buturo said the step was taken because foreign journalists had become a "security threat." On March 9, Canadian freelance journalist Blake Lambert was denied reentry to the country following a visit to South Africa. Lambert's international reporting and his domestic radio commentary included criticism of the government; no official reason was given by authorities for denying him entry. However, in a positive move, a new regulation restricting in-country travel by international journalists was rescinded soon after it was promulgated.

A number of media outlets were harassed, intimidated, and censored throughout the year, particularly those entertaining perspectives from the Forum for Democratic Change (FDC), the primary opposition party, during the election or giving voice to the Lord's Resistance Army in the north. In March, the Mbale offices of the private radio station Open Gate

FM were raided by police, who confiscated equipment and arrested two journalists for failing to produce a record of their March 18 interview with Nathan Mafabi Nandala, a parliamentarian and senior leader of the FDC. The two employees were later released without being formally charged. Also in March, two journalists with the private tabloid *Red Pepper* were temporarily detained and eventually released without charge after they published a leaked cabinet list. Shortly thereafter, Martin Ojara Mapenduzi, program manager of the private radio station Choice FM, was detained temporarily by police without charge after broadcasting a piece in February that the government deemed threatening to national security. In fact, soon after the election, Choice FM was forcibly shut by police on accusations of operating without a license. The station adamantly denies operating illegally but was permitted to reopen in July only after paying a fine in excess of US$2,700. In 2005, the government passed a ban on coverage of the trial of opposition leader Kizza Besigye; this ban continued in 2006, even though it was widely disregarded in practice without penalty. Two journalists from the respected Kampala-based *Weekly Observer* faced charges of "promoting sectarianism" in connection with a 2005 article criticizing the government's prosecution of Besigye.

Independent media outlets—including more than two dozen daily and weekly newspapers as well as about 100 private radio and television stations—have mushroomed since the government loosened control in 1993, and they are often highly critical of the government and offer a range of opposition views. However, high annual licensing fees for radio and television stations place some financial restraints on the broadcast media. A ban on new radio stations, which was imposed in 2003 and was widely disregarded in practice without penalty, was lifted this year for up-country radio stations; however, it still holds for Kampala. The state broadcasters, including Radio Uganda, the only national radio station, wield considerable clout and are generally viewed as sympathetic to the government. Self-censorship is widespread. There are no official restrictions on internet access, although on February 13 the government directed Uganda Telecom to block internal access to www.radiokatwe. com, a U.S.–based website that published antigovernment gossip. Use of the internet increased during the year, with 1.7 percent of the population accessing this new media during 2006.

LEGAL ENVIRONMENT: 13

POLITICAL ENVIRONMENT: 19

Ukraine

ECONOMIC ENVIRONMENT: 21

Status: Partly Free

TOTAL SCORE: 53

Survey Edition	2002	2003	2004	2005	2006
Total Score, Status	60,PF	67,NF	68,NF	59,PF	53,PF

Months of political conflict within the government, including the dissolution of President Viktor Yushchenko's ruling coalition and the approval of his former rival Viktor Yanukovych as prime minister in August 2006, stalled the achievement of greater press freedom in Ukraine. The legal framework, which provides for freedom of the press and speech, has generally been respected in practice following the 2004 Orange Revolution, in which Yushchenko won the presidency. However, international agencies such as the Organization for Security and Cooperation in Europe have reiterated the need to further develop a free and professional media environment and bring Ukrainian laws into line with European standards. Particular priorities include drafting and amending legislation on access to information and the ownership of media, as well as measures involving the broadcasting market and the creation of independent public service broadcasting. Libel was eliminated as a criminal offense in 2001, but lawmakers in 2006 offered a draft bill that would reestablish the charge, and officials continued to use civil libel suits to deter and punish journalists and media outlets.

Despite Yushchenko's promise to make the high-profile case of murdered journalist Heorhiy Gongadze a priority of his administration, the trial of the three men charged with the 2000 slaying—Valery Kostenko, Mykola Protasov, and Oleksandr Popovych—made little progress in 2006. (A fourth suspect, senior police official General Oleksiy Pukach, remained a fugitive.) The Kyiv Court of Appeals closed major parts of the trial to the public and press, including the testimony of the defendants and government security agents. Gongadze's family and media watchdogs criticized the move for undermining the integrity of the process and curbing public attention. An appellate panel also rejected as premature the defense's request to seek testimony from such important individuals as former president Leonid Kuchma and Parliament Speaker Volodymyr Lytvyn, both of whom had been accused in a parliamentary inquiry of ordering the murder, and Mykola Melnychenko, the former presidential bodyguard whose secret audio recordings implicated them.

Reports of harassment and physical abuse of journalists who covered sensitive stories continued around the country in 2006, notably prior to the March 26 parliamentary elections. In March, unidentified men attacked Irina Ovsy, editor of *Sotsialisticheskaya Kharkovshchina*, a weekly newspaper of the For Union political coalition in the Kharkiv region, telling her to stop publishing the paper. Three other journalists also suffered physical attacks, one of whom was kidnapped in broad daylight, taken to a forest and beaten. Fires were also set in order to intimidate the media. One occurred in February at the office building of the independent internet newspaper *Vgolos*, which also contained the offices of local news agency Press-time in Lviv, both of which had criticized local politicians and reported on environmental problems. Similar attacks occurred against journalists' homes, presumably in retaliation for criticisms aimed at local politicians. In March, the basement of Lilia Budjurova was set on fire by unidentified individuals. Budjurova, a journalist for the local TV station STB and editor of the weekly *Pervaya Krymshaya*, believed the fire to be retribution for a recently published list of parliament members with criminal records. The apartment of Sergei Yanovsky, a correspondent of the *Kievskiye Vedomosti* newspaper, was set on fire by arsonists in June; Yanovsky had previously reported on election campaign irregularities and also published exposés of local corruption.

With hundreds of state and private television and radio stations and numerous print and electronic news outlets, Ukraine's media remained diverse. However, because many major outlets are owned by business magnates and individuals with close ties to the government, coverage is often slanted in favor of specific economic or political interests. Additionally, Ukraine's print distribution system remains problematic and dependent on the national postal service. The government did not restrict internet access or require internet publications to register in 2006, but it had the ability to monitor websites and the e-mails of the 11.5 percent of the population that used the internet regularly.

United Arab Emirates

LEGAL ENVIRONMENT: 23
POLITICAL ENVIRONMENT: 23
ECONOMIC ENVIRONMENT: 22

Status: Not Free

TOTAL SCORE: 68

Survey Edition	2002	2003	2004	2005	2006
Total Score, Status	74,NF	74,NF	75,NF	72,NF	65,NF

While the constitution of the United Arab Emirates (UAE) provides, at least in principle, for freedom of speech and of the press, in practice the government uses its judicial and executive branches to restrict those rights. UAE Federal Law No. 15 of 1980 for Printed Matter and Publications, which extends to all aspects of the media, including book publishing, is considered one of the toughest in the Arab world. The law gives the government control over content and prohibits any criticism of government, rulers and ruling families, and friendly governments. The law also subjects all publications to state licensing; journalists are forbidden from leveling any criticism against authorities and can be prosecuted under the penal code. Press law in the UAE authorizes the state to censor both domestic and foreign publications prior to distribution. In 2006, the UAE abolished the Ministry of Information, the government's arm of media control and censorship, and replaced it with the National Media Council. This council has the task of controlling and overseeing the press, enforcing media-related laws, issuing licenses, and approving editors. Both the larger press and private associations' publications are censored by the government.

Journalists in the UAE suffer from several forms of intimidation. While native journalists usually face warnings and threats whenever the government feels they have crossed a line, non-citizen journalists, who account for more than 90 percent of all journalists in the UAE, face harsher measures, including termination and deportation. Extreme forms of self-censorship are widely practiced whenever journalists write or broadcast about topics such as politics, culture, religion, friendly governments, or any topic that the government could deem to be politically or culturally sensitive. The only place where an amount of press freedom exists is the much celebrated Dubai Media City (DMC), a zone where foreign media outlets that produce content intended for audiences outside the country operate relatively freely. Media outlets and journalists based in the DMC are regulated by the Technology and Media Free Zone Authority. While such outlets generally focus solely on international issues and refrain from covering any local concerns, they too are subject to the 1980 law and penal code whenever they transgress in their coverage of local issues. There were no physical attacks on the press in the UAE in 2006.

All media outlets are either owned outright by the government or closely affiliated with it. Privately owned newspapers, such as the Arabic daily *Al-Khaleej* and its sister, the English-language *Gulf News*, are heavily influenced by the government, which provides subsidies, and both rely heavily on the official UAE news agencies for content. All broadcast media, also solely state-owned, provide only the official view on local issues. In 2005, the government of Dubai formed the Arab Media Group to operate as its media arm. The group publishes two newspapers and controls two local radio stations. Even though it promises a freer and more professional outlook, the group is still operating under the 1980 Press Law. This concentration of media ownership in the hands of the government and its close business allies has hindered the country's ability to practice freedom of speech and develop media independence. The close alliance between the few business owners and the ruling families makes any criticism of the government and its laws impossible.

Furthermore, the UAE is considered a regional leader in its ability to censor the internet. Thirty-five percent of the population uses the internet and the only internet service provider in the country is owned and operated by a government corporation, the Emirates Telecommunications Corporation (Etisalat). Both high-speed and dial-up users find themselves directed to a proxy server that blocks materials deemed inconsistent with the "religious, cultural, political, and moral values of the country" and that also maintains a list of banned websites and blocks users from accessing them. In January, the government enacted a sweeping Information and Privacy Cybercrime Law. The new law criminalizes use of the internet to commit a range of crimes—including violating political, social, and religious norms—and subjects offenders to prison terms and fines.

United Kingdom

LEGAL ENVIRONMENT: 5
POLITICAL ENVIRONMENT: 8
ECONOMIC ENVIRONMENT: 6
TOTAL SCORE: 19

Status: Free

Survey Edition	2002	2003	2004	2005	2006
Total Score, Status	18,F	18,F	19,F	18,F	19,F

With a history of aggressive reporting and an editorially independent public broadcasting system, the United Kingdom maintained its free press environment in 2006. The law provides for freedom of the press, and the government generally respects this right in practice. However, legislation is in place under which journalists deemed to have information vital to a police investigation can be forced to give evidence at trial. In the aftermath of the July 2005 bombings on the London underground, the government passed the Prevention of Terrorism Act 2005 (which came into effect in April 2006) that includes provisions for the criminalization of forms of free speech considered by the government to be "encouragements of terrorism," even without proof of a direct link to a terrorist act. A religious hatred bill introduced in January 2006 criminalizes incitement of religious hatred or violence, although the bill that passed was weakened from its original form, allowing for rights to ridicule or cause offense to religious groups. The Freedom of Information Act has drawn criticism in the past year owing to several exemptions for sensitive issues related to national security and health and safety, along with frequent bureaucratic delays in responding to requests. Government proposals to introduce fees for certain time-consuming requests have also inspired media criticism. Figures released in December 2006 revealed that 40 percent of information requests were turned down by the government.

The United Kingdom's stringent libel laws were reformed in 2006 as the result of a law lords ruling in a libel case. Libel laws traditionally have heavily favored the plaintiff in the United Kingdom, with the burden of truth placed solely on the defendant. In deciding a libel case in October, however, the law lords chose in favor of the defendant—*The Wall Street Journal Europe*—despite the paper's lack of evidence in its defense. The lords justified their decision by arguing that the article in question was in the public interest, a ruling that should afford journalists greater freedom to report allegations against public figures without fear of reprisal. Further, in December the government introduced the Defamation bill, which will reportedly make it more difficult to bring unsubstantiated libel cases.

There were no physical attacks on the media during the year. However, in Northern Ireland, journalists routinely face intimidation, especially while investigating sensitive political issues. In 2006, a reporter from the *Sunday World* investigating paramilitary activities received several death threats. Press freedom groups expressed concern regarding a new law that would extend the powers of the police to search and seize documents, which could jeopardize the ability of journalists to protect their sources. Continuing investigations into the 2001 murder of journalist Martin O'Hagan have produced few results, with eight separate suspects arrested and released owing to lack of evidence. It is believed that O'Hagan was killed for his investigations into cooperation among Northern Irish police, military intelligence, armed groups, and drug gangs.

British media are free and largely independent from government interference. The United Kingdom has a strong tradition of public broadcasting, and the British Broadcasting Corporation, although funded by the government, is editorially independent. Ownership of independent media outlets is concentrated in the hands of a few large companies, including those headed by Rupert Murdoch, and many of the private national papers remain aligned with political parties. Few commercial radio news stations exist—in fact, 8 of the 11 radio news stations are affiliated with the BBC—but several independent news television channels operate throughout the country, including ITV and British Sky Broadcasting. Authorities may monitor internet messages and e-mail without judicial permission in the name of national security and "well-being." However, surveillance must be approved by the secretary of state, and there are departments in place to handle public complaints of abuse as well as interception warrants. An estimated 62 percent of the population was able to access the internet without restriction in 2006.

United States

LEGAL ENVIRONMENT: 6
POLITICAL ENVIRONMENT: 6
ECONOMIC ENVIRONMENT: 4

Status: Free

TOTAL SCORE: 16

Survey Edition	2002	2003	2004	2005	2006
Total Score, Status	16,F	17,F	13,F	17,F	16,F

The press remains aggressive in covering scandals involving government figures, including high-ranking members of the Bush administration, and in its coverage of the Iraq war. At the same time, the United States continued to face a controversy over growing demands by prosecutors that journalists reveal confidential sources or provide access to research material in the course of criminal investigations.

Press freedom enjoys a strong foundation of legal protection in the federal Constitution, in state and federal laws, and in court decisions. The Supreme Court has repeatedly issued decisions that take an expansive view of freedom of expression and of the press. In particular, court decisions have given broad protection to the press from libel or defamation suits that involve commentary on public figures. An exception to judicial support for press freedom involves demands by prosecutors for information gathered by reporters in the course of their journalistic investigations, including material from confidential sources. In the most high-profile recent case, *New York Times* reporter Judith Miller was jailed for 85 days in 2005 for refusing to testify before a federal grand jury in a case involving the leaking of the identity of a Central Intelligence Agency employee, Valerie Plame. In 2006, it was revealed that the special prosecutor for the Plame case knew early on that the source for the leak was Deputy Secretary of State Richard Armitage. In the end, no one was charged with leaking the information; the only person charged in the case was the chief of staff to Vice President Dick Cheney, Lewis "Scooter" Libby, who was indicted on allegations of perjury and obstruction of justice. As a result of the high-profile nature of the Plame case and the actual imprisonment of Miller, many within the media are concerned that this has put a chill on investigative reporting by making potential sources more reluctant to come forward and confide in journalists who may no longer be able to ensure their anonymity. In 2005, the Miller case provoked members of Congress to propose legislation that would shield reporters from being compelled to reveal confidential sources. Although there was considerable bipartisan support for the legislation at the time and more than 30 states already have such "shield laws," no legislative progress had been made at the federal level by the end of the year.

Judges continued to take an aggressive stance against journalists who refused to cooperate with the prosecution. In two unrelated cases in California, journalists faced contempt charges during 2006. In September, a judge ordered two journalists for the *San Francisco Chronicle* to jail in a criminal case relating to allegations of steroid use by professional athletes after they published a story based on leaked grand jury testimony. Their appeal was still pending at year's end, and neither reporter served time in jail. In a separate incident, blogger and freelance journalist Josh Wolf was imprisoned in August after refusing to hand over a videotape documenting clashes between police and demonstrators during a rally protesting a G8 economic conference held in San Francisco in 2005. After spending a month in prison, Wolf was released—only to return there in September upon losing his appeal. He remained in prison at year's end. Sami Al-Haj, a Somali-born Al-Jazeera journalist, continued to be held without charge by U.S. forces at Guantanamo Bay. He was originally arrested in Pakistan in 2001 in the initial push for results in the war on terror. However, Al-Haj's lawyer contends that his detention is based on the U.S. government's belief that a link exists between Al-Jazeera and al-Qaeda and that no evidence has been produced against his client.

In recent years, reporters from several prominent newspapers, including *The New York Times, The Washington Post*, and *The Wall Street Journal*, have published a series of investigative articles that have called into question various aspects of the Bush administration's war on terror and its conduct in the Iraq war. In June, several newspapers published articles revealing that the administration had gained access to the Society for Worldwide Interbank Financial Telecommunication in search of material that might involve money transfers by terrorists. Publication of the articles drew sharp criticism from President Bush and members of Congress and a threat by Attorney General Alberto Gonzales that *The New York Times* could face criminal prosecutions and potentially charges of treason. In 2005, the Bush administration was criticized for having paid several political commentators who supported certain domestic policy initiatives through grants from agencies of the federal government; a report by federal auditors concluded that the administration's efforts amounted to "covert propaganda." However, there were no further reports of such incidents in 2006.

Media coverage of political affairs is aggressive and often polarized. The press itself is frequently a source of controversy, with conservatives and supporters of the Bush administration accusing the media of anti-administration bias and liberals accusing the press of timidity in coverage of administration misdeeds. The appearance of enhanced polarization is driven to some degree by the growing influence of blog sites, many of which are aggressively partisan. Nonetheless, most American newspapers make a serious effort to keep a wall of separation between news reporting, commentary, and editorials. Ironically, the trend toward fewer family-owned newspapers and more newspapers under corporate control has contributed to a less partisan, if blander, editorial tone.

The media in the United States are overwhelmingly under private ownership. Nevertheless, National Public Radio, an entity funded partly by the government and partly by private contributions, enjoys a substantial audience. In 2005, the chairman of the Corporation for Public Broadcasting (CPB) stepped down amid charges that he had attempted to politicize the agency. A report by the CPB's inspector general charged that former chairman Kenneth Tomlinson had violated the agency's code of nonpartisanship through personnel and program decisions. Tomlinson remains chairman of the Broadcasting Board of Governors (BBG), the agency that administers America's foreign broadcasting services. In August, the inspector general for the State Department criticized Tomlinson for having improperly hired a friend on the public BBG payroll. Under U.S. law, radio and television airwaves are considered public property and are leased to private stations, which determine content. The Federal Communications Commission (FCC) is charged with administering licenses and reviewing content to ensure that it complies with federal limits on indecent or offensive material. On several occasions, the FCC has issued fines against radio and television outlets for what the agency deemed acts of indecency.

The United States is home to more than 1,500 daily newspapers geared primarily toward local readerships. Many of the country's largest and most prestigious newspapers have encountered financial difficulties in recent years, owing mainly to competition from the internet. Newspapers have instituted staff reductions and, in some cases, have cut back on their coverage of national and international news (and on maintaining foreign news bureaus) in favor of a more local focus. Many predict a major transformation of the newspaper business in coming years, with some newspapers closing and others focused increasingly on bolstering their electronic editions. However, the primary form of news dissemination in the country is through television news networks both cable and satellite, like CNN, Fox News, and CBS. Media concentration is an ongoing concern in the United States. This controversy has intensified in recent years following the purchase of media entities, especially television networks, by large corporations with no previous experience in journalism. At the same time, diversity of the U.S. media has expanded somewhat with the mushrooming of cable television and, especially, the internet. The number and influence of internet sites and blogs have expanded greatly in recent years, and blogs have proven to be an important source of information in certain political controversies. Blogs devoted to public policy questions often lean to the highly partisan, and though their proliferation adds to the richness of press diversity, it also contributes to ideological polarization. On two occasions, the U.S. Congress has tried to impose legislation that could lead to censorship of internet content, but both attempts were ruled unconstitutional by the courts. In a positive test of internet independence in November, a California state supreme court ruled in a defamation case that internet service providers could not be held responsible for the content of their customers' posts. In 2006, the internet was used by more than 210 million Americans, roughly 70 percent of the nation's population.

LEGAL ENVIRONMENT: 10
POLITICAL ENVIRONMENT: 10

Uruguay

ECONOMIC ENVIRONMENT: 10

Status: Free
TOTAL SCORE: 30

Survey Edition	2002	2003	2004	2005	2006
Total Score, Status	25,F	30,F	26,F	29,F	28,F

Although Uruguay is usually considered to have one of the freest media environments in South America, some negative trends in 2006 raised concern. The constitution provides for freedom of speech and of the press, and the government generally respects the law. On September 18, the Supreme Court reinstated the criminal defamation conviction of journalist Carlos Dogliani Staricco, who had written reports denouncing irregularities by a local mayor. The Court's ruling placed the honor of public officials above freedom of expression, reversing its own decision in a 1997 ruling. In this way, the Supreme Court reinforced a troubling trend of criminalizing reports that criticize government authorities.

Although Uruguayans witnessed few cases of physical attacks on media professionals and organizations in 2006, there was a noticeable increase in the number of verbal harassments of news organizations by public officials, including one incident when President Tabare Vazquez accused major media outlets of conspiring against the government. The military occasionally threatens journalists investigating human rights abuses that took place during the military dictatorship of the 1970s and 1980s. In March, confidential military documents were stolen from investigative reporter Eduardo Preve. It was widely believed that the military was behind the theft because the documents reportedly supported claims that the military protected individuals accused of human rights abuses during the military dictatorship. In a separate incident in September, a group of journalists was assaulted when they attempted to approach General Gregoria Alvarez, who was de facto president of Uruguay during the military dictatorship, in order to question him about his alleged past human rights abuses. When the reporters tried to question Alvarez, unidentified persons dressed as civilians began to beat the reporters.

Media ownership continued to be relatively concentrated, but Uruguay has a diverse media system, with more than 100 privately owned papers, though some are linked directly to political parties. There are over 100 private radio stations and at least 20 television stations, as well as one state-owned radio station and one television station that are regulated by the official broadcasting service, SODRE. Advertising is often used by the government to either reward or punish media outlets, and in December the Uruguayan Press Association released a report documenting the government's manipulation of advertisements to favor media outlets sympathetic to the administration. There are no government restrictions on the internet, which is used by over 20 percent of the population.

Uzbekistan

Status: Not Free

LEGAL ENVIRONMENT: 29
POLITICAL ENVIRONMENT: 37
ECONOMIC ENVIRONMENT: 25
TOTAL SCORE: 91

Survey Edition	2002	2003	2004	2005	2006
Total Score, Status	84,NF	86,NF	84,NF	85,NF	90,NF

The government maintained its tight grip on the press in 2006 as it continued to systematically attack media freedoms. Uzbek authorities do not respect freedom of speech or of the press, despite nominal constitutional guarantees. A number of ambiguously phrased statutes broadly prohibited incitement of religious or ethnic strife and statements advocating the subversion or overthrow of the constitutional order. A new media resolution in 2006 tightened a system of laws that already allowed penalties of up to five years in prison for publicly criticizing the president. Aside from this new resolution, the legal situation for the media, though restrictive, remained largely unchanged from previous years.

After domestic unrest in 2005, the Uzbek authorities undertook a concerted campaign against foreign-funded media, and in 2006 the British Broadcasting Corporation, Radio Free Europe/Radio Liberty, and Voice of America remained unable to broadcast from within Uzbekistan. A resolution passed in 2006 by the government, aimed at shutting down criticisms published abroad, stressed that foreign correspondents were forbidden "to insult the honor and dignity of Uzbek citizens, [or] to interfere in their personal lives." It also expressly forbade native Uzbeks from working for foreign outlets that had not been accredited by the government.

Although there was little independent media activity left in the wake of the government's repressive efforts in 2005, harassment continued in 2006. In January, rights activist Saidjahon Zainabiddinov was reportedly sentenced to a seven-year prison term for speaking with foreign journalists about the Uzbek security services' violent suppression of the May 2005 Andijan uprising. Several other journalists were stripped of their accreditation, deported, or fired because of criticisms of the government while the independent news website tribune-uz.info was shut down following direct harassment. In October, a court sentenced independent journalist Ulughbek Haydarov to a six-year prison term for extortion, but he was released in November. He had reported on local government corruption. Sobirdjon Yakubov, a journalist with the newspaper *Hurriyat* who had been jailed in 2005 after calling for democratic reforms, was released in April and allowed to return to work.

There are no private publishing houses or printing presses, and the establishment of new periodicals is subject to political approval. The government in 2006 continued to control national dailies and television stations, which routinely denounced foreign-funded media as aggressors in an "information war" against Uzbekistan and portrayed Western-style democratization as a plot to undermine Uzbek identity. Virtually all media were controlled either directly or indirectly by the state and the government continues to use them to present a positive distortion of the reality in the country, with occasional forays into carefully controlled criticism. With foreign-funded broadcast media barred from the country, the internet was a critical source of information, and a number of exiled Uzbek journalists were able to operate news sites from abroad with a focus on rights issues. However, only 3.3 percent of the population accessed the internet in 2006, and consistent reports indicated that the authorities tried to block critical news and opposition sites, although some remained available through proxy servers. An Uzbek court in January 2006 suspended Freedom House's operations in the country, finding that the group had provided internet access without a license.

Vanuatu

LEGAL ENVIRONMENT: 6
POLITICAL ENVIRONMENT: 9
ECONOMIC ENVIRONMENT: 9

Status: Free

TOTAL SCORE: 24

Survey Edition	2002	2003	2004	2005	2006
Total Score, Status	24,F	21,F	23,F	24,F	25,F

The island nation of Vanuatu continues have a small, but vibrant press. Freedom of expression is protected under Article 5.1.g of the constitution, and this right is generally respected in practice. As the result of a media workshop in August, Transparency International Vanuatu and Media Association blong Vanuatu (MAV) agreed to draft Vanuatu's first freedom of information bill. The draft was pending at year's end. Although officials do not actively interfere with media coverage, journalists have been censored or intimidated on occasion. In March, the Pacific Islands News Association condemned the actions of the Vanuatu police when they assaulted photographer Samuel Taffo and imprisoned *Vanuatu Daily Post* publisher

Marc Neil-Jones in separate incidents. Police Commissioner Arthur Caulton promptly apologized for the incidents and launched investigations. There are private print media, but only one radio and one television station on the island, both state-owned. Radio broadcasts have increased since the installation of new transmitters at the beginning of 2006. In October, the MAV expressed concern over political interference at the Vanuatu Broadcasting and Television Corporation, including the suspension of its general manager by Prime Minister Ham Lini, who is also the minister for media. The internet is not restricted by the government, though it is accessed by only 3.4 percent of the population.

Venezuela

LEGAL ENVIRONMENT: 26
POLITICAL ENVIRONMENT: 30
ECONOMIC ENVIRONMENT: 18

Status: Not Free

TOTAL SCORE: 74

Survey Edition	2002	2003	2004	2005	2006
Total Score, Status	44,PF	68,NF	68,NF	72,NF	72,NF

A hostile political atmosphere under the government of President Hugo Chavez has fostered a steady decline in press freedom over the past several years, and that trend continued in 2006. State initiatives have eroded the influence of private media, in which the previous dominance of pro-opposition outlets has been dwindling. Among other actions, the government has enacted legislation prohibiting the broadcast of certain material, intimidated and denied access to private media, attempted to shut down pro-opposition outlets, and harassed journalists employed at such outlets.

The legal environment for the press remains poor. The Law of Social Responsibility in Radio and Television, signed in December 2004, contains vaguely worded restrictions that can be used to severely limit freedom of expression. For example, the law forbids graphic depictions of violence between 5 a.m. and 11 p.m. on both television and radio. In March 2005, the penal code was revised to make insulting the president punishable by 6 to 30 months in prison. Furthermore, comments that could "expose another person to contempt or public hatred" are subject to one to three years in prison as well as a severe fine. Inaccurate reporting that "disturbs the public peace" carries a prison sentence of two to five years. In January 2006, a judge issued a gag order barring the media from reporting on the investigation into the high-profile murder of prosecutor Danilo Anderson, including descriptions of the key witness's credibility problems. At least three journalists were convicted and sentenced for defamation in 2006, with several others under investigation.

Government *cadenas* (announcements) require that broadcasters cease regular programming to transmit official messages; 182 such *cadenas* were issued in 2006. Independent journalists complained that a lack of access impeded their reporting; they were often denied entry to military ceremonies and other official events that state media representatives were allowed to attend. In June, Chavez announced his intention to review the licenses of private broadcasters. The year's most dramatic media event occurred on December 28, when the authorities announced that the license of RCTV, a prominent pro-opposition network, would not be renewed and the channel would go off the air by May 2007. The decision was decried by media watchdogs, who questioned the decision's motivation, legality, and lack of transparency. In May, the governor of Bolivar state called for the eviction of the newspaper *El Correo del Caroni*, which had been critical of his administration; in June, the paper's power was cut for five hours

Direct assaults on the media continued to occur regularly in 2006. Local media watchdog Instituto Prensa y Sociedad issued eight alerts throughout the year regarding aggression against the television channel Globovision alone. Three journalists were murdered, including a photographer who captured his killer, a policeman, in one of his last photos. Many other journalists reported beatings and threats. Tension rose throughout the preelection period, with both opposition and government reporters facing assaults by ideological opponents. In the days leading up to the election, Chavez warned that private stations would be closed if they violated bans on the release of exit poll data. In a related incident, prominent congresswoman Iris Varela called on Chavez supporters to be ready to seize control of private media if they announced an opposition victory. The European Union reported that while both pro-opposition and pro-government media reflected strong partisan tendencies throughout their campaign coverage, Chavez dominated "institutional publicity" by a margin of 19 to 1.

The government controls four national television stations, a national radio network, and a wire service, all of which have benefited from budget increases. Such government-run stations operate alongside multiple private television and radio stations in the country. Local and regional media are particularly dependent on government advertising revenue, leaving them vulnerable to economic retaliation for criticism. The president has a weekly television show (scheduled to switch to a nightly radio program in 2007) and exercises his power to preempt programming to ensure extensive coverage of government announcements in private media. In November, the mayor of the city of Maturin imposed a "publicity ban" on several newspapers and radio stations. There are no government restrictions on the internet, which had over three million users (nearly 13 percent of the population) by the end of 2006.

LEGAL ENVIRONMENT: 27
POLITICAL ENVIRONMENT: 28

Vietnam

ECONOMIC ENVIRONMENT: 22

Status: Not Free

TOTAL SCORE: 77

Survey Edition	2002	2003	2004	2005	2006
Total Score, Status	82,NF	82,NF	82,NF	82,NF	79,NF

The year 2006 was marked by increased tension between the government and journalists, as activists pushed for a more open media while the government cracked down on freedom of expression, particularly on the internet. Although the 1992 constitution recognizes the rights to freedom of opinion, expression, and association for all citizens, the propaganda and training departments of the ruling Communist Party of Vietnam (CPV) control all media and set press guidelines. In addition, a 1999 law requires journalists to pay damages to individuals or groups found to have been harmed by press articles, even if they are true. Reporting considered to be against the national interest can be charged under the criminal code and anti-defamation provisions. On July 1, 2006, in response to increasingly vibrant reporting by both the traditional and internet-based news media, the government passed a decree which defined over 2,000 additional violations of the law in the areas of culture and information and imposed hefty fines for offenders, with a particular focus on protecting "national security." In October, two newspapers were temporarily suspended and a third was banned under the new regulations after publishing articles on sensitive subjects.

Although journalists cannot cover sensitive political or economic matters or openly question the CPV's single-party rule without fear of legal or violent reprisals, they are more often allowed to report on crime and official corruption, and such reports have become increasingly common. Nevertheless, a number of print journalists were harassed and arrested during the year. Several reporters were beaten in March after covering a high-level corruption case. In April, two journalists departing for a freedom of expression seminar in the Philippines, Duong Phu Cuong and Nguyen Huy Cuong, were detained and interrogated by plainclothes police who claimed the reporters had violated departure laws. They had been under police surveillance for months prior to the arrest. In 2006, the government also cracked down harshly on Vietnam's fledgling community of internet dissidents, making several arrests throughout the year. Foreign journalists are monitored closely, and their movements within the country are restricted.

There is only one national television station in the country, state-owned Vietnam Television, although cable does carry some foreign channels. Radio is mainly controlled by the government-run Voice of Vietnam; only one other national private station operates in the country. All print media outlets are owned by or under the effective control of the CPV, government organs, or the army, although several newspapers, including *Thanh Nien, Nguoi Lao Dong,* and *Tuoi Tre* (owned by the Youth Union under the CPV), have attempted to become financially sustainable and to stop relying on state subsidies. According to Human Rights Watch, Vietnamese activists launched an unsanctioned newspaper, *Tu Do Ngon Luan (Free Expression),* which has published two editions since April 2006. Additionally, reporters and bloggers formed an unofficial media group, the Free Journalists Association of Vietnam. Local journalists are generally optimistic that private ownership of the media will expand sooner rather than later, particularly with regard to the internet, though competition for advertising among the more than 500 newspapers and 200 digital news sites remains stiff. Foreign periodicals, although widely available, are sometimes censored, and the broadcasts of stations such as Radio Free Asia are periodically jammed.

Access to satellite television broadcasts and the internet is growing. Currently, more than 17 percent of Vietnamese have internet access. The first online news site, vietnamnet.vn, publishes in Vietnamese and English, while vietnamjournalism.com, a blog run by a local journalist, discusses professional and ethical issues. Website operators continue to go through internet service providers (ISPs) that are either public or part public owned, like Vietnam Data Communications, which is controlled by the Ministry of Post and Telecommunications and caters to nearly a third of all internet users. It is required by law that ISPs block access to designated websites that the government considers politically unacceptable. In its crackdown against internet opposition, the government arrested three cyberdissidents in September for expressing democratic views; the journalist, Tran Khai

Thanh, was interrogated and placed under house arrest in November as a result of his essays published on the internet.

Yemen

LEGAL ENVIRONMENT: 28
POLITICAL ENVIRONMENT: 31
ECONOMIC ENVIRONMENT: 21

Status: Not Free

TOTAL SCORE: 80

Survey Edition	2002	2003	2004	2005	2006
Total Score, Status	65,NF	69,NF	67,NF	76,NF	81,NF

Genuine press freedom continued to be absent in Yemen due to the government's vigilance in silencing dissent. The constitution supports free speech "within the limits of the law," and Article 3 of the 1990 Press and Publication Law supports the right to "freedom of knowledge, thought, the press, personal expression, communication, and access to information." Nevertheless, the government does not respect these rights in practice, and few legal or social protections exist for journalists. Debates around the creation of a new Press Law continued in 2006, after the Ministry of Information submitted a draft to the Parliament in 2005. While the draft Press Law under consideration removes jail terms for press offenses, journalists can still face imprisonment under the country's penal code. In addition, restrictions remain in place against criticizing the president and harming national interests, more stringent regulations on entering the field of journalism have been introduced, and the capital required to launch a print publication has been increased.

Meanwhile, journalists faced criminal charges under the 1990 Press Law, continuing an alarming trend that began in 2004, partly in reaction to the media's increasing coverage of sensitive topics such as state policies toward the southern region of the country, relations with neighboring Arab states, corruption, security issues, and antiterrorism policy. In 2006, public officials, ministries, corporations, and the president of the republic all filed lawsuits against the press, charging criminal defamation and libel. In February, three journalists were imprisoned temporarily and charged (under both the penal code and the Press Law) with insulting the prophet Muhammad after they reprinted cartoons caricaturing Muhammad that originally appeared in a Danish daily in September 2005. Kamal al-Olufi of *Al-Rai al-Am*, Mohammed al-Assadi, editor of the *Yemen Observer*, and two journalists from *Al-Hurriya* were all convicted at the end of the year and received various sentences including the suspension of their papers, temporary writing bans, fines, and prison terms. One opposition paper, *Al-Thawri,* and its editor in chief, Khalid Salman, were involved in 14 separate civil lawsuits in 2006.

In addition to legal harassment, journalists faced direct and indirect attacks at the hands of both state and non-state actors, including assaults, travel bans, and smear campaigns. Government censors also targeted newspaper offices. A noticeable increase in offenses against the press occurred in the months leading up to the September presidential elections. The Yemeni organization, Women Journalists Without Chains, reported 67 cases of violations committed against journalists in 2006 solely for expressing their opinions. Jamal Amer, editor in chief of the independent newspaper *Al-Wasat,* who was abducted, beaten, and threatened by suspected government agents in August 2005, continued to be harassed in 2006. Abed al-Osaily, a journalist from the newspaper *Al-Nahar,* was murdered in July after writing an article that criticized government handling of a local irrigation project. Police failed to arrest the perpetrators. A number of other journalists were physically attacked both on and off the job, often while covering protests, sit-ins, political rallies, and sensitive topics. In one such instance in March, Qaed al-Tairi of *Al-Thawri* was kidnapped and assaulted for articles criticizing public figures. Perpetrators of violence against the press are rarely prosecuted, and the government seems to support an environment of complete impunity for these crimes, failing to conduct serious investigations or denounce the assaults. There were few developments in the cases of crimes committed in 2005, such as the November stabbing of journalist Nabil Sabaie, the December attack on journalist Muhammed Sadiq al-Odaini, or the injury of *Al-Nahar* editor Haga' al-Jehafi caused by an exploding file folder. The president and the defense minister continued to instigate violence toward oppositional journalists through speeches that insinuated they were traitors or separatists financed by external enemies.

Yemen offers a wide and diverse range of print publications that express the different perspectives of the government and the opposition, as well as independent and international views. Nevertheless, more than 70 percent of the population lives in rural areas where newspapers are not distributed, and the country has a high rate of illiteracy. Most people receive their news from the radio and television; however, the state maintains a monopoly on all broadcast media. There is currently no procedure for licensing independent media. Satellite television and the internet provide sources of uncensored domestic and international news but are available primarily in urban areas. Little more than 1 percent of the population accesses the internet. The government inspects all printed material that arrives from abroad and filters internet content. Websites were blocked in the months surrounding the September presidential elections.

Zambia

LEGAL ENVIRONMENT: 19
POLITICAL ENVIRONMENT: 24
ECONOMIC ENVIRONMENT: 21

Status: Not Free   TOTAL SCORE: 64

Survey Edition	2002	2003	2004	2005	2006
Total Score, Status	65,NF	63,NF	63,NF	65,NF	64,NF

An oppressive legal environment and biased government media all served to restrict freedom of the press in Zambia in 2006. Freedom of speech is constitutionally guaranteed, but the government often restricts this right in practice. The Independent Broadcasting Authority and Zambia National Broadcasting Corporation (ZNBC) Acts, which set up independent boards for the regulatory body and the national broadcaster, have not yet been fully implemented despite being passed in December 2003. A draft Freedom of Information bill has also yet to be passed. Under Section 69 of the penal code, it is a criminal offense for any media outlet to defame the president. Journalists have regularly been subject to criminal libel and defamation suits brought by ruling party leaders under this and other legal provisions. In November 2005, Fred M'membe, editor of Zambia's only private daily, *The Post*, was charged with defamation after writing a series of editorials that were critical of President Levy Patrick Mwanawasa. In February 2006, the state finally dropped all charges. The Public Order Act, among other statutes, has at times been used to harass journalists. In March 2006, two journalists working for the Chikuni community radio station were charged with the "publication of false news with intent to cause fear and alarm to the public" after covering a suspected ritual murder of a young boy.

On August 26, two media workers were harassed by a crowd after a speech made by Michael Sata, president of the opposition party, the Patriotic Front (PF), in which Sata called the licensing fee paid to the reporters' employer, Zambia National Broadcasting Corporation (ZNBC), an "unfair tax." The PF later issued a statement condemning the comments and urging Zambians not to harass or intimidate members of the press. In 2006, the Media Institute of Southern Africa–Zambia released a study revealing imbalance and bias in favor of the ruling party by the ZNBC in its coverage of news during the current election campaigns. This was found to be the case despite the legal provisions requiring equitable coverage of all political candidates. Separately, there were also reports of harassment of ZNBC journalists by opposition supporters. As a result of prepublication review at government-controlled newspapers, journalists commonly practice self-censorship. Opposition political parties and nongovernmental organizations complained of inadequate access to media resources.

The government controls two widely circulated newspapers, the *Times of Zambia* and *Zambia Daily,* and the state-owned, pro-government ZNBC dominates the broadcast sector. However, a group of independent newspapers widely criticize the government, and an independent radio station, Radio Phoenix, presents nongovernmental views. Most other private radio stations offer little political reporting, focusing instead on religious issues and music. There are no private television stations, except on expensive foreign satellite services. In March, the government passed an amendment to the Value-Added Tax Act that would have increased the standard rate applicable to the supply of newspapers and magazines and raised the costs of production by 25 percent. The amendment was later withdrawn after protests from local media organizations. Internet access is not restricted by the government, though its use is hindered by socioeconomic conditions and only 2 percent of the population was able to access it regularly in 2006.

Zimbabwe

LEGAL ENVIRONMENT: 29
POLITICAL ENVIRONMENT: 33
ECONOMIC ENVIRONMENT: 27

Status: Not Free

TOTAL SCORE: 89

Survey Edition	2002	2003	2004	2005	2006
Total Score, Status	83,NF	88,NF	89,NF	89,NF	90,NF

Press freedom in Zimbabwe remained extremely restricted in 2006, as President Robert Mugabe's government continued to tighten control over domestic media and attempted to block the efforts of foreign outlets to circulate unfiltered news within the country. Despite constitutional provisions for freedom of expression, officials display an openly hostile attitude toward media freedom, and a draconian legislative framework continues to effectively inhibit the activities of journalists and media outlets. The 2002 Access to Information and Protection of Privacy Act (AIPPA) requires all journalists and media companies to register with the government-controlled Media and Information Commission (MIC). It also gives the information minister sweeping powers to decide who is able to work as a journalist, and a 2005 amendment to the law introduced prison sentences of up to two years for journalists working without accreditation. A number of private newspapers have been denied licenses since the AIPPA came into force. The *Daily News,* the country's only independent daily, was shuttered in 2003 for not adhering to the AIPPA, and the MIC continued to deny it a license in 2006. Constitutional challenges to the AIPPA by affiliates of the *Daily News* have proven unsuccessful. However, the high court in February ruled that the July 2005 MIC decision to deny registration to the banned papers must be reconsidered and in March ruled that the MIC should rescue itself from the decision owing to the obvious bias of its chairman.

Authorities continue to employ a range of restrictive legislation—including the Official Secrets Act, the AIPPA, the Public Order and Security Act (POSA), and criminal defamation laws—to harass journalists. Section 15 of the POSA and Section 80 of the AIPPA criminalize the publication of "inaccurate" information, and both laws have been used to intimidate, arrest, and prosecute reporters. The 2005 Criminal Law (Codification and Reform Bill) increased prison sentences for similar violations to a maximum of 20 years. The General Laws Amendment Act, which tightened the "presidential insult" and "communication of falsehoods" provisions of the POSA, was signed into law in February. Several times during the year, the AIPPA was used to threaten the remaining independent press. In January, the weekly *Financial Gazette* withdrew an article suggesting that the MIC was controlled by intelligence officers after the commission threatened to revoke the paper's license. Later that month, the MIC refused to renew the accreditation of 15 journalists working for the *Zimbabwe Independent* until the paper retracted a similar story. A number of former *Daily News* employees continued to face charges of working without accreditation, although none of those charged under the AIPPA so far have been convicted. In January, freelance journalist Sidney Saize was detained for three days on charges of practicing journalism without a license and filing a "false story" for the Voice of America news service. In December 2005, police and government officials had raided the Harare office of the independent Voice of the People (VOP) radio station, which broadcasts locally produced programs into the country from the Netherlands. The authorities confiscated equipment and files and arrested three employees.

Six members of the VOP's board of trustees were also arrested and charged in January 2006 with broadcasting without a license, but after several court appearances, a judge dismissed the case in September.

Professional and media monitoring organizations—such as the Zimbabwe Union of Journalists, the Media Monitoring Project of Zimbabwe, and the local chapter of the Media Institute of Southern Africa (MISA)–Zimbabwe—were subject to official harassment during 2006. These three groups were jointly involved in advocating for the introduction of an independent media council, intended to replace the MIC as part of a self-regulatory system.

Journalists are routinely subjected to verbal intimidation, physical attacks, arrest and detention, and financial pressure at the hands of the police, government officials, and supporters of the ruling party. In February, freelance journalist Gift Phiri was brutally beaten by attackers who accused him of working for foreign news outlets. Instances of arbitrary arrest and detention occur primarily when reporters are trying to cover politically charged stories. In July, two journalists covering an antigovernment demonstration were arrested, detained, and then released after paying a fine. Mike Saburi, a cameraman with Reuters Television, was assaulted by police officers and jailed in September after he filmed the police beating people involved in a banned trade union march in Harare. During the past several years, dozens of Zimbabwean journalists have fled the country, and according to a report by the Committee to Protect Journalists (CPJ), more than 90 currently live in exile, predominantly in South Africa and the United Kingdom.

Foreign journalists are not allowed to reside full-time in the country and are regularly denied visas to file stories from Zimbabwe. Locally based correspondents for foreign publications, particularly those whose reporting has portrayed the regime in an unfavorable light, have been refused accreditation or threatened with lawsuits and deportation. CPJ reported that in April police arrested two journalists from BTV, the state broadcaster of neighboring Botswana; they were accused of practicing journalism without a license and violating Zimbabwean immigration law, and in November they were convicted and fined roughly US$20 each. Publisher Trevor Ncube, who owns several newspapers in both Zimbabwe and South Africa, faced repeated harassment as authorities attempted to strip him of his citizenship and confiscate his passport.

The government, through the Mass Media Trust holding company, controls several major daily newspapers, including the *Chronicle* and the *Herald*; coverage in these news outlets consists of favorable portrayals of Mugabe and the ruling party and attacks on perceived critics of the regime. Several independent weeklies such as the *Standard* and the *Zimbabwe Independent* continue to publish, although many journalists practice extensive self-censorship. Others, such as the privately owned *Daily Mirror*, have been effectively bought up and infiltrated by the intelligence service; during 2006, this new ownership engineered the forced dismissal of several journalists. Some foreign newspapers, mostly from South Africa, are available, although the authorities have threatened to restrict their importation. In October, police raided the Harare distribution offices of the *Zimbabwean*, an independent weekly printed in South Africa, and confiscated documents.

In general, newspapers have poor distribution networks outside the urban areas and have become relatively expensive, placing them beyond the reach of most Zimbabweans. Printing expenses have increased dramatically because of soaring prices for newsprint and paper, causing many outlets to restrict their print runs. According to the MISA's Africa Media Barometer, state-run companies do not advertise in private papers, and state-run media outlets do not accept advertising from companies known to be aligned with the opposition. Owing to poor economic conditions and salaries that do not keep pace with inflation, corruption and cash incentives for coverage have become rampant.

The state-controlled Zimbabwe Broadcasting Corporation runs all broadcast media, which are seen as mouthpieces of the regime. The Broadcasting Services Act bans foreign funding and investment in this capital-intensive sector, making it very difficult for private players to enter the market. In addition, broadcasting licenses have been consistently denied to independently owned radio stations, although a parliamentary committee did call for an opening up of the broadcast sector in 2006. Access to broadcast media in rural areas is hampered by deteriorating equipment and a lack of transmission sites; according to the MISA, only 30 percent of the country receives radio and television coverage from the state-controlled broadcaster, although the government has reached an agreement with China to help upgrade this infrastructure. Meanwhile, also using Chinese technology, authorities have begun to focus on jamming the signals of the increasingly popular foreign-based radio stations that broadcast into Zimbabwe. The short-wave signal of SW Radio Africa, a London–based station run by exiled Zimbabwean journalists, was blocked around the time of the March 2005 parliamentary elections; the station then added a medium-wave broadcast, but this was blocked in the Harare area in June 2006. Similarly, the Voice of America's Studio 7 service, although it remains accessible within Zimbabwe, has been periodically blocked on different frequencies. Although satellite television services that provide international news programming remain largely uncensored, their prohibitive cost places them out of reach for most of the population.

Access to the internet is not restricted by the government, but it is limited by the high costs at internet cafés and service disruptions caused by frequent power outages. Nonetheless, almost 10 percent of Zimbabwe's population accessed this new medium in 2006, one of the highest rates of internet access in all of Africa. The law allows the government to monitor e-mail content. In April, the government proposed new legislation, the Interception of Communications bill, which would allow officials to intercept electronic communications to prevent a "serious offense" or a "threat to national security"; the bill would require internet service providers (ISPs) to pay the cost of surveillance. In August, media advocates and ISP representatives uniformly opposed the bill at a parliamentary hearing. While technology for implementing the legislation is already undergoing tests, officials said in November that the bill would be amended to reflect the concerns of the parliamentary legal committee. However, a revised version of the bill released that month was also criticized by the MISA–Zimbabwe for containing undemocratic provisions. Online newspapers run by Zimbabweans living abroad are popular among those with internet access.

About Freedom House

Freedom House is an independent private organization supporting the expansion of freedom throughout the world.

Freedom is possible only in democratic political systems in which governments are accountable to their own people, the rule of law prevails, and freedoms of expression, association and belief are guaranteed. Working directly with courageous men and women around the world to support nonviolent civic initiatives in societies where freedom is threatened, Freedom House functions as a catalyst for change through its unique mix of analysis, advocacy and action.

▌ **Analysis.** Freedom House's rigorous research methodology has earned the organization a reputation as the leading source of information on the state of freedom around the globe. Since 1972, Freedom House has published *Freedom in the World*, an annual survey of political rights and civil liberties experienced in every country of the world. The survey is complemented by an annual review of press freedom, an analysis of transitions in the post-communist world, and other publications.

▌ **Advocacy.** Freedom House seeks to encourage American policymakers, as well as other governments and international institutions, to adopt policies that advance human rights and democracy around the world. Freedom House has been instrumental in the founding of the worldwide Community of Democracies, has actively campaigned for a reformed Human Rights Council at the United Nations, and presses the Millennium Challenge Corporation to adhere to high standards of eligibility for recipient countries.

▮ **Action.** Through exchanges, grants, and technical assistance, Freedom House provides training and support to human rights defenders, civil society organizations, and members of the media in order to strengthen indigenous reform efforts in countries around the globe.

Founded in 1941 by Eleanor Roosevelt, Wendell Willkie, and other Americans concerned with mounting threats to peace and democracy, Freedom House has long been a vigorous proponent of democratic values and a steadfast opponent of dictatorships of the far left and the far right. The organization's diverse Board of Trustees is composed of a bipartisan mix of business and labor leaders, former senior government officials, scholars, and journalists who agree that the promotion of democracy and human rights abroad is vital to America's interests abroad.

1301 Connecticut Avenue, NW, Floor 6
Washington, DC 20036
(202) 296-5101

120 Wall Street, Floor 26
New York, NY 10005
(212) 514-8040

www.freedomhouse.org